Exploring Morgan's Metaphors

SAGE was founded in 1965 by Sara Miller McCune to support the dissemination of usable knowledge by publishing innovative and high-quality research and teaching content. Today, we publish over 900 journals, including those of more than 400 learned societies, more than 800 new books per year, and a growing range of library products including archives, data, case studies, reports, and video. SAGE remains majority-owned by our founder, and after Sara's lifetime will become owned by a charitable trust that secures our continued independence.

Los Angeles | London | New Delhi | Singapore | Washington DC | Melbourne

Exploring Morgan's Metaphors

Theory, Research, and Practice in Organizational Studies

Editors

Anders Örtenblad
Nord University, Norway

Kiran Trehan
University of Birmingham Business School, UK

Linda L. Putnam
University of California, Santa Barbara, USA

Los Angeles | London | New Delhi
Singapore | Washington DC | Melbourne

FOR INFORMATION:

SAGE Publications, Inc.
2455 Teller Road
Thousand Oaks, California 91320
E-mail: order@sagepub.com

SAGE Publications Ltd.
1 Oliver's Yard
55 City Road
London, EC1Y 1SP
United Kingdom

SAGE Publications India Pvt. Ltd.
B 1/I 1 Mohan Cooperative Industrial Area
Mathura Road, New Delhi 110 044
India

SAGE Publications Asia-Pacific Pte. Ltd.
3 Church Street
#10-04 Samsung Hub
Singapore 049483

Printed in the United States of America

Library of Congress Cataloging-in-Publication Data

Names: Örtenblad, Anders, editor. | Trehan, Kiran, editor. | Putnam, Linda, editor.

Title: Exploring Morgan's metaphors : theory, research, and practice in organizational studies / edited by Anders Örtenblad, Kiran Trehan, Linda Putnam.

Description: Thousand Oaks, California : SAGE, [2017] | Includes bibliographical references and index.

Identifiers: LCCN 2016005369 | ISBN 978-1-5063-1877-6 (pbk. : alk. paper)

Subjects: LCSH: Morgan, Gareth, 1943- Images of organization. | Organization. | Organizational behavior. | Organizational sociology. | Metaphor.

Classification: LCC HD31.M6282 A67 20017 | DDC 658.4—dc23
LC record available at http://lccn.loc.gov/2016005369

This book is printed on acid-free paper.

Acquisitions Editor: Maggie Stanley
Editorial Assistant: Neda Dallal
Production Editor: Kelly DeRosa
Copy Editor: Christina West
Typesetter: C&M Digitals (P) Ltd.
Proofreader: Sarah J. Duffy
Indexer: Jeanne R. Busemeyer
Cover Designer: Gail Buschman
Marketing Manager: Ashlee Blunk

SUSTAINABLE FORESTRY INITIATIVE

Certified Chain of Custody
Promoting Sustainable Forestry
www.sfiprogram.org
SFI-01268

SFI label applies to text stock

16 17 18 19 20 10 9 8 7 6 5 4 3 2 1

• Brief Contents •

• Detailed Contents •

PART II • USING METAPHORS IN ORGANIZATIONAL ANALYSIS

• Foreword •

Gareth Morgan

Let me begin with a word of thanks and appreciation.

It's wonderful and at the same time humbling to have one's work and ideas provide the focus of a book such as this, and I am truly grateful to the editors for initiating and steering the project, and to all the contributors for the insights, critiques, and ideas for future development provided in their various papers. There are many powerful voices and perspectives represented here. They all stand as important and provocative contributions on their own account and, collectively, demonstrate the depth and sophistication of current thinking about the role of metaphor in theory, research, and practice in the field of organization studies. They also illustrate many of the controversies and debates currently in play.

The editors have asked me to write this brief foreword to create a bridge between my early work on metaphor, especially as presented in the various editions of *Images of Organization* (1986, 1997, 1998, and 2006) and I'm delighted to do so. That said, it is by no means an easy task because of the huge amount of circularity of interpretation that's involved. Simply put, authors write books which are then effectively re-authored through the interpretations of the readers from *their* point of view. Hence any commentary on the interpretations, which is effectively what I am being asked to provide here, always runs the danger of running full circle and simply restating what has already been said, perhaps in just another form. This, in turn, then typically provides the basis for another round of reinterpretation. And so it goes.

I want to avoid this circularity as far as I possibly can, and recognize that all I can really do here is offer a personal point of view on how I see some of the current challenges relating to the use of metaphor in the field of organization studies, while making as many links as I can to some of the ideas presented in the papers in this volume. A warning, though—there are so many diverse points of view and insights being expressed that I can't possibly do justice to them all. In other words, no shortcuts here! You have to read the papers. And I know that you will be well rewarded in doing so.

On the Paradoxical Nature of Metaphor and Its Use in *Images of Organization*

So let's start with a few "bridging" comments on what I was seeking to do in writing *Images of Organization*. The detailed story is presented in a paper I wrote on this topic in 2011, now reproduced here in Chapter 2. In essence, the main purpose of the book was to illustrate how all of organization and management theory and practice is shaped by metaphors that have simultaneous strengths and limitations. Though theorists and practitioners often believe that they are viewing and acting in relation to the world *as it is,* they are in fact relating to a world that's filtered and shaped through creative metaphors that have become embedded in their thinking, language, and everyday practice. This creates ways of seeing and acting that are simultaneously *ways of not seeing and of not acting.* No surprise, therefore, that the theory and practice of organization and management—as with other areas of professional practice—often has many unintended consequences that typically create new problems with which we then have to deal.

To understand the deeper issues and problems that are involved here, it is important to recognize at least three things. First, that while we are living in a complex, multidimensional world where any given situation combines many different elements and dimensions existing at one and the same time, most of our thinking, theories, and acting tends to be unidimensional—because we are typically just engaging and acting in relation to small elements of what's actually present. In other words, we are always dealing with partial understandings and need to recognize that no single theory or perspective will ever be giving us a comprehensive and fully accurate view of the situations with which we are involved.

Second, because our theories are metaphorical, our ways of seeing always involve simultaneous insights and distortions. Hence, we are not just seeing and acting in relation to fractions of what's actually present. We are also doing so in a way that has *inherent* blind spots and distortions. We tend to get attracted by the insights conveyed by the metaphorical way of seeing while ignoring or dismissing the limitations and potential downsides. As discussed in Chapter 2, this is what I describe as the paradox of metaphor. Insights and distortions are intertwined. You can't have one without the other. Your favored implicit or explicit metaphor (e.g., treating an organization as if it is a machine, an organism, a brain, a culture, a political system, an instrument of domination) may be helping you to understand and deal with the issues that are a focus of your attention. But there will also likely be some kind of intrinsic downside, because the organization is *not* a machine, an organism, a brain, etc.

Third, and a corollary of the above, this means that our seeing, understanding, and acting is always biased. It's skewed by the partiality of the engagement, and by the interests or intent that lead us to favor one particular metaphorical way of engaging situations over others. The skewing plays a major role in generating future issues and problems with which we then have to deal, since in acting on the insights associated with our modes of engagement we often have impacts on the hidden or neglected dimensions of the multidimensionality. This can catalyze all kinds of actions and reactions that reverberate in unexpected ways as other human and nonhuman stakeholders in the overall situation adjust and respond to what we are doing.

These paradoxical qualities and impacts of metaphor are illustrated throughout *Images of Organization.* For example, each chapter exploring how a given metaphor has shaped the nature of organization and management theory and practice shows how the specific strengths of its way of thinking are always accompanied by inherent limitations *that are a direct consequence of the strengths.* To take a simple example, if you think about organizations in mechanistic terms and organize in a mechanistic way you can create an efficient operational structure. But you also *create* rigidities and patterns of behavior that hamper the ability to adapt to change. In other words, the actual strength creates a limitation. The book as a whole constantly plays with the paradox that if you are theorizing and acting in one way, you are failing to see and act in another, and how the benefits resulting from one's way of seeing and acting may be creating negative impacts elsewhere. Consider, for example, how the instrumental form of rationality embedded in management orthodoxy through use of mechanical, biological, and a variety of supporting metaphors (e.g., brain, culture, and political) can simultaneously create institutionalized modes of domination that can exploit the workforce, local communities, society, and the planet at large. This dynamic continues to be played out at a global level as the *strengths* of the mechanical and other metaphors powering industrialization and much of modern corporate life *simultaneously create* new social and planetary problems, (e.g. in the form of structural unemployment, inequality, global imbalance, various kinds of social decay and dysfunction, air, water and land pollution, and climate change).

While the focus of *Images of Organization* is on the role of metaphor in shaping organization and management theory and practice, it is important to recognize that its relevance goes beyond this particular domain. The basic thesis is that all theory, all thinking, and all acting relating to that thinking is shaped metaphorically. Hence the corollary is that all of science and all of our understandings and actions in everyday life are shaped by processes that create simultaneous insights and distortions.

To appreciate the significance of these claims it is important to recognize and understand the nature of metaphor and the role it plays in everyday life. As argued in *Images of Organization* (and further discussed in my article in Chapter 2, and in the excellent papers by Cornelissen [Chapter 3] and Tsoukas [Chapter 11]), while metaphor is commonly seen as just a linguistic device for embellishing discourse, its significance is much greater than this. Metaphor is ontological. It is a way of being in the world where we fuse one element of experience with another, using the one to engage, grasp, understand, and deal with the other. In other words, metaphor is fundamental. It's not optional. It captures the way we are! This ontological process produces metaphors (note the "s") as epistemological constructs that shape the *content* of our knowledge.

Viewed in this way, we are obliged to see that all our theories are just social constructs, tapping into the world in different and partial ways with different effects according to the metaphors that are used. And, as discussed earlier, because of the ontological multidimensionality that's involved in any given situation, we should always act on the premise that no single approach can ever give us a complete, all-purpose point of view.

This is the epistemological position taken in *Images of Organization*, leading to the argument that the best we can do is to learn to *read* the ontological complexity of the situations with which we are faced through the medium of multiple theoretical perspectives. Hence the book counter-poses the insights of one metaphorical view of organization with another . . . then another, then another . . . highlighting the potential strengths and limitations of each, without ever advocating the intrinsic superiority of any given view. The invitation, in short, is to embrace rather than deny the complexity of organizational life, and be open to the learning and action opportunities that can emerge from different and potentially contradictory points of view.

To understand the spirit of *Images of Organization* and the overall objectives that I was trying to achieve, I can do no better than refer you to the essay by Hari Tsoukas in this volume (Chapter 11). It provides an excellent and truly insightful account of the general intent of my work in promoting a more reflective way of thinking that can begin to deal with the relativistic and contingent nature of knowledge. I particularly appreciate the parallels that he draws with the work of John Dewey and the challenge of developing the art of "suspended conclusion"—by simultaneously engaging and remaining open to new interpretations of a situation that may provide better ways of dealing with the situations we face. This is precisely what my approach to "reading" organizations seeks to achieve. As Tsoukas shows so well, the challenge is to overcome the "mental inertia" that's so often associated with conventional thinking and acceptance of "received categories" of interpretation, and actively deal with the complementary and contradictory insights that can emerge by approaching situations with an open mind that can lead to deeper understandings and a broader range of action possibilities.

Joep Cornelissen (Chapter 3) also adds very important insights here, showing us how our metaphors connect us with our realities and are always driven by some kind of intent. In effect, our favored metaphors act as tools that help us get things done in ways that other metaphors are unable to do. Thus in addition to their practical contributions, they also have ideological, ethical, and political dimensions. The metaphors that become established in public consciousness tend to be those that rationalize particular ways of viewing the world and that can mobilize and justify action in relation to shared beliefs, aspirations, or needs. As Cornelissen suggests, we see this in how so much organization and management theory is built around concrete, instrumental metaphors that put managers or powerful individuals "in the driving seat," offering the hope of at least some measure of control of the situations being faced.

Consider, for example, the current dominance of institutional theory in organization studies, which, in its various forms, tends to view organizations as institutional actors and/or economic agents striking agreements and contracts, having specific corporate identities and legal rights, and acting in general pursuit of various corporate goals *as if* they are abstract human beings. As Cornelissen notes, this underlying metaphorical view is ideally suited for CEOs and others in power who want to emphasize their agency role in exercising control over people, resources, and at times, government legislation—all in the interests of the corporate "being" that they are appointed to lead. Just as the image of rational economic man has exerted an incredible influence on overall economic and social life, the parallel metaphor of the organization as a rational economic entity is having an equal, if not more important, impact. Yet the fundamental metaphorical assumptions involved here are often hidden and unquestioned, unless challenged by theorists, commentators, and practitioners favoring completely different metaphorical ways of representing what is happening in the corporate world—especially through variations of what I have described as the "psychic prison" and instrument of domination metaphors.

Our discussion here leads us into the issue of critique and why different metaphors come into play and have their day, and in terms of organization studies and science at large, the question of whose biases and interests are being served. These are obviously huge topics, raised in various ways in several papers in this volume. (See, for example, Cornelissen [Chapter 3], Bhatnagar [Chapter 5], Klein and Huber [Chapter 9], and Case et al. [Chapter 12]). Space constraints prevent full discussion here. So I'm going to tackle the issues by restricting myself to some general comments in relation to *Images of Organization* with regard to (a) potential biases in its view, use, and selection of metaphors; and (b) the continuing relevance of its "eight metaphors" for understanding organizations and organizational life in today's world.

On the Issue of Bias

The issue of bias is an important one and can mean many things (e.g., prejudice, partiality of perspective, unfairness, favoritism, predisposition, preconception, preference, a blocked view, and so on). As discussed at various points above, in a multidimensional world bias is inevitable in trying to make a definitive statement about anything because of both the partiality of perspective and the general intent in relation to what one is seeking to achieve. It is useful to think about the former as kind of *bias by default*—a bias that arises because of what we leave out, because, for one reason or another, it is outside our horizon of awareness and understanding. The second—*bias by intent*—may incorporate the former but also involves explicit omission or disregard of elements of a situation that are not consistent with our conscious prejudices and beliefs or the specific objectives we may be seeking to achieve. Both types of bias are often in play and, as we all know, the critique of any given position (e.g., of a statement, a viewpoint, a judgment, a theory, or appropriateness of a given metaphor) typically involves some kind of evaluation of what has been left out of account, or has been explicitly distorted in some way.

Critique of any position is thus crucially important. But it is also important to realize that the position of the critic can be critiqued in a similar way, because all critique typically involves one or both types of bias. Hence, the really important questions on both sides of any discussion hinge on whether one is aware of one's biases, and whether one can consciously take them into account in what one is saying and doing, as opposed to locking into "I am right . . . you are wrong" circular and self-fulfilling arguments of justification based on the assumptions underpinning each proponent's point of view. In other words, critique as an end in itself is not enough. If one is interested in some form of genuine inquiry it is also important to find what's missing from *both* points of view and deal with the paradoxes that are involved when one way of seeing and understanding the situation at hand precludes the other.

If we view *Images of Organization* and the debates generated by its publication in these terms, we see the relationship between bias and critique being played out in many forms.[1] And, as pointed out in several papers in this volume, the book can be

---

[1] As discussed in Morgan (1996) and in the *Reflections* paper reproduced here in Chapter 2, *Images of Organization* has been critiqued from many perspectives. For example: because it gives too much attention to organizations as physical entities; because it encourages the use of metaphor as opposed to promoting more literal modes of understanding; because it does not offer a definitive view and is open to many interpretations; because responsibility for interpretation is left with the reader; because it overplays the role of metaphor as opposed to other tropes; because it is too

seen as incomplete or biased in several specific ways. For example, as Bhatnagar points out in Chapter 5, my choice of metaphors can be seen as overemphasizing the negative side of organizations and human nature, as opposed to focusing on hope and optimism and the potential for organizations to be "enablers of happiness." Klein and Huber in Chapter 9 argue that I do not give enough attention to the political use of metaphors. Case et al. in Chapter 12 point out the Anglo and potentially colonial bias, and how the use and interpretation of metaphors is crucially dependent on cultural context. And so on.

There are many great points of specific critique here and, clearly, there is a lot more that *Images of Organization* could have said on all these issues. But, for immediate purposes, I am going to focus on two related but more general themes found in many critical discussions of the book. First, the issue of whether it is overly biased toward a managerial perspective. Second, whether it overplays the significance of seeing and "reading" organizational life, as opposed to "authoring," feeling, and other tactile modes of experience.

The issue of managerial bias is a really interesting one, since the book is often critiqued from *outside* management circles for endorsing and promoting a Western management view that gives too little attention to gender, race, and a variety of class-based ideological, material, and political issues. It is also frequently critiqued from *within* conventional management theory for having a subversive influence that undermines the authority of established management thinking. Interestingly, I agree with elements of both.

There is definitely a management bias in that the primary aim of the book was to demonstrate the metaphorical basis of organization and management theory, which, at the time of writing the original edition in 1986, was overwhelmingly dominated

---

relativist and subjectivist in approach; because it is too idealistic; because it encourages a form of "libertarian anarchism"; because it implies there is a "supermarket" of metaphors open to selection according to consumer choice; because it creates superficial as opposed to depth understandings; because it undermines rational explanations of social life; because it can foster and support ideological distortions; because it ignores or underplays the role of power in shaping all aspects of life; because it attributes too much power to individuals in shaping their realities; because it gives too much attention to "reading" as opposed to "authoring" situations; because it underplays the role of gender; because it does not give prominence to racial issues; because it has a Western bias; because it is too oriented to a management view. And so on.

While these may all be valid points that can contribute to valuable learning—especially when gaps in knowledge and argument and various forms of intent / interest-based bias are being pointed out—all I want to suggest here is that in evaluating the critique we also take a close look at the metaphors and biases shaping the critic's point of view since bias exists on both sides of the argument in question (i.e., with both critic and critiqued). The interesting question is whether it is possible to embrace key elements of both points of view without throwing out the proverbial "baby with the bath water." However, that said, while it may be possible to learn from each other's views, complete reconciliation or consensus often remains beyond reach if the protagonists are locked into fundamentally different ontological and epistemological positions. In these circumstances the one side often fails to "hear" the other because what is said is typically heard and interpreted within the dominant frame of the hearer. And vice versa. (See Chapter 2 in this volume, Morgan (1980, 1983a, 1996), and Burrell and Morgan (1979) for further discussion of this issue in relation to the nature of organization and management theory in a multi-paradigm world.)

by a management view.[2] There is also a second source of managerial bias, in that to gain the attention of organization and management theorists and practitioners as a core audience, the whole book was framed around a core challenge facing managers and decision makers in all walks of life: that of effectively reading and acting in relation to the situations being faced. In order to do this, I also formulated a method of "diagnostic reading" through which one can improve the art of reading and re-reading organizational situations with effective action in mind. This was illustrated through the "Multicom case" using an approach that parallels the process of open-ended interpretation described by Hari Tsoukas in Chapter 11 of this volume.

That said, in doing the above I also sought to write a book that, simultaneously, could play a role in *deconstructing* existing organization and management theory and thinking. (See my article in Chapter 2 for further discussion.) This was achieved in four ways:

First, and most obviously, by showing how all management views are metaphorical social constructions with no absolute claims to authority (achieved by counter-posing the insights of different metaphors, highlighting strengths and limitations while trying to minimize absolute judgment on my part, and trusting that the counter-positioning could itself help to deconstruct dominant thinking and theoretical perspectives).

Second, by extending the range of metaphors explored beyond what was typically covered in conventional organization theory at the time. (The psychic prison, flux and transformation, and instrument of domination metaphors were explicitly developed to challenge the core premises of traditional organization and management.)

Third, my analysis of the "Multicom case" also showed how *all* metaphors of organization can be used to serve completely different objectives according to the intent of the user. (To do this, I counter-posed the readings and actions that could emerge from a diagnostic reading on the part of a conventional manager or management consultant on the one hand, as opposed to that of a social critic on the other.)

---

[2] It is important to note that the last thirty years have seen a huge extension of organization theory into the domain of critical management studies building on a variety of Marxian, Radical Weberian, and other social critiques developed through the Frankfurt School and the work of Foucault and other deconstructionist critics. See, for example, Adler (2010), Alvesson (1992, 2003), Alvesson and Willmott (2012), Alvesson et al. (2009), Grey and Willmott (2005), Townley (1995). Though sometimes incorporated within mainstream organization and management theory, the insights of the critical management theorists often remain in a kind of parallel universe because of the underlying differences in worldview, ideology, and the paradigm issues discussed in Burrell and Morgan (1979). My discussion of the psychic prison, flux, and transformation and instrument of domination metaphors in *Images of Organization* specifically drew on some of these alternative theoretical foundations and, as discussed in Chapter 2 of this volume, sought through a counter-position of perspectives to provide some measure of deconstruction of more accepted organization and management metaphors (i.e., offering a form of critique from within not just from outside).

Fourth, as discussed by Tsoukas in Chapter 11, the book as a whole sought to offer an alternative kind of text that could encourage and support a different approach to teaching in the field of organization and management studies. Instead of offering a definitive position on what organizations *are* and *how* to manage them using conventional concepts focused, for example, on relations between organizational structure, strategy, culture, technology, leadership, power, group behavior, etc., I suggested that (a) all of these factors are intertwined, not discrete entities ; (b) given the absence of an absolute, authoritative, non-metaphorical base that all of organization and management theory should be just seen as offering a *way of thinking*; and (c) that responsibility for interpretation and action ultimately rests with the reader-practitioner as opposed to being found in specific recommendations or instructions within the book itself. The aim was to "foster a kind of critical thinking that encourages us to understand and grasp the multiple meanings of situations and to confront and manage contradiction and paradox rather than pretend that they do not exist" (Morgan 1986: 339).

So these are among the main reasons why the book can be simultaneously critiqued by management theorists who see it as a subversive text, and also by more "radical" critics who feel that it is overly biased toward a managerial view. Personally, I am very comfortable with the tensions here, and recognize that there may be substance in the critiques from all sides. Different readers and different critics tend to engage with different elements or potentialities of the text according to their interests, objectives, and the organizational situations and challenges with which they are involved. It's exactly the same issue that I mentioned above in relation to the Multicom case. What resonates, what one learns, what one embraces or critiques, and the conclusions that are drawn are always the product of two-way processes involving both the reader and the text. The really important questions here seem to hinge on what we can learn from this, how we can add meaningful insight to each other's positions; how we can overcome the oversimplifications and biases present on all sides. For example, what can the conventional management theorist or practitioner learn from "radical" criticism of the exploitative consequences of their thinking and practice? What can the radical critic learn from excellent management practice that enhances the quality of human life? Or just staying with the aims of radical critique, how can one take it further? How can one "flip" its orientation and potential impact? For example, instead of just settling for a critique of the exploitative aspects of existing organization and management, can one develop a new kind of pragmatic organization and management theory for the exploited? In other words, how can we go beyond polarized critique to launch powerful new possibilities?

So with this in mind, let's move now to discussion of the second theme relating to potential bias: whether *Images of Organization* overplays the significance of seeing and "reading" organizational life, as opposed to authoring, feeling, and other tactile modes of experience. The issue is raised specifically in the paper by Case et. al. in Chapter 12, and also underpins some of the discussions of metaphor found in the papers by Cornelissen (Chapter 3), Kerr et. al. (Chapter 8), and in the excellent work that they and others have done in adding to the general literature on the role of metaphor more generally.[3] My view is that there is definitely a visual bias in my treatment of metaphor that gets played out in many different ways. For example, in *Images of Organization* and my other work, I make a great deal of the notion that metaphors give us "ways of seeing, and of not seeing"; can "reveal," "illuminate," "obscure," or "hide"; can generate different kinds of "insight"; provide different interpretive "lenses". And in the first edition, I also discussed how use of different metaphors can provide us with a kind of "binocular vision" that can add to our depth of insight in understanding a phenomenon. I actually say that "when we look at the world with our two eyes we get a different view from that gained by using each eye independently. Each eye sees the same reality in a different way, and when working together, the two combine to produce another way" (Morgan, 1986, p. 340). The visual dimension also underpins the whole idea of "reading" organizations and social life as a kind of text. As Marshall McLuhan (1962, 1964) observed, the printed word is an extension of the eye and in effect privileges the visual sense as opposed to audio, oral, and tactile modes of experience. When we read something we in effect create some kind of visual image of what we are reading about in what is sometimes described as the "mind's eye."

So the visual bias gets played out in many ways, and as John Shotter (1990) pointed out in an early commentary, my emphasis on "reading" organizational life inevitably raises the question of "authoring." This latter metaphor takes us much more into the detailed processes through which we actively *"write"* and produce organizational life—a topic that easily justifies a book on its own account. It is also explored in work related to the social construction of reality and the creation and maintenance of different forms of dialogue in various organizational contexts. (See, for example, Cooren, 2004; Gergen, 2001; Grant, Hardy, Oswick & Putnam, 2004, Putnam 1996, Shotter; 2008 & Taylor & Van Every 2000).

Hence my overall conclusion with regard to all these issues is that while the visual bias underlying my work has served useful purposes in helping us use different metaphors to see, highlight, and read dimensions of organizations that we often don't see, it does run the danger of overemphasizing the seeing dimension. Hence, I agree fully with the spirit of Shotter's critique. If we restrict ourselves to using metaphors as just lenses—as often happens in the teaching of these ideas—we implicitly put ourselves in the role of an external observer "looking at" something exterior, and underplaying the ongoing relationship between seeing and acting, and also the reverse. The important challenge, and one that I have recognized in all editions of *Images of Organization,* is to emphasize the interconnection between seeing, thinking, and acting without asserting any particular sequence here. Seeing can lead to particular ways of thinking and acting. Acting can lead to new ways of seeing and thinking. And so on. All are intertwined.

---

[3] See, for example, Alvesson & Spicer, 2011; Boxenbaum & Rouleau, 2011; Cornelissen, 2004, 2005, 2006; Cornelissen and Durand, 2014; Cornelissen and Kafouros, 2008; Cornelissen, et al., 2005, 2008; Grant and Oswick, 1996; Inns, 2002; Lakoff, 1994; Lakoff and Johnson, 1980; Mangham and Overington, 1987; Morgan, 1983, 1996, 2016; Oswick and Grant, 1996; Oswick et.al., 2002, 2004, 2011; Putnam and Boys, 2006; Putnam et al., 1996; Sackmann, 1989; Sandberg and Tsoukas, 2011; Schon, 1963, 1979; Tsoukas, 1991, 1993, 1994, 2005. A lot of work has also been conducted on the significance of other tropes alongside metaphor, (i.e., metonymy, synecdoche, and irony, For further discussion see Cornelissen, 2008; Morgan, 2011, 2016; Oswick et al., 2004; Pinto, 2016; Schoeneborn et. al., 2016.

For these reasons, and as discussed earlier and in Chapter 2 of this volume, it is important that we treat metaphor as an ontological process of engagement linking interior and exterior worlds, generating metaphors as frames (i.e., epistemological constructs) that shape the nature of specific modes of engagement. I have developed my ideas on the nature of engagement in various ways, most notably in Morgan (1983a, 1996, 2011) and at a practical level in *Imaginization: New Mindsets for Seeing Organizing and Managing*. This book explicitly develops and illustrates the relationship between reading and writing organizational life with managerial practice in mind. The aim is to show how we are active readers and authors at one and the same time, and how the process of organizing always embodies some form of creative human imagination. These and related issues are also explored in various ways in the discussions and refinements of metaphor offered by Cornelissen (Chapter 3), Grant and Oswick (Chapter 10), and Tsoukas (Chapter 11) (e.g., in emphasizing the "blending" of relations between subject and object, '"source and target domains," etc. In our various ways, we are all emphasizing the interconnected nature of ontology and epistemology, illustrated, for example, in Tsoukas's discussion in Chapter 11 of the emergent nature of interpretation and action and how the insights generated through metaphor are not just subjective readings but also belong to the nature of the situation explored. Stated in the words I used in *Images of Organization*, "reality has a tendency to reveal itself in accordance with the perspectives through which it is engaged" (2006, p 339). Different metaphors help us to engage and deal with different aspects of the multidimensionality that's present. Or as Tsoukas puts it "multiple interpretations of organization-as-text belong to the possibility of the text: the interpretation is not external to the text." The issues involved here are important ones defining, in the terms used by Grant and Oswick (Chapter 10), an important point of our "journey" in understanding metaphor and its role in understanding organizational life.

The Continuing Relevance of the Original Eight Metaphors

This discussion brings us to an issue raised in several papers in this volume about the continuing appropriateness of the frames of analysis offered in *Images of Organization* (for various perspectives here, see Cornelissen [Chapter 3], Bhatnagar [Chapter 5], Grant and Oswick [Chapter 10], and Case et al. [Chapter 12]). For example, Grant and Oswick suggest that given the rapidly changing world in which we live, it is important to ask whether the eight metaphors of organization are as relevant as they used to be. Case et al. highlight the Western Anglo-bias of these metaphors and do an excellent job deconstructing their meaning and ethical implications when viewed from a variety of international perspectives. They also rightly point out that there is a danger of reifying the metaphors if we see them as static, self-referential entities, as opposed to appreciating their role in more dynamic forms of thought and interpretation.

My position here is that I fully agree there is danger in treating the eight metaphors as offering a fixed framework, or as offering some definitive "set" with predefined meanings. Though my work has sometimes been interpreted in this way, I have always presented the eight metaphors as just illustrative, inviting people to recognize and embrace the role of metaphor in our thinking and acting, and to use my method of analysis flexibly in reading and understanding the contextual nuance of the situations we are dealing with. (See Tsoukas [Chapter 11] for a clear exposition of this.) While the discussion in *Images of Organization* inevitably evokes and describes a particular configuration of meaning in connection with each metaphor that's explored, there can be no doubt that the significance and meaning of any metaphor, hence its resonance and power in understanding and shaping situations, is always going to be context dependent, and needs to be understood in this way. To endorse the relevance and importance of this message, you need look no further than the international analysis presented by Case et al. (Chapter 12). This clearly demonstrates how the meanings of metaphors can always vary. For example, as they illustrate, when we evoke and use what may seem to be a fairly straightforward metaphor in an Anglo Western context (e.g., viewing organizations as machines or organisms) in other ethnic contexts the partner to our conversation or analysis may have great difficulty in making sense of what is being said. Often, the metaphor in question can only be grasped or made intelligible through a constellation of other metaphors that often have very different meanings. In other words, user beware—there are always important social constructions involved in the use of metaphor.

That said, and recognizing that all metaphors and analytical schemes should be used flexibly with the above considerations in mind, I think that the eight metaphors discussed in *Images of Organization* are still of considerable relevance because they continue to tap into key elements of the multidimensionality shaping the evolution and character of so much of social, economic, and political life. As Grant and Oswick suggest in Chapter 10, new metaphors are definitely needed to capture and deal with how organizations and the global economy have changed over the last thirty years. But this does not necessarily negate the existence and value of many of the metaphors we already know and use. To illustrate, consider the contemporary relevance of the machine metaphor. If we just associate it with traditional bureaucratic, hierarchical forms of organization, then yes, we may feel that it is getting out of date. But looking more closely to the new, flatter, and more automated forms of organization that have emerged, we can often see mechanistic principles shaping the very basis of what they do. Nobody may be talking about Frederick Taylor's Scientific Management or the principles of Classical Management Theorists anymore. But their thinking has become deeply sedimented in everyday mindsets on what it means to streamline and organize efficiently, and in the operation of many of the automated information and control systems being used to achieve cost effectiveness and customer service as a primary goal. As we know, Frederick Taylor was an engineer whose breakthrough contribution rested in explicitly using his engineering mindset to engineer the conduct of work. He would be truly astonished to see how his conscious and unconscious aims continue to be realized in the modern workplace.

We could examine the relevance of all eight metaphors in similar terms. Space limitations preclude this here, but it is clear how the organismic metaphor is relevant for understanding the different species of organization that have emerged and their success and failure in dealing with the rapidly changing environment; how brain-like learning is a key for success in times of change; how all organizations are cultures comprised of a network of subcultures, operating within national or international cultural milieu; how political dynamics shape organizational life and the contexts in which they operate; how different approaches to organization and leadership styles may embody deep psychoanalytic and other dimensions; how many organizations continue to use and exploit people and the resources of the planet for selfish corporate ends. And so on.

Hence, the fundamental issue is not whether the eight metaphors are still relevant as frames for understanding the multidimensionality of organizational life, so much as what new metaphors are *also* needed to deal with new or neglected challenges. The papers by Cornelissen (Chapter 3), Örtenblad (Chapter 4), Bhatnagar (Chapter 5), Süße et al. (Chapter 6), Virtanen (Chapter 7), Kerr et al. (Chapter 8), and Grant and Oswick (Chapter 10) all address this issue, adding valuable ideas for making progress here.

However, that said, it is important to realize that we do not need new metaphors for the sake of finding new metaphors. This typically just results in new free-standing epistemological constructs generating new epistemological debate. I agree fully with what Grant and Oswick say in relation to these issues. The fundamental challenge is to find ways of engaging what's new and of overcoming the deficiencies of our existing modes of understanding. In other words, the quest should be driven ontologically by the phenomena that we are seeking to understand; not just by an epistemological concern for novel theory. The resonance of new generative metaphors in fostering meaningful understanding and action (i.e., in what they allow us to see, capture, and create) is what's key, along with deep appreciation of their strengths and limitations, and associated ethical, political, ideological, and other considerations.

Some Concluding Remarks With Regard to Teaching, Research and Future Development

One of the major aims of the current volume is to bridge *Images of Organization* with day-to-day teaching in the domain of organization studies and the conduct of future research. So, by way of conclusion, what are some of the key points that need to be made here?

On the teaching front, I'm just going to refer you again to the paper by Tsoukas in Chapter 11. This summarizes the challenges so well. In today's world, the most valuable thing we can do for our students, whether they are studying on academic courses or in professional settings, is to help them see, think, and act reflectively, with broad appreciations in mind. As Tsoukas shows, this kind of openness is an eminently achievable goal if we can help them develop the art of "suspended conclusion." As he puts it, when we recognize that given the multidimensionality of organizational life "there is no Olympian summit from which we may obtain a definitive view," we are encouraged to adopt multiple perspectives that can bring "extra informational depth" from which new more holistic insights and actions can emerge. This, in a nutshell, is what the use of metaphor and the "reading" methodology offered in *Images of Organization* helps us to do.

At a practical level, I see the process of helping students and practitioners gain skill in open-ended reading of the situations being faced as a two-stage challenge. The first and most important objective is to help them appreciate the legitimacy and value of adopting multiple perspectives in understanding any complex situation. They already know this in everyday life. But when it comes to any domain of academic or professional study, a belief about expertise often seems to take hold (e.g., in the idea that there is some definitive theory or technique that will sort out the issues). By using simple case studies or situations from daily life to engage and illustrate the multidimensionality and show and discuss how different metaphors bring different kinds of insights, each with their own inherent limitations and blind spots, the way can be opened to more flexible thinking. In achieving this one has already made a major pedagogical breakthrough compared with more conventional modes of teaching focused on communicating research on specific theories or sets of abstract concepts that, more often than not, just oversimplify how we see and deal with a much more complex reality. In contrast, I believe that it is far more important to invite students to a way of thinking. If one can do this the second objective flows—students become more aware that they have, in effect, to *become their own theorists*, taking responsibility for interpretations and actions as opposed to relying on abstract concepts and the theories in and of themselves. When given the opportunity to apply ideas in understanding *their own* situations, with a little luck and encouragement, this empowering message really hits home.

Moving on to the issue of the role of metaphor in future theory development in organization studies, it is clear that significant developments still need to be made. As Cornelissen notes in Chapter 3, while the metaphorical basis of theory and research is now well recognized in the field at large, relatively little attention has been given in mainstream theory to the fundamental implications of this. As will be evident from virtually every chapter in this volume, great work has been done in understanding more about the operation of metaphor and related tropes by specialists in this area. But as far as mainstream theorists are concerned, many just seem content to recognize that their theory and research is using a metaphor and leave it at that.

Clearly, this is insufficient. If we recognize that theory is metaphorical, and that because of the multidimensional nature of what we are studying no single theory will ever give us a comprehensive, correct, authoritative point of view, this is something with which mainstream theory needs to deal. As I have discussed throughout this foreword, at minimum, it means that we need to give explicit attention to the partial nature of our theories and what we are doing; to recognize and deal with the inherent limitations of any given point of view and the consequences that result; and be more explicit about the biases that always accompany our theorizing and research because of the personal and institutional intent underlying what we are trying to do.

On one level, these issues can just be seen as highlighting the socially constructed, ethical, political, and ideological implications of our craft, and be dismissed as providing just one more radical critique. But, more fundamentally, they speak to the essence of what is required to create a more reflective approach to our discipline that can deal with the emerging challenges of our time. As discussed earlier, this requires that we find ways of engaging what's new in the world, and also overcome the deficiencies of our existing modes of understanding.

The former is often seen as the more attractive path because it opens the possibility of new theoretical vistas. But the latter is equally important because of the deficiencies and unintended consequences of our existing theories and points of view. As noted earlier, these deficiencies often generate lots of critique. But more often than not it gets polarized in terms of "I am right . . . you are wrong" positions instead of recognizing that both stances can have strengths and inherent limitations. In appreciating this we can often create springboards for more holistic modes of understanding that can help us overcome the blind spots, distortions, and unintended consequences of our thinking. Consensus may never be achieved, especially given the multidimensionality with which we are typically dealing. But something of value can usually be learned from the process. If we can move closer to a view that as theorists and researchers we are just developing and using imperfect tools for understanding the phenomena with which we are engaged, the way can be opened to a degree of constructive self-criticism on which the art of "suspended conclusion" depends and thrives. One of the most important resources that we have as human beings rests in our ability to see, think, and act reflectively with broad appreciations of situations in mind, and to have the wisdom and flexibility to modify and deal with the limits and distortions of our thinking when the world is in effect "telling us," via the consequences of our actions, that other approaches may be more appropriate. This, in my opinion, captures the open and reflective stance that needs to be further developed in our approach to theory, research, and all aspects of organization, leadership, management, and decision-making practice.

Finally, to close our general discussion here, I'd like to return to my views on the overall nature and aims of Images of Organization. In their paper in Chapter 12, Case et al make a very interesting comment on the book, suggesting that it can be seen as "the last *modern* organization theory text and also one of the first *postmodern* texts." They also provocatively suggest that while appreciating its contributions it "might ultimately go down as the last gasp of modernist organization studies." They do a great job deconstructing the Western Anglo bias of the book's eight metaphors, and I love the modern–post-modern contradiction they highlight because I think they are absolutely right. One can see *Images of Organization* as an attempt to make a comprehensive statement on the nature of organization theory as a discipline, and its "reading methodology" as offering an integrative perspective that seeks to mobilize competing viewpoints as part of a coherent whole. Very modernist indeed. But for me, just a strategy for gaining the attention of mainstream modernist theory while at the same time deconstructing it.

As I have noted earlier in this foreword in my discussion of managerial bias, I sought to achieve this deconstructionist aim through all kinds of counter-positioning within a book that ultimately invites us to a mode of thinking that offers a measure of deconstruction of each theory or position it presents, while avoiding final closure around any individual point of view. As discussed in my paper in Chapter 2 of this volume, I like to position my approach as that of a *constructive postmodernist*—one who recognizes the tentative, biased, incomplete, and contradictory nature of knowledge, but who at the same time seeks to embrace the relativism and do more than just critique every other's point of view. I am going to leave that essay to give more detail on what I mean here.

And as to the specific issue of whether *Images of Organization* represents "the last gasp of modernist organization studies"? In line with what I have said above I'd prefer it to be seen as a work seeking to advance organization and management theory while deconstructing it. The challenge is whether the approach initiated in 1986 can continue to encourage and legitimize a more diverse and open approach to inquiry that respects the complexity and competing interests embodied in the phenomena with which we have to deal. Needless to say, I think we can continue to rely on a loyal ally here. It's called metaphor—a process that helps us to construct and deconstruct our thinking at one and the same time.

References

Adler, P. (Ed). (2010). *The Oxford handbook of organization studies*. Oxford, England: Oxford University Press.

Alvesson, M. (1992). *Critical management studies*. London, England: Sage.

Alvesson, M. (2003). *Studying management critically*. London, England: Sage.

Alvesson, M., Bridgman, T., & Willmott, H. (Eds.). (2009). *The Oxford handbook of critical management studies*. Oxford, England: Oxford University Press.

Alvesson, M., & Willmott, H. (2012). *Making sense of management*. London, England: Sage.

Alvesson, M., & Spicer, A. (Eds.). (2011). *Metaphors we lead by: Understanding leadership in the real world*. New York, NY: Routledge.

Boxenbaum, E., & Rouleau, L. (2011). New knowledge products as bricolage: Metaphors and scripts in organizational theory. *Academy of Management Review, 36*, 272–296.

Burrell, G., & Morgan, G. (1979). *Sociological paradigms and organisational analysis*. London, England: Ashgate.

Cooren, F. (2004). Textual agency: How texts do things in organizational settings. *Organization, 11*, 373–393.

Cornelissen, J. P. (2004). What are we playing at? Theatre, organization, and the use of metaphor. *Organization Studies, 25*, 705–726.

Cornelissen, J. P. (2005). Beyond compare: Metaphor in organization theory. *Academy of Management Review, 30*, 751–764.

Cornelissen, J. P. (2006). Metaphor and the dynamics of knowledge in organization theory: A case study of the organizational identity metaphor. *Journal of Management Studies, 43*, 683–709.

Cornelissen, J. P. (2008). Metonymy in language about organizations. *Journal of Management Studies, 45*(1), 79–99.

Cornelissen, J. P., & Durand, R. (2014). Moving forward: Developing theoretical contributions in management studies. *Journal of Management Studies, 51*, 995–1022.

Cornelissen, J. P., & Kafouros, M. (2008). The emergent organization: Primary and complex metaphors in theorizing about organizations. *Organization Studies, 29*, 957–978.

Cornelissen, J. P., Kafouros, M., & Lock, A. R. (2005). Metaphorical images of organization: How organizational researchers develop and select organizational metaphors. *Human Relations, 58*, 1545–1578.

Cornelissen, J. P., Oswick, C., Thoger Christensen, L., & Phillips, N. (2008). Metaphor in organizational research: Context, modalities and implications for research introduction. *Organization Studies, 29*(1), 7–22.

Gergen, K. (2001). *Social construction in context*. London, England: Sage.

Grant, D. C., Hardy, C. Oswick, & L. Putnam. (Eds.). (2004). *The Sage handbook of organizational discourse*. London, England: Sage.

Grant, D., & Oswick, C. (Eds.). (1996). *Metaphor and organizations*. London, England: Sage.

Grey, C., & Willmott, H. (Eds.). (2005). *Critical management studies: A reader*. Oxford, England: Oxford University Press.

Inns, D. (2002). Metaphor in the literature of organizational analysis: A preliminary taxonomy and a glimpse at a humanities-based perspective. *Organization, 9*, 305–330.

Inns, D., & Jones, P. J. (1996). Metaphor in organization theory: Following in the footsteps of the poet? In D. Grant & C. Oswick (Eds.), *Metaphor and organizations* (pp. 110–126). London, England: Sage.

Lakoff, G. (1993). The contemporary theory of metaphor. *Metaphor and Thought, 2*, 202–251.

Lakoff, G., & Johnson, M. (1980). *Metaphors we live by*. Chicago, IL: University of Chicago Press.

Mangham, I., & Overington, M. A. (1987). *Organizations as theatre: A social psychology of dramatic appearances*. Chichester, England: Wiley.

McLuhan, M. (1962). *The Gutenberg galaxy*. London, England: Routledge and Kegan Paul.

McLuhan, M. (1964). *Understanding media*. London, England: Routledge and Kegan Paul.

Morgan, G. (1980). Paradigms, metaphors and puzzle solving in organization theory. *Administrative Science Quarterly, 25*, 605–622.

Morgan, G. (Ed.). (1983a). *Beyond method: Strategies for social research*. Thousand Oaks, CA: Sage.

Morgan, G. (1983b). More on metaphor: Why we cannot control tropes in administrative science. *Administrative Science Quarterly, 27*, 601–607.

Morgan, G. (1986, 1997, 2006). *Images of organization*. Thousand Oaks, CA: Sage.

Morgan, G. (1993). *Imaginization: The art of creative management*. Thousand Oaks, CA: Sage. (Republished as *Imaginization: New mindsets for seeing, thinking and organizing, and managing*, San Francisco, CA: Berrett-Koehler, 1997).

Morgan, G. (1996). Is there anything more to be said about metaphor? In D. Grant & C. Oswick (Eds.), *Metaphor and organizations*. London, England: Sage.

Morgan, G. (1998). *Images of organization: The executive edition*. San Francisco, CA: Berrett-Koehler.

Morgan, G. (2011). Reflections on images of organization and its implications for organization and environment. *Organization & Environment, 24*, 459–478.

Morgan G. (2016). Commentary: Beyond Morgan's eight metaphors. *Human Relations, 69*, 1029–1042.

Oswick, C., & Grant, D. (1996). *Organization development: Metaphorical explorations*. London, England: Pitman.

Oswick, C., Keenoy, T., & Grant, D. (2002). Metaphor and analogical reasoning in organization theory: Beyond orthodoxy. *Academy of Management Review, 27*, 294–303.

Oswick, C., Putnam, L. L., & Keenoy, T. (2004). Tropes, discourse and organizing. In D. Grant, C. Hardy, C. Oswick, & L. L. Putnam (Eds.), *The Sage handbook of organizational discourse* (pp. 105–127). London, England: Sage.

Pinto, J. (2016). "Wow! That's so cool!" The Icehotel as organizational trope. *Human Relations, 69*, 891–914.

Putnam, L. L. (1996). Commentary: Situating the author and text. *Journal of Management Inquiry, 5*, 382–386.

Putnam, L. L., & Boys, S. (2006). Revisiting metaphors of organizational communication. In S. R. Clegg, C. Hardy, T. B. Lawrence, & W. R. Nord (Eds.), *Sage handbook of organization studies* (pp. 541–576). London, England: Sage.

Putnam, L. L., Phillips, N., & Chapman, P. (1996). Metaphors of communication and organization. In S. R. Clegg, C. Hardy, & W. R. Nord (Eds.), *Handbook of organization studies* (pp. 375–408). London, England: Sage.

Sackmann, S. (1989). The role of metaphors in organisation transformation. *Human Relations, 42,* 463–485.

Sandberg, J., & Tsoukas, H. (2011). Grasping the logic of practice: Theorizing through practical rationality. *Academy of Management Review, 36,* 338–360.

Schoeneborn, D., Vasquez, C., & Cornelissen, J. P. (2016). Imagining organization through metaphor and metonymy: Unpacking the process-entity paradox. *Human Relations, 69,* 915–944.

Schön, D. A. (1963). *Invention and the evolution of ideas.* London, England: Tavistock.

Schön, D. A. (1993). Generative metaphor: A perspective on problem-setting in social policy. In A. Ortony (Ed.), *Metaphor and thought* (2nd ed., pp. 137–163). Cambridge, England: Cambridge University Press. (Original work published 1979)

Shotter, J. (1990). The manager as author. In: Knowing of the Third Kind, Utrecht, 217–26.

Shotter, J. (2008). Dialogism and polyphony in organizing theorizing in organization studies: Action guiding anticipations and the continuous creation of novelty. *Organization Studies, 29,* 501–524.

Taylor, J. R., & Van Every, E. J. (2000). *The emergent organization: Communication as its site and surface.* Mahwah, NJ: Lawrence Erlbaum.

Townley, B. (1994). Reframing human resource management. London, England: Sage.

Tsoukas, H. (1991). The missing link: A transformational view of metaphors in organizational science. *Academy of Management Review, 16,* 566–585.

Tsoukas, H. (1993). Analogical reasoning and knowledge generation in organization theory. *Organization Studies, 14,* 323–346.

Tsoukas, H. (1994). Refining common sense: Types of knowledge in management studies. *Journal of Management Studies, 31,* 761–780.

Tsoukas, H. (2005). *Complex knowledge: Studies in organizational epistemology.* Oxford, England: Oxford University Press.

• Preface •

This edited volume serves two main purposes. First, it pays tribute to Gareth Morgan's seminal book, *Images of Organization*, on its 30th anniversary. In particular, it recognizes the critical role that this book has played in management circles, especially its reach to a broad audience of readers—students, scholars, and practitioners. To this end, the editors asked the contributors to this volume to reflect on 1) how they first came in contact with *Images of Organization* (hereafter *Images*), 2) how they used the book, and 3) what the book meant to them and to the field of organizational studies. While page limits prohibit reproducing the full set of responses, the comments that contributors made clustered into five key categories of influence: inspiring scholars and students, developing teaching and training strategies, bridging disciplinary boundaries, enriching theoretical and conceptual discussions, and reflecting on the field at large.

Inspiring Scholars and Students

A number of contributors pointed out how *Images* served as a source of inspiration for them and their students through "opening their eyes," "developing curiosity," "questioning," and "challenging dominant thinking."

Joep Cornelissen: The book was a real eye opener, in that in a single master stroke, it laid out how our theories and thinking about organizations [are] fundamentally metaphorical.

Turo Virtanen: [*Images*] is a source of inspiration. . . . [It] opened my eyes for metaphorical thinking . . . [and] shows that there are alternative ways to do research.

David Grant: I liked the way that *Images* posed as many questions as it provided answers, and [I was] inspired by its use of metaphor in playful, provocative, and imaginative ways that opened up new possibilities. Since those days, whether in relation to my teaching or research, I've always been grateful to the book (and therefore to Gareth) for giving me the courage to question and challenge dominant thinking about organizational theory and practice.

Cliff Oswick: I first read *Images* in 1988 when I was an HR practitioner and part-time lecturer. For me, [it] acted as an intellectual tipping point. Within a year, I was [a] full-time academic and my love affair with metaphor as a central theme of my research and critical component of my teaching had started (and it shows no signs of abating). It is fair to say that Gareth Morgan's work has impacted my thinking in a very deep and profound way.

Developing Teaching and Training Strategies

Related to this inspiration, several contributors recognized Morgan's *Images* as "the best textbook" in organizational studies. It achieved this acclaim through its accessibility, novel approach, engaging rhetorical style, and translation of complex ideas for novices and for multiple audiences. In this way, the book has been adopted in a variety of pedagogical and training circles.

Ron Kerr, Sarah K. Robinson, and Carole Elliott: We have used *Images* extensively in our teaching, for example, [with] second-year students about how [the field] characterizes organizations. We wrote it into Open University courses. . . . It's an important contribution because it makes organizational studies accessible. Some of our Open University students found studying the metaphors [in Morgan's book] to be the watershed moment [for them that] enabled them to move from experiencing organizations to studying and theorizing about them.

Vitor Hugo Klein Jr.: [*Images*] was extremely important in our training . . . it presents a wide range of perspectives in the field of organization theory in an accessible way. At the same time, its rhetorical style and the many examples used in the book were, from a practitioner's point of view, very important in making complex issues within theory useful . . . for organizational analysis.

Bernd-Friedrich Voigt: *Images* has guided a number of my international executive trainings. Participants, especially from Asian countries, value Morgan`s mind-opening variety of unbiased organizational perspectives.

Vikas Rai Bhatnagar: As a practitioner [who was] leading the HR function of a multinational corporation, . . . I was mesmerized by *Images* and drew immense insights for strategizing HR interventions. I remember carrying out an action research project . . . in which I operated from the adaptive metaphor of an organism . . . and the group executive officer operated from a strong metaphor of a machine. . . . [In this situation, I asked] "How do I create a process that blends two opposing metaphors . . . and make an impact to the initiative of leadership development?" We were successfully able to develop leadership as well as create knowledge by being informed on how metaphors play in the context of organizations. . . . [*Images* is] one of the finest books in the field of organization behavior . . . [and has] immense practical implications for making a difference to the lives of people in organizations.

Bridging Disciplinary Boundaries

Our contributors also pointed out how Morgan's *Images* crossed disciplinary boundaries and became an excellent resource for interdisciplinary teaching, research, and practice.

Uta Wilkens: The book is of high value for interdisciplinary teaching. It helps us understand different mental models and bridge different views, especially between business and engineering . . . or business studies and linguistics.

Bernd-Friedrich Voigt: Today the book also enhances our interdisciplinary research activities on understanding the logics of organizing for integrated solutions.

Christian Huber: I find [the book] inspirational for looking at the ways [that] management accountants see the world—which is one of numbers, not always just a machine. I think this illustrates part of the power and appeal of the book—its ideas are not restricted to a single discipline or field.

Enriching Theoretical and Conceptual Discussions

Scholars also employed *Images* to engage in theory building and develop new concepts in an array of organizational arenas, such as corporate identity, organizational communication, organizational transformation, imagination, and the nature of metaphor itself.

Thomas Süße: For me, this book enriches the theoretical discourse of organizational research by its highly inspiring style of discussing and reflecting on organizational phenomena.

Linda L. Putnam: *Images* was the inspiration for several chapters that I co-authored on the role of communication in organizational studies. It enabled me to challenge the dominant notion that communication is merely a conduit for transmitting or exchanging information and to embrace the critical role of multiple metaphors, such as symbol, voice, linkages, and performance in the development of a field.

Uta Wilkens: Since the time when we were students, Morgan's *Images* have always been a guideline for understanding and distinguishing organizations. But it took a while until we started to make use of the concept actively in our empirical research. That was when we had to explain the organizational transformation from product-based companies to integrated product-service systems (IPSS) with their ambiguous demands.

Vitor Hugo Klein Jr.: My interest in Morgan's work was renewed . . . when I started to develop a curiosity about the role of imagination in organizations. Reading *Images of Organization* again and, this time [with] an understanding [of] other studies of metaphors produced since Morgan's seminal work, I was surprise[ed] to find out that very little was written about imagination.

Reflecting on the Field

These theoretical discussions led to ways of using *Images* to reflect on the field of organizational studies. Contributors to this volume employed Morgan's *Images* as "a summary of perspectives," "a map of the field," and "an analytical tool" for reading organizations. Some of them highlighted how the pluralistic stance of this book

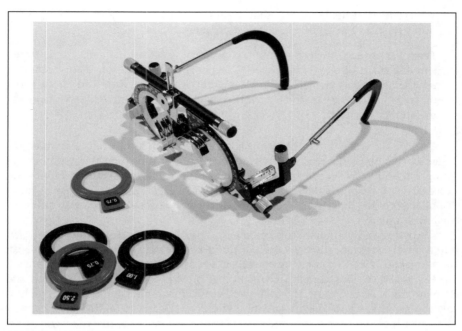

©iStockphoto.com/avalon1973

illuminated the notion of paradigms and the role of multiple lenses in depicting the development of a field.

Bernd-Friedrich Voigt: *Images* provides an easy access [and] overall summary of perspectives in organizational studies. . . . The book is placed on my desk—not in the book shelf.

Anders Örtenblad: As an undergraduate student in 1989, I [took] a course on organization theory [and used *Images* as the textbook]. It felt as if the book was written directly for me. . . . Immediately I felt that I had gotten "adjustable multiple glasses"/"trial frame" to understand all the other literatures. . . . Since then, these glasses have been my map of organization theory (even of the world).

Vitor Hugo Klein Jr.: Published in the 80s when writing (and talking) about metaphors was considered something rather eccentric in the field of organization theory, *Images* came as an insightful contribution. The book . . . gave way to a vision of pluralism of perspectives. Despite being harshly criticized at the time, Morgan's option for pluralism was fortunate. Organizational studies are marked today much more by pluralism than by paradigmatic consensus.

Christian Huber: When PhDs in Germany or Austria receive their training in methodology, the story almost always starts with Kuhn's paradigms. That's a nice idea but usually students find it difficult to see the point. [Morgan's *Images*] makes this point vivid and understandable. . . . If I had to highlight one single

achievement of the book, it is that it has enabled a pluralistic form of organization studies as a discipline to become legitimate.

Turo Virtanen: [*Images* provides] a conceptual structure that makes understandable the main differences between . . . schools of organization theory; students
use the metaphors as analytical tools in group work when they read a book about
organizations and try to find elements consistent with the main ideas of Morgan's
metaphors.

Overall, the collective voices of the contributors to this volume underscored the
value of this book, the reason it has stood the test of time, and the many uses of
Morgan's *Images*. As several authors pointed out, prior to the 1980s, metaphor was
a literary and linguistic device that was foreign to organizational studies. Now, as
Tsoukas notes in Chapter 11, metaphor has become normalized as a way "to read"
organizational life.

A second main purpose of this volume is to provide exemplars of the vastly different ways that scholars, students, and practitioners have used *Images* to engage in organizational analysis, to conduct research, and to extend theory/concept development.
To this end, the book contains chapters that provide theoretical explanations and
frameworks, such as Chapter 2 on Morgan's views of metaphor and Chapter 3 on how
metaphors work. It also contains empirical studies (see Chapter 6 on IPSS and Chapter 7
on leadership) and case studies and exemplars that examine the role of images in the
visual and digital turns in organizations (Chapter 8) and in the international arena
(Chapter 12). It includes essays that set forth new metaphors (Chapters 5 and 10),
presents typologies for using metaphors in organizational analysis (Chapter 4), and
sing praises as well as provide critiques of *Images* (Chapters 11 and 9, respectively).

To aid in using this edited volume, each chapter provides a list of key terms and
learning points that capture insights from the readings. Furthermore, the volume contains an overall glossary that consolidates definitions of key concepts across the book.
In this way, it could be used as a companion to Morgan's *Images*. In particular,
Chapters 2 (Morgan) and 3 (Cornelissen) of this volume expand on and develop ideas
from Chapter 1 of *Images,* particularly in updating Morgan's insights on how metaphors function as ways of seeing and shaping organizational life. Chapter 4 (Örtenblad)
of this volume also extends Chapter 10 of *Images* and explicates alternative ways to use
metaphor for conducting diagnostic readings and organizational analyses.

Chapters in this volume also illustrate as well as apply key concepts from
Morgan's book. Specifically, Chapter 5 (Bhatnagar) applies action research to predate,
inform, and contribute to culture as a metaphor and thus, it could be used in conjunction with Chapter 5 of *Images*. Chapter 6 (Süße, Voigt, & Wilkens) develops a
triangle of three mutually reinforcing metaphors (i.e., the brain, organism, flux and
transformation) to explain connectivity and information flows in organizational
environments and could be used in conjunction with Chapters 3, 4, and 8 in
Morgan's book.

Both Chapters 7 and 8 of this volume interface with multiple chapters in
Morgan's *Images*. Chapter 7 (Viranen) applies the machine, organism, brain, political
system, and culture metaphors (Chapters 2–6 of *Images*) to an analysis of leadership
and Chapter 8 (Kerr, Robinson, & Elliott) develops a case exemplar that draws on

TABLE 1 ● **Alignment of Chapters With Morgan's *Images***

Chapter and Author	Brief Title of Chapter	Corresponding Chapter(s) in *Images*	Metaphors Emphasized
Chapter 2 (Morgan)	Reflections on *Images*	Chapter 10; entire book	All metaphors
Chapter 3 (Cornelissen)	Morgan's Legacy	Chapter 1	All metaphors
Chapter 4 (Örtenblad)	Metaphors in Organizational Analysis	Chapters 10 and 11; entire book	All metaphors
Chapter 5 (Bhatnagar)	Organizations as Enablers of Happiness	Chapter 5	Culture
Chapter 6 (Süße, Voigt, & Wilkens)	Combining Metaphors	Chapters 3, 4, and 8	Brain, organism, flux and transformation
Chapter 7 (Viranen)	Leadership Metaphors	Chapters 2, 3, 4, 5, and 6	Machine, organism, brain, culture, political systems
Chapter 8 (Kerr, Robinson, & Elliott)	Metaphors in Visual and Digital Turns	Chapters 4, 7, 8, 10, and 11	Brain, psychic prisons, flux and transformation
Chapter 9 (Klein & Huber)	Political Uses of Images	Chapters 6 and 9; entire book	Political systems, instruments of domination, all metaphors
Chapter 10 Grant & Oswick	Organizations as Affect	Chapters 8 and 10	Flux and transformation
Chapter 11 (Tsoukas)	Reflective Judgment	Chapter 10	All metaphors
Chapter 12 (Case, Gaggiotti, Gosling, & Caicedo)	Of Tropes, Totems, and Taboos	Chapter 10	All metaphors

Chapters 4 (brain), 7 (psychic prisons), and 8 (flux and transformation) of *Images* and offers an example similar to Morgan's Chapter 11.

In the final section on reflections and commentaries, Chapter 9 (Klein & Huber) sets forth a critique of imagination that could be used in conjunction with Chapter 6 (political systems metaphor) and Chapter 9 (instruments of domination) of *Images* as well as the entire book. Exploring a new metaphor, Chapter 10 (Grant & Oswick) extends ideas developed in Chapter 8 (flux and transformation) of Morgan's book.

The last two chapters of the edited volume (Chapters 11 and 12 by Tsoukas and Case et al., respectively) also address applications of Morgan's book for reflective thinking, reading organizations as *texts*, and using *Images* in international contexts.

In summary, we hope that the readers of this book might see metaphors and Morgan's *Images* in a new light. Chapters in this volume serve as a compendium for the vast work on metaphors and organizations and as stimulus to explore new terrains that might lead to the development of alternative metaphors. It also provides exemplars of the multifaceted ways that scholars are using Morgan's *Images* for organizational analysis, research, and theory development. Above all, it pays tribute to a seminal book that in many ways has transformed management thinking about the complexities of and possibilities for organizations.

We close this preface with a special thanks to our contributors, our publisher, and our reviewers who helped make this book possible. The following reviewers vetted manuscripts that scholars submitted for possible publication in this volume and provided excellent feedback to the authors in revising their chapters. Special thanks to the following reviewers:

Andrea Bernardi, *Manchester Metropolitan University*

Orlando E. Blake, *University of Arizona, South*

Pavel Bogolyubov, *Lancaster University Management School*

Gibson Burrell, *Leeds University*

Marya Doefel, *Rutgers University*

Albert G. Elam, *International Business Academy*

Tammy Fitzpatrick, *Argosy University*

Steve Fox, *Queen Mary University*

Christeen George, *University of Hertfordshire*

Francis Green, *University of Birmingham*

Jim Gritton, *University of Greenwich*

James E. Harris, *St. Norbert College*

Mary Jo Hatch, *University of Virginia*

John Johnson, *University of Kentucky*

Sue Kavli, *Dallas Baptist University*

Yeonsoo Kim, *University of Nevada Las Vegas*

Melrona Kirrane, *Dublin City University*

Joseph Kretovics, *Western Michigan University*

Jeffrey Lewis, *Pitzer College*

Renee Maday, *Arizona State University*

Sarah Marshall, *Central Michigan University*

Ivan Matic, *University of Split*

Regina L. Garza Mitchell, *Western Michigan University*

John Nirenberg, *Walden University*
Östen Ohlsson, *University of Gothenburg*
Anita Pankake, *University of Texas Pan-American*
Gary Pheiffer, *London Metropolitan University*
Roberto Hugh Potter, *University of Central Florida*
Murray James Pyle, *Marywood University*
Joe Raelin, *Northeastern University*
Hans Petter Saxi, *Nord University*
Chrysavgi Sklaveniti, *Strathclyde University Business School*
Patricia Sotirin, *Michigan Technological University*
Basak Ucanok Tan, *Istanbul Bilgi University*
Scott Taylor, *University of Birmingham*
Jeffrey Treem, *University of Texas at Austin*
Richard Vail, *Colorado Mesa University*

Our thanks as well to Niels Pflaeging for the idea to include a quote by Gareth Morgan alongside his photo.

—Anders Örtenblad, Linda L. Putnam, and
Kiran Trehan

• About the Editors •

Anders Örtenblad is professor of organization and leadership at the Faculty of Social Sciences, Nord University, Norway. His main research interests are fashionable management ideas and their travel in space and time, organizational learning and the learning organization, management education, and the use of metaphors for and in the study of organizations and education. He has published articles in journals such as *Human Relations, Management Learning,* and *International Journal of Management Reviews* and he has edited books published by Edward Elgar, Routledge, and SAGE.

Kiran Trehan is professor of leadership and enterprise development at Birmingham University. Her research interests are leadership, emotions, and diversity in organizations. She has published a number of journal articles, policy reports, books, and book chapters in the field. Her work has been supported by grants from research councils, government departments, regional and local agencies, and the private sector. She has been a guest editor for multiple journals and serves in national advisory roles that shape debates and policy in leadership, diversity, and enterprise development.

Linda L. Putnam is a research professor in the Department of Communication at the University of California, Santa Barbara. Her current research interests include discourse analysis in organizations, negotiation and organizational conflict, and gender. She is the co-editor of 12 books, including The *Sage Handbook of Organizational Communication* (2014) and *Building Theories of Organization: The Constitutive Role of Communication* (2009), and she is the author/co-author of over 180 journal articles and book chapters. She is a Distinguished Scholar of the National Communication Association, a Fellow of the International Communication Association, and a recipient of the Distinguished Service Award from the Academy of Management.

"It is impossible to develop new styles of organization and management while continuing to think in old ways."

Gareth Morgan

Gareth Morgan is Distinguished Research Professor at the Schulich School of Business, York University, Toronto, Canada. He is author or co-author of several books on social and organizational theory and research, including *Sociological Paradigms and Organizational Analysis* (with Gibson Burrell), *Beyond Method, Images of Organization, Riding the Waves of Change*, and *Imaginization: New Ways of Seeing, Organizing and Managing*. His work has been published in numerous leading journals including *Academy of Management Review, Administrative Science Quarterly, Human Relations, Organization and Environment*, and *Organization Studies*. He has a particular research interest in the challenges of turbulent environments and transformations related to digital technology and been elected Life Fellow of the International Academy of Management for his international contributions to the science and art of management.

• About the Contributors •

Vikas Rai Bhatnagar is a visiting faculty member at the Indian Institute of Management (Indore) and the Jaipuria School of Business (Indirapuram), both in India. His research interests include leadership, employee happiness, and organizational change. He was the recipient of the World HRD Congress HR, Researcher of the Year Award in 2013. Prior to this, he held key roles in multinational corporations such as GE, Aventis, and Bayer. He leads an action research firm in India, providing action research services to diverse organizations.

Mikael Holmgren Caicedo is associate professor at Stockholm Business School, Stockholm University, Sweden. His research interests are on the organization of management accounting and control and the poetics and rhetoric of organizational and accounting practices, specifically the structures and forms that are advocated by formal and informal standard-setting communities. His work has been published in journals including *Culture and Organization, Critical Perspectives on Accounting*, and *Journal of Contemporary Accounting & Organizational Change*.

Peter Case is professor of organization studies, Bristol Business School, University of the West of England. He also holds a part time chair at James Cook University, Australia. His research interests encompass organization theory, organizational ethics and international development. He served as general editor of *Culture & Organization* (2007-10) and has published widely in such journals as *Organization, Human Relations, Journal of Management Studies and Management Learning*.

Joep Cornelissen is professor of corporate communication and management at Rotterdam School of Management, Erasmus University, The Netherlands. His research focuses on the role of corporate and managerial communication in the context of innovation, entrepreneurship and change, and social evaluations of the legitimacy and reputation of firms. His work has been published in the *Academy of Management Review, Journal of Management Studies, Organization Science*, and *Organization Studies*, and he has written a general text on corporate communication (*Corporate Communication: A Guide to Theory and Practice*, Sage) that is now in its fourth edition.

Carole Elliott is professor of HRD at the University of Roehampton Business School, UK, and a Visiting Fellow at George Washington University, Washington, DC. Her research interests are in management and leadership learning, with a focus on the critical examination of women's leadership. Other projects include the development of critical hermeneutic and visual methods; this work is now extending to examinations of the role of websites in creating revisionist histories of organizations. She is editor-in-chief of *Human Resource Development International.*

Hugo Gaggiotti is principal lecturer at Bristol Business School, University of the West of England, UK. His current research centers on issues relating to ethnographic analysis of professional mobility, nomadic management, and forms of organizing in the borderlands. His work has appeared in a range of interdisciplinary journals, including *Annals of Anthropological Practice, Culture and Organization, Journal of Organizational Change Management* and *Journal of Qualitative Research in Organizations and Management.* His latest book is *Un Lugar en su Sitio: Narrativas y Organización Cultural Urbana en El Espacio Latinoamericano* (Doble J, 2006).

Jonathan Gosling is an independent academic, Emeritus Professor at Exeter University, and visiting positions at universities in Canada, China, Denmark, and Slovenia. His current research examines the leadership of malaria elimination programs, Chinese philosophical influences on management and business, and the relations of shame and remorse to "responsible leadership." His most recent books are a study of power tactics, based on the career of Napoleon Bonaparte and modern comparators; and a textbook on "One Planet Business." He is lead faculty at the Forward. Institute, co-founder of coachingourselves.com, and a director of Pelumbra Ltd.

David Grant is pro-vice chancellor at Griffith Business School, Griffith University, Australia. His research focuses on how language and other symbolic media influence the practice of leadership and organization-wide, group, and individual-level change. He is a co-editor of the *SAGE Handbook of Organizational Discourse* (2004), *Metaphor and Organizations* (1996), and *Organisation Development: Metaphorical Explorations* (1996) and is a co-founder of the International Centre for Organizational Discourse Strategy and Change.

Christian Huber is a lecturer at the Helmut Schmidt University–University of the Federal Armed Forces, Hamburg, Germany. His research interests include imagination, mindfulness, management accounting, risk management, public sector organizations, valuation, and the use of literature in organizational theory. His work has been published in journals such as *Human Relations, Management Accounting Research, Critical Perspectives on Accounting, Journal of Management Inquiry,* and the *Journal of Business Ethics.*

Ron Kerr is senior lecturer at the University of Edinburgh Business School. His research interests include the application of Bourdieu's concepts to management and organizations, discourse and leadership in organizations, and the role of the Scottish banks in the global financial crisis. He has published in journals including *Critical Discourse Studies, Human Relations, Organization Studies, Organization,* and the *British Journal of Management.*

Vitor Hugo Klein Jr. is assistant professor at the Department of Public Governance at the Universidade do Estado de Santa Catarina, Brazil. He is a member of Strategos (Strategy and Organizations) research group at the Escola Superior de Administração e Gerência (Esag). His research interests include organizational behavior, leadership, and risk management. He is currently investigating the role of imagination in organizations.

Cliff Oswick is professor of organization theory at Cass Business School, City University London. His research interests focus on the application of aspects of discourse, dramaturgy, tropes, narrative, and rhetoric to the study of management, organizations, organizing processes, and organizational change. He has published over 140 academic articles and contributions to edited volumes. He is the European editor for *Journal of Organizational Change Management* and associate editor for *Journal of Change Management*.

Sarah K. Robinson is a reader in management and organization studies at the Adam Smith Business School, University of Glasgow. She has a long-standing interest in visual and digital approaches to organizational analysis and her research includes applications of critical hermeneutics to management and organization studies. She has published widely, including in *Human Relations, Organization Studies, Organization, British Journal of Management*, and *Management Learning*.

Thomas Süße Research and Teaching Fellow at the Chair for Human Resources and Work Process Management at the Institute of Work Science, Ruhr-Universität Bochum, Germany. His research particularly concentrates on issues about organizational learning and renewal in the context of highly ambiguous and dynamic business environments. In that regard, he mainly focuses on the trend of servitization of production toward integrated product-service systems (IPSS), on digitalization of work processes and the emergence of new forms of organizing.

Haridimos Tsoukas is the Columbia Ship Management Professor of Strategic Management in the University of Cyprus in Cyprus and a Distinguished Research Environment Professor at University of Warwick, UK. His research interests include knowledge-based perspectives on organizations, the management of organizational change and social reforms, organizational becoming; practical reason and the epistemology of practice, and meta-theoretical issues in organizational theory. He is the co-founder with Ann Langley of the annual International Symposium on Process Organization and co-editor of the *Perspectives on Process Organization Studies*, published annually by Oxford University Press. He is the author of *Complex Knowledge: Studies in Organizational Epistemology* (Oxford University Press, 2005), *If Aristotle were a CEO* (in Greek, Kastaniotis, 2012, 4th edition), and *Philosophical Organization Theory* (Oxford University Press, forthcoming).

Turo Virtanen is adjunct professor at the University of Helsinki. His research interests are in management and leadership of universities, knowledge management, human resource management, theory of social action and power, organizational and leadership culture, and public management. He has undertaken numerous external roles as a member or chair of many panels assessing the quality of academic research, accrediting study programs, reviewing institutions, and assessing quality assurance systems in Finland and many European countries.

Bernd-Friedrich Voigt is a research and teaching fellow at the Chair for Human Resources and Work Process Management at the Institute of Work Science, Ruhr-Universität Bochum, Germany. His research focuses on measuring and managing heterogeneity. He is also founder and owner of Managing Organizations, an internationally operating consulting, training, and researching company that engages in executive leadership development, competence portfolio management, and diversity management.

Uta Wilkens is professor of human resources and work process management at the Institute of Work Science, Ruhr-Universität Bochum, Germany, and was a research fellow at MIT and the Japan Advanced Institute of Science and Technology. Her research is on dynamic capabilities, organizational change, individual competencies, new employment relationships, and new fields of business such as product-service systems. From 2008 to 2015, she was the Ruhr-Universität Bochum vice rector for teaching, continuous education, and international affairs. She is a reviewer for international journals in management studies.

Making Sense of *Images of Organization*

Introduction

From Theory to Application of Metaphor in Organizational Analysis

Linda L. Putnam, Anders Örtenblad, and Kiran Trehan

M ost scholars would agree that Gareth Morgan's book *Images of Organization* has made a major impact on organizational studies (Morgan, 1986). It has been 30 years since the first publication of the book. During that time, *Images of Organization* has been cited over 15,496 times (Google Scholar, 2015) and was translated into 14 languages (Morgan, 2015). For the English-language versions alone, the first edition sold over 250,000 copies (Oswick & Grant, 2015) and the 1996 and 2006 editions sold more than 100,000 copies (Maggie Stanley, Sage, August 2015, personal communication). In addition, Morgan has produced two substantial revisions of the book (Morgan, 1996a, 2006), a book on imagination (Morgan, 1993), and a special edition for executives (Morgan, 1998). As Case et al. note later in Chapter 12, "it is nothing short of an organizational tour de force."

This edited volume pays tribute to Gareth Morgan and his seminal contribution of *Images of Organization*. As Grant and Oswick (1996, p. 11) noted on the 10th anniversary of this book, "It remains a highly influential piece doing exactly what it sets out to achieve—encouraging new ways of thinking and seeing organizations." Not much has been written about the ways that scholars and practitioners use Morgan's book for theory development, research, and practical reflection. This volume aims to fill this gap by providing specific exemplars of how contributors have applied Morgan's metaphors to research, theory, and organizational analysis. Its overall aim is to help practitioners, theorists, and students employ Morgan's book for critical evaluation and for ways to see organizations differently. To this end, this introduction offers a brief summary of Morgan's *Images of Organization*, explores uses and critiques of this book, highlights recent developments on the evaluation of metaphors, and offers an overview of the chapters in this volume. As a companion to *Images,* the preface suggests ways that chapters in this volume could be used in conjunction with Morgan's book.

Overview of Morgan's *Images of Organization*

Images of Organization (hereafter referred to as *Images*) was first published in 1986 and grew out of Morgan's work on the links between organizational theories and the fundamental assumptions on which they were based (see Morgan, 2011; reprinted in Chapter 2 of this volume). As Morgan (2011) points out in Chapter 2 of this volume, he came to the idea of metaphor by reflecting back on his co-authored book, *Sociological Paradigms and Organizational Analysis* (Burrell & Morgan, 1979), particularly how a given metaphor or theory sometimes locks scholars into narrow assumptions about the nature of organizations. As he began to "run with the idea" of "theory as metaphor," Morgan developed *Images* not simply as a set of different lenses for viewing organizations but to explicate the philosophical foundations for generating knowledge and analyzing complex organizations (Jermier & Forbes, 2011).

Metaphor then is a process that drives knowledge generation as well as puzzle solving. Defined as a way of understanding one situation in terms of another, metaphor asserts that A is like B by transferring information from a well-known source to a relatively unfamiliar target. When we say that an organization is like a sports team, we transfer information from what we know about sports teams (e.g., competitive, winners and losers, strives to outdo the other side, makes end runs) to a particular organization as the target.

Yet, as Morgan (1986) explicitly contends, metaphor yields only partial insights in that it accents some features while it distorts others; for example, a sports team may also create stress and anxiety among members in terms of "making the team." The typical use of a sports metaphor rarely captures the psychological aspects of this image; hence, features remain hidden in the background. In this way, the use of metaphor is inherently paradoxical in that it promotes both seeing and not seeing (Morgan, 1996b).

Thus, to uncover hidden features, Morgan (1986, 1996a, 2006) adopts a pluralistic approach that includes multiple metaphors—each of them simultaneously revealing while concealing the nature of an organization. In this way, he presents a different model of knowing and exploring complex organizations. Consistent with this stance, Morgan (2011, p. 467) treats "organizations [as] multidimensional, socially constructed realities where different aspects can coexist in complementary, conflicting, hence paradoxical ways." Therefore, he views puzzle solving about issues and developing knowledge about organizations as stemming from the dynamic interplay of multiple perspectives—comparing and contrasting, challenging, critically assessing, and deeply reflecting on the metaphorical foundations of the field (Jermier & Forbes, 2011).

Consistent with this foundation, Morgan (1986) sets forth eight images of organizations that function as root metaphors. Each metaphor embodies its own concepts and images that could splinter and develop into categories and submetaphors as ways to broaden or deepen organizational understanding. In effect, each metaphor is robust, encompasses its own vocabulary of images, and brings into focus particular features of an organization. The eight metaphors are machines, organisms, brains, cultures, political systems, psychic prisons, flux and transformation, and instruments of domination.

1. The *machine* metaphor highlights efficient production through focusing on inputs and outputs, organizational design, and routinized procedures. It covers organizational theories such as classical management, bureaucracy, and scientific management.
2. The *organism* metaphor casts an organization as a living system by focusing on life cycles, species, ecology, birth and death, adaptation, and survival. It encompasses open systems theory, contingency theories, population ecology, and evolutionary theories of organizations.
3. The *brain* metaphor centers on the learning capacities of organizations by emphasizing information processing, cognitive functioning, right and left brain functioning, memory, and holographic images. It embraces cybernetics, learning theories, and information theory.
4. The *culture* metaphor underscores values, beliefs, symbols, norms, and shared meanings and treats organizations as accomplishments that are socially constructed.
5. The *political systems* metaphor aligns organizations with governance systems, interest-based needs, conflicts, gender and race, and power. This metaphor draws on stakeholder theories, control theories, resource dependency, uncertainty, and boundary management perspectives.
6. The *psychic prisons* metaphor highlights the unconscious, psychological states, anxiety, and defense mechanisms. It embraces psychodynamic views of organizing, Freudian theory, paradoxes and traps, and patriarchy.
7. The *flux and transformation* metaphor accents process, flows, logics of change, circular patterns, and self-production. It includes chaos and complexity theories, mutual causality, feedback loops, and dialectical theories.
8. The *instrument of domination* metaphor highlights exploitation, alienation, class systems, and organizational control, and it draws from Marxist and critical theories.

The appeal of *Images* resides not only in its philosophical foundations but also in its rich tapestry of examples, innovative images, and alignments of abstract and concrete explanations. Consistent with the interplay of perspectives, each chapter ends with a review of the strengths and limitations of that particular metaphor. Each one also emphasizes what that metaphor does in the process of theorizing and how it produces partial, conflicting, and distorted insights about organizations. In doing so, Morgan (2011) has cast both problem solving and theory construction as dialectical processes that make us uncomfortable with our taken-for-granted views and leads us to expand our horizons.

Uses and Critiques of *Images of Organization*

To this end, scholars and practitioners have used Morgan's *Images* in a wide variety of ways, including analysis, reflective thinking, mapping the field, and developing organization theory (Cornelissen, 2005). They have conducted empirical studies on one or more of the eight images (Alvesson, 1995), categorized literature within a particular area of study (Müller, Mathiassen, & Balshøj, 2010), and examined the role of metaphors in leadership (Alvesson & Spicer, 2011) and project management (Winter, 2009). These uses have helped to instantiate the concept of metaphor in the field, embrace the interpretive and critical turns in management studies, and provide a bridge between theory and practice. *criticism**

These diverse applications, however, have generated several critiques of Morgan's book, particularly regarding the relativism and pluralism in his use of metaphors. *Relativism* refers to the ease and readiness of applying multiple metaphors to particular organizational situations. For example, VrMeer (1994) highlights the potentially rampant and naïve use of metaphors in conceptualizing organizational phenomenon, whereas Reed (1990, p. 38) contends that Morgan's *Images* promotes a form of relativism grounded in cognitions and shared interpretations that ignore economic and material realities. Furthermore, Tinker (1986, p. 364) contends that Morgan adopts a stance of "supportive, tolerant, uncritical, [and] scientific free-for-all" in his use of metaphors, and McCourt (1997) charges that Morgan's metaphors are ready-made products that are too easy to use, substitute, and reconstitute the nature of organizations. This notion of relativism then addresses two concerns: 1) an ethical relativism that stems from Morgan's lack of commitment to a political or moral stance and 2) an ontological relativism that endorses the legitimacy and interplay among multiple metaphors.

In response to these critiques, Morgan (see Chapter 2 of this volume) argues that although he embraces a way of knowing grounded in the interplay among perspectives, this process does not mean that any metaphor is as good as any other image in theory development and organizational analysis (see Tsoukas, Chapter 11). Knowledge generation, for Morgan (2011), is always context based and arises from practical situations in which the dynamic interplay among metaphors becomes embedded in people, their circumstances, and their interpretations. Some scholars, however, claim that Morgan's approach in *Images* remains abstract and removed from the embodied enactments of organizational practices (see Case et al., Chapter 12). Yet, for Morgan, context sensitivity should govern the use of particular metaphors in situations that call for different meanings and interpretations. Scholars and practitioners then need to avoid abstracting, generalizing, and decontextualizing metaphors as well as treating them as interchangeable lenses for analyzing organizations writ large.

Pluralism refers to Morgan's use of multiple metaphors to avoid simplifying organizations. To enter into analysis and knowledge building, Morgan (1996a) recommends aligning, engaging, and contrasting multiple perspectives. Yet some scholars view this pluralism as homogenizing radically different orientations to organizational reality (McCourt, 1997; Reed, 1990). Other critics contend that the pluralistic use of metaphors turns a blind eye to the role of power in shaping organizational realities (Reed, 1990; Tinker, 1986).

For Morgan (2011), however, organizations are complex phenomena that require a multifaceted view to capture their complexity. He further contends that the very process of knowledge generation is both opened and constrained, and thus, power enters into the very activity of developing insights about organizations. In his use of multiple images, Morgan (1996b) advocates employing a dialectical interplay among

"metaphors highlight factors while overshadowing others"
+ metaphors, + views

opposites and not simply integrating, combining, or reassembling parts back into the whole. In response to his critics, Morgan (2011) affirms his belief that organizations are socially constructed, multidimensional phenomena in which diverse and conflicting elements coexist. To understand organizational problems and issues, Morgan (1986, pp. 371–372) suggests that organizational actors develop the art of *reading* metaphors. *Reading* in this sense refers to applying and integrating insights from competing metaphors to gain a pragmatic understanding of a particular situation. By being open to the frames aligned with each metaphor, organizational members can shift figure-ground relationships between what is visible and what is hidden. In doing so, they become open to new opportunities or courses of action. Reading an organization, as Morgan (2006) suggests, requires disciplined imagination (Weick, 1989) and diagnostic processes that are as complex as the phenomenon itself.

Generating Organizational Metaphors in Theory and Practice

The issue of relativism closely relates to the criteria for evaluating metaphors. Cornelissen (2004) sets forth two criteria for selecting and evaluating new metaphors: 1) making a robust correspondence between the selected concepts (e.g., organizations and machines) and 2) selecting ones that are distant and distinct from each other in their domains (e.g., machines reside in a different category of phenomena than do organizations). These two criteria signal the extent to which a metaphor is likely to break new ground, have heuristic value, and reveal surprising or unexpected insights.

For example, Cornelissen (2004) demonstrates that the metaphor of *organization as theater*, although commonplace in the literature (Czarniawska, 1997; Mangham & Overington, 1987), demonstrates a strong correspondence between target and domain concepts but draws from very similar category domains. In effect, theater and organizations fall into the same broad category of "human collectives." Even though the metaphor of *organization as theater* highlights the performative, ritualistic, dramatic, and audience-oriented nature of organizations, Cornelissen suggests that it lacks heuristic value and, consequentially, is less useful in problem solving. Moreover, he contends that the insights the metaphor reveals are not particularly surprising.

These criteria are useful in distinguishing between generative and surface metaphors (see Morgan's discussion in Chapter 2 of this book). *Generative metaphors* "broaden and deepen understanding of the phenomena . . . and create important problem solving ideas" (Morgan, 2011, p. 468), whereas *surface metaphors* may enrich understanding but they often fail to break new ground or create new value for users. Developing new metaphors then stems from disciplined imagination (Weick, 1989) linked to problem statements that grow out of particular puzzles. As Morgan (2011, p. 468) cautions, "innovative theory building and problem solving do not just rest on finding cute new metaphors." Rather, scholars should strive to develop generative metaphors that encompass multiple related images and create value for users.

Given these guidelines, what are some potential avenues for developing generative metaphors in organizational theory and practice? To address this question, we edited a special issue of *Human Relations* (Örtenblad, Putnam, & Trehan, 2016) titled "Beyond Morgan's Eight Metaphors: Adding to and Developing Organizational Theory." From this issue, two particular processes stood out as potential avenues for generating metaphors: 1) engaging in critical reflection that is context based and 2) exploring links between metaphors and metonymy.

Metaphors often grow out of critical reflection grounded in organizational contexts; that is, scholars focus on a problem or puzzle, reflect on and critique current practices, and challenge status quo thinking. When Morgan's (1986) book first entered the scene in the 1980s, the very notion of metaphor as theory was a revolutionary idea. In many ways, scholars and practitioners viewed his eight metaphors as radical, unconventional, and even emancipatory (e.g., organizations as *psychic prisons* or *instruments of domination*). Today, these metaphors may seem commonplace in organizational studies and management education.

Embracing a puzzle that has the potential to challenge dominant thinking is important in developing new metaphors. Drawn from publications that appear in the *Human Relations* special issue, we highlight several articles that generate metaphors and submetaphors through challenging dominant thinking. Specifically, McCabe (2016) sets forth the metaphor of *Wonderland,* drawn from Lewis Carroll's (1865) work on *Alice's Adventures in Wonderland,* to challenge the common-sense assumptions that organizations are shaped by order and rationality. The *Wonderland* metaphor highlights the ridiculous, contradictory, irrational, and nonsensical aspects of everyday organizational life. In reflecting on routine organizational experiences, McCabe makes a correspondence between this fictional work and the absurdity of organizational life. Thus, in terms of critical reflection, this metaphor represents a radical shift in organizational thinking. Yet, based on Cornelissen's (2004) criteria of distance in category domains, *Wonderland* and fiction may be too similar to organizational reality to provide heuristic value.

Two other articles in the special issue of *Human Relations* create metaphors from focusing on problem-centered issues in organizational contexts. Specifically, Kemp (2016) contends that Morgan's traditional eight images are gender-less and consequently perpetuate status quo inequality through neutralizing gender. Embracing this problem, she develops submetaphors of *femicide* and *justice* as ways to make gender equality central to organizational theory and practice. In a similar way, Jermier and Forbes (2016) challenge the traditional roles that organizations play in responding to the natural environment. Working within the *instruments of domination* metaphor, the authors develop subimages of organizations as *water exploiters, water keepers,* and *ecological partners.* Importantly, these metaphors emanate from critical reflection on particular organizational practices and from grounding images in context-based problems of real concern. Moreover, they draw images from categories that have distinct domains (i.e., organizations and water).

A second practice for generating new metaphors stems from the interplay between parts of an image and the metaphor as a whole. *Metonymy* refers to using particular words as parts to substitute for relationships as wholes, such as using the word *sisters* to signify *the feminist movement* or the term *crown* to refer to the *kingdom* (Oswick, Putnam, & Keenoy, 2004). Metaphor depends on metonymy or the process of making specific and concrete attributes of an image into a signified whole. For Morgan (2016), this relationship gets at the heart of how metaphor works in practice. Specifically, metaphor functions through expansion or broaden ways of thinking, whereas metonymy relies on reduction through identifying the details of images (Oswick, Keenoy, & Grant, 2002; Oswick et al., 2004).

Scholars have explored the relationship between metaphor and metonymy, both in generating images and using in them in practice (Cornelissen, 2008). In generating new metaphors, Schoeneborn, Vasquez, and Cornelissen (2016) explicate the features of flux and transformation, ones grounded in metonymy to make this image concrete. Their efforts reveal new submetaphors of organizations as practice, as process, and as communication. A comparison among those submetaphors shows how the image of *organization as entity* works in tandem with its conception as a process.

As an example of using the metonymy–metaphor relationship in practice, Pinto (2016) explores a puzzle of how an actual Icehotel, located in Sweden, is paradoxically temporary and yet permanent, different and yet the same, and regularly destroyed only to be reborn. The edifice of the Icehotel is torn down every year and reconstructed the next winter season. Using attributes of the edifice itself and the operations of the Icehotel as an organization (e.g., the purity of the ice, the multiskilled teams, and time pressures), Pinto details the concrete features of the metaphor that show how temporary organizations can be effective, high performers. As Morgan (2016) notes in his commentary, "It is the metonymical reduction that gives the metaphor grounded meaning and relevance beyond the fact that it is a large block of ice that's constantly coming and going and functioning as a 'wonder of the world' in Northern Sweden."

In essence, given the importance of metaphors in management theory, scholars need to generate new metaphors and focus on what makes them take hold in theory and practice. For the most part, robust metaphors break new ground, reveal new insights, and have heuristic value for practice. They reach beyond the surface, generate new knowledge, embody a repertoire of their own images, and hold value for how they can be used. In generating new metaphors, two avenues offer promise for developing insightful and useful images: namely, engaging in critical reflections on puzzles and problems in context-rooted situations and exploring the links between metonymy and metaphor.

Moving From Theory to Application: The Structure of This Book

This book contributes to discussions of metaphor through examining how researchers and practitioners use Morgan's *Images* in concept development, research, and arenas of practice. This book is divided into three parts. Part I contains three chapters that introduce the reader to Morgan's *Images*, including this introduction and the issues that it raises. Part II forms the heart of the book and focuses on the different ways that scholars have used Morgan's metaphors to analyze situations, solve problems, and make sense of complex organizations. Part III consists of four chapters that offer reflection, commentary, and constructive critique.

Part I: Making Sense of *Images of Organization*

The three chapters in this section provide a background for the remainder of the book by focusing on what metaphor is, why it is important to organizational studies, how metaphors work, and how they are linked to theory construction. Chapter 1 ("Introduction: From Theory to Application of Metaphor in Organizational Analysis") sets the stage for the book and builds the groundwork for examining different ways that scholars have used Morgan's *Images*. Chapter 2 ("Reflections on *Images of Organization*") is a reprint of Morgan's (2011) article in which he reflects on the origin, aims, and intensions in writing *Images*. The original article appeared in a special issue of *Organization & Environment*, edited by Linda Forbes and John Jermier. In this article, as reprinted in Chapter 2, Morgan not only provides a background for developing *Images*, but he also sets forth his view of metaphor, its connection to metonymy, and the role that it plays in organizational studies. In this chapter, Morgan distinguishes between choosing a particular metaphor and the process of using it, specifically in theory construction. He concludes Chapter 2 by responding to the critics of his book and suggesting the possibility of new metaphors.

Elaborating on Morgan's views of images, in Chapter 3 ("Morgan's Legacy in Theorizing and Understanding Organizations"), Joep Cornelissen treats metaphors as essential to reasoning about abstract and complex phenomena; hence, individuals use language that evokes images as they conceptualize organizations in their everyday discourse. Metaphor fleshes out what an organization is through how it works as a cognitive process.

Specifically, Cornelissen departs from the notion that metaphor works through making comparisons from a known source to an unknown target (Tsoukas, 1991, 1993). Claiming that Morgan (1986) adopts this comparison model, Cornelissen sets forth a constitutive view in which scholars construct metaphor through creating a blend between the target and domain (see Cornelissen's discussion in Chapter 3). From this view, he suggests that individuals develop an organizing frame; elaborate on the blend between concepts; and generate emergent, unique meanings in which both domains come together. In this way, new metaphors emerge through an active process in which people start with a primary or basic metaphor that arises automatically and then engage in elaboration and conceptual blending to develop complex images.

Part II: Using Metaphors in Organizational Analysis

Focusing on the use of metaphors, Part II of this book shifts from theory to application. In Chapter 4 ("Approaches to Using Metaphors in Organizational Analysis: Morgan's Metaphors and Beyond"), Anders Örtenblad overviews and distinguishes among seven ways in which people use metaphors, specifically as 1) a *color map* to reveal features of organizations, 2) *colored lenses* for applying different perspectives in organizational analysis, 3) *pigeon-holes* or categories for how to classify organizations and understandings of organizations, 5) a means for *self-diagnosis*, 6) an *eye-opener* for what is happening in organizations, and 7) *cognitive innovations* for developing creativity. These approaches differ in the ways that they align with binaries, including descriptive versus generative metaphors, metaphor as a variable versus metaphor as "seeing as," root versus surface metaphors, analyst metaphors versus those being studied, and metaphors that stem from organizational research versus development. Using these seven approaches, Örtenblad applies them to the chapters in this section and shows how patterns emerge in the application of Morgan's *Images*.

In Chapter 5 ("Viewing Organizations as Enablers of Happiness"), Vikas Rai Bhatnagar illustrates the generative use of metaphor by treating it as predating, informing, and contributing to organizational culture. He contends that metaphor shapes organizational reality through artifacts that reveal espoused values and shared assumptions, ones often linked to a company's designer. Moreover, traditional images of organization, particularly ones that parallel Morgan's eight metaphors, often align with negative affect and the dehumanizing aspects of organizational cultures. Drawing on positive psychology, he calls for designers to conceptualize organizations as enablers of happiness through emphasizing employee well-being and focusing on activities that stress good intentions.

Moving from generative to descriptive uses of metaphors, Thomas Süße, Bernd-Friedrich Voigt, and Uta Wilkens examine the role of images in the emergence of integrated product-service systems (IPSS) in Chapter 6 ("Combining Metaphors to Understand New Organizational Phenomena"). In changing from production to mass consumption, the IPSS focuses on how to deliver customized and individual solutions to problems through integrating products and services. Based on a survey of problem-solving behaviors of engineers, Süße et al. coded responses to open-ended questions into categories drawn from Morgan's eight metaphors. Their analyses show how a triangulation of three mutually enforcing metaphors best captures the nature of integrated product-services. Arrayed in a triangle, these multimetaphors serve as design principles for organizations that are engaged in developing the integration of products and services.

Also relying on quantitative data, Turo Virtanen examines the relationships between metaphors of organizations and images of leadership in Chapter 7 ("Exploring Metaphors of Leadership"). Drawing from five of Morgan's images, Virtanen develops 30 metaphorical expressions (e.g., *gardener* as nurturing and supporting growth and *confessor* as listening to problems and protecting confidentiality) to depict five leadership styles. Then he conducts a survey in which he asks respondents to link the metaphorical expressions to the behaviors of two superiors in their organizations. The results demonstrate an overlap between the metaphorical expressions and four of the five leadership styles. Virtanen's study also reveals a clear segmentation between positive and negative images of leadership and an alignment of metaphors into two clusters—charismatic and solidarity images. He concludes that a bridge of latent meaning structures exists between leadership metaphors and images of organizations.

Drawing from recent organizational changes, in Chapter 8 ("Developing Metaphors in Light of the Visual and Digital Turns in Organizational Studies: Toward a Methodological Framework)," Ron Kerr, Sarah K. Robinson, and Carole Elliott question whether Morgan's *Images* can capture the complex and decentralized nature of contemporary organizations, specifically the visual and the digital turns. The visual turn highlights the creation of objects to view organizations through promoting and branding, whereas the digital turn centers on the role of new media in communicating with stakeholders and widening the sphere of organizational influence. To explore these features of organizations, the authors examine the webpages of a new transnational corporation and conduct informal and formal analyses of what the visuals and texts are doing. Their analyses suggest that Morgan's metaphors of psychic prison, brain, and flux are useful in capturing both the digital and visual aspects of corporate identities. This application, however, does not address how visual and digital media interact to construct deception or trickery in casting objects as real. In effect, the authors call for developing a new metaphor that goes beyond depicting visuals and focuses on how new media constitute contemporary organizational realities.

Part III: Reflections, Commentaries, and Constructive Critique

The previous chapters highlight ways that organizations are changing through developing new social and economic structures, making rapid advances in technology, and focusing on branding and digital media to extend organizational influence. Chapters 9–12 provide commentary, reflection, and constructive critique of Morgan's *Images*.

Specifically, in Chapter 9 ("Imagination and the Political Use of Images"), Vitor Hugo Klein Jr. and Christian Huber contend that Morgan's metaphor of *organizations as political systems* fails to capture the imagination of actors in legitimating, reproducing, challenging, and deceiving organizations. Focusing on the relationship between imagination and image, the authors call for a theory to assess how metaphors hide vested interests in promoting creative ways of thinking. They draw from two different theorists, Ricoeur (1976) and Castoriadis (1987), to develop this theory and to situate politics as a negative outgrowth of employing metaphors in organizational analysis.

Chapter 10 ("Organization as Affect: Moving on Metaphorically"), by David Grant and Cliff Oswick, embraces the challenge to develop new images that capture current organizational changes. The authors propose the metaphor of *organization as affect* to capture online processes of organizing and to yield insights about virtual organizations. Affect focuses on trans-personal activities in which organizational members interact and connect with one another in seemingly illogical and unpredictable ways. Moreover, it relies on visual cues, incorporates immediate and involuntary responses, and moves beyond the idea of nontraditional forms of organizing. It also exhibits sufficient, but not excessive overlap between source (affect) and target (organization), selects concepts from unique domains, and meets the criteria of being vivid and compact. As an *applied metaphor*, affect serves as a way to analyze organizational phenomena and to employ other tropes associated with the use of metaphor. Importantly, Grant and Oswick treat this suggestion as only one of a number of possible new metaphors. They challenge scholars to develop bold and imaginative images, ones that move away from an overreliance on literal targets.

In Chapter 11 ("The 'Metaphor' Metaphor: Educating Practitioners for Reflective Judgement"), Haridimos Tsoukas aligns literal as the familiar and metaphor as the unfamiliar. He notes that the term *metaphor* has become normalized in organizational studies as a way "to read" organizational life and that Morgan's *Images* enables a broad audience of scholars, practitioners, and students to engage in this type of reading. For scholars, Tsoukas sees metaphor as a tool that disrupts traditional classification systems by generating new concepts.

For practitioners, metaphor triggers unrest, fosters reflective thinking, and sharpens practical understanding of situations. Tsoukas points out how the reflective manager employs metaphor to increase his or her sensitivity to the organizational context, observe subtle cues, and attend to the big picture. He claims that by treating organizations as texts, a practitioner can complicate understandings through using metaphor to suspend conclusions and to observe how language reveals while it conceals. He observes that *Images* has helped students improve their initial readings of a case and refine their taken-for-granted understandings as they reformulate interpretations to yield insights. For Tsoukas, Morgan's reach to a broad audience attests to the impact of *Images* and why he regards it as the best textbook in organizational studies to date.

Reaching a broad audience is a central concern for Peter Case, Hugo Gaggiotti, Jonathan Gosling, and Mikael Holmgren Caicedo in Chapter 12 ("Of Tropes, Totems, and Taboos: Reflections on Morgan's *Images* From a Cross-Cultural Perspective"). Case et al. situate Morgan's *Images* as totems, a concept that refers to presupposing particular translations of language, objects, and forms across cultures. They claim that metaphors, like totems, function by imbuing an object with a distinct reality, like a *coat of arms* identifies people in a family heritage. The concept of totem grows out of anthropological sensitivity in which scholars explore the qualities of an image through adopting a cultural stance. The authors caution that cultural assumptions of particular metaphors carry the danger of conveying ethnocentric views of organizations and organizing. Rather than accepting Morgan's eight images as orthodoxy, they recommend that scholars use metaphors as totems to enhance cultural sensitivity.

To illustrate the challenges of linguistic and cultural translations, Case et al. present exemplars from the use of Morgan's metaphors in Finnish, Albanian, Catalan, and Malaysian cultures. For example, the organism metaphor in Finnish culture denotes a nonliving being, a compound of parts, and a multifaceted instrument—not a biological system. In effect, they contend that metaphors are not value free or independent of a cultural context. Scholars in international settings then need to develop multiethnic interpretations that guard against ethnocentric use of Morgan's metaphors.

In summary, this edited volume offers a potpourri of chapters that illustrate how scholars and practitioners have used Morgan's (1986) *Images of Organization* in theory building, research, and analysis. These chapters focus on how metaphors work; ways of using them in organizational analysis; and the roles that they play in organizational culture, IPSS, and leadership. These essays explore new terrain, including capturing the visual, digital, and affect metaphors that characterize branding; widening corporate influence; and developing virtual means of organizing. They also caution scholars and practitioners to avoid assuming that other cultures use metaphors in the same ways and with the same meanings that Anglo-Saxon readers do.

Overall, these chapters promote a reflexive, imaginative, and even political rethinking of how we use *Images of Organization* as a book as well as employ metaphors generically in organizational analysis. As scholarship advances, new images will surface and as they do, we urge theorists and practitioners to develop generative metaphors through relying on context-based problems and puzzles and through assessing the vital role that metaphors play in organizational life.

References

Alvesson, M. (1995). *Management of knowledge-intensive companies*. Berlin, Germany: Walter de Gruyter.

Alvesson, M., & Spicer, A. (Eds.). (2011). *Metaphors we lead by*. London, England: Routledge.

Burrell, G., & Morgan, G. (1979). *Sociological paradigms and organizational analysis*. London, England: Heinemann.

Carroll, L. (1865). *Alice's adventures in Wonderland*. London, England: Macmillan.

Castoriadis, C. (1987). *The imaginary institution of society*. Cambridge, MA: MIT Press.

Cornelissen, J. P. (2004). What are we playing at? Theatre, organization, and the use of metaphor. *Organization Studies, 25*(5), 705–726.

Cornelissen, J. P. (2005). Beyond compare: Metaphor in organization theory. *Academy of Management Review, 30*(4), 751–764.

Cornelissen, J. P. (2008). Metonymy in language about organizations: A corpus-based study of company names. *Journal of Management Studies, 45*(1), 79–99.

Czarniawska, B. (1997). *Narrating the organization: Dramas of institutional identities*. Chicago, IL: University of Chicago Press.

Google Scholar. (2015). *Gareth Morgan*. Retrieved November 14, 2015 from https://scholar.google.com/citations?user=gsyNMpgAAAAJ&hl=en&oi=sra

Grant, D., & Oswick, C. (1996). Introduction: Getting the measure of metaphors. In D. Grant, & C. Oswick (Eds.), *Metaphor and organizations* (pp. 1–20). London, England: Sage.

Jermier, J. M., & Forbes, L. C. (2011). Metaphor as the foundation of organizational studies: Images of organization and beyond. *Organization & Environment, 24*(4), 444–458.

Jermier, J. M., & Forbes, L. C. (2016). Metaphors, organizations and water: Generating new images for environmental sustainability. *Human Relations, 69*(4), 1001–1028.

Kemp, L. (2016). "Trapped" by metaphors for organizations: Thinking and seeing women's equality and inequality. *Human Relations, 69*(4), 975–1000.

Mangham, I. L., & Overington, M. A. (1987). *Organizations as theatre: A social psychology of dramatic appearances*. Chichester, England: Wiley.

McCabe, D. (2016). "Curiouser and curiouser!" Organizations as Wonderland—A metaphorical alternative to the rational model. *Human Relations, 69*(4), 945–974.

McCourt, W. (1997). Discussion note: Using metaphors to understand and to change organizations: A critique of Gareth Morgan's approach. *Organization Studies, 18*(3), 511–522.

Morgan, G. (1986). *Images of organization*. London, England: Sage.

Morgan, G. (1993). *Imaginization: The art of creative management*. Newbury Park, CA: Sage.

Morgan, G. (1996a). *Images of organization* (2nd ed.). London, England: sage.

Morgan, G. (1996b). Is there anything more to be said about metaphor? In D. Grant, & C. Oswick (Eds.), *Metaphor and organizations* (pp. 227–240). London, England: Sage.

Morgan, G. (1998). *Images of organization: The executive edition*. San Francisco, CA: Berrett-Koehler.

Morgan, G. (2006). *Images of organization* (3rd ed.). London, England: Sage.

Morgan, G. (2011). Reflections on *Images of Organization* and its implications for organization and environment. *Organization & Environment, 24*(4), 459–478.

Morgan, G. (2015). *Major books*. Retrieved November 15, 2016, from http://imaginiz.com/?page_id=6

Morgan, G. (2016). Commentary: Beyond Morgan's eight metaphors. *Human Relations, 69*(4), 1029-1042.

Müller, S.D., Mathiassen, L., & Balshøj, H.H. (2010). Software process improvement as organizational change: A metaphorical analysis of the literature. *Journal of Systems and Software, 83*(11), 2128–2146.

Örtenblad, A., Putnam, L.L., & Trehan K. (2016). Beyond Morgan's eight metaphors: Adding to and developing organizational theory. *Human Relations, 69*(4), 875–890.

Oswick, C., & Grant, D. (2015). Re-imagining images of organization: A conversation with Gareth Morgan. *Journal of Management Inquiry.* Advance online publication. doi: 10.1177/1056492615591854

Oswick, C., Keenoy, T., & Grant, D. (2002). Metaphor and analogical reasoning in organization theory: Beyond orthodoxy. *Academy of Management Review, 27*(2), 294–303.

Oswick, C., Putnam, L. L., & Keenoy, T. (2004). Tropes, discourse and organizing. In D. Grant, C. Hardy, C. Oswick, & L. L. Putnam (Eds.), *The Sage handbook of organizational discourse* (pp. 105–128). London, England: Sage.

Pinto, J. (2016). "Wow! That's so cool!" The icehotel as organizational trope. *Human Relations, 69*(4), 891–914.

Reed, M. (1990). From paradigms to images: The paradigm warrior turns postmodernist guru. *Personnel Review, 19*(3), 35–40.

Ricoeur, P. (1994). Imagination in discourse and in action. In G. Robinson & J. Rundell (Eds.), *Rethinking imagination* (pp. 118–135). London, England: Routledge.

Schoeneborn, D., Vasquez, C., & Cornelissen, J. (2016). Imagining organization through metaphor and metonymy: Unpacking the process-entity paradox. *Human Relations, 69*(4), 915–944.

Tinker, T. (1986). Metaphor or reification: Are radical humanists really libertarian anarchists? *Journal of Management Studies, 23*(4), 363–384.

Tsoukas, H. (1991). The missing link: A transformational view of metaphors in organizational science. *Academy of Management Review, 16*(3), 566–585.

Tsoukas, H. (1993). Analogical reasoning and knowledge generation in organization theory. *Organization Studies, 14*(3), 323–346.

VrMeer, R. (1994). Postmodernism: A polemic commentary on continuity and discontinuity in contemporary thought. *Administrative Theory & Praxis, 16*(1), 85–91.

Weick, K. E. (1989). Theory construction as disciplined imagination. *Academy of Management Review, 14*(4), 516–531.

Winter, M. (2009). *Images of projects*. London, England: Gower Press.

Reflections on *Images of Organization*

Gareth Morgan

This chapter is reprinted from Gareth Morgan's feature article "Reflections on Images of Organization and Its Implications for Organizations and Environment," published in 2011 in Organization & Environment, *24(4), 459–478. The title has been abbreviated for this book and the editors have inserted new headings to signal the content of each section.*

In developing this feature, we asked Gareth Morgan to reflect on his classic book, *Images of Organization* (1986), a work known for its innovative framework for understanding and using metaphors in organizational studies. We asked him to comment on whether, adding up what has been written in the last 25 years, effective use has been made of the framework. As our exchange unfolded, the invitation to write this piece developed into a series of more detailed questions that embraced the origin, aims, and intentions of *Images of Organization* as a contribution to organizational studies and its particular relevance for the issues addressed by Organization and Environment scholars. These questions are now reflected in the overall structure of his article.

—Linda Forbes and John Jermier,
CCFW Guest Editors

On the Genesis of *Images of Organization*

What was the genesis of the project leading to Images of Organization?

The genesis of *Images of Organization* (1986) rests in the work that I wrote with Gibson Burrell (*Sociological Paradigms and Organizational Analysis*, 1979), which sought to put the development of organization theory in a philosophical and sociological context. The core thesis of that work was that all theories of organization (and all social theory in general) have implicit core assumptions about the nature of the social world. Following Kuhn (1962/1970), we characterized these underlying assumptions as "paradigms" (in the sense of worldviews or alternative realities) and mapped social theory and organizational analysis as a domain of competing paradigms based on conflicting meta-theoretical assumptions about the nature of social science and of society. In our view, the conflicts in the underlying worldviews were generating conflicting theories that could not be understood or reconciled without understanding the implicit (and often hidden) assumptions on which they were based.

Sociological Paradigms was very successful in opening discussion across several disciplines about the contributions of different paradigms and the need for a more pluralistic and open view of organizational theory and research. It also succeeded in providing important legitimization of nontraditional methods of research characteristic of what we called the Interpretive, Radical Humanist, and Radical Structuralist paradigms, alongside the dominant Functionalist paradigm.[1]

However, as with all controversial work the book also attracted its fair share of critics. Some were upset that we took such a strong stand on the mutually exclusive nature of our paradigms and that the views from one paradigm tended to exclude those of another, creating opposing kinds of theory and research. Others mistakenly saw our work as just providing a classificatory device, as opposed to the deep challenge to fundamental assumptions that we intended. Gibson and I defended our work in a spirited way, and we were gratified by the book's acceptance and growing impact. But one challenge, voiced casually to me while writing the book by a colleague waiting for a coffee in the Faculty Lounge at Lancaster University, lingered on. "Gareth," he asked, "how can my work be in one of your paradigms if I don't even know what the paradigms are?"

This comment was clearly intended as one of critique. And it was one for which I did not have an immediate answer. My first inclination was to consider it as merely an attempt to dismiss what *Sociological Paradigms* was seeking to do. It just lingered as a background concern. But, the more I took it seriously, "Yes," I thought, "How can one be developing social theories, or theories of organization, without really knowing the fundamental assumptions on which one's theories are based?"

The moment of insight came quite randomly as a result of an invitation to take up a visiting faculty position at Penn State University—an invitation with one major requirement: that in addition to some graduate-level teaching, I would also teach a core undergraduate management course. This created a huge personal dilemma. I wanted to accept the invitation. But I had absolutely no idea how I could teach a conventional undergraduate management course while being true to the principles of *Sociological Paradigms*. Then it hit me. I could teach organization theory through metaphor, illustrating a range of different theories by presenting them as metaphors, each of which had both strengths and weaknesses.

The idea truly came as an intuitive flash of insight. There was no specific mention of metaphor in *Sociological Paradigms*. But in our analysis of systems theory, much had been made of the distinction between closed (mechanical) and open (organismic) systems, as was common in the sociological and organizational literature of the time.[2] The focus was on how these theories were shaped by models and analogies that reinforced an equilibrium or homeostatic ("steady state") view of the world. The book also suggested that there was no reason to be confined by these analogies and that fundamental systems principles could be challenged and extended by adopting new models. For example, we offered a diagram (Figure 2.1) illustrating how new or emerging system analogies (morphogenic, factional, and catastrophic) could be used to develop systems theories that saw change and transformation as a primary driving force. But it had never struck me that these analogies were really metaphors, accompanied by all the strengths and weaknesses of metaphor. I just saw them as offering different ways of model building.

In retrospect, this seems strange. But I had always seen an analogy as just a way of drawing simple comparisons between two phenomena. In the context of the arguments being developed in *Sociological Paradigms*, the concept was just used to point out how factional and catastrophic systems model could help systems theory break free of the Functionalist paradigm, towards the Radical Structuralist one.

The Penn State opportunity put all this work into a new frame: If theories at the most fundamental level were just metaphors, with all the limitations of metaphor, then metaphor could help explain the detailed structure of organization theory and disciplines. I had an answer to my colleague's question. In implicitly or explicitly selecting a metaphor as a basis for theorizing, one would also be implicitly locking into the assumptions on which the metaphor was based. Hence, in using a particular metaphor, consciously or unconsciously, one could also end up adopting the assumptions of an underlying sociological paradigm.

I felt I had to immediately test this hypothesis, and within a couple of hours of the Penn State telephone call, I found myself in the management section of Lancaster University's library, checking virtually every book on the shelves to see if

FIGURE 2.1 ● Some Possible Types of System Models

Type of system analogy	Mechanical	Organismic	Morphogenic	Factional	Catastrophic
Principal tendency	Equilibrium	Homeostasis	Structure elaboration	Turbulent division	Complete reorganization

←——————————————————————————————————→

Order and stability   **Conflict and change**

Source: Burrell and Morgan (1979), p. 61.

the ideas they presented were shaped by a dominant metaphor. Three hours later I was absolutely convinced, and very excited. This very crude and instinctive act of hypothesis testing convinced me that in developing management theory we are just developing the implications of a favoured metaphor. My academic career was now on a completely new trajectory, investigating the role of metaphor in a systematic way. Within a couple of years of intensive research, I had configured and taught my Penn State undergraduate course through metaphor; wrote an article for *Administrative Science Quarterly* on the links between paradigms, metaphors, and puzzle solving in organization theory (Morgan, 1980); developed some of the implications of the ideas for approaches to research (Morgan, 1983; Morgan & Smircich, 1980); and begun work on a series of projects that led to *Images of Organization* (1986).

On the Inspiration for Writing This Book

Whose work inspired and ultimately most influenced your thinking as you developed your framework for understanding metaphor?

That's an interesting question because all my work on metaphor became a completely emergent project shaped by the original problem-solving insight that "all theories are metaphors." If I look for the specific roots, they are definitely located in the work, conversations, and friendship with Gibson Burrell leading to our "relativist" view of social science as an enterprise driven by conflicting sets of assumptions. The Sociological Paradigms work was a real "game changer" for us. It was impossible to see or engage in social research as before, and our roles as academics were fundamentally changed.

What's interesting, in retrospect, is that there was no obvious single way forward. Basically, Gibson and I were both fairly fresh academics trying to find our feet in the social sciences. Neither of us had a single significant academic publication to our name, nor had we completed a PhD when we wrote *Sociological Paradigms*. The whole project was driven by a desire to decode what was happening in the social sciences in the 1970s as a process of self-education. Basically, we wanted to clarify the major debates and where we fit in. As a former accountant, I was very dependent on Gibson in introducing me to the sociological literature as we launched on what became a major journey of discovery. The culture of our host Department at Lancaster (Behaviour in Organizations), and friendship and conversations with our colleagues Bob Cooper, Colin Brown, and Frank Blackler, were also important, as was the open leadership of Department Head Sylvia Shimmin, who gave us all a huge amount of freedom to innovate as we wished. We were truly working in a culture where the pursuit of new knowledge was a driving force for us all, regardless of the career and other risks involved.

In terms of a very precise source of inspiration that put me on the metaphor track, in retrospect, I think I found it in Buckley's (1967) critique of systems theory and the distinctions he drew between mechanistic and organismic models as opposed to his morphogenetic (structure elaborating) alternative. It catalyzed the possibilities for systems theory that Gibson and I captured in Figure 2.1, and this was the image that came to my mind in response to the Penn State telephone call. The insight quickly drove me to investigate existing writings on metaphor, and I soon found the work of Black (1962),

Brown (1977), Cassirer (1946), Hesse (1966), Lakoff and Johnson (1980), Mueller (1871), Ortony (1979), Pepper (1942), Schon (1963), and others cited in Morgan (1980).

But, to be perfectly honest, I just "ran with the idea" of theory as metaphor without too much regard for the formal details presented in the literature. I am very much an idea-driven person, and I am inclined to plunge into issues on instinct, take them as far as I can, and then look to see what others have said about the same issue. I primarily use the literature to pay homage to work that has already been done, to test and refine emerging theory, and to ensure that I am not just "reinventing the wheel." I am greatly in favour of this approach to theory building and research, since if one grounds one's work too heavily in what already exists, it is difficult to escape from the status quo. This style of discovery was definitely the driver behind the work that Gibson and I did in writing *Sociological Paradigms* and is, I believe, one of the main factors leading to my specific approach to metaphor and why I was able to add a novel dimension to what has obviously been a very well-worked concept in the fields of literature, linguistics, philosophy, communications, and postmodernism.

I see my primary contribution as resting in how I have focused on the interrelationship between the insight and distortion embedded in the use of metaphor (more crudely put as the interplay between what is "true" and "false") and the epistemological, ideological, and political implications that flow from this (Figure 2.2). The approach, in short, emphasizes how we are always trying to understand the world through images, ideas, theories, and concepts that are simultaneously both insightful and distorting. Other writers and philosophers have got to this conclusion through other means, for example, Heisenberg's (1958) work on the uncertainty principle and Rorty's (1979) work on the impossibility of foundational truth. My journey, expressed most fully in the writing of *Images of Organization*, just took the paradoxical nature of metaphor to a logical conclusion, creating a dialectic between the strengths and limitations of different metaphorical perspectives to advocate ways of seeing, thinking, and acting that can create a broader, more creative, and more critical mode of understanding organizations than is usually the case.[3]

On Metaphor and How It Works

Can you tell us more about your view of metaphor and how it works?

The essence is captured in Figure 2.2. At its simplest level, metaphor operates as an implicit or explicit process that asserts "A is B," for example, "the man is a lion," "the organization is a machine." In the process, one point of reference is used to understand the other. For example, we look for and see the machine-like aspects of the organization or the lion-like aspects of the man. In so doing, we generate partial "truths"—insights that may resonate and produce genuine understanding but, if taken literally or to an extreme, are patently distorting and false. The man is not a lion; the organization is not a machine. This is what I call the paradox of metaphor.

I see this process as fundamental to human knowing and experience as we carry over one element of life to understand and cope with another, typically using *what we know* to negotiate and understand the unknown. As I have described at length elsewhere (Morgan, 1996), the "crossing over" that underlies metaphor is ontological—a primal cognitive process that, in part, defines our very nature as human beings.[4]

FIGURE 2.2 ● Metaphor—A Process of Seeing A as B

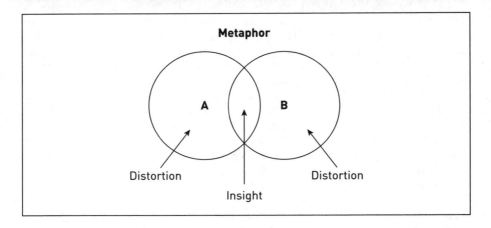

This ontological process results in metaphors (note the "s")—as images or words that are used to evoke and capture meaning. When we are talking about *metaphors*, we are in the domain of epistemology—dealing with constructs through which we are attempting to know and negotiate the world. I believe that the distinction between the ontological and epistemological aspects of metaphor is crucial, because it highlights that while our *metaphors* (the *content* of our knowledge and discourse) may be the subject of choice, the *process* of metaphor is not.

As illustrated in *Images of Organization*, I believe that *metaphor* is the process that drives theory construction and science, generating *metaphors* that create *theories* and associated research that always have inherent strengths and limitations because of the creative insights and distortions that characterize the very nature of the metaphorical process. The book makes its point by exploring eight generative metaphors, viewing organizations as machines, organisms, brains, cultures, political systems, psychic prisons, processes of change and transformation, and instruments of domination. As I note in the book, the choice of metaphors is intended to illustrate *a range of possibilities* for organizational theorizing and is by no means exhaustive. The aim was to present a treatise on "theory as metaphor" that shows the inherent incompleteness of any particular point of view. Every metaphor is presented as a framework that generates both strengths and limitations, with the juxtaposition of different metaphors being used to show how the limitations of one particular metaphor may be addressed by the strengths of others. As stated in *Images*, "Think 'structure' and you'll see structure. Think 'culture' and you'll see all kinds of cultural dimensions. Think 'politics' and you'll find politics. Think in terms of system patterns and loops, and you'll find a whole range of them" (Morgan, 1997, p. 349; Morgan, 2006, p. 339).

In this way, the book plays on the paradox of metaphor to challenge our ways of thinking in the hope of extending horizons of understanding—in how we understand organizations as theorists/managers/practitioners; in terms of how theory and research are constructed; and in terms of the implications of these ideas for how we act and shape organizations and organizational life in practice.

Through the juxtaposition of images the aim is to create an *experience* for readers that throws them back on themselves and their modes of understanding as they are enticed by the insights of a metaphor, only to find that these insights may be in conflict and challenged by what they read next. In this way, I have sought to create a form of "constructive deconstruction," challenging thinking in a way that encourages one to go beyond the confines of one's favoured point of view to explore others. By showing how any given theory is just generating partial insights that are in essence an oversimplification of what is being studied, it seeks to advance the cause of a more open and reflective approach to social science. By creating a kind of dialectic between the insights of competing points of view, it sets the basis for a broader and more integrated approach.[5]

While this is the basic aim and message of the book, interpretations and reactions vary, according to how different people relate to the whole idea of metaphor. For example, managers may just see metaphor as an abstract or fluffy concept of no direct relevance to their immediate work; theorists and researchers may see it as belonging to art and literature rather than science. These reactions have motivated me to think further about the metaphorical process and how it can be communicated.

The essence of my current view is captured schematically in Figure 2.3, which illustrates how metaphorical concepts can end up being seen as real "nonmetaphorical" ways of thinking about the world. In Section (A) of Figure 2.3, I have illustrated how metaphor can create a domain of understanding (as illustrated earlier in Figure 2.2 and related discussion—for example, the organization is a machine). The image, if it resonates, gets us thinking about the ways in which the organization is like a machine to tie down its specific (machine-like) characteristics. These are illustrated in Section (B) in Figure 2.3. For example, the mechanical view may lead us to see the organization as a *structure of interrelated parts*, as having *inputs* that are converted into *outputs*, as employing people that become *cogs in wheels*, that the organization can be *designed* and run for *efficiency* and evaluated in terms of *efficient performance*, and so on. In other words, the metaphor generates detailed elements of a machine theory of organization.

This process of tying down the details is fundamental for the operation of metaphor—otherwise we would have an image without any intrinsic or detailed meaning (if, indeed, one can imagine such a situation). The concretization or "tying down" of the metaphor is, in fact, what is described in linguistics and literature as "metonymy"—a process whereby the names of elements or parts of a phenomenon can be used to represent the whole.[6] As a result of this process, we may now arrive at a stage where the concepts stand as *concepts in their own right* as the generative metaphor gets lost from view (see Section [C] of Figure 2.3). The focus now is exclusively on "metonymical elements" that may be viewed as literal representations of the phenomena to which they are applied, for example, as managers and organizational theorists focus on the structuring of organization, the clear definition of roles, concerns for efficiency, etc.

Figure 2.3 thus captures the links between metaphor and what is often seen as concrete, literal thinking and is important for understanding the generative process that underlies detailed theory and research, which often inhabits Section (C) of Figure 2.3, without understanding what has gone before (i.e., in Sections [A] and [B]). This results in an overly reductive approach to both organizational research and management practice and to science generally. For example, if one

FIGURE 2.3 ● Metaphor and the Generation of Scientific Concepts

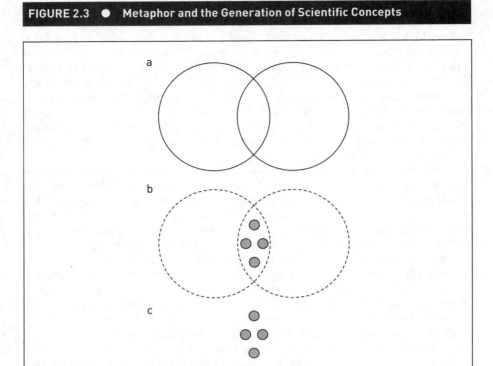

ignores the metaphorical genesis of the concepts one is using, one can get locked into the details, ignore the bias that the underlying metaphor may have generated, and miss other potentials, for example, from other metaphors that have been eliminated from view.

We are now clearly back to the epistemological aspects of metaphor discussed earlier and the importance of obtaining a reflective understanding of the process in which one is engaged—whether as a manager, theorist, or detailed researcher.[7]

On the Contributions That *Images* Makes

Images of Organization is a book about organization theory, and also offers a specific diagnostic scheme for the analysis of organizations. Which do you think has made the most important contribution to organization studies, and did you foresee something in writing the book that is greater than what has been accomplished to date?

This is an important question and one that I've reflected on a great deal. In order to write *Images* I had to make a specific decision on what I wanted to achieve and faced two main options with distinctive messages for the future development of organization studies. One option was to write a book on organization theory, specifically addressed to organization theorists and other social scientists. The other was to pursue the practical implications in the hope of also engaging a practitioner audience. I decided to combine both, using the majority of chapters to address organization theorists, concluding with two chapters that mobilized the insights of the book into a diagnostic method for reading and shaping organizational life. In order to achieve this aim, I framed the whole book within the context of a specific metaphor—the idea that one can "read" organization as if it were a kind of living text. I made this decision because I had already devoted so much work to the *theory* of organizations and felt that I could shift the grounds of my arguments and open new possibilities by speaking more directly to practitioners and educators of practitioners, albeit at a fairly theoretical level. The first unpublished draft of *Images* did in fact focus on the research and epistemological aspects of my ideas. It was only later that I decided to make the shift towards a more diagnostic, practice-oriented view.

In terms of impact, the practical educational implications of the work have clearly taken hold, especially through the work of educators and organizational consultants who are interested in helping people grasp richer understandings of organizations and organizational problems. The value of *Images of Organization* from this perspective is as an educational tool that helps one tap into different dimensions of organizations and to act with an appreciation of these in mind. The specific method for "reading organization" (illustrated through the Multicom Case in a preliminary form in the 1986 edition, and refined in subsequent editions) highlights how one can develop a "diagnostic reading" embracing multiple perspectives that then can be integrated through a "critical evaluation" with specific aims in mind. As such, it has been seen and used as a tool for developing skills in creative framing and reframing, ways of seeing, and as a form of critical thinking that can explore the multidimensional and often paradoxical nature of organizational life.

The book has also had an impact on organization theory, encouraging theorists and researchers to become more aware of their favoured metaphors and to explore the possibilities of finding new ones (e.g., Alvesson, 1993; Cornelissen, 2005; Cornelissen, Oswick, Christensen, & Phillips, 2008; Grant, 2004; Grant & Oswick, 1996; Oswick & Grant, 1996; Oswick, Keenoy, & Grant, 2002; Tsoukas 1991, 1993). The approach has also been applied to the analysis of specific aspects of organization and management, for example, on strategy (Mintzberg, Ahlstrand, & Lampel, 2005), on managing projects (Winter, 2009), on leadership (Avesson & Spicer, 2011). But the area in which I think it is possible to go a lot further rests in pursuing the epistemological implications of metaphor captured in Figure 2.3.

For example, if we explicitly pursue the idea that the ultimate challenge of metaphor to scientific investigation is to recognize how our concepts are grasping at very limited aspects of the realities we are trying to understand, this could open the way to a very different approach. What if we took *really* seriously the points made in Note 3 that

> metaphors provide partial insights; that different metaphors can produce conflicting insights; that in elevating one insight others are downplayed; that a way of seeing becomes a way of not seeing; and that any attempt to understand the complex nature of organizations (as with any other complex subject) always requires an open and pluralistic approach based on the interplay of multiple perspectives?

What if we actively sought to tackle the limitations of an abstracted "metonymical science," as captured in Level (C) of Figure 2.3?

This would require a much more reflective and self-critical approach to scientific inquiry. It would lead us to deal with the complexity of what we are studying by actively recognizing *the limits and downsides of our concepts* rather than just settling for the insights. This would immediately take us into better recognition of multidimensionality and help us anticipate and deal with potentially negative implications of our point of view. Of course, this requires a degree of reflexivity and self-deconstruction of one's approach that is not encouraged by the existing institutional research system.[8] Interestingly though, the openness and self-critique required here is perfectly consistent with the logic of science advocated by Popper (1958), with its emphasis on the role of refutation as the main driver of scientific knowledge. I also feel that we are going to see shifts in this direction as the current structure of science, thought, and understanding is transformed by the new forms of consciousness and communication accompanying widespread use of digital media.[9] The shift may be generational and take a while to realize, but I feel that it is sure to come.

I was not able to articulate this challenge in *Images of Organization* in the way I have above. But I believe it is one of the major implications of my work and an area where there is something greater to be accomplished than has been achieved to date.

On Responses to Critiques of *Images*

What do you think of the critiques that have been made of your work (e.g., scientism, anti-relativism, anti-postmodernism) and have any of your positions changed?

One of the interesting things about the critique is that it has come from lots of different directions. The advocates of traditional positivist (metonymical) science see my use of metaphor as too intangible and relativistic. Radical critics who wish to champion a particular metaphor or point of view (e.g., that organizations are ultimately class-based phenomena best understood as instruments of domination) also critique the relativism from an ideological as opposed to science-based perspective. Postmodernists often see the deconstruction embedded in my multidimensional methodology as being undermined by the way I seek to put "Humpty Dumpty together again" in the form an integrated diagnostic method. Others critique the emphasis I place on "reading" organization as opposed to the authorship role through which organizations are brought into being and continuously shaped and reshaped.

I have sought to learn from them all and to incorporate the merits of their arguments as far as possible.[10] But ultimately I have to stand on the fundamentals of my point of view. As noted above, I operate on the premise that ontologically, organizations are multidimensional, socially constructed realities where different aspects can coexist in complementary, conflicting, hence paradoxical ways. Consistent with this, I adopt a relativist view of epistemology that is open to multiple ways of engaging the fundamental complexity, recognizing that the different views can be combined, integrated, or used dialectically for a multiple of different ends. The process can create multiple forms of perspective-based knowledge that is always context based, in the sense that it is a direct product of the mode of engagement embedded in the perspective and objectives that the would-be knower brings to the phenomenon of study. Because of the complex, paradoxical nature of organizations, I side with Bohr's (1958) view that the opposite of a profound truth can be another profound truth. Hence, my view of knowledge and research is essentially pluralistic and open to multiple approaches to overcome the oversimplification of narrow views.

Obviously, this context-based view of knowledge obliges us to recognize that power relations have a major influence on the process, for example, in the sense that we do not always act in circumstances of our own choosing and that the knowledge we desire or produce may not always resonate with the dominant interests shaping the broader context and be discouraged or denied. Hence, the knowledge-generating process is both open and constrained and at times can become completely distorted. It is this concern about power relations that perhaps makes many of my critics most uncomfortable with the position taken in *Images of Organization*, that is, that in advocating a pluralist use of metaphor, I am ignoring this important contextual factor. My response: what is the alternative, since any editing of the knowledge-creating process or advocacy of specific metaphorical views leads directly into the realm of ideology?

That, in a nutshell, is my fundamental position, and how I would seek to answer my critics in relation to the overall message of *Images of Organization*.

On Developing New Metaphors for Research

One interpretation of your work is that you are calling for new liberating metaphors as a basis of research. Is this accurate?

The call for new metaphors was definitely a force driving the writing of *Images of Organization*, particularly the 1986 edition, when mainstream organization theory was very much in the hold of mechanical and organismic thinking. One of my definite aims was to help break the bounds of existing thinking and open inquiry to more radical metaphors, such as those captured in the chapters on psychic prisons, instruments of domination, and the image of transformation and change.[11] Since 1986, interest in and the exploration of metaphor across many disciplines has grown at a rapid pace, and it's interesting to reflect on some of the patterns here.[12] While there have been many important developments, I don't think it is a good idea to celebrate the search for new metaphors as an end in itself.

When we are talking about the exploration of new metaphors in theory development, it is important to distinguish between *generative "root metaphors"* that can broaden and deepen understanding of the phenomena we are investigating and create important new problem-solving ideas, as opposed to more *surface or decorative metaphors* that just embellish communication. Or, to put the point more directly, innovative theory building and problem solving does not just rest in finding a cute new metaphor, and many of the critics of the use of metaphor in social research are correct in criticizing the superficiality and diversion that this can create. Effective use of metaphor in theory building and problem solving should always create new value for the user and ultimately be judged in these terms.

Hence, in *Images of Organization* I focused on unfolding the implications of eight generative metaphors, each of which led to the development of ideas and concepts that could often be developed as metaphors in their own right. For example, when you start to explore organizations as organisms you quickly get into thinking about life cycles, health, birth and death, species, population growth and survival rates, evolution, ecologies and subecologies, and hosts of other organic images and ideas. When you view organizations as brains, you find yourself thinking about information processing systems, learning capacities and disabilities, right and left brain intelligence, holographic capacity distribution, and a host of images that can take brain-like thinking beyond the spongy mass of material that comprises an actual brain. When you start to explore organizations as political systems you quickly get into images of autocracy and democracy, Machiavellianism, gender, racial and social power imbalances, images of exploiting and exploited groups, subtle or crude power plays, and so on. The point is that the generative metaphor opens up a whole range of potential discourse with lots of concrete implications that can truly bring attention to core aspects of the phenomenon being studied, and open important new horizons for understanding and action.[13]

Decorative or surface metaphor does not do this. The metaphor may help you see some parallels with the phenomenon being studied, but the process will not really take you anywhere in terms of creating deeper insight and value. Of course, one can't always know from the start whether a metaphor is going to prove truly valuable and one often has to try and see. The important point is to have an investigative and critical attitude that encourages one to pursue the implications of the metaphor and to recognize if it isn't really taking you anywhere. This involves a judgment call, and is an art rather than a science. I have illustrated this approach to metaphor in my book *Imaginization: New Mindsets for Seeing, Organizing and Managing* (1993),[14] written as a sequel to *Images of Organization* to illustrate the role that metaphor can play in detailed management practice and problem solving. It shows how metaphor can be used in an emergent, spontaneous way, and how unlikely metaphors that on the surface do not seem to be very serious ones can have major implications. My discussion of how I have used the "spider plant" metaphor to help executives think about processes of organizational decentralization provides a case in point.

So the call for new metaphors is an interesting one and has to be approached with both a creative and critical attitude. Interestingly, I do not think it is just a question of sitting down and coming up with new ideas. Generative metaphor often emerges quite naturally if one tries to really investigate and understand the nature of the issues that one is dealing with and wrestle with problems of real concern. In other words, metaphorical theory often emerges from critical reflection on practice as a way of capturing or communicating key issues in a new way.

A recent example of this is found in Roger Martin's (2011) view that the problems associated with the runaway nature of senior executive rewards (which in the current context of criticism relating to corporate greed, the widening gaps between rich and poor, and the growing reward discrepancies between senior and lower levels of organizations is of growing concern), can be critically understood and remedied through lessons drawn from the National Football League (NFL). His metaphorical argument distinguishes between rewards for *actual* results and rewards for *expected* results. The former requires real performance on the field of play and for which players and coaches receive rich rewards. The latter rests in the domain of Las Vegas and the betting scene, and from which members of the NFL are deliberately excluded through anti-betting rules. Carrying the metaphor to corporate life it raises the question: why reward CEOs and other senior executives for Las Vegas–style expectations (e.g., through stock options and other rewards where the value is affected by share price on the stock exchange that their actions can directly impact) as opposed to the real value that they and their organizations deliver on the field of play.[15]

It is a brilliant new problem-solving metaphor for thinking about an important social issue and has the ability to challenge and change the bounds of current thinking about executive pay and, in the process, provide possible new methods of compensation based on real achievements. It will, of course, be interesting to see if it is adopted in practice given the power structures that have allowed the problem to arise in the first place. Either way, it is a great illustration of the power of a generative metaphor, and how new metaphor can emerge quite naturally from tackling important issues as one connects one domain of experience with another, in this case executive boardrooms, Las Vegas, and professional football.

On Criteria for Evaluating a Metaphor

What are your personal criteria for evaluating a metaphor?

I have to frame my answer to this question by returning to the distinction I made earlier between metaphor as the medium through which we create insights and metaphors (with the "s") that generate the content of thinking. The question here relates primarily to how we judge the power of the latter.

One line of potential evaluation is to reflect on what may be called the "truth value" of a particular metaphor in terms of the degree to which it informs or corresponds with the phenomenon to which it is applied. My personal view is that this is fraught with difficulty, because the use and meaning of a metaphor is ultimately in the mind and interpretation of the user, and to generate any real evocation or power the image underlying the metaphor must be significantly different from the phenomenon to which it is applied. Hence, there are real problems in thinking about the "truth," correctness, or accuracy of a metaphor in any literal or absolute sense.

Hence, I prefer to think about the evaluation of metaphors in terms of the value of the general and specific insights that are generated, and the value of what the metaphor allows one to do. Insight, value, and action potentials are the key evaluative elements for me.

Of course, the value across all these dimensions will vary according to the aims and objectives of the person using the metaphor, and the very same metaphor may create positive value and outcomes for some, while creating negative value and outcomes for others. There thus seem to be no absolute criteria for judgment that can be unequivocally applied. Metaphor, in the most basic sense, provides a mode of engagement through which we shape our relationship with our world, and ultimately has to be judged in terms of its practical impacts. Does a metaphor generate valuable insights that allow us to understand what's happening in a more informed way? Does it help us to act more appropriately or effectively in terms of what we are seeking to do? What practical downsides does the use of the metaphor produce?

Interestingly, these are similar questions that one would ask in evaluating some form of technology, and I think this is where my view of metaphor takes us. Images and concepts of all kinds are a form of cognitive technology that directly shapes our relations with the world, guiding how we think and act, hence the practical impacts/consequences of those actions.

On Dominant Metaphors in the Field

What forces keep or maintain a metaphor in a dominant position in a field?

This is a subject worthy of detailed study, but my hunch is that it is an issue of power, in two senses: the power that metaphors (as a form of cognitive technology) create for their users in terms of what they allow them to do and the role played by institutional power in encouraging or discouraging the use of particular metaphors. For example, a lot of the fads and fashions in management are driven by the rise of different metaphors promising to tackle specific problems or general issues of concern, and remain current so long as they seem to provide a relevant way of thinking and/or deliver practical results.

Take, for example, the rise of the reengineering movement that served the purpose of leaders seeking to restructure their organizations in the late 1980s and 1990s, but which commands little direct *public* attention now.[16] In an academic context, we see the same rise and fall phenomenon, often driven by a demand for novelty, and I imagine that a systematic study of the popularity of different metaphors would take us into different forms of institutional power embedded in gate-keeping roles and the structuring of publishing, research funding, and the tenure and promotion system. But ultimately these are empirical questions, worthy of systematic research.

On Additional Generative Metaphors

Are there any additional "generative metaphors" that you wish you had covered in writing Images of Organization?

In writing a book like Images, it is impossible to cover everything relating to one's topic, and I am often asked if I can fill the gaps. I have resisted this and only produced two really significant updates (Morgan, 1997, 1998). But in both I decided to stick with my original eight metaphors because part of the objective of the book was to demonstrate the role of metaphor in organization theory with an invitation to readers to explore metaphors of their own. This has proved an effective strategy in creating new opportunities for instructors and organizational consultants who wish to use Images as a platform for getting their students or their colleagues to think beyond the confines of the book to embrace new perspectives, for example, as an exercise in creative and critical thinking. In other words, the incompleteness can be seen as a means of opening inquiry rather than seeking to close it around a fixed framework.

The other consideration relating to retention of the original structure related to the extent to which the original eight metaphors—because they are broad and generative in nature—have been able to incorporate, or at least provide an umbrella for addressing many of the recent developments in the field of organization and social theory.

Take, for example, how four prominent developments—the rise of social networking, the image of organizations as psychopaths, the rise of a stakeholder perspective, and the emergence of many aspects of the theory of chaos and complexity—can be seen as being consistent with four of my original metaphors, that is, of the brain, psychic prison, political system, and flux and transformation. One can argue that at least three[17] of these developments are worthy of chapters of their own. But isn't social networking using digital media an extension of our information processing brains? Isn't the psychopathic metaphor another illustration of how our institutional frameworks can imprison us in unconscious patterns capable of producing great harm? Isn't the stakeholder approach another way of exploring the relations between the interests, conflict, and power that lie at the heart of political analysis.

The fundamental point: yes, we can see organizations as networks, psychopaths, and stakeholder domains and treat these images as generative metaphors on their own account, and write excellent books on each topic, as many have already done.[18] But for my own purposes I am happy to see them as very important theories and perspectives consistent with my original metaphors. This can be viewed as an arbitrary decision, as it is—in my case driven by a very pragmatic concern to limit the number of distinct chapters in my book in a way that's illustrative rather than exhaustive and absolutely complete.

However, that said and done, there are also several metaphors that are not addressed by *Images* that certainly have a strong case for inclusion. For example, there's the metaphor of organizations as economic systems—which embraces the whole field of economics, the theory of the firm, and agency theory. We could also make the case for discussing organizations as legal systems in their own right, or at least as an important aspect of the economic model. There's also a case to be made for viewing organizations through the lenses of gender and race, and for including the generative metaphor of organizations as text and discourse. The last seems a particularly obvious choice since I chose to frame the whole argument presented in *Images* around the process of "reading organization."[19]

But, if I had a single choice, the metaphor that I most wish that I had included would be one based on communications theorist Marshall McLuhan's view that all forms of technology are best understood as extensions of human senses and that "the medium is the message."[20] More specifically, the metaphor would explore "Organizations as Media" with a particular focus on the transformations created in the wake of phonetic literacy and the rise of new electronic media, particularly the digital forms that are currently unfolding. I believe this metaphor will put the history of formal organizations in new perspective and raise some interesting questions and challenges on how we can expect new organizational forms and associated economic systems to unfold in the years ahead.

To elaborate, the basic argument would build on the work of McLuhan and the anthropologists, historians, and literary scholars on which his ideas draw, to explore the links between the interconnected rise of the phonetic alphabet, abstraction, individualism, deductive logic, reductive science, mechanization, and the general rise of formal organizations supported by phonetic literacy and writing as primarily a Western phenomenon. If McLuhan's ideas are correct, we are already in the midst of a major revolution that will completely transform the nature of contemporary organizations and how they operate. Of course, the first effects are already well known since they are already being experienced. But the interesting thing from a McLuhan perspective is that the transformation and challenges raised will not just be about technology but about the nature of consciousness and human interconnection itself. Crudely put, just as we can see the bureaucratic model as an extension of the *written word*, and see electronic media as creating new forms of literacy that are facilitating new forms of thinking, acting, connecting, and organizing, we can expect our organizations and the broader economic system of which they are part to be transformed in the most fundamental ways. I am only able to hint at the possibilities here, but I am confident that anyone interested in pursuing this line of inquiry will be richly rewarded. It is also my belief, as suggested in my discussion on the role of metaphor and the dominance of metonymical science, that our concept of science and modes of knowledge creation will also undergo major transformation as electronic media continue to extend our collective brain at a global level in the way that McLuhan so clearly envisaged.

We have here, a generative metaphor that can put the mechanistic era and our emerging future in a completely new perspective. In my view, it has the potential to provide a deep structural explanation of social life that may prove as powerful as that offered to the late 19th and 20th century by the work of Marx, but with a focus on a different generative logic of change.

On Metaphors and the Natural Environment

What about metaphors of organizations and the natural environment? How can the exploratory aspects of metaphor offer insight into this relatively new, but critically important area in organizational studies?

I think the key here is to focus on metaphors that specifically address the *relationship between* organizations and the natural environment. Clearly we have a problem. The jury doesn't even need to leave the room—the natural environment is definitely not a winner in terms of organization—environment relations, at least as far as history to date is concerned. The metaphors of "organizations as instruments of domination" and, if one wishes to be charitable and attribute negative effects to unintended consequences, "organizations as psychic prisons," clearly have a role to play here in highlighting the exploitative and destructive aspects. They provide general frames for thinking about the problems that can also be approached by exploring the limitations and hidden downsides of some of the conventional organizational metaphors, most notably those of machine and organism. If one wants to be really comprehensive about the issue, I am sure it is possible to write as broad a work as *Images of Organization* on the topic—there are so many interesting aspects to organization–environment relations.

But, for immediate purposes, let's take a closer look at some detailed metaphors that can help us think about specific problems and challenges. Take, for example, the image/ideology of "development" or "progress" that's used to justify so many negative organizational and social impacts on the natural environment. The idea of progress is associated with the view that humans are on a pedestal as part of "the ascent of man," which is associated with various interpretations of the theory of evolution on the one hand, or with the creationist view that humans are on a pedestal in the broader order of things through a creative act of God who has made man in his own image, or as creationist critics would assert, because of the reverse.[21] Either way, this image creates an overassertive relationship between "man as figure" and "nature as ground" in which the importance of human acts take precedence over the interests and well-being of nature as a whole. Nature becomes a resource to be used for human ends, with modern organizations a primary instrument for achieving desired goals.[22]

Many of the problems here have been clearly addressed in the work of Stephen Jay Gould (1996), which shows us as that the very idea of the ascent of man as a symbol of progress represents a distortion of the total evolutionary picture where relatively few species have become part of a runaway pattern against the context of a much larger context or ground, which has remained largely unchanged, *and on which the so-called higher forms ultimately depend.*

Gould also points out that use of images of evolution to explain and justify human progress has another distorting effect because whereas evolution in the natural world has taken place over many millions of years, creating an amazing pattern of *mutual* adaptation, human social evolution is accelerating at a much faster pace in the course of decades, and in the process, destroying many aspects of the contextual pattern on which it ultimately depends. The point is that the differences in time scale of natural and social evolution are completely different and make the use of simple evolutionary metaphors of progress extremely problematic. The "inconvenient truth" is that we are in very dangerous territory indeed. As far as the social world is concerned, as Gould notes, we are in a situation akin to "Lamarckian development" based on the acquisition of inherited characteristics as human innovations build on one another and rapidly become building blocks for runaway patterns, resulting in so many of the problems we are currently experiencing, both socially and environmentally. For example, as I write the news is that global population has just passed the 7 billion mark and [is] growing rapidly, producing huge challenges for the years ahead.

The basic message that I am making here is that we can produce many important insights and action opportunities by addressing *the limitations of existing metaphors* relating to social evolution and progress; we don't necessarily have to look for new ones!

I have addressed some of the fundamental issues here in *Images of Organization* under the umbrella of the flux and transformation metaphor, for example, through my discussion of autopoiesis and related "logics of change." Specifically, the contrasts I drew between the logics of "ego-centricism" and "systemic wisdom," and between the "survival of the fittest" as opposed to the "survival of the fitting," directly speak to the distortions and pathologies created when humans have an overassertive relationship with the broader environment. Egocentric interactions with the natural environment through narcissistic processes and projections that "edit out" inconvenient aspects of the broader context, create the greatest environmental disruption and harm. Many recent environmental catastrophes illustrate this in practice. Consider, for example, BP's deep-sea drilling activities in the Gulf of Mexico and the associated environmental catastrophe. BP's over-assertion of corporate interests, reinforced by its associated risk management evaluation decisions, effectively "edited" and downgraded the importance of potential impacts on other stakeholders, such as the Gulf shrimp industry, other fishermen, the tourist industry, general social context, wildlife, and other aspects of the natural environment. It provides a classic illustration of the egocentric view in practice and the rationale for the alternative ecocentric paradigm advocated by Catton and Dunlap (1978, 1980) and other environmentalists.

These and other problems between organization and environment can also be explored through dozens of different exploratory and problem-solving metaphors that systematically focus on the flaws and downsides of progress through variations on a domination and exploitation theme. Interestingly, many of these are already in play in response to the crises and problems that have emerged over the years. For example, stakeholder metaphors provide a means of exploring patterns of interest and exploitation; ecological metaphors highlight the importance of self-regenerating life cycles; images of "cradle to cradle" technology and production processes can help give life-cycle models an especially evocative turn; images of the triple bottom line, especially in highlighting cases of excessive externalization of social and environmental costs, can provide a way of accounting for organizational activities in a broader frame; and so on.

Taking another tack, we can pursue diverse metaphors of runaway growth, cancer, greed, parasites that destroy their hosts, the impact of invasive species (a particularly resonant metaphor for studying the impact of modern organizations in undeveloped parts of the world), and other social and organic metaphors that explicitly seek to understand imbalanced or pathological patterns of development. Or let's go to the movies and see *Avatar* in 3D to experience a modern commentary on environmental degradation that speaks directly to how many resource extraction industries are destroying the natural and social environment in an irreparable way.

Or consider the metaphor that views modern organizations as psychopaths (Bakan, 2004)—that is, as institutions that pursue private gain while rendering public pain. Bakan's work here provides a particularly powerful way of studying how self-interest at the expense of the broader social and natural environment has actually been built into the fabric and functioning of modern organizations through the legal concept of limited liability. In other words, if one wanted to create a method for developing organizations that are systematically motivated to put the individual interests of "the part" ahead of "the whole," one could not have a more effective approach.[23] It will be interesting to see how the debate around this issue evolves in the public attack on corporate and other forms of greed stemming from the 2007–2008 financial, economic, and global debt restructuring crises, and the "99% versus the 1%" social movement to which it has given rise.[24]

In summary, the challenge ahead as far as the use of new metaphor is concerned seems to rest in finding images and ideas that will have real power in constraining and reversing the overassertive relationship between organizations and their broader context. Anything that asserts the priority and privilege of a single individual or institution at the expense of the collective or broader ground enhances the "survival of the fittest" as opposed to the "survival of the fitting." In the process it undermines the mosaic-like fabric and interconnectedness that the best in ecological thinking has shown to be so central to the nature of life.

Notes

1. I spent several years pursuing this line of inquiry, seeking to legitimize and create more scope for nontraditional research in several publications—Discussed in Note 3.

2. See the discussion on Systems Theory in Burrell and Morgan (1979, pp. 57–68).

3. To provide a little more background on this, the story of *Images of Organization* has a lot of different strands. In addition to what I have said above, it is important to understand how all the different projects that I was working on were interconnected. For example, the importance of the links between *Sociological Paradigms* and *Images of Organization* can't be overemphasized. The latter would not have been possible without the former because all my work from 1979 to 1986 was driven by a desire to unfold the implications of what Gibson Burrell and I had started in *Sociological Paradigms*. My most important publications in this intervening period were (a) my *Administrative Science Quarterly* article "Paradigms, Metaphors and Puzzle Solving in Organization Theory" (Morgan, 1980), which sketched the initial links that I saw between paradigms and metaphors and which was written primarily to introduce and legitimize the ideas in *Sociological Paradigms* for a North American audience; (b) the article I wrote with Linda Smircich, "The Case for Qualitative Research" (Morgan & Smircich, 1980), which provided the rationale for nontraditional research methods using the ontological, epistemological, and methodological framework created in *Sociological Paradigms*; and (c) *Beyond Method* (Morgan, 1983), which presented research as a process of engagement and conversation with the subject of study that's driven and shaped by the frame of reference and assumptions of the researcher. The fundamental aim of *Beyond Method* was (a) to provide a *methodological* companion to *Sociological Paradigms* (the 21 research strategies presented in the book take the reader on a circular tour around the paradigms) and (b) to outline my emerging view of epistemology and how researcher and researched are locked into a loop of interaction where research realizes the perspective of the researcher and what he or she is looking for. In other words, in research we "meet ourselves"—not just the subject of study! My ideas on metaphor had a major influence on the *Beyond Method* volume, but, for the sake of simplification, were kept in the background—because I wanted the focus to be on the *logics of social research, the choice of method,* and how *all* research is ultimately driven and *shaped by the assumptions and perspectives of the researcher,* not just the phenomenon researched. *Images of Organization* extended and applied these views using metaphor as a focus for understanding the socially constructed nature of organization theory. For example, the view that metaphors provide partial insights; that different metaphors can produce conflicting insights; that in elevating one insight others are downplayed; that a way of seeing becomes a way of not seeing; and that any attempt to understand the complex nature of organizations (as with any other complex subject) always requires an open and pluralistic approach based on the interplay of multiple perspectives are common integrating themes.

4. A word of caution is necessary here. We have to tread carefully on this issue as the concept of metaphor has itself become a metaphor (taken from language, literature, poetry, etc.) and through which we are now trying to understand ourselves (see Morgan, 1996, pp. 233–235). In time, the physical experiments of neuroscientists may provide another way of informing us on this issue as they study dynamics of the human brain. Note also that the representation of metaphor in Figure 2.2 is also metaphorical in the sense that the concept of metaphor is presented spatially through overlapping circles.

5. The implications here are fully explored in *Beyond Method* (1983), which, as noted in Note 3, develops my epistemological position, viewing research as a mode of engagement that encourages reflective forms of scientific conversation.

6. For a more detailed discussion of this point, see Morgan (1996, pp. 228–233).

7. This discussion leads us directly into a long-standing critique of modern science and modern thinking, generally in terms of the excessive reductionism (or oversimplification)

that stems from excessive attention to (metonymic) concepts alone at the expense of seeing and understanding the larger picture. The harsh fact is that much of science (and everyday thought) oversimplifies. The process can lead to major insights and breakthroughs (such as the way an understanding of bacteria set the basis for antibiotics), but which can also have major negative effects (the evolution of stronger bacteria, now commonly described as "super-bugs"). Metaphor warns us of the inherent problems by inviting us to see the limitations of one's viewpoint, that is, what's being lost from view. Or, put slightly differently, in dealing with any complex phenomenon we have to realize that there is always a danger that the ontological complexity of the phenomenon itself is going to get oversimplified because of metonymical reductions and that the phenomenon will "often push back." To take another example, switching to the realm of organization theory and practice consider the implications of the metonymical concept of "organization structure" and how an excessive focus on mechanical structuring can create organizational rigidities; an inability to cope with changing circumstances; a backlash from employees who consciously or unconsciously resent being treated as "cogs in wheels"; political dynamics associated with the hierarchical mechanistic structure; and so on. The context in which the concept is used "pushes back!"

8. The emphasis in institutionalized research, for example, through the structure of research funding, journals, and university tenure systems (with minority exceptions), reinforces the need for abstracted concept development and testing and the discovery of evidence based "truth," that is, the metonymical mode of study illustrated in Level (C) of Figure 2.3.

9. My argument here is rooted in the work of Marshall McLuhan (1964) and the idea that the whole institution of science with its emphasis and its concern for fixed perspectives and fragmented literal truths is a product of the printed word and the fragmentation and mechanization of consciousness that it brings. As we shift further from a world dominated by print and associated linear modes of thought into the more relativistic and fluid environment now rapidly unfolding, this is very likely to change. In the meantime, more exploration of multiple views, listening, and active inquiry as opposed to excessive metonymical reduction will help greatly—even if only as a frame through which we begin to see and evaluate the results of existing metonymical research.

10. For example, see the 1997 and 2006 editions of *Images of Organization* and the Executive Edition of 1998. The issue of "authoring" is also explored in Morgan (1993).

11. One of the aims in exploring these metaphors was to give concrete ways of thinking about organizations through the lens of the Radical Humanist and Radical Structuralist paradigms explored in Burrell and Morgan (1979).

12. For example, see the review and discussion presented in the introductory article for this feature by John Jermier and Linda Forbes.

13. In line with my explanation of metaphor presented earlier in relation to Figure 2.3, it is important to note that the elaboration of a generative metaphor can take place through metonymical reduction or through the generation of related images that can become generative metaphors in themselves.

14. The original book title was *Imaginization: The Art of Creative Management*. The book provides many illustrations of the use of metaphor in reading and authoring organizational life.

15. Martin's argument and the implications of his metaphor goes well beyond what I am summarizing here and is worth exploring in much more detail.

16. This, of course, does not mean the metaphor has disappeared or has ceased to have a major influence—because the implications of the metaphor now inhabit the domain of Section (C) in Figure 2.3 in the business process reengineering concepts built into common management and consulting practice.

17. Regarding the fourth: important aspects of the theory of chaos and complexity was anticipated in part in the original 1986 edition through a discussion of complex systems

as "loops not lines" shaped by patterns of mutual causality. It has been given more explicit treatment in subsequent editions as a logical extension of the chapter on Organizations as Flux and Transformation.

18. See, for example, Kilduff and Tsai (2003) on networks; Bakan (2004) on psychopathic organizations (also see Bakan's movie *The Corporation*, 2003); and Freeman (1984) and Freeman, Harrison, Wicks, Parmar, and deColle (2010) on stakeholders.

19. A case can also be made for treating institutional theory as a frame in its own right. But this can also be seen as fusing elements of population ecology, cultural, and political metaphors and discussed under any of these umbrellas. A clear case can also be made for treating gender and race as frames for thinking about fundamental aspects of organization, as opposed to subsuming them under the umbrellas of cultural, political, psychic prison, and instrument of domination metaphors. All these issues relate to the incompleteness point made earlier. There are dozens of metaphors that could have been developed in *Images of Organization* in their own right. We also have here a perfect illustration of why I extended the invitation to explore new metaphors, and how I see the role incompleteness can play in raising issues and opening debate on the nature and significance of any specific theoretical/metaphorical approach.

20. The classic works here are McLuhan (1962, 1964) and McLuhan and McLuhan (2011). Unfortunately, McLuhan's ideas are difficult to untangle because of his aphorismic nonlinear writing style and the unconventional ways in which he seeks to communicate his ideas. The lack of clarity has often led people to view his work as just a form of technological determinism. But, there is more to it than this. He is really speaking about how we shape technological forms that then, invisibly, shape us; he is addressing the hidden power of technology at a contextual level, not just its surface manifestations or unfolding effects. There are fundamental insights to be drawn from the above sources and from the work of his interpreters. See, for example, Logan (2004, 2010).

21. I am deliberately using the word "man" instead of human here to reflect common usage in this discourse, for example, in the sense of man versus (mother) nature. No unintended gender bias intended.

22. This assertion of the elevated status of the human being, hence of formal organizations as extensions of humans, can be explained, at least in part, by the ideas of McLuhan (1964) in terms of how the sense of individualism that occupies centre stage in popularized stories of human evolution is associated with the rise of phonetic literacy and the printed word. It is no accident, for example, that the assertion of the interests of humans against nature has developed most fully as a Western phenomenon and continues at an accelerated pace as the East now follows the Western industrial model. The work of Gregory Bateson (1972, 1979) is also very important here, especially for his approach to understanding contexts and what he calls "the pathology of conscious purpose" and its systemic disruptions (for a comprehensive discussion of Bateson's work, see Harries-Jones, 1995). In organization-environment studies, the work of Catton and Dunlap (1978, 1980) drew early attention to these issues in their call for a new ecocentric paradigm as opposed to the dominant anthropocentric one (see Jermier, 2008, for an overview of the issues here, and Shrivastava's (1994) important article on neglect of the environment in organization studies).

23. Legal liability was of course introduced in a much simpler context, where its effects were much more limited. Now, with the rise of gigantic global organizations, or even of small organizations that are capable of having dramatic negative effects on the social and natural environment, the very concept of limited liability is extremely problematic.

24. Interestingly, the image of "99%:1%" itself provides a powerful metaphor for capturing key aspects of our times, and is likely worth exploring in many dimensions—just as the popular "80:20 rule" has created an understanding of a wide range of socioeconomic phenomena.

References

Alvesson, M. (1993). The play of metaphors. In J. Hassard & M. Parker (Eds.), *Postmodernism and organizations* (pp. 114–131). London, England: Sage.

Alvesson, M., & Spicer, A. (Eds.). (2011). *Metaphors we lead by.* London, England: Routledge.

Bakan, J. (2004). *The corporation: The pathological pursuit of profit and power.* New York, NY: Free Press.

Bateson, G. (1972). *Steps to an ecology of mind.* New York, NY: Ballantine.

Bateson, G. (1979). *Mind and nature.* New York, NY: Bantam.

Black, M. (1962). *Models and metaphors.* Ithaca, NY: Cornell University Press.

Bohr, N. (1958). *Atomic theory and human knowledge.* New York, NY: Wiley.

Brown, R. H. (1977). *A poetic for sociology.* New York, NY: Cambridge University Press.

Buckley, W. (1967). *Sociology and modern systems theory.* Englewood Cliffs, NJ: Prentice Hall.

Burrell, G., & Morgan, G. (1979). *Sociological paradigms and organizational analysis.* London, England: Heinemann.

Cassirer, E. (1946). *Language and myth.* New York, NY: Dover.

Catton, W. R., & Dunlap, R. E. (1978). Environmental sociology: A new paradigm. *American Sociologist, 13,* 41–49.

Catton, W. R., & Dunlap, R. E. (1980). A new ecological paradigm for a post-exuberant sociology. *American Behavioral Scientist, 24,* 15–47.

Cornelissen, J. P. (2005). Beyond compare: Metaphor in organization theory. *Academy of Management Review, 30,* 751–764.

Cornelissen, J. P., Oswick, C., Christensen, L. T., & Phillips, N. (2008). Metaphor in organizational research: Context, modalities and implications for research. *Organization Studies, 29,* 7–22.

Freeman, E. (1984). *Strategic management: A stakeholder approach.* Marshfield, MA: Pitman.

Freeman, R. E., Harrison, J., Wicks, A., Parmar, B., & deColle, S. (2010). *Stakeholder theory: The state of the art.* Cambridge, England: Cambridge University Press.

Gould, S. J. (1996). *Full house: The spread of excellence from Plato to Darwin.* New York, NY: Harmony Press.

Grant, D. (Ed.). (2004). *The Sage handbook of organizational discourse.* London, England: Sage.

Grant, D., & Oswick, C. (Eds.). (1996). *Metaphor and organizations.* London, England: Sage.

Harries-Jones, P. (1995). *Ecological understanding and Gregory Bateson.* Toronto, Ontario, Canada: University of Toronto Press.

Heisenberg, W. (1958). *Physics and philosophy.* New York, NY: Harper.

Hesse, M. (1966). *Models and analogies in science.* Notre Dame, IN: University of Notre Dame Press.

Jermier, J. (2008). Exploring deep subjectivity in sociology and organizational studies: The contributions of William Catton and Riley Dunlap on paradigm change. *Organization & Environment, 21,* 460–469.

Kilduff, M., & Tsai, W. (2003). *Social networks and organizations.* Thousand Oaks, CA: Sage.

Kuhn, T. S. (1970). *The structure of scientific revolutions.* Chicago, IL: University of Chicago Press. (Original work published 1962)

Lakoff, G., & Johnson, M. (1980). *Metaphors we live by.* Chicago, IL: University of Chicago Press.

Logan, R. (2004). *The alphabet effect: A media ecology understanding of the making of western civilization.* New York, NY: Hampton Press.

Logan, R. (2010). *Understanding new media: Extending Marshall McLuhan.* New York, NY: Peter Lang.

Martin, R. (2011). *Fixing the game: Bubbles, crashes and what capitalism can learn from the NFL.* Cambridge, MA: Harvard Business Review Press.

McLuhan, M. (1962). *The Gutenberg galaxy.* London, England: Routledge & Kegan Paul.

McLuhan, M. (1964). *Understanding media*. London, England: Routledge & Kegan Paul.
McLuhan, M., & McLuhan, E. (2011). *Media and formal cause*. Houston, TX: NeoPoieis Press.
Mintzberg, H., Ahlstrand, B., & Lampel, J. (2005). *Strategy safari: A guided tour through the wilds of strategic management*. New York, NY: Free Press.
Morgan, G. (1980). Paradigms, metaphors and puzzle solving in organization theory. *Administrative Science Quarterly, 25*, 605–622.
Morgan, G. (Ed.). (1983). *Beyond method: Strategies for social research*. Thousand Oaks, CA: Sage.
Morgan, G. (1986). *Images of organization* (1st ed.). Thousand Oaks, CA: Sage.
Morgan, G. (1993). *Imaginization: The art of creative management*. Thousand Oaks, CA: Sage.
Morgan, G. (1996). Is there anything more to be said about metaphor? In D. Grant & C. Oswick (Eds.), *Metaphor and organizations* (pp. 227–240). London, England: Sage.
Morgan, G. (1997). *Images of organization* (2nd ed.). Thousand Oaks, CA: Sage.
Morgan G. (1998). *Images of organization: The executive edition*. San Francisco, CA: Berrett-Koehler.
Morgan, G. (2006). *Images of organization* (3rd ed.). Thousand Oaks, CA: Sage.
Morgan, G., & Smircich, L. (1980). The case for qualitative research. *Academy of Management Review, 5*, 491–500.
Mueller, M. (1871). *Metaphor: Lectures on the science of language*. New York, NY: Scribners.
Ortony, A. (Ed.). (1979). *Metaphor and thought*. Cambridge, England: Cambridge University Press.
Oswick, C., & Grant, D. (1996). *Organization development: Metaphorical explorations*. London, England: Pitman.
Oswick, C., Keenoy, T., & Grant, D. (2002). Metaphor and analogical reasoning in organization theory: Beyond orthodoxy. *Academy of Management Review, 27*, 294–303.
Pepper, S. C. (1942). *World hypotheses*. Berkley, CA: University of California Press.
Popper, K. R. (1958). *The logic of scientific discovery*. London, England: Hutchinson.
Rorty, R. (1979). *Philosophy and the mirror of nature*. Princeton, NJ: Princeton University Press.
Schön, D. A. (1963). *Invention and the evolution of ideas*. London, England: Tavistock.
Shrivastava, P. (1994). Castrated environment: Greening organizational studies. *Organization Studies, 15*, 705–726.
Tsoukas, H. (1991). The missing link: A transformational view of metaphors in organizational science. *Academy of Management Review, 16*, 566–585.
Tsoukas, H. (1993). Analogical reasoning and knowledge generation in organization theory. *Organization Studies, 14*, 323–346.
Winter, M. (2009). *Images of projects*. London, England: Gower Press.

Morgan's Legacy in Theorizing and Understanding Organizations

Joep Cornelissen

Key Learning Points

- Understand the difference between diverse ways of viewing metaphor, including cognitive and discursive perspectives.
- Be able to compare different and creative ways of using metaphor practically for organizational analysis.
- Understand the basic characteristics of metaphors that make them more likely to be used by managers and people within organizations.
- Foster critical reflection on the possibility of alternative and future metaphors as images of organization.

A classic but still widespread idea of organizations is based on an **image** of organizations as if they are machines that are efficiently designed to produce certain outputs and meet predefined targets. This particular image, which Morgan (1986) describes in *Images of Organization* as one of eight **master tropes**, goes back to Frederick Winslow Taylor's formulation of industrial bureaucracy in the early 1900s, better known as scientific management, which involved a mixture of ideas and principles from mechanical engineering and **"social physics."** The assumption underlying this image was that productivity could be enhanced by specifying cause and effect in the production process, similar to the controlled mechanics of a machine. This particular image laid the foundation for many of the technical approaches to understanding and managing organizations (e.g., control systems, cost-savings, "human resources" management) that are still with us today and are, perhaps somewhat ironically, making a comeback in this digital age (*Economist*, 2015).

What this example suggests is that people use images to conceptualize and think of organizations. Different people may also use different images or alternate between images, an observation that tells us that the nature of reality does not dictate the way that reality is represented in people's minds and articulated to one another. Our **imagination** allows us to frame the same phenomenon in different and at times incompatible ways (Searle, 2010). An organization can be thought of as a machine, organism, brain, culture, political system, psychic prison, flux, or instrument of domination (among many other things) depending on how we mentally imagine it for ourselves (Morgan, 1986), which in turn depends on what we choose to focus on and what we choose to ignore—something that Morgan describes so well in his book (see Chapter 10 in Morgan, 2006). The way in which we imagine an organization in alternative ways in turn leads to alternative decisions and courses of actions with direct consequences for ourselves as well as for the economy and society at large. Alternative images also reveal different ideological positions on how organizations can best accomplish their ends and on how workers and employees, based on their abilities and motivations, should be controlled (Barley & Kunda, 1992). Often, alternative ways of **imagining** and **framing** an organization are pitted against each other, and the disputants struggle to show that their framing is more apt. At this point, one may wonder what it all matters that people in general produce these images as rival accounts or even as fully fledged theories of organizations.

As Morgan (1980, 1983) showed so astutely, these different images are not just in a strictly academic sense about how we use words and entire vocabularies such as "business process reengineering" or "corporate citizen" to conceptualize organizations and to think about them. Using these words says something more generally about the relation of words to reality—the way that managers, employees, consultants, politicians, and everyone else commit themselves to a shared understanding of what organizations are, and the ways their thoughts are anchored to developments and situations in the world. It is also about the relation of words and vocabularies to a community—how words when they are introduced come to evoke the same idea in an entire community, so that people can understand one another when they use them. Words and the language that we use to define organizations evoke images of what we believe organizations are or indeed should or can be.

Morgan (1980, 1983) also made the intriguing observation that our vocabulary to describe organizations is inherently **metaphorical**, as opposed to literal. **Linguistically**, a metaphor is a "figure of speech in which a word or phrase is applied to something to which it is not literally applicable" (Oxford English Dictionary). Our words disclose conceptions of organizations *as if* they are machines, social structures, computers, or corporate citizens (among many other things). Organizations are of course not literally machines or citizens (at least not in how we originally understand these concepts). However, as Morgan showed, by transferring these words from their original **domain** to the sphere of organizations, we are able to extend our thinking. In other words, mobilizing words from other domains enables us to cognitively frame and understand organizations in novel and multiple ways. It opens up possibilities for seeing and understanding organizations that would otherwise not be there if we restricted ourselves to a set of literal words and a fixed set of categories for understanding organizations (Morgan, 1980, 1983). In other words, metaphors give us alternative ways of imagining and framing organizations, a feat of language and thought that explains how and why there is such wide variety and change in our thinking about organizations.

In this chapter, I build on Morgan's initial and revealing observations about the metaphorical nature of our talk and thought about organizations. I describe from a **cognitive perspective** how metaphors work and persist, and I suggest some reasons for why certain metaphors, compared with others, are more likely to fall into favor with larger groups of people, including policy makers, managers, entrepreneurs, and employees in organizations. These reasons all boil down to whether a metaphor, and the image that it produces, offers an easily imaginable and controllable picture of organizations—one that in effect brings it into the purview of human understanding. I end the chapter with some reflections on the hold of such images over our collective imagination and the implications that this has for theory and practice.

Morgan and Metaphors

Past research has suggested that the dynamics by which new metaphors are introduced and become common usage are stubbornly chaotic (Cornelissen, 2006; Cornelissen & Kafouros, 2007). The reason for this, it has been suggested, is that it follows a cultural pattern of diffusion with some metaphors surviving, while others are lost. Like practices in a culture (e.g., fashions, rituals, beliefs), words in a language must originate with an innovator, must then appeal to the innovator's social contacts and then to the social contacts' contacts, and so on, until a word becomes endemic to a community. The variety and changing nature of our images of organizations similarly depends on the extent to which a new metaphor resonates with already common and socially shared understandings of organizations. Resonance occurs because of a similarity between the novel metaphor and our existing understanding or because the metaphor offers a striking contrast with our present language and thought (Oswick et al., 2004). The recent metaphor of organizations as networked forms of distributed intelligence (e.g., Gore, 1996) caught on because it not only built on but also contrasted with traditional mechanistic and computational images. This cultural mechanism holds a lesson for our understanding of organizations more generally. Our language and thought tends to branch out to the extent that it is conditioned by prior, socially shared understandings. For example, images of **social systems** followed machine images of organization, **connectionist images** of distributed intelligence elaborated on computational images, evolutionary images of organization were challenged by images of organizations as chaotic and complex adaptive systems, and so on. Such a stacking of metaphors is also the name of the game in academic research, in which scholars are pressed to find contrasting images with earlier work (Boxenbaum & Rouleau, 2011; Cornelissen & Durand, 2014).

A cognitive interpretation of metaphor casts a different but complementary light on the application of metaphor to organizations. Amid the cultural dynamics at play, metaphors are not simply markers or empty vessels in a cultural **language game**. Instead, metaphors are cognitively useful and essential in our reasoning about abstract or complex subjects such as organizations. This cognitive interpretation is the one that I associate most closely with Morgan (1980, 1983, 1986), compared with more discursive or even **philosophical accounts of metaphor** (see Putnam et al., 2004). Morgan is essentially concerned with metaphors as cognitively coherent constellations of ideas and is far less bothered about more linguistic questions of how metaphor is identified in speech (see Cornelissen, Oswick, Christensen, & Phillips, 2008). Like Lakoff and Johnson (1980, 1999) before him, Morgan is mostly concerned with the practical reality of metaphor, as a basic form of human cognition.

From this cognitive perspective, metaphors point in fact to an obvious way in which people learn to reason about abstract or complex concepts. They would notice, or have pointed out to them, a parallel between a realm that they already understand and an abstract or complex realm that they do not yet understand. By accessing and transferring knowledge from a known domain to an as yet unknown or difficult to know complex or abstract domain, people can understand otherwise inaccessible concepts. For this reason, metaphor is not considered an ornamental flourish of language; rather, it is an essential part of thought: "Our ordinary conceptual system, in terms of which we both think and act, is fundamentally metaphorical in nature" (Lakoff & Johnson, 1980, p. 3). In this cognitive view, metaphors are not only useful but also essential as ways of thinking about abstract and complex subjects such as organizations (Morgan, 1980). They bring organizations into the confines of a single image by drawing on parallels between organizations and other, concrete domains of knowledge (Cornelissen & Kafouros, 2008). Thus, when we liken an organization to a machine, we use our knowledge of machines to form an image of what an organization is like. The metaphor frames our understanding of the organization in a distinctive but partial way. Metaphors tend to produce partial insights because a particular image highlights certain interpretations at the expense of others. The image of an organization as a machine brings aspects of efficiency and engineering into focus but ignores the human aspects. The metaphor is thus enlightening and biased or limiting at the same time (Morgan, 1986); this assumption is also shared by **discursive approaches**, although they highlight the nature of partial emphasis as dissonance and resonance (in speech and texts) versus the emphasis that is placed here on partial forms of cognitive understanding.

Metaphors also aid our reasoning as tools of inference that can be carried over from a conventional to novel domain, where they can do real work. They can power sophisticated inferences (Cornelissen, 2005, 2012; Cornelissen & Clarke, 2010). For example, when an organization is seen as a machine, it is cast as a functional unity or assembly serving various purposes and consisting of distinct, although interconnected, mechanical parts that are not themselves self-adapting. Hence, to make an organization work, managers need to specify the functional connections between the parts (and document these in an organizational chart or process documents), they must control the energy source or force (i.e., "human resources") that gets it to operate, and they need to redesign specific parts or connections between parts whenever these are faulty or malfunctioning. Such redesign may result in job losses, but the machine image suggests that such losses are not problematic because an employee is merely a resource or commodity that can be acquired and traded. The employment relationship, in turn, is an arm's-length transaction based on market conditions and the value of the resource or commodity for organizational operations.

When managers **enact** such an image of the organization and the employment relationship, it has predictable consequences that may be self-reinforcing: just as organizations feel no particular social obligation or moral tie to their employees, employees, now told to look out for themselves, do precisely that (e.g., Haran, 2013). In other words, metaphors are not merely rival frames but have real-world consequences whenever they are enacted—a point that Morgan has stressed on numerous occasions (see Chapter 10 in Morgan, 2006).

How Metaphors Work

Having outlined some reasons for why metaphorical language and thought plays a central role in our understanding of organizations, the logical next question to ask is how metaphors emerge and *work*. Every metaphor has to come from somewhere. Perhaps one might think that they are thought out and disseminated by an elite corps of academic writers, consultants, and business gurus and are then hoarded by the wider populace. Given the prevalence of metaphor in our language about organizations, it seems more likely that they are the natural products of the way everyone's mind works. If so, we should be able to account for how people in the act of sensing deep correspondences between superficially different realms construct useful metaphors for thinking about organizations.

In his groundbreaking text, Morgan (1986, 1997, 2006) argued that people sense the connection by "seeing" or identifying a single dimension that relates to the combined realms. He argued that metaphor proceeds through implicit or explicit assertions that A *is* (or is like) B. For example, when we say "the man is a lion," we assert that the man shares features or characteristics with the lion, such as being strong and ferocious (Morgan, 2006, pp. 4–5). Morgan's account of metaphor follows a so-called **comparison model** of how metaphor works (Black, 1962; Cornelissen, 2005). In this model, which goes back to Aristotle's earliest writings, the development and interpretation of a metaphor is assumed to involve a comparison of concepts or domains to determine what discrete properties or relations that apply to the one can also apply to the other in the same or a similar sense. In short, metaphor is seen as a comparison in which the first concept A (i.e., the **target**) is asserted to bear a partial resemblance to the second concept B (i.e., the source). Figure 3.1 (from Morgan, 2006, p. 5) illustrates this model of how metaphor works. In Morgan's traditional view, a metaphor is understood when we "see" the connection between two concepts or domains and are able to "visualize" the "**ground**"—namely, those features that are shared by both. In other words, we understand metaphors when the source allows us to identify a feature (or set of features) already present in our understanding of the target, albeit that those features may initially not have been that salient to us. The productive force of metaphors, in other words, comes from making connections between domains "salient" or "visible."

The key limitation of the comparison account is that it is unable to account for how people discern such *new* metaphorical connections involving a set of entities that **interact** in particular ways. Recall that metaphors are powerful to the extent that they *create* new insights and new ways of analyzing and managing organizations; they do not simply uncover already existing similarities. Metaphors do not just draw out mere aspects of sameness; if they did, they would only make "the familiar more familiar" (Oswick, Keenoy, & Grant, 2002, p. 295). Instead, this comparison account suggests that metaphorical thinking is severely constrained to picking up hackneyed metaphors that already permeate our language about organizations and capture all there is to capture about organizations (Cornelissen, 2005).

Metaphors, by their very nature, are creative tools of human cognition for drawing parallels between domains of knowledge in order to expand our current knowledge into previously unrecognized possibilities (Morgan, 1997). A metaphor cannot be reduced to already present features or attributes because when these are specified, one does not get the metaphorical effect in question. This is the case because the characteristics or features of the source often cannot be applied directly to the target, as the features they "share" are often only shared metaphorically (and not literally). For example, the connection between organizations and machines is only a metaphorical one that aids our thinking about organizations. These concepts do not literally share any features or characteristics (which is why the Venn diagram in Figure 3.1 is misleading). Prior to their metaphorical comparison, we did not even conceive of a connection between organizations and machines. Thus, a metaphor *creates* similarity (as a correspondence is *constructed*) instead of simply emphasizing and visualizing preexisting (but previously unnoticed) similarities in the features of the constituent concepts or domains.

Now, a more useful model of metaphor is one that recognizes the creative potential of metaphor and accounts for how new insights and understandings emerge from using a metaphor (Cornelissen, 2005). This approach focuses on correspondences between two concepts or domains that emerge as counterpart connections that we construct between the two concepts or domains. Once a correspondence is constructed, the two concepts or domains are in turn "blended" with one another as a way of reordering our understanding of the target or by creating an emergent meaning that did not exist in each of the two concepts or domains separately. For example, when we say "the man is a lion" (the classic example that Morgan uses), we reorder our understanding of the kind of bravery and ferocity that we think a man is capable of based on our understanding of lions. The metaphor, in other words, leads us to reorder and reexamine our understanding of this particular man. Similarly, when we think of organizations as machines, we completely

FIGURE 3.1 ● Metaphor as Seeing Similarities

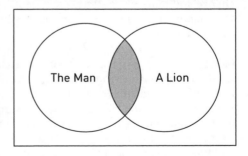

Source: Reproduced from Morgan (2006, p. 5).

recast our understanding of organizations. We blend the two domains to conceive of an organization as a functional unity with distinct, although interconnected, parts; to conceive of work as controlled and automated motions; and to conceive of employees as human resources or commodities. The intricate blending or mixing of these two domains into one and the same image also means that it is often difficult for people to still recognize the active metaphorical nature of the image whenever we use it to think about organizations. In other words, blending contributes to the belief that an organization *is* a machine and not just a useful way of thinking about organizations.

In some cases, the blending of the two domains is elaborated by people in such a way that new meanings or insights are created that did not exist in them previously. To illustrate, consider the popular idea that an organization has an identity, similar to a human being. The initial correspondence that informed this metaphor was that within a public context, third parties ascribe identity traits to both entities—organizations and individuals—in order to form an image of both of them. Indeed, organizational psychologists have long pointed out that stakeholders of an organization are inclined to perceive an organization in corporeal terms and to credit it with identity traits, just as they would an individual person (Bakan, 2004; Marchand, 1998). Based on this correspondence, ideas about identity in social psychology were transferred and blended with elements in our understanding of organization.

For example, the idea that in displays of our identity as human beings we express a sense of personal distinctness, a sense of personal continuity, and a sense of personal autonomy was used to reorder our understanding of organizations. Organizations were subsequently understood to have an identity consisting of 1) a claimed central character (corporate characteristics that are seen as the essence), 2) a claimed distinctiveness (corporate characteristics that distinguish the organization from others), and 3) a claimed **temporal continuity** (corporate characteristics that exhibit sameness over time) (e.g., Albert & Whetten, 1985).

However, academic writers and managers soon realized that organizations are not human beings. The blend was therefore elaborated with the idea that the identity of an organization is less enduring and more flexible than the identities of human beings (e.g., Gioia, Schultz, & Corley, 2000). The identity of an organization mutates as a result of internal organizational changes (e.g., a restructuring or the introduction of new technologies) and interactions with stakeholders. As organizations change and mutate over time, their identities will similarly evolve. Thus, the idea of the adaptive nature of an organization's identity emerged from the elaboration of the blend.

Figure 3.2 visualizes this process of how metaphor creates meaning through the blending of two concepts or domains. First, when people develop a metaphor, or have one pointed out to them, they start with constructing a basic correspondence between two domains. For example, the correspondence between the man and a lion may be that they are both male creatures that inhabit our planet. Once a correspondence is constructed, people may then blend the two domains into one and the same image, which means that they transfer information from both the target ("the man") and the source ("a lion") and use the information to elaborate and complete a coherent, blended image of the man *as* a lion. The novel image, in turn, leads us to rethink

FIGURE 3.2 ● Metaphor as the Blending of Two Concepts or Domains

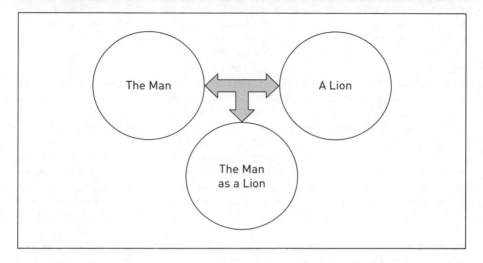

our concept of the man, which has been recast as a result of the blend. When we recognize this ability of metaphors to completely change our understanding of a particular subject, we begin to appreciate their true power as a way of bringing progressive viewpoints to bear upon the subject of organization.

Metaphors and Theories of Organization

Given the central role of metaphors for conceptualizing and understanding organizations, one would expect a large amount of time and energy being devoted within academic circles to understanding the very processes by which they are generated and the outcomes they have for everyone involved with organizations. Yet research on the topic over the years has been scant; in many ways, it is still seen as a fringe subject compared with other more "mainstream" subjects and research questions. There are the occasional bursts of attention, such as the special issue on theory building in the *Academy of Management Review* in 2011, with virtually all articles in that issue acknowledging the foundational role of metaphors for thinking about organizations (e.g., Alvesson & Sandberg, 2011; Boxenbaum & Rouleau, 2011; Oswick, Fleming, & Hanlon, 2011; Shepherd & Sutcliffe, 2011). However, by and large, the significance of metaphor to our understanding of organizations is not matched with a similar amount of research and attempts at a more detailed understanding. To some extent, this lack of attention reflects the usual ebb and flow of scholarly research, in which metaphor as a subject had its heyday in the 1980s amid broader meta-theoretical discussions on paradigms, methods, and theory but ebbed away in the decades afterward. Those who, in fact, were still writing about metaphor afterward were genuine enthusiasts or were heavily influenced by Morgan, with his work leaving a formative and lasting imprint on their own scholarship (e.g., Alvesson & Sandberg, 2011).

This lack of attention has a wider bearing on the academic community. One direct consequence is that prominent scholars in economics, sociology, and organizational theory do not routinely reflect on the theories and the assumptions they work from *as* metaphors. To give one example, economists and economic sociologists tend to define organizations in figurative terms as natural, self-constituted individuals underpinned by a nexus of specific treaties and contracts (e.g., Fama & Jensen, 1985). For example, Fama and Jensen (1985, p. 101) simply assume that organizations can be modeled as economic agents and "'as if' they come from the maximization of an objective function—for example, the value maximization rule of the financial economics literature." Somewhat similarly, institutional sociologists cast organizations in the image of unitary social actors (e.g., King, Felin, & Whetten, 2010), who have an intentionality and agency that transcends any of its members who instead merely act "'as if' the organization is willing the action to be so" (King et al., 2010, p. 295). In both instances, researchers implicitly assign a role to metaphor (note the "as if" in their reasoning) as part of their theorizing and use such metaphors as part of their research. Yet they hardly reflect on such metaphors, nor do they think about whether those same metaphors are used by individuals interacting with, or acting on behalf of, an organization in the real world. In fact, these researchers often go out of their way to suggest that their theorizing about organizations is not in the slightest metaphorical (e.g., see Hannan & Freeman, 1989), as if that would mean that their credibility as serious academics who write "literal" and formal theory would be challenged.

Writing about the image of organizations as economic agents, Fama and Jensen (1985) stress that they are using a "literal" analogy rather than a metaphor, arguing that their thinking involves a simple extension of the economic agency of natural persons to that of the organization, who as an agency-bearing "individual" by law (Ghoshal, 2005; Jensen & Meckling, 1994) is able to engage in economic transactions and form contract relationships. In another article, Jensen and Meckling stress the importance of limiting the analogy so that it does not further metaphorically "personify" the organization "by thinking about organizations *as if* they were persons with motivations and intentions" (Jensen & Meckling, 1976, p. 311) but simply adopt the economic analogy that the decisions and transactions of an organization can be modeled "'as if' they follow the value maximization rule of a single economic agent" (Fama & Jensen, 1985, p. 101). These twists and turns hide, rather than reveal, the underlying metaphor of economic utility and may be seen to "objectify" and naturalize its premise. The overall consequence is very little reflection within academic circles on images and models of organizations—images that, as in this case, form the basis for much economic thought in both theory and practice.

This is in fact unfortunate, because our theoretical language of organizations is laden with metaphors (Morgan, 2006). Instead of purging them from our theories, it would make more sense to devote our energies toward a more detailed understanding of how metaphors work and toward harnessing their generative potential. Without such reflection, we miss thinking about the fundamental assumptions, or grounds, on which we reason about organizations in our research and explain individual and collective behaviors. It also limits us in our ability to be truly generative by shifting grounds or by inverting the logic of an image into a counterfactual image (Cornelissen & Durand, 2014; Putnam & Boys, 2006). Unfortunately, Morgan's pioneering work was published three decades ago and we still do not reap the benefits of a truly reflective approach to our metaphors, applying our metaphors instead in a largely habitual and rote manner (Morgan, 1997).

A direct consequence of this lack of reflection is that to some extent we are out of step with the demands of our times, which need much more complex and dynamic metaphorical images than many of their forebears. Where the contemporary global, digital, and distributed nature of organizations and organizing would require us to produce new images or new assemblages of images, academics, managers, policy makers, and industry analysts seem instead to have returned to old stalwarts such as the machine image (*Economist*, 2015). The machine image is again used for managing large (e.g., Amazon) and small organizations alike, in both manufacturing and high-tech and service sectors. What this dogged persistence of the machine image shows (with hardly anyone questioning its aptness) is something that applies to all metaphors.

In the context of organizations, there is a strong preference not only for concrete images but also for images that emphasize the agency and control of people—as opposed to a more abstract image that is less specific on agency or might even put the control and management of organizations outside of the hands of single individuals. As we know, concreteness is important and is a core basis for metaphors to be considered as apt and useful (Cornelissen & Kafouros, 2007). This is, for example, why the machine image fares better than more abstract societal images such as corporate citizenship and corporate democracy or sustenance metaphors such as organizational development and growth. In addition to concreteness, another key feature is whether a metaphor puts the individual or individuals using the image in the scenario in the driver's seat, something that is particularly important for managers who want to see themselves (and who want to be seen by others) as being in charge and in control. Managers want to believe they can *leverage* assets, *structure* the organization, and *streamline* its operation to *drive* results (a manager's metaphorical dream scenario). To some extent, this agentic or control aspect of metaphors may be seen to be related to the **embodiment hypothesis** (Lakoff & Johnson, 1980), the idea that metaphors with embodied source domains (e.g., human-initiated motor actions or human sense experiences) are preferred over other usually more complex cultural source domains. Even beyond the embodiment hypothesis, the control feature is about having an image that is "human scale" and manipulable, as opposed to abstract and thus beyond immediate comprehension and control. Such control allows people individually and collectively to mentally simulate a scenario in their heads of what organizations are like, and in a way, that makes it "real" and tied to their own being and actions.

To illustrate this a bit more, it is instructive to relate the feature of control to Morgan's image of flux and transformation (based on a metaphor of **complexity science**), and we get an immediate sense of why an image such as that of the machine persists over time, although the idea of flux and transformation is constantly being touted and reintroduced as the next big thing—without ever being widely embraced. (Although who knows? The digital age may create a more fertile ground for the metaphor to finally take hold.) The difficulty here is that the image of flux does not concretely say how individuals fit in the picture. It also offers a very complex causal picture that any one of us struggles with, with organizations being produced and reproduced as emerging accomplishments out of a complex causal interplay of forces. Certainly, a manager may then simply use a machine image as a much more easily understood and *manageable* proxy. However, although the combination of concreteness and control may provide an explanation for the implicit preference for certain metaphors over others, it should not be seen as a rule or standard for selecting certain metaphors. It simply reveals a bias, or human tendency, that we should recognize and at times make the most of, but one that we should also sometimes challenge or actively circumvent.

In particular, when our times ask for complex and coordinated solutions to grand challenges such as climate change, it arguably does not work to keep debating whether climate change is "man-made" or not. This may not be the right imagery because the issue probably cannot be reduced (in its entirety, at least) to human size. This is probably easier said than done, but being aware and reflective (Morgan, 1986) is already an important first step. The next and following step will be to take up Morgan's quest for a truly **metaphorical theory (or *theorizing*) of organization** and reenergize research on how we are able to methodologically or practically metaphorize alternative images of organizations and thus alternative futures.

In the penultimate chapter of his 2006 book, Morgan describes the importance of navigating across alternative metaphors, as ways of seeing and knowing, and to become reflective and skilled in the use of metaphor: to find ways of conceptualizing, understanding, and shaping the situations that we want to organize and manage (Chapter 10 in Morgan, 2006). As he writes:

> As we gain comfort in using the implications of different metaphors . . . , we quickly learn that the insights of one metaphor can help us overcome the limitations of another. This, in turn, encourages us to recognize and, indeed, search for the limitations of existing insights: so that we can use them as springboard for new insight. (Morgan, 2006, p. 342)

In other words, Morgan (2006) suggests that the way forward is in reflection and learning, with all of us studying, managing or working in, or otherwise interacting with organizations, being mindful of the assumptions that we are working from when approaching the same organization, or at least our understanding of that organization, in different ways. He primarily uses the **metaphor of "reading"** (Chapter 11 in Morgan, 2006) to describe this process, which he feels captures how through an attitude of learning, we come to reflect on our assumptions and open ourselves up to new horizons of understanding. It is a very powerful metaphor, and one that he has since devoted much of his life's work to—in order to, as I understand it, extend the power of metaphor to foster learning and education.

What is interesting is that Morgan believes in the unleashing power of education, with individuals striving to enhance their understanding by actively working through alternative metaphors. He also seems to believe that this is a progressive process such that through learning, individuals gain a progressively more nuanced and complex understanding of organizations. I also in part subscribe to this reading metaphor and have in actual fact seen evidence for it in classrooms. At the same time, I think that it does not directly address the persistent tendency that I described, in which individuals (mostly outside of a classroom) opt for the most concrete and controlled image and may thus not be encouraged to push themselves any further in their education and learning. This tendency is real, and we see it all over the place today.

One way to address this tendency is not fostering a lateral approach, but instead, encouraging people to work through and across various metaphors as vantage points. Instead, the solution may be that we advocate an active process in which individuals start with a concrete image but gradually complicate such images by combining ideas into ever bigger assemblies, thus extending their reach beyond the basic image with which they started. The idea is that individuals can build up more complex metaphorical images that as complex systems of thought are in a "molecular" way made up of "atomic" metaphorical parts called **primary metaphors** (Cornelissen & Kafouros, 2008). A primary metaphor is the most basic metaphorical description of a target domain and has a minimal structure. A primary metaphor arises in a very basic and automatic manner through everyday experience by means of conflation, during which cross-domain associations have been formed between a target domain and other domains. **Complex metaphors** are formed from primary ones through further conceptual blending and elaboration—that is, the fitting together of small metaphorical "pieces" into larger wholes (Cornelissen, 2005).

For example, returning to the flux image (Morgan, 2006), seeing "organizations as complex adaptive systems" sees them as having the qualitative properties of complex and chaotic systems such as self-organizing networks sustained by importing energy, co-evolution to the edge of *chaos*, nonlinear interactions within and between organizations, irreversibility, and system evolution based on recombination—a real headache to fathom for any individual, particularly without any preparation. However, the primary metaphorical parts that are combined in this complex metaphor include "actions are self-propelled motions," whereby actions of organizations are metaphorically structured as movements of one's body through space; "relationships are enclosures," which likens interactions between organizations as happening in an enclosed space; "change is motion," which sees change or development as a movement in a direction (down a path) and makes it irreversible; and "organizational landscape as natural systems," which likens the surroundings of an organization to a complex natural system such as weather systems or thermodynamics and leads us to see it as an entity that is subject to natural forces.

When they are broken down in this manner, we can see how such basic, primary metaphors lead to a complex metaphorical image wherein organizations, although "emergent" and "constantly changing," act as bodily "agents" and move in a "path-dependent" way in a "space" or "landscape" that is "chaotic" and "constantly evolving." There is also an evolutionary intention in such moves as they may lead to a better "adaptation" (i.e., a "form" or "configuration" of the organization that "[co]evolved" with the "ecology" of the "changing space" or "landscape"). As illustrated by Carley (2002, p. 214), "through a process of synthetic adaptation, groups and organizations become more than the simple aggregate of the constituent personnel and become complex, computational and adaptive agents in their own right." This final inference is the one that people would arrive at, but they can in effect only get there if they have done the more basic primary metaphorical work beforehand.

As this example illustrates, images of organizations may involve complex meta-phorical thought that is made up of smaller metaphorical parts. When combined together, such metaphorical parts may lead to a complex metaphor scene that, although elaborate in detail and inferential capacity, can be easily understood and manipulated by individual scholars, managers, and others interested in understanding organizations (Cornelissen, 2005). Although it involves different primary metaphors, the imagined complex metaphor is often still coherent in terms of underlying metaphoric mappings of agency (i.e., who initiates the action[s]), causality (i.e. relationships between cause and effect), and the position of the act (and its consequences) in time and space. The "organizations as complex adaptive systems" metaphor, for example, involves a coherent image of organizations as agents who direct and initiate actions and move in response to constantly evolving environmental circumstances.

In other words, besides a process of **metaphorical imagination** that laterally works across alternative metaphors (Morgan, 2006), the additional suggestion I have would be to horizontally "scale up" from basic, primary metaphors to more complex constellations that are fit for our times. Both moves together may be particularly powerful to foster imagination and to encourage all of us to work with and embrace more complex and dynamic images of organizations.

Conclusions

I have one final note for those doubters who might still be out there. One may reasonably ask whether the text in this chapter means that the very notion of organization can only be represented and reasoned about in metaphorical terms, and not in literal terms. In other words, can we represent organizations without metaphorical thinking? The answer is hardly. If we consciously make the enormous effort to separate out our metaphorical from nonmetaphorical thought, we probably can do some very minimal and unsophisticated nonmetaphorical reasoning about organizations. However, as scholars, we do not do this, and such reasoning would never capture the full inferential capacity of complex metaphorical thought. The concept of organization can, if pushed, indeed be described and unpacked in literal terms, such as a "collective of people working together." However, without metaphor, the literal concept of organization is relatively impoverished and has only a minimal "skeletal" structure (Lakoff & Johnson, 1999). Metaphor fleshes out the skeleton in a variety of ways and adds **inferential structure**. In fact, so much of the **ontology** and inferential structure of the concept of organization is metaphorical, such that if one somehow managed to eliminate metaphorical thought, the remaining skeletal concept would be so impoverished that none of us could do any substantial reasoning about organizations. Morgan realized this point more than 30 years ago and called for an approach to studying and managing organizations that put metaphor at the center. Although he had a resounding impact on the field in the 1980s, the subject has received far less attention in recent years, and it would make sense to restore metaphor as an important research program in the field.

Key Terms

Cognitive perspective
Comparison model
Complex metaphors
Complexity science
Connectionist images
Discursive approaches
Domain
Embodiment hypothesis
Enact
Framing
Ground
Image
Imagination
Inferential structure
Interact
Language game

Linguistically
Master tropes
Metaphorical
Metaphorical
    imagination
Metaphorical theory
Ontology
Philosophical accounts of
    metaphor
Primary metaphors
Reading as metaphor
Social physics
Social systems
Source domain
Target domain
Temporal continuity

References

Albert, S., & Whetten, D. A. (1985). Organizational identity. In L. L. Cummings & B. M. Staw (Eds.), *Research in organizational behavior* (Vol. 7, pp. 263–295). Greenwich, CT: JAI Press.

Alvesson, M., & Sandberg, J. (2011). Generating research questions through problematization. *Academy of Management Review, 36*(2), 247–271.

Bakan, J. (2004). *The corporation: The pathological pursuit of profit and power*. London, England: Constable.

Barley, S. R., & Kunda, G. (1992). Design and devotion: Surges of rational and normative ideologies of control in managerial discourse. *Administrative Science Quarterly, 37*(3), 363–400.

Black, M. (1962). *Models and metaphors*. Ithaca, NY: Cornell University Press.

Boxenbaum, E., & Rouleau, L. (2011). New knowledge products as bricolage: Metaphors and scripts in organizational theory. *Academy of Management Review, 36*(2), 272–296.

Carley, K. M. (2002). Intra-organizational computation and complexity. In J. A. C. Buam (Ed.), *Companion to organizations* (pp. 208–232). Oxford, England: Blackwell.

Cornelissen, J. P. (2005). Beyond compare: Metaphor in organization theory. *Academy of Management Review, 30*(4), 751–764.

Cornelissen, J. P. (2006). Metaphor and the dynamics of knowledge in organization theory: A case study of the organizational identity metaphor. *Journal of Management Studies, 43*(4), 683–709.

Cornelissen, J. P. (2012). Sensemaking under pressure: The influence of professional roles and social accountability on the creation of sense. *Organization Science, 23*, 118–137.

Cornelissen, J. P., & Clarke, J. S. (2010). Imagining and rationalizing opportunities: Inductive reasoning and the creation and justification of new ventures. *Academy of Management Review, 35*(4), 539–557.

Cornelissen, J. P., & Durand, R. (2014). Moving forward: Developing theoretical contributions in management studies. *Journal of Management Studies, 51*(6), 995–1022.

Cornelissen, J. P., & Kafouros, M. (2008). The emergent organization: Primary and complex metaphors in theorizing about organizations. *Organization Studies, 29*(7), 957–978.

Cornelissen, J. P., Oswick, C., Christensen, L. T., & Phillips, N. (2008). Metaphor in organizational research: Context, modalities and implications for research. *Organization Studies, 29*(1), 7–22.

Economist. (2015, September 12). Digital Taylorism: A modern version of "scientific management" threatens to dehumanize the workplace [Web log post]. Retrieved from http://www.economist.com/news/business/21664190-modern-version-scientific-management-threatens-dehumanize-workplace-digital

Fama, E. F., & Jensen, M. (1985). Organizational forms and investment decisions. *Journal of Financial Economics, 14*(1), 101–119.

Ghoshal, S. (2005). Bad management theories are destroying good management practices. *Academy of Management Learning and Education, 4*(1), 75–91.

Gioia, D. A., Schultz, M., & Corley, K. G. (2000). Organizational identity, image and adaptive instability. *Academy of Management Review, 25*(1), 63–81.

Gore, A. (1996). The metaphor of distributed intelligence. *Science, 272*(5259), 177.

Hannan, M. T., & Freeman, J. (1989). *Organizational ecology.* Cambridge, MA: Harvard University Press.

Haran, U. (2013). A person-organization discontinuity in contract perception: Why corporations can get away with breaking contracts but individuals cannot. *Management Science, 59*(12), 2837–2853.

Jensen, M. C., & Meckling, W. H. (1974). The theory of the firm: Managerial behavior, agency costs, and ownership structure. *Journal of Financial Economics, 3*(4), 305–360.

King, B. G., Felin, T., & Whetten, D. A. (2010). Finding the organization in organizational theory: A meta-theory of the organization as a social actor. *Organization Science, 21*(1), 290–305.

Lakoff, G., & Johnson, M. (1980). *Metaphors we live by.* Chicago, IL: University of Chicago Press.

Lakoff, G., & Johnson, M. (1999). *Philosophy in the flesh: The embodied mind and its challenge to Western thought.* New York, NY: Basic Books.

Marchand, R. (1998). *Creating the corporate soul: The rise of public relations and corporate imagery in American big business.* Berkeley: University of California Press.

Morgan, G. (1980). Paradigms, metaphors and puzzle solving in organizational theory. *Administrative Science Quarterly, 25*(4), 605–622.

Morgan, G. (1983). More on metaphor: Why we cannot control tropes in administrative science. *Administrative Science Quarterly, 28*(4), 601–607.

Morgan, G. (1986). *Images of organization.* Beverly Hills, CA: Sage.

Morgan, G. (1997). *Imaginization.* San Francisco, CA: Berrett-Koehler.

Morgan, G. (2006). *Images of organization* (3rd ed.). Thousand Oaks, CA: Sage.

Oswick, C., Fleming, P., & Hanlon, G. (2011). From borrowing to blending: Rethinking the processes of organizational theory-building. *Academy of Management Review, 36*(2), 318–337.

Oswick, C., Keenoy, T., & Grant, D. (2002). Metaphor and analogical reasoning in organization theory: Beyond orthodoxy. *Academy of Management Review, 27*(2), 294–303.

Oswick, C., Putnam, L. L., & Keenoy, T. (2004). Tropes, discourse and organizing. In D. Grant, C. Hardy, C. Oswick, & L. L. Putnam (Eds.), *Handbook of organizational discourse* (pp. 105–127). London, England: Sage.

Putnam, L. L., & Boys, S. (2006). Revisiting metaphors of organizational communication. In S. R. Clegg, C. Hardy, T. B. Lawrence, & W. R. Nord (Eds.), *The Sage handbook of organization studies* (pp. 541–576). London, England: Sage.

Schoeneborn, D., Vasquez, C., & Cornelissen, J. P. (2016). Imagining organization as flux: Unpacking the process-entity paradox through metaphor and metonymy. *Human Relations, 69*(4), 915–944.

Searle, J. R. (2010). *Making the social world: The structure of human civilization.* New York, NY: Oxford University Press.

Shepherd, D. A., & Sutcliffe, K. M. (2011). Inductive top down theorizing: A source of new theories of organization. *Academy of Management Review, 36*(2), 361–380.

Williamson, O. E. (1985). *The economic institutions of capitalism.* New York, NY: Free Press.

Using Metaphors in Organizational Analysis

4

Approaches to Using Metaphors in Organizational Analysis

Morgan's Metaphors and Beyond

Anders Örtenblad

Key Learning Points

- Understand that Morgan's metaphors as well as any other metaphors can be used in several different ways in both developing and researching organizations.
- Know that there is not any one approach to using metaphors that is always the best one; which approach is most relevant depends on what you want to achieve.
- Identify six ideal-typical approaches to how to use metaphors in organizational analysis: A) the color map approach; B) the colored lens approach; C) the pigeon-holes approach; D) the self-diagnosis approach; E) the eye-opener approach; and F) the cognitive innovation approach.
- Realize that metaphors can, when used in organizational analysis, have different functions; they can help to improve things, they can help to better understand something, or they can be used for the purpose of liberation.
- Assist in choosing which approach to use. You can decide whether your aim is to develop an individual organization or conduct research on organizations and which knowledge interest comes closest to what you want to achieve.

- Know that some of the approaches to using metaphors involve metaphors suggested by the analyst, whereas other approaches involve metaphors suggested by those being studied.
- Recognize that in a few of the approaches, the analyst starts in a single metaphor or a set of metaphors; in the majority of the approaches, the analyst starts in the object(s) of study (e.g., an organization) and chooses thereafter metaphors that are relevant in relation to what the analyst has found when studying the object(s).
- Understand that metaphors can be used either as variables, and thus uncover only those aspects of the organization that are similar to the source domain, or in terms of "seeing as," implying that the source domain is used as a colored lens through which everything in the organization is viewed and understood.

This chapter presents an overview of some possible ways to use metaphors in the development of organizations as well as in research of organizations.[1,2] The term **organizational analysis** is used to denote the study of organizations both for reasons of developing organizations and for conducting research on them. Consequently, this chapter brings together two streams of literature that too rarely are brought together. One of these literature streams deals with how metaphors can be used when developing organizations (e.g., Akin & Palmer, 2000) and the other stream addresses how metaphors can be used when doing research on organizations (e.g., Cornelissen, Oswick, Thøger Christensen, & Phillips, 2008). Thus, this chapter should appeal both to those who take interest in helping single organizations as internal or external consultants as well as to those with an interest in analyzing organizations for scientific purposes.

It is not that uncommon that metaphors are used when people conduct organizational analysis. Metaphors are frequently used in both the development of and research on organizations. The exact way that such work is conducted varies; there are a number of studies and different ways to use metaphors in organizational analysis. The aim here is not to create an all-inclusive **taxonomy** that covers all of these exact variations; rather, the aim is to present a **typology** containing some typical approaches (which can be regarded as **ideal types**) about how to use metaphors in organizational analysis. This set of approaches on how to conduct organizational analysis using metaphors offers a fairly comprehensible map that we can use to categorize the many varied methods on how to develop or conduct research on organizations with the help of metaphors that others actually have used. Some of these methods are quite similar to a single approach, whereas other methods can be understood with two or more approaches. Thus, the approaches can be said to be refined versions of methods that have actually been used in organizational analysis. For this reason, some may be easily identifiable in organizational literature, whereas others may not be identified as easily.

The presentation of the set of approaches in this chapter is meant to not only stimulate the reader to use metaphors in conducting organizational analysis, through giving examples of how such analyses can be conducted. The ambition is also to increase the readability of the rest of this book, especially the remaining chapters in Part II, by positioning these in relation to the set of approaches. This will be undertaken toward the end of this chapter.

The area of "using metaphors in organizational analysis" is quite complex; simplifying things too much would decrease understanding. Therefore, to increase readability and improve the possibility of comparing the approaches, the following seven distinctions are used as a framework:

1. Descriptive metaphors versus generative metaphors
2. Root metaphor versus metaphorical expression
3. Metaphors of those being studied versus metaphors of the analyst
4. Variable versus seeing as
5. Starting in metaphor versus starting in object of study
6. A set of metaphors versus single metaphors
7. Developing organizations versus researching organizations

Each approach addressed in this chapter is related to and positioned on each of these seven distinctions, which are presented more in depth and explained in the next section. There are, of course, myriad ways that these seven distinctions could be combined. However, the typology of approaches to using metaphors in organizational analysis will be limited to six approaches.

It must be mentioned that many of the approaches can be used in analyzing not only whole organizations (one or more) but also more or less any kind of aspect of or situation in organizations. Thus, the approaches work just as well for analyzing divisions, departments, or groups in organizations as they do for any other unit, meetings, kick-off events, and so forth. However, for reasons of simplifying the presentation, I often refer to the analysis of "organizations" in general.

Higher educational institutions (HEIs) (e.g., universities) and their practice (frequently in terms of a class and/or the classroom and group of students) are referred to as a fictive case example throughout the chapter because an HEI is an example of an organization with which the reader can be assumed to have experience.[3] However, examples of other types of organizations are also addressed because they occur in the literature to which I refer. The chapter is structured as follows. First, the seven distinctions are presented and thus some concepts central for this chapter are defined (also see the key terms at the end of this chapter). Second, the typology containing the six approaches to the use of metaphors in organizational analysis is presented. Third, the question is raised regarding which approach to using metaphors is preferable and this chapter demonstrates that the answer depends on what you want to achieve. Fourth, the remaining chapters in Part II of the book (along with one chapter in Part III) are positioned on the typology of approaches. Finally, a brief discussion of how to view sets of metaphors and approaches to the use of metaphors from a meta-perspective is provided.

Framework: Seven Distinctions

This section presents seven distinctions between different types of metaphors as well as different ways of using or approaching metaphors. These distinctions are used in the remainder of the chapter in order to position the approaches that will be placed on these distinctions. It should be noted that even if they are distinctions, they are not mutually exclusive. Thus, when a particular approach is positioned so that it looks as though it is in accordance with only one of the alternatives on the distinction at stake, it should be interpreted as if it is *more* in accordance with that alternative rather than *only* in accordance with it.

The alternative that is true for the approach at stake is shown in bold type. In a few cases, both alternatives are in bold, which means that the approach at stake involves both alternatives. In cases in which none of the alternatives is bolded, the distinction is not that relevant for the approach at stake.

A few concepts must be explained before I present the distinctions. The concepts of **source domain** and **target domain** are used to denote the two "parts" of metaphor. Source domain is the more well-known domain that is used as a source to understand the domain that we want to make understood (i.e., the target of our analysis [target domain]). For instance, we may want to use the "debating arena" or "church" as a source domain to say something about the target domain, which may be any particular classroom or the classroom in general. The seven distinctions are presented in detail below.

Distinction 1: Descriptive Metaphors Versus Generative Metaphors

There are different reasons why people use metaphors. The purpose can be said to depend on the context in which metaphors are used. In novels and poetry, for instance, metaphors are often used in an artistic way to make the language "sexier," whereas a researcher may use metaphors in order to gain knowledge. People may occasionally use metaphors without a certain reason—they may not even be aware that the words that they use are metaphoric at all.

However, we can still identify some general reasons for why people use metaphors. A distinction can be made between a **descriptive metaphor** (e.g., Yanow, 2005) and a **generative metaphor** (Schön, 1979/1993; Srivastva & Barrett, 1988). A descriptive metaphor implies that a metaphor is used for something that would be more difficult to describe using other language. For example, instead of saying "she is a very good swimmer," we may instead want to express ourselves in the following way: "She is a dolphin in the water." When it comes to higher education, we may, for instance, want to state about a particular university lecturer that "she or he is a guru," instead of explaining, more literally, how knowledgeable the lecturer is and the extent to which students and colleagues seem to look up to her or him. This is to make the less familiar more familiar and thus that which is difficult to describe a bit easier to describe. Therefore, descriptive metaphor means that a source domain that is close to or similar to the target domain is chosen.

A generative metaphor is used for the purpose of making the familiar unfamiliar. An example would be if we choose to view "charity" as an "instrument of domination." We would do this in order to generate new, creative knowledge on something that may be familiar to us, but not from the new light that we shed on "charity" by viewing it as an "instrument of domination." An example from higher education would be to suggest that "higher education is manipulation" instead of explaining that we believe that it would be fruitful and interesting to question whether higher education really is as enlightening as it often is assumed to be. Thus, in this case, a source domain that is more dissimilar to the target domain is chosen.

Distinction 2: Root Metaphor Versus Metaphorical Expression

Another distinction can be made between **root metaphor** and **metaphorical expression** (see Brown, 1977; Smith & Eisenberg, 1987). A root metaphor is one that lies underneath the understanding of something (e.g., of "organization") and is thus the "root" for our understanding of it. In this case, the source can be said to be the domain from which knowledge of something originates. Our knowledge of organizations originated from, as Morgan (1986, 1996, 2006, 2016) has shown in *Images of Organization*, areas such as biological systems (the organism metaphor) and cultural anthropology (the culture metaphor). Hence, Morgan's book can be understood as presenting eight root metaphors of "organization."

A metaphorical expression is one that involves metaphor (i.e., a phrase in which one or some of the words are more or less explicitly metaphorical). The root metaphor is thus on a deeper level and is not necessarily explicit, whereas a metaphorical expression is explicit and on a more surface level. For instance, when talking about her or his company, a manager might say, "We need more oil in the machinery." We could reasonably argue that the manager's root metaphor, which lies beneath how she or he views the company, is the "organization as machine" metaphor. Another, similar example is when a manager says that "there is a need for more blood in the bloodstream"; in this metaphorical expression, the manager's root metaphor could be said to be "organization as organism." Likewise, we may say about higher education that "I am not sure exactly where my education is taking me" (a metaphorical expression) and conclude that this expression is rooted in the metaphor "education is a journey" (the root metaphor).

In addition to metaphorical expressions, other types of expression can be said to be rooted in a particular root metaphor. For instance, a literal expression such as "increased productivity" may also be said to be based on the machine metaphor as a root for the person's understanding of "organization," even if the expression is literal and thus contains no explicit metaphor. Let us call these expressions **"semi-metaphorical expressions."**

In the above examples of metaphorical expressions and root metaphors, it was assumed that there is a strong connection between the two. Accordingly, some regard the connection between root metaphor and metaphorical/semi-metaphorical expressions as a relatively unproblematic connection. They claim that the root metaphor of a person relatively easily can be studied and identified through studying her or his metaphorical and/or semi-metaphorical expressions. One can even go as far as to suggest that the use of the word "information" implies that the person who uses this word refers to putting something *in form* because the word contains the metaphor "in-form" (Deetz, 1986, p. 177).

Others are not as convinced that the connection is as unproblematic (e.g., Shen & Balaban, 1999). You could, for instance, argue that we as humans are schooled into using certain words such as "information" and that the use of these words therefore does not at all mirror our root metaphor. The use of the metaphorical expression "oil in the machinery" about an organization would, according to this perspective, not necessarily mean that this person's root metaphor is "organization as machine." Another type of critique is that humans are too complex to be categorized into merely one single root metaphor. Any particular individual may not always use the same metaphorical/semi-metaphorical expressions. Yet another critique is that the relation between metaphorical expressions and root metaphor may be more problematic than it seems. For instance, it could be questioned whether it would be fair to claim that metaphorical expressions such as "she was a dolphin in the water" and "you are a pig" are actually based on the root metaphor "humans as animals."

Distinction 3: Metaphors of Those Being Studied Versus Metaphors of the Analyst

A distinction could be made between metaphors that are suggested by those who are being studied, such as **organizational actors**,[4] and metaphors suggested by **analysts** (i.e., those who study and analyze the organization, such as researchers, students, consultants, etc.). A similar distinction has previously been made between theoretical metaphors and "**metaphors of the field**" (see Manning, 1979; Meyer, 1984). However, within the "analyst" group, I include not only researchers but also groups such as internal and external consultants, students, and so forth. Within the "studied" group, I include organizational actors as well as authors of the literature that the analyst studies.

The analyst can listen to the metaphors appearing among those who are being studied, such as by the people who are being interviewed by the analyst, or by authors of books and articles that the analyst studies. A student whom the analyst studies may claim that her or his lecturer is a pathfinder or guide.

Conversely, the analyst may suggest metaphors. For instance, the analyst may want to suggest that it would increase our understanding of a certain university if we view it as a prison, whereas another university more reasonably may be understood as a garden. The analyst could also suggest metaphors that could help us to create better universities for the future. An example could be "universities as political systems," with an aim to claim that universities should be turned into places where different opinions are shared openly. These would all be metaphors of the analyst.

There may sometimes be borderline cases, such as when the analyst draws conclusions of an individual's root metaphor by listening to metaphorical and nonmetaphorical expressions in the individual's talk. This can be interpreted as being a combination of metaphors offered by those who are studied and metaphors offered by the analyst.

Distinction 4: Variable Versus Seeing As

All of Morgan's metaphors can be used either as "**variable**" or as "**seeing as**" (cf. Smircich, 1983). The same is also potentially true for any other metaphor. When using a metaphor as variable, it works like a simile and only that which is similar between the source domain and the target domain is identified through the metaphor. For example, when using the brain as a metaphor for a university class in this way, only that which is similar when comparing "brain" and "university class" is noticed, such as all of the learning that takes place both in brains and in university classes. That which is not similar to brain, however, is left out. Thus, issues such as who in the classroom has the most power—the lecturer, one student, or a particular group of students—would not be dealt with or would not be "seen." By using more than one metaphor as variable, we can uncover various "parts" or "aspects" of what takes place in the classroom in case we want to offer a more diverse (or even a complete) presentation of the organization. For instance, with the help of the political systems metaphor (and possibly also the instrument of domination metaphor), the issue of who has the most power in the classroom would be addressed.

If we are instead using metaphor as "seeing as," then everything in the target domain would be interpreted *as if it were* the source domain. In this case, the classroom that is studied would be seen as if it were a brain. Therefore, everything in the studied classroom—even that which is very unlike "brain"—would be interpreted in terms of knowledge about the brain. For instance, the question of who it is in the class who has the most power, which we can barely make sense of using the brain metaphor as variable, could be interpreted as if some people have more relevant cognitive maps or knowledge than other people with the help of the brain as root metaphor.

Distinction 5: Starting in Metaphor
Versus Starting in Object of Study

In some cases, the analyst takes a particular metaphor or a particular set of metaphors as the starting point for a study; on other occasions, the analyst starts in the empirical data and thereafter connects to suitable metaphors. For instance, when studying a particular class, we may already have chosen a certain metaphor through which we view the class.

Alternatively, we may instead start in the class and let what we observe guide our decision on which metaphor we choose in order to, for instance, claim that the class can be likened to. Perhaps we found that the students attentively listened to the lecturer and therefore want to suggest that the class was a divine service.

Distinction 6: A Set of Metaphors Versus Single Metaphors

A distinction can be made between using a set of metaphors (e.g., Morgan's eight metaphors in *Images of Organization*) and using one single metaphor (or a few). If we study one single university and want to use a metaphor to characterize it, a single metaphor may very well be enough. If, on the other hand, we want to study a handful of universities and want to be able to draw comparisons between them, we would certainly need a set of metaphors that can help us detect differences.

Likewise, when using metaphors as variables to uncover various aspects of a university, we definitely need a set of metaphors, but one metaphor would be enough if we are using it as a way of seeing each and every aspect of the studied university ("seeing as"). The difference between a set of metaphors and "a few single metaphors" is that there is a clear connection between the metaphors within the set, whereas the single metaphors may be more or less unconnected to each other.

Distinction 7: Developing Organizations Versus Researching Organizations

The approaches addressed in this chapter may be more relevant for developing individual organizations, an activity that may not always result in research or may be more relevant for doing research. There are, of course, different views on what exactly research is; however, most scholars would probably agree that solving an individual organization's problems per se is not research, although it is of course important. To be considered as "research," the project should not only deal with curing/repairing the single organization, but there must also be some kind of contribution to existing theory within the area from the project. Nevertheless, understanding and solving problems in organizations can still be an important aspect in or the basis for projects that, in addition to helping the single organization, also contribute to theory by viewing the organization as a case that, after having been studied, can contribute to existing knowledge on how problems of a certain *type* can be understood and/or solved.

For example, we may choose to use metaphors when trying to improve the climate in a class by first suggesting that "there is a very cold atmosphere in this class" and then suggesting that "all students and the lecturer need to help in creating a warmer atmosphere" (i.e., for developing organizations). Alternatively, we may instead want to use metaphors when analyzing the impact that different teaching styles may have on class climate, and we conclude, for instance, that "an authoritative teaching style generally results in a cold class climate" (i.e., for doing research on organizations). It is now time to turn our attention to the six approaches to using metaphors in organizational analysis.

A Typology of Approaches to Using Metaphors in Organizational Analysis

If we view Morgan's *Images of Organization* as a historical odyssey of organizational theory, then the book can simply be used as a *smorgasbord* from which a relevant theory for doing research can be selected. However, the approaches that are taken up here are a bit more complex than that. Each of the six approaches has been given a name inspired by one metaphor or another:

A. (A set of metaphors as a) *color map*
B. (A metaphor as a) *colored lens*
C. (A set of metaphors as) *pigeon-holes*
D. (Using metaphors in) *self-diagnosis*
E. (A metaphor as an) *eye-opener*
F. (Metaphor as) *cognitive innovation*

Each of these approaches is presented in more depth below.

Approach A: A Color Map
for Uncovering Aspects of Organizations

With an effort to study organizations in as multiperspectival a manner as possible, a set of metaphors (i.e., Morgan's set of metaphors) could be approached as a color map for the uncovering of a variety of aspects of an organization (Figure 4.1). This approach to using metaphors is perhaps the one that Morgan himself puts the most emphasis on. It is similar to what he terms "diagnostic reading"[5] (Morgan, 2006, p. 349). The approach implies the uncovering of aspects of an organization with help of a set of metaphors. Each metaphor covers one aspect or a set of aspects. For instance, instead of taking interest only in the efficiency of the studied organization stemming from a common goal, which the machine metaphor would help to uncover, you could (by using all eight metaphors) also study the effectiveness of the structure (uncovered through the organism metaphor), the values and norms of the organization (uncovered through the culture metaphor), learning in and by the organization (uncovered through the brain metaphor), different interests within the organization (uncovered through the political systems metaphor), people's psyches and their effect on the organization (uncovered by the psychic prison metaphor), the control over the employees that the management pursues (uncovered through the instrument of domination metaphor), and continuous change within the organization (uncovered through the flux and transformation metaphor).

& vice versa

This approach implies that the metaphors are used as similes/variables, focusing only on obvious similarities between the source domains (e.g., the organism, machine, and culture) and the target domain (the organization). Therefore, one would not view everything in the organization as if it were, for instance, an organism, but would instead uncover the obvious organism-like aspects of the organization, such as people (yes, we are often referred to as organisms), the economic systems in the organization (organisms contain systems), and structure (an important aspect of organisms as systems). Everything that is not obviously organismic is neglected—it will instead be covered by the other source domains (i.e., the machine, culture, etc.). Thus, the metaphors help to remind the analyst to cover a variety of aspects of the organization.

If we were to study a lecture in mathematics using Morgan's eight metaphors as a color map, we may find the following: with the help of the machine metaphor, we get an opportunity to analyze the efficiency of the lecture in terms of, for instance, the number of equations that the teacher goes through. The organism metaphor helps to analyze the effectiveness of the lecture, such as to what extent the students have learned something that they can use outside of the lecture room. The brain metaphor will help us to analyze the meta-learning in terms of what the students have learned about learning (i.e., how to learn mathematics). The culture metaphor assists us in analyzing the norms that are developed in the classroom, such as whether it is okay to wear a hat or if the students have to raise their hands before asking questions.

The political systems metaphor helps to analyze the different interests that the students and the lecturer may have; for example, the lecturer's main interests may be to get paid or see to it that the students learn enough to pass the exam so that it will be easy to mark the exam. By contrast, some students' main interest may be to

THE COLOR MAP APPROACH

GENERAL DESCRIPTION: The analyst starts in a set of metaphors; each metaphor helps uncover certain aspects of the organization, and together they uncover everything.

EXAMPLE: An internal consultant uses Morgan's eight metaphors to uncover different aspects of the studied class.

FIGURE 4.1 ●   A Set of Metaphors as a Color Map for Uncovering Aspects of Organizations

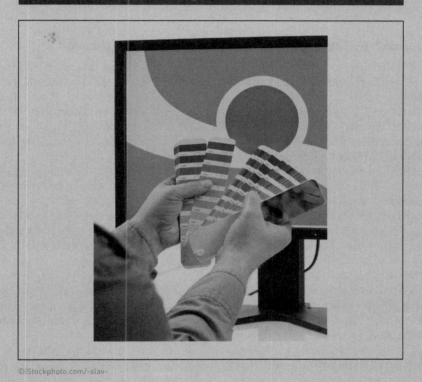

©iStockphoto.com/~slav~

learn as much as possible for life and others' main interest may be to get a good career. The psychic prison metaphor would help us to analyze the impact that the psyches of the students and lecturer have on the whole group during the class. It may, for instance, be that a few students are depressed and this may add a gloomy mood to the class. The instrument of domination metaphor would help us to analyze whether there are any measures taken by the lecturer that run the risk of abusing the students, such as using her or his power to get favors from the students. Finally, the flux and transformation metaphor could help us to analyze the small, almost invisible changes that the group of students goes through during the lecture, such as increasingly coming to respect their lecturer.

The "color map" approach in relation to the seven distinctions:

1. **Descriptive metaphors** versus generative metaphors
2. Root metaphor versus metaphorical expression
3. Metaphors of those being studied versus **metaphors of the analyst**
4. **Variable** versus seeing as
5. **Starting in metaphor** versus starting in object of study
6. **A set of metaphors** versus single metaphors
7. **Developing organizations** versus researching organizations

Approach B: Colored Lenses to See Organizations Through

With an effort to explore new perspectives and for gaining new, interesting, and creative understanding of organizational phenomena, a single metaphor could be used as a colored lens through which every aspect of the organization is viewed and understood (cf. colored sunglasses) (Figure 4.2). The lens that is used as a starting point colors everything in the same color as the lens. Therefore, even that which is not obviously similar between the source domain and the target domain is interpreted *as if it were* the source domain.

Often, in this approach to using metaphors, you would use one single metaphor through which you would describe everything in the organization. One reason why it may be a good idea to use one metaphor only is that it may be difficult to see everything through more than one metaphor at a time and do all of them justice (e.g., Pinder & Bourgeois, 1982; Sanford, 1987; Tsoukas, 1993). Some critics claim that you cannot really do justice to any metaphor that does not correlate with your own paradigm (cf. Morgan, 1980). Therefore, these critics doubt that we are actually really fully free to choose research perspective.

Morgan's metaphors would be a good start for choosing a metaphor because there is a lot of theory backing up each of the eight metaphors that he presents and there is often also an accompanying methodology for each metaphor (e.g., "**ethnography**" accompanies the metaphor of organization as culture).

The culture metaphor is likely the one of Morgan's metaphors that has been used most commonly in studies that explicitly start in a certain metaphor as a lens through which everything in the organization is studied. Smircich (1983) described the difference between viewing culture as a subsystem (cf. variable) in the organization, and culture as a root metaphor. One of the scholars who took this further is Alvesson (1995), who studied an information and communications technology consultancy firm through the lens of the culture metaphor. Thus, even if something was not obviously culture, Alvesson examined it as if it were culture nonetheless. Thus, for instance, he analyzed both the firm's business idea and its formal structure (none of which has obvious similarities with "culture") *as if they were* culture (i.e., symbols). Alvesson's book *Management of Knowledge-Intensive Companies* is interesting and well worth reading and successfully illustrates the "seeing as" perspective to using metaphors and thus the "metaphor as colored lens" approach.

Even if the culture metaphor is perhaps the one of Morgan's metaphors that is most commonly used in this kind of research, and even if it is the metaphor with which this approach works best, all of Morgan's metaphors can be used in this way. For instance, if we study an organization where a lot of interpersonal conflicts are going on and we base our study on the organism metaphor, then we may view the conflicts as abscesses that either will be cured automatically (by the "immune system") or need to be cured by medicine. By contrast, a study using the organism as variable would hardly uncover the conflicts at all (these would instead be uncovered by metaphors such as the political systems and instrument of domination).

Another example of such a generative use of one of Morgan's metaphors as a root metaphor is to study an organization that is well known for taking very good care of its employees on the basis of the instrument of domination metaphor to get an understanding of which new, interesting things we could learn. Similarly, we could also study other organizations that at first glance have very few similarities with the instrument of domination metaphor, such as the Red Cross or a church, and we could interpret all of the good they do for other people as if these were measures to preserve existing inequalities and injustice in the world.

The one of Morgan's metaphors that may be the most similar to the common understanding of HEIs is the brain metaphor, so we may instead want to view a university as if it were a machine, thereby exploring everything about that university as if it were a "machine." Even that which is not obviously cold, rational, and machine-like would be interpreted as if it were. For instance, the university library may be interpreted as a cog in the knowledge production process.

You could, of course, instead use a metaphor that is similar to the organization that you aim to study or even the metaphor that is the most similar to the organization. By doing so, you would find fewer issues that are obviously different between the source domain and the target domain when comparing these, but there would always be issues that are not obviously similar between the studied organization and the source domain, in that everything in the organization—also that which is not that similar to the chosen source domain—is seen and interpreted through the frame at stake. For this reason, this way of using Morgan's metaphors is always more generative than descriptive.

The "colored lens" approach in relation to the seven distinctions:

1. Descriptive metaphors versus **generative metaphors**
2. **Root metaphor** versus metaphorical expression
3. Metaphors of those being studied versus **metaphors of the analyst**
4. Variable versus **seeing as**
5. **Starting in metaphor** versus starting in object of study
6. A set of metaphors versus **single metaphors**
7. Developing organizations versus **researching organizations**

THE COLORED LENS APPROACH

GENERAL DESCRIPTION: The analyst starts in a single metaphor and views everything of the organization as if it were whatever the chosen metaphor prescribes.

EXAMPLE: A researcher uses academic literature on culture to form a colored lens and concludes that "from seeing a university as if it were culture, it appears that university education is about socialization."

FIGURE 4.2 ● Metaphors as Colored Lenses to View Organizations Through

Approach C: A Set of Pigeon-Holes to Categorize Into

With an intention to point out and offer an overview of differences between a number of units, metaphors can be used as a set of pigeon-holes with which to categorize these units (but in some situations, a few single metaphors or even one single metaphor—in case one unit only is categorized—would be sufficient) (Figure 4.3).

THE PIGEON-HOLES APPROACH

GENERAL DESCRIPTION: The analyst starts studying a number of objects and chooses a relevant set of metaphors to categorize these objects into.

EXAMPLE: A student-as-researcher studies three classrooms and concludes that classroom 1 is a prison, classroom 2 is a garden, and classroom 3 is a factory.

FIGURE 4.3 ● Metaphors as a Set of Pigeon-Holes Into Which to Categorize the Units of Study

©iStockphoto.com/JohnatAPW

The units may be organizations, subunits of organizations, or any situation or phenomena in organizations such as meetings, events, lunchroom talk, activities, and so forth. The units may also be people's understandings of organizations, which, for instance, can be studied through verbal accounts or written texts.

The main difference between categorizing organizations and categorizing people's understandings of organizations (inclusive of texts) is that, when categorizing organizations, the decision on which metaphor to categorize into relies much more heavily on the analyst, whereas when categorizing people's understandings of organizations, the analyst usually makes more effort to keep to the understanding of the people or text studied. When categorizing organizations per se, what the analyst does here is ultimately to categorize her or his own understanding of the organizations at stake.

Let us start to look at what this approach implies when the analyst is about to categorize organizations per se. The analyst starts in the objects of study, such as the organizations, and categorizes these on the basis of an existing set of metaphors or creates a new set of metaphors into which to categorize the organizations. Morgan's metaphors can be used to categorize the units that are being studied, but any existing set of metaphors will work and there is even room to create a new set of metaphors that fulfills the purpose. When creating a new set of metaphors to categorize into, the analyst may be more or less inspired by the units of study. In the normal case, each unit of study would be categorized according to one of the metaphors within the chosen set of metaphors.

Let us now say that the analyst intends to categorize three different university classes with the help of Morgan's metaphors. The analyst may find that one of the classes has many similarities with a machine (e.g., that the lecturer teaches in a traditional way, emphasizes punctuality, and clearly shows that she or he expects the students to memorize the information taught), that another class has many similarities with a political system (e.g., that the lecturer lets the students debate various issues that are connected to the course content and emphasizes the importance of different opinions brought forward), and that the third class has many similarities with a brain (e.g., that the lecturer lets the students learn in self-managed teams without any fixed course literature).

If the analyst instead were to use any metaphors when categorizing three other classes, she or he may conclude that one class is a church service in that the students praise everything that their lecturer says; another class is a garden in that the lecturer seems to make efforts to facilitate each individual's growth by encouraging the students to come up with their own thoughts about the subject being taught; and a third class is a prison in that the lecturer in an assiduous manner controls that the students are punctual, that they do not speak without having been given the permission to do so, and that they have done the homework that the lecturer has given them.

Let us now take a closer look at the categorization of people's understandings of organizations with the help of metaphors. A common method used is to interview the people whose understandings are being studied, but observing them or studying documents that these people have authored may also be of interest. The analyst would normally identify metaphorical and semi-metaphorical expressions that the studied people use, but behavior signifying a certain metaphor (i.e., "**metaphorical behavior**") may also be of interest. The less explicitly metaphorical the expressions or behavior are, the more difficult it is for the analyst to tell whether the suggested metaphors actually are metaphors of those being studied or if they rather are metaphors of the analyst.

The analyst would, on the basis of the metaphorical and semi-metaphorical expressions and on the metaphorical behavior in case such has been identified, draw conclusions about the individual's deep-down understanding of, or root metaphor for, whatever is at stake. For instance, for an individual who repeatedly uses expressions such as "face-loosing," "jaw dropping," and "hold your head cold," the analyst may want to conclude that this individual's root metaphor of human interaction is that of the "human body." For an individual who talks about her or his organization in terms of "a need for more blood in the bloodstream," "there is a need to adapt to the environment," and "systems in the organization," the analyst may conclude that the individual's root metaphor is that of "organization as organism."

Going back to the university example, you may want to categorize your classmates' understandings of the university where you study or of a particular class that you take on the basis of Morgan's set of metaphors or on the basis of a set of metaphors that you construct yourself. It may be, for instance, that some of your classmates understand your university as a prison, others understand it as a factory, and yet others understand it as a garden.

For those who do not believe that individuals in general have one root metaphor or that it is not possible to identify such, then there is another option. You could instead categorize each of a particular individual's accounts to the certain metaphor that it is most similar to and thus outline a list of metaphors that represents the specific individual's perspective of (the) organization. For instance, you may notice that, for one of your classmates, the university where you study is a garden on occasions when she or he takes part in extracurricular activities, a prison during the compulsory lectures, and a factory during the summer vacation. In this case, the metaphors would be treated as variables, whereas if you made an effort to identify your classmate's one root metaphor of the university, you would rather treat the metaphor as "seeing as" (i.e., a root for the person's understanding through which she or he views everything). Perhaps you would find that, even if you could argue for the existence of different metaphors within your classmate's expressions, her or his root metaphor is "university as factory."

To categorize published texts such as academic literature or newspaper articles is a special case of categorizing people's understandings of organizations in that it is mainly the author(s) who is categorized (although, in some cases, the editor and/or publisher may have also had some influence over the text). To categorize literature within a certain area is, in fact, what Gareth Morgan did in *Images of Organization*. To a certain extent, he identified from which area various organizational theories had borrowed knowledge, such as the fact that some organizational theorists had used knowledge on systems theory from biology to understand organizations, something that Morgan positioned within the "organization as organism" metaphor. In the works that Morgan categorized into the set of eight metaphors, there may very well be several expressions that suggest metaphors other than the one into which Morgan categorized the text at stake. A reasonable interpretation of what he did is that he made an effort to identify a single root metaphor in each of the texts that he categorized.

The same thing can be done with other texts. It is, for instance, interesting to study newspaper articles about a particular organization and to interpret the metaphor(s) of the articles' authors. It can be especially interesting to compare articles about the same organization (or about a particular incident, such as the collapse of Lehman Brothers or the treatment of employees by Foxconn in China) published in newspapers that have different political views.

The "pigeon-holes" approach in relation to the seven distinctions:

1. **Descriptive** metaphors versus generative metaphors
2. **Root metaphor** versus **metaphorical expression**
3. **Metaphors of those being studied** versus **metaphors of the analyst**

4. **Variable** versus **seeing as**
5. Starting in metaphor versus **starting in object of study**
6. **A set of metaphors** versus **single metaphors**
7. **Developing organizations** versus **researching organizations**

Approach D: Metaphors by Invitation: Mentored Self-Diagnosis

In an effort to help people express their own (more or less unconscious) beliefs and feelings about things in their organization, metaphors can be used in mentored self-diagnosis (Figure 4.4). The analyst typically leads some kind of workshop and invites the participants to express themselves through metaphors. The analyst would

THE SELF-DIAGNOSIS APPROACH

GENERAL DESCRIPTION: The analyst asks people in the organization to describe both how things are in their organization and how things ideally could be.

EXAMPLE: An external consultant invites metaphors from students on how things are/could be in the classroom, who suggest "this class is a candy shop while it should be a vegetarian food store."

FIGURE 4.4   ●   Using Metaphors as an Instrument in Mentored Self-Diagnosis

©iStockphoto.com/ATIC12

primarily encourage the participants to suggest metaphors for the current state but could also invite metaphors that may help to improve the organization or solve the problem at stake. The analyst may leave it totally up to the participants to use any metaphor or may lead them in a certain direction by, for instance, asking them to "think of your university as an animal—which animal would it be?"

Morgan's metaphors are not that relevant when using this approach. The main reason for this is that when using metaphors in this way, it is important not to delimit the imagination of the participants; they must be given the freedom to associate to any source domain that they prefer. However, occasionally, some of the offered metaphors may be the same as or similar to any of Morgan's eight metaphors. It may also be that Morgan's eight metaphors can be used to categorize the metaphors that the participants suggest because the pigeon-holes approach is often used as a complement to the self-diagnosis approach.

An example of a student or scholar who is encouraged to suggest a metaphor for the university where she or he studies or works and which she or he finds problematic might be that "my university is like a church—all students believe blindly in what they read and what the teacher says."

The "self-diagnosis" approach in relation to the seven distinctions:

1. **Descriptive metaphors** versus **generative metaphors**
2. **Root metaphor** versus **metaphorical expression**
3. **Metaphors of those being studied** versus metaphors of the analyst
4. Variable versus seeing as
5. Starting in metaphor versus **starting in object of study**
6. A set of metaphors versus **single metaphors**
7. **Developing organizations** versus researching organizations

Approach E: Metaphors as Eye-Openers

In an effort to suggest alternative ways of understanding organizational actors' reality, metaphors can serve as eye-openers (Figure 4.5). This approach is primarily used in the development of organizations. The analyst would first make efforts to understand the organization in general or look at a particular problem from the organizational actors' perspective (this may take place through the self-diagnosis approach or in any other way). Metaphors are thereafter used to suggest alternative ways of conceiving the organization or problem at stake. Therefore, through the help of metaphors, the analyst offers alternative realities with the intention of improving conditions for the organizational actors. The offered realities/metaphors may also help the organizational actors to overcome or even solve problems.

Metaphors may, to this end, be a very relevant device to use in that they may speak not only to the intellect but also to the organizational actors' emotions. Therefore, internal or external consultants (or anyone else, for that matter, such as workmates or managers) can use metaphors to get an instant reaction and to offer an alternative understanding of an organization or subunit of it. For instance, it may be that the employees at a university view their university as a garden, but this understanding from an outsider's perspective may appear merely as an illusion; therefore, an external consultant may suggest that "this university is not a garden, it is a prison."

As a student, you could point out for your lecturer that she or he treats the class as if it were a machine, or you could point out for your vice chancellor that she or he treats the whole university as if it were a church. Occasionally, university lecturers may say to their students, "to you, this is a kindergarten," and they may suggest that their students "grow up" and "become your own teachers." The lecturers may even suggest that "this is a knowledge temple."

The "eye-opener" approach in relation to the seven distinctions:

1. Descriptive metaphors versus **generative metaphors**
2. **Root metaphor** versus metaphorical expression
3. Metaphors of those being studied versus **metaphors of the analyst**
4. Variable versus **seeing as**
5. Starting in metaphor versus **starting in object of study**
6. A set of metaphors versus **single metaphors**
7. **Developing organizations** versus researching organizations

THE EYE-OPENER APPROACH

GENERAL DESCRIPTION: The analyst starts in those being studied and their understanding(s) of their organization and then suggests contrasting metaphor(s).

EXAMPLE: An internal consultant interviews students who claim that their lecturer is bad, so the internal consultant contrasts their understanding by suggesting that "your lecturer is no demon, she or he is a considerate parent."

FIGURE 4.5 ● Using Metaphors as Eye-Openers

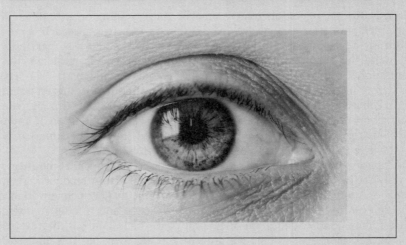

©iStockphoto.com/simarik

Approach F: Metaphors as Cognitive Innovations

Metaphors can also be used in an effort to suggest new ways to conceptualize and, in general terms, to make sense of organizations (Figure 4.6). It is especially valuable to suggest metaphors that cannot easily be understood in terms of any of Morgan's eight metaphors because these have become a common frame of reference for many organizational analysts.

This innovative task should, however, not be considered as anything that can be undertaken with too much ease. If it were only a question of quantity, then we could easily list a number of metaphors that may or may not be relevant for our understanding of HEIs and higher education (e.g., HEIs as sofas, candles, ice cream, carpets, curtains, etc.). There is a clear risk that such "brainstormed" lists of metaphors would appear a bit suspect. On the other hand, creativity must be encouraged. The art here is to come up with metaphors that can help us to say something interesting about organizations. Therefore, a good idea could be to evaluate any metaphor that comes to one's mind (see Cornelissen, Chapter 3 in this volume).

As we mentioned in Chapter 1, the three editors of this book also previously edited a special issue of an academic journal titled *Human Relations* (Örtenblad, Putnam, & Trehan, 2016). In that special issue, various contributors suggested metaphors that could complement the set of eight metaphors that Morgan suggested in *Images of Organization*. In our introduction to the special issue (Örtenblad et al., 2016), we suggested, on the basis of metaphors suggested by our contributors, that there are different grounds for suggesting new metaphors.

Here, I will stick to the following (somewhat simplified) categories of means to suggesting new metaphors: covering emergent organizational theories, covering emergent organizational practice, and food for thought. The first two categories imply descriptive metaphor, rather than generative metaphor, in that both categories include occasions in which metaphors are suggested to cover up for something that already exists. However, these metaphors can still appear to be generative to those who have not yet come across the theories or practices that the metaphors are intended to cover. The third category is the only category that can be said to involve truly generative metaphors.

The first category of means, covering emergent organizational theories, includes occasions when new metaphors are suggested for a theory or group of theories that cannot be understood with, for instance, any of Morgan's eight metaphors. Examples of theories are those on time and organizations (Ancona, Goodman, Lawrence, & Tushman, 2001), humor and irony in organizations (Hatch, 1997), and voice and silence in organizations (e.g., Morrison & Milliken, 2003). (Judge for yourselves if you think that these theories can be understood with any of Morgan's eight metaphors.) The second category, covering emergent organizational practice, includes occasions when metaphors are suggested to understand new kinds of organizations that have appeared lately (e.g., space stations, online reputation management consultancy firms, and climate change associations), which were uncommon when *Images of Organization* was first published in 1986 (if they existed at all). This category also includes the suggestion of new metaphors for new phenomena in organizations and new situations in which organizations appear. One example could be the increased appearance of new public

THE COGNITIVE INNOVATION APPROACH

GENERAL DESCRIPTION: The analyst starts in a perceived lack and suggests a metaphor to fill the perceived lack.

EXAMPLE: A students-as-researcher finds that there is no metaphor for understanding the fact that managers at many universities are appointed on the basis of an election process among the faculty, and suggests the "university leadership as mirage" metaphor.

FIGURE 4.6 ● Metaphors as Cognitive Innovations

©iStockphoto.com/AndrewRich

management at HEIs and many other similar organizations. The third category (food for thought) includes those occasions when new metaphors are suggested on no other particular ground than that the metaphor is a new one and that it may stimulate new thoughts.

Among the contributions to the above-mentioned special issue, McCabe (2016) was mainly covering emergent organizational practice when suggesting the metaphor of "Wonderland," which puts the focus on and makes sense of the quite irrational and chaotic reality many of us nowadays experience in our everyday life in organizations. Pinto (2016) also covered emergent organizational practice when suggesting the metaphor of "organization as icehotel," which points to the paradoxical aspect of some organizations of our time.

The "cognitive innovation" approach in relation to the seven distinctions:

1. **Descriptive metaphors** versus **generative metaphors**
2. **Root metaphor** versus metaphorical expression
3. Metaphors of those being studied versus **metaphors of the analyst**
4. Variable versus seeing as
5. Starting in metaphor versus **starting in object of study**
6. A set of metaphors versus **single metaphors**
7. Developing organizations versus **researching organizations**

Which Approach Is Preferable?

It is now time to discuss the value of the approaches in relation to each other. In accordance with a contingency perspective, my strong belief is that there is no approach to using metaphors in organizational analysis that is always better than all of the other approaches. Instead, as a contingency perspective prescribes, which approach is the most relevant is contingent upon several factors, the most important of which is, of course, what you want to achieve with your organizational analysis.

One distinction that relates to what you may want to achieve with your study is actually apparent in one of the distinctions: you may either want to develop a single organization or do research on any organizational aspect in general. If you, for instance, intend to develop a single organization, you are recommended to use any of the approaches with the main function of developing organizations described in the above text and in Table 4.1.

A complementary factor that can help in advising which approach is the most relevant one in a certain situation is to involve Habermas's (1966) **knowledge interests**. One knowledge interest is the technical, in which the researcher is normative and thus tries to make something better. Another knowledge interest is interpretative, in which the researcher seeks to understand. The third of Habermas's knowledge interests is the critical, in which emancipation is at the forefront (i.e., to liberate people either from physical oppression or to "free people's minds"). Habermas's theory is primarily relevant for understanding researching organizations, but I apply it here also for developing organizations.

As is illustrated in Table 4.1, all three knowledge interests are represented among those approaches that are suggested to be relevant mainly for developing organizations. For instance, the "metaphors as color map" approach is connected with both a technical knowledge interest and an interpretative knowledge interest, whereas the "metaphor as eye-opener" approach is mainly connected with the emancipatory knowledge interest. Likewise, two of the three knowledge interests are represented among the approaches with the main function of researching organizations. Therefore, knowledge interest can complement the distinction between "development" and "research" in that different approaches that are relevant for development and research, respectively, are connected to different knowledge interests.

TABLE 4.1 ● An Overview of the Six Approaches. For Each of the Approaches, the Main Role of the Analyst Is Briefly Outlined, the Main Knowledge Interest Is Indicated, and the Positioning on Each of the Seven Distinctions Is Illustrated								
			Descriptive Metaphor Versus Generative Metaphor		Root Metaphor Versus Metaphorical Expression		Metaphors of Those Being Studied Versus Metaphors of the Analyst	
Approach	Main Role of Analyst (When It Comes to Using Metaphors)	Main Knowledge Interest	Descriptive Metaphor	Generative Metaphor	Root Metaphor	Metaphorical Expressions	Metaphors of Those Being Studied	Metaphors of the Analyst
Color map	Uncovering different aspects of an organization with the help of a set of metaphors	Interpretive/ technical	X					X
Colored lens	Describing an organization as if each and every aspect of it were what the source domain of the chosen metaphor prescribes	Emancipation		X	X			X
Pigeon-holes	Categorizing organizations or understandings of organizations with the help of a set of metaphors	Interpretive	X		X	X	X	X
Self-diagnosis	Inviting organizational actors to express their organizational problems or to describe their organization in terms of metaphors	Emancipation	X	X	X	X	X	
Eye-opener	Suggesting metaphors that go beyond the organizational actors' current understanding of themselves and/or their organization	Emancipation		X	X			X
Cognitive innovation	Suggesting metaphors that are new in relation to existing knowledge about organizations in general	Interpretive	X	X	X			X

Variable Versus Seeing As		Starting in Metaphor Versus Starting in Object of Study		A Set of Metaphors Versus Single Metaphors		Developing Organizations Versus Researching Organizations	
Variable	Seeing As	Starting in Metaphor	Starting in Object of Study	A Set of Metaphors	Single Metaphors	Developing Organizations	Researching Organizations
X		X		X		X	
	X	X			X		X
X	X		X	X	X	X	X
	X		X		X	X	
			X		X	X	
			X		X		X

As illustrated in Table 4.1, some of the approaches have many similarities. For instance, the "metaphors as color map" approach and the "metaphor as eye-opener" approach are similar in many respects. To make it easier to distinguish between the approaches, the main role of the analyst when it comes to the use of metaphors is briefly outlined for each of the approaches in Table 4.1.

Readers are encouraged to find their own favorite approach by trying them out, refining them, combining them, and so forth. Students especially are encouraged to try out the approaches in practice. However, the use of metaphors for organizational analysis (or, for that matter, in any other context) should not be limited to these six typical approaches. The reader is encouraged to explore new ways of using metaphors in areas such as organizational analysis.

The Chapters in Part II of This Book

In this section, those chapters in the book that use metaphors in organizational analysis are positioned in relation to the six approaches. The chapters that are relevant here are all of the remaining chapters in Part II and one chapter in Part III. As a matter of fact, the chapters have more or less stuck to two of the six approaches. As is illustrated in Table 4.2, all five chapters have used the "metaphor as cognitive innovation" approach. Three of these chapters have also used the "metaphors as pigeon-holes" approach. In the following, justifications for the positioning of each of these five chapters are offered. It must be mentioned that the authors of the categorized chapters, as well as the other literature that I categorize in this section, may or may not have been aware that they used any certain approach when they conducted their studies (at least, they may not have been aware of the particular approaches taken up in this chapter).

In Chapter 5 ("Viewing Organizations as Enablers of Happiness"), Vikas Rai Bhatnagar suggests a new (mainly generative) metaphor. By doing so, Chapter 5 can be read as an example of the "metaphor as cognitive innovation" approach. The suggestion of the metaphor "organizations as enablers of happiness" can mainly be understood as "food for thought." It is true that the suggested metaphor to some extent is also based on organizational practice, as Bhatnagar himself claims, but not to such an extent that I would see it as being a measure to "covering emergent organizational practice." The rudimentary theory of organizations as enablers of happiness did, in fact, develop as Bhatnagar was carrying out action research, but it was hardly a question of mapping existing organizational practice even if the author implemented happiness through the action research. However, "happiness" is rather to be seen as some kind of ideal that Bhatnagar suggests. In this sense, the approach to suggesting a new metaphor seems here to be most in accordance with "food for thought," although the suggested metaphor also covers theory—such as positive psychology applied to organizations (and thus could be regarded as a measure to "covering emergent organizational theory")—as well as emerging practice.

In Chapter 6 ("Combining Metaphors to Understand New Organizational Phenomena"), Thomas Süße, Bernd-Friedrich Voigt, and Uta Wilkens use not only the "metaphor as cognitive innovation" approach but also the "metaphors as pigeon-holes" approach. The approach that is most apparent in this chapter is the

Reference / This volume	Color Map	Colored Lens	Pigeon-Holes	Self-Diagnosis	Eye-Opener	Cognitive Innovation
Chapter 5 ("Viewing Organizations as Enablers of Happiness"), Vikas Rai Bhatnagar						X
Chapter 6 ("Combining Metaphors to Understand New Organizational Phenomena"), Thomas Süße, Bernd-Friedrich Voigt, and Uta Wilkens			X			X
Chapter 7 ("Exploring Metaphors of Leadership"), Turo Virtanen			X			X
Chapter 8 ("Developing Metaphors in Light of the Visual and Digital Turns in Organizational Studies: Toward a Methodological Framework"), Ron Kerr, Sarah K. Robinson, and Carole Elliott			X			X
Chapter 10 ("Organization as Affect: Moving on Metaphorically"), David Grant and Cliff Oswick						X

(Continued)

TABLE 4.2 ● (Continued)

Reference Additional publications	Color Map	Colored Lens	Pigeon-Holes	Self-Diagnosis	Eye-Opener	Cognitive Innovation
"Using Metaphor to Read the Organization of the NHS," Elkind (1998)	X					
"Analogical Reasoning Is the Way to Go Beyond Orthodoxy in Formulating Organisational Problems: The Use of An Improved Version of Morgan's Metaphors Revisited," Torlak (2007)	X					
"Management of Knowledge-Intensive Companies," Alvesson (1995)		X				
"Metaphor Analysis of Social Reality in Organizations," Koch & Deetz (1981)			X			
"Systemizing the Organizational Scenario Literature Using Morgan's Metaphors," Lang (2008)			X			
"Analysing Metaphor in Human Resource Development," Short (2000)			X			
"Method and Metaphor in Organizational Analysis," Boland & Greenberg (1992)			X	X		

Reference	Color Map	Colored Lens	Pigeon-Holes	Self-Diagnosis	Eye-Opener	Cognitive Innovation
"Images of an Organization: The Use of Metaphor in a Multinational Company," Oswick & Montgomery (1999)			X	X		
"Metaphorical Images of an Organization: The Power of Symbolic Constructs in Reading Change in Higher Education Organizations," Simsek (1997)			X	X		
"The Transforming Nature of Metaphors in Group Development: A Study in Group Theory," Srivastva & Barrett (1988)			X		X	
"Generative Metaphor Intervention: A New Approach for Working With Systems Divided by Conflict and Caught in Defensive Perception," Barrett & Cooperrider (1990)					X	
"Glass Cages and Glass Palaces: Images of Organization in Image-Conscious Times," Gabriel (2005)						X
"'Curiouser and Curiouser!' Organizations as Wonderland — A Metaphorical Alternative to the Rational Model," McCabe (2016)						X
"'Wow! That's So Cool!' The Icehotel as Organizational Trope," Pinto (2016)						X

former, in that the authors make efforts to identify a new metaphor for an emergent organizational phenomenon called integrated product-service systems (IPSS). Therefore, the basis for suggesting a new metaphor is "covering emergent organizational practice." However, Süße et al. never actually identify any truly new metaphor, but they instead combine three of Morgan's existing metaphors. This could be said to be in accordance with the "metaphors as pigeon-holes" approach in that they categorized the studied phenomenon (IPSS) into the three metaphors (or, more accurately, they categorized engineers' reflections on actions in relation to IPSS).

In Chapter 7 ("Exploring Metaphors of Leadership"), Turo Virtanen uses some of Morgan's metaphors as a starting point when developing metaphors for leadership. This relates to at least a few of the approaches presented in this chapter. We could say that it is a way of categorizing people's understandings and thus can be considered as the "metaphors as pigeon-holes" approach at least indirectly, in that it was the respondents who, when asked by Virtanen, categorized their superiors by the help of metaphors. However, the main aim in Virtanen's chapter is hardly to categorize people; this is merely a means to an end. The end is rather to explore the relationship between organizational metaphors and leadership metaphors. When Virtanen suggests the six metaphors per the five chosen ones of Morgan's metaphors, he could be said to use metaphors as cognitive innovations and indirectly and implicitly perhaps also to use a set of metaphors to categorize (texts within) another field (leadership). Therefore, my impression of Chapter 7 is that it illustrates some kind of combination of the "metaphors as pigeon-holes" approach and the "metaphor as cognitive innovation" approach.

An interesting aspect of Virtanen's chapter is his reasoning when it comes to operationalizing deeper metaphor structures into metaphorical and nonmetaphorical, everyday expressions (cf. distinction 2, above, on root metaphor versus metaphorical expression). Would you agree with his assumptions regarding the connections between expressions and leadership metaphors, between leadership metaphors and leadership styles/groups of leadership metaphors, and between leadership styles/ groups of leadership metaphors and metaphors for organizations?

Like Chapters 6 and 7, Chapter 8 ("Developing Metaphors in Light of the Visual and Digital Turns in Organizational Studies: Toward a Methodological Framework") illustrates a combination between the "metaphors as pigeon-holes" approach and the "metaphor as cognitive innovation" approach. Ron Kerr, Sarah K. Robinson, and Carole Elliott provide a complex method of analysis; the part that refers to metaphors can be said to be most inspired by "metaphors as pigeon-holes," in that they categorized both text and images at the studied website according to certain metaphors. Furthermore, they can also be said to have used the "metaphor as cognitive innovation" approach when they suggested a new, descriptive metaphor that can describe a transnational corporation such as Mondelēz International and its visual and digital projections, namely the "*trompe l'oeil*."

There is at least one more chapter that deserves to be positioned in relation to the six approaches, even if it appears in Part III of the book; therefore, the chapter's role in this book is not primarily to illustrate any approach to using metaphors in organizational analysis. In Chapter 10 ("Organization as Affect: Moving on Metaphorically"), David Grant and Cliff Oswick illustrate the approach of "metaphor as cognitive innovation." Their suggestion of the metaphor of "organization as affect" seems to be based on "covering for emerging organizational practice."

A Comment on Meta-Metaphors:
Understanding How We Approach Metaphors

As I mentioned in the introduction to this chapter and as the reader has probably noticed, I have used metaphors to frame the various approaches addressed here. As a matter of fact, metaphors could be used not only to understand and analyze organizations but to also make sense of metaphors per se and even of approaches to the use of metaphors. These, we could call "**meta-metaphors**." As suggested above, especially (but not only) in the headings of the six approaches, metaphors may be used as "color maps," "smorgasbords," "colored lenses," "pigeon-holes," "eye-openers," and "cognitive innovations."

Each one of Morgan's metaphors can be said to imply a certain way of relating to metaphor use and even to the very metaphors that Morgan has suggested. Therefore, the organism as meta-metaphor, for instance, would imply that each metaphor is represented by and uncovers a certain subsystem of the organization; for example, that the culture metaphor uncovers the culture as a subsystem of the organization, the political systems metaphor uncovers power as a subsystem, and so forth. The machine as meta-metaphor suggests that Morgan's set of metaphors is a toolbox, whereas the political systems as meta-metaphor suggests that Morgan's set of metaphors is a palette of political colors or interests. The flux and transformation as meta-metaphor could suggest that each metaphor as well as the set of eight metaphors is in continuous change. The psychic prison as meta-metaphor may suggest not only that each of the eight metaphors is a psychic prison, but also that the set per se is a psychic prison for how to view organization that it is not easy to break free from, an issue that Morgan himself actually has touched on (see, e.g., Morgan, 2016; see also Kemp, 2016).

How do you view Morgan's set of eight metaphors? Which is your meta-metaphor for understanding Morgan's metaphors and for understanding approaches to using metaphors in organizational analysis?

Key Terms

Analyst	Organizational analysis
Descriptive metaphor	Root metaphor
Ethnography	Seeing as
Generative metaphor	Semi-metaphorical expressions
Ideal types	Source domain
Knowledge interest	Target domain
Meta-metaphor	Taxonomy
Metaphorical behaviors	Tropes
Metaphorical expression	Typology
Metaphors of the field	Variable
Organizational actor	

Notes

1. Dr. Örtenblad thanks Lars Norén for inspiration, particularly his book about interpretative research methodologies within the area of business administration (Norén, 1995).
2. It should be acknowledged that metaphors can be used for negative reasons, such as seducing people (for a recent and fun-to-read publication in this area, see Ohlsson & Rombach, 2015); however, this chapter focuses on some of the more constructive ways that metaphors can be used (namely, in analyzing organizations).
3. There are a vast number of studies that have used metaphors for analyzing various phenomena in the area of higher education. Thus, there are, for instance, works on metaphors for teaching and learning at HEIs (Northcote & Fetherston, 2006; Wegner & Nückles, 2015), metaphors for higher education (Colonnese, 2000; Ritchie, 2002), and metaphors for HEIs (Argon, 2015; Cantor & Schomberg, 2003; Finkelstein, 2007; Firat & Kabakçi Yurdakul, 2012; Fuller, 1985; Valentine & Valentine, 1994).
4. Note that "organizational actor" in itself is a metaphor, potentially originating from the "organization as theater" metaphor. Likewise, another expression that is often used to denote people in organizations (at least among organizational researchers), "organizational members," is also a metaphor, with a potential origin in the "organization as association" metaphor (it is true that some organizations de facto are associations, but far from all are associations).
5. It should be noted, though, that Morgan at least in Exhibit 11.1 (Morgan, 2006, p. 350) uses the metaphors more as root metaphors than what is the case in this approach, where the metaphors typically are used as variables.

References

Akin, G., & Palmer, I. (2000). Putting metaphors to work for change in organizations. *Organizational Dynamics, 28*(3), 67–79.

Alvesson, M. (1995). *Management of knowledge-intensive companies*. Berlin, Germany: Walter de Gruyter.

Ancona, D. G., Goodman, P. S., Lawrence, B. S., & Tushman, M. L. (2001). Time: A new research lens. *Academy of Management Review, 26*(4), 645–663.

Argon, T. (2015). Longitudinal Investigation of perceptions towards university concept through metaphors: A university sample in Turkey. *Educational Research and Reviews, 10*(1), 36–49.

Barrett, F. J., & Cooperrider, D. L. (1990). Generative metaphor intervention: A new approach for working with systems divided by conflict and caught in defensive perception. *Journal of Applied Behavioral Science, 26*(2), 219–239.

Boland R. J., Jr., & Greenberg, R. H. (1992). Method and metaphor in organizational analysis. *Accounting, Management and Information Technologies, 2*(2), 117–141.

Brown, R. H. (1977). *A poetic for sociology: Toward a logic of discovery for the human sciences*. Cambridge, England: Cambridge University Press.

Cantor, N., & Schomberg, S. (2003 March/April). Poised between two worlds: The university as monastery and marketplace. *EDUCAUSE Review*, 12–21. Retrieved from http://surface.syr.edu/cgi/viewcontent.cgi?article=1018&context=chancellor

Colonnese, M. (2000). Business metaphors in higher education: Students as products/ students as customers. *Journal of Thought, 35*(2), 19–23.

Cornelissen, J. P., Oswick, C., Thøger Christensen, L., & Phillips, N. (2008). Metaphor in organizational research: Context, modalities and implications for research — Introduction. *Organization Studies, 29*(1), 7–22.

Deetz, S. (1986). Metaphors and the discursive production and reproduction of organization. In L. Thayer (Ed.), *Communication — Organization* (pp. 168–182). Norwood, NJ: Ablex.

Elkind, A. (1998). Using metaphor to read the organization of the NHS. *Social Science & Medicine, 47*(11), 1715–1727.

Finkelstein, M. (2007). The ivory tower in a flat world: The university and applied sociology in the global economy. *Journal of Applied Social Science, 1*(1), 16–22.

Firat, M., & Kabakçi Yurdakul, I. (2012). University metaphors: A study of academicians' perspectives. *International Journal of Social Sciences and Education, 2*(2), 194–206.

Fuller, R. (1985). *What you think is what you get: Metaphors for the university, e.g. the land grant university as a feedlot.* Lincoln: University of Nebraska. Retrieved from http://digitalcommons.unl.edu/cgi/viewcontent.cgi?article=1039&context=adaptessays

Gabriel, Y. (2005). Glass cages and glass palaces: Images of organization in image-conscious times. *Organization, 12*(1), 9–27.

Habermas, J. (1966). Knowledge and interest. *Inquiry, 9*(1–4), 285–300.

Hatch, M. J. (1997). Irony and the social construction of contradiction in the humor of a management team. *Organization Science, 8*(3), 275–288.

Kemp, L. (2016). "Trapped" by metaphors for organizations: Thinking and seeing women's equality and inequality. *Human Relations, 69*(4), 975-1000.

Koch, S., & Deetz, S. (1981). Metaphor analysis of social reality in organizations. *Journal of Applied Communication Research, 9*(1), 1–15.

Lang, T. (2008). Systemizing the organizational scenario literature using Morgan's metaphors. *Academy of Management Proceedings* (Meeting Abstract Supplement), 1–6.

Manning, P. K. (1979). Language and social analysis. *Administrative Science Quarterly, 24*(4), 660–671.

McCabe, D. (2016). "Curiouser and curiouser!" Organizations as Wonderland — A metaphorical alternative to the rational model. *Human Relations, 69*(4), 945-974.

Meyer, A. D. (1984). Mingling decision making metaphors. *Academy of Management Review, 9*(1), 6–17.

Morgan, G. (1980). Paradigms, metaphors, and puzzle solving in organization theory. *Administrative Science Quarterly, 25*(4), 605–622.

Morgan, G. (1986). *Images of organization.* London, England: Sage.

Morgan, G. (1996). *Images of organization* (2nd ed.). London, England: Sage.

Morgan, G. (2006). *Images of organization* (3rd ed.). London, England: Sage.

Morgan, G. (2016). *Images of organization* (30th Anniversary Edition.). London, England: SAGE.

Morrison, E. W., & Milliken, F. J. (2003). Speaking up, remaining silent: The dynamics of voice and silence in organizations. *Journal of Management Studies, 40*(6), 1353–1358.

Norén, L. (1995). *Tolkande företagsekonomisk forskning — en metodbok: Social konstruktionism, metaforsynsätt, aktörssynsätt.* Lund, Sweden: Studentlitteratur.

Northcote, M. T., & Fetherston, T. (2006). New metaphors for teaching and learning in a university context. In *Critical visions,* Proceedings of the 29th Higher Education Research and Development Society of Australasia Annual Conference, Western Australia, July 10–12, 2006 pp. 251–258. Retrieved from http://research.avondale.edu.au/cgi/viewcontent.cgi?article=1018&context=edu_conferences

Ohlsson, Ö., & Rombach, B. (2015). *The tyranny of metaphors.* Stockholm, Sweden: Santérus Academic Press.

Örtenblad, A., Putnam, L. L. & Trehan, K. (2016). Beyond Morgan's eight metaphors: Adding to and developing organizational theory. *Human Relations, 69*(4), 875–890.

Oswick, C., & Montgomery, J. (1999). Images of an organization: The use of metaphor in a multinational company. *Journal of Organizational Change Management, 12*(6), 501–523.

Pinder, C. C., & Bourgeois, V. W. (1982). Controlling tropes in administrative science. *Administrative Science Quarterly, 27*(4), 641–652.

Pinto, J. (2016). "Wow! That's so cool!" The Icehotel as organizational trope. *Human Relations, 69*(4), 891-914.

Ritchie, D. (2002). Monastery or economic enterprise: Opposing or complementary metaphors of higher education? *Metaphor and Symbol, 17*(1), 45–55.

Sanford, A. J. (1987). *The mind of man: Models of human understanding.* Brighton, England: Harvester Press.

Schön, D. A. (1979/1993). Generative metaphor: A perspective on problem-setting in social policy. In A. Ortony (Ed.), *Metaphor and thought* (2nd ed., pp. 137–163). Cambridge, England: Cambridge University Press.

Shen, Y., & Balaban, N. (1999). Metaphorical (in)coherence in discourse. *Discourse Processes, 28*(2), 139–153.

Short, D. C. (2000). Analysing metaphor in human resource development. *Human Resource Development International, 3*(3), 323–341.

Simsek, H. (1997). Metaphorical images of an organization: The power of symbolic constructs in reading change in higher education organizations. *Higher Education, 33*(3), 283–307.

Smircich, L. (1983). Concepts of culture and organizational analysis. *Administrative Science Quarterly, 28*(3), 339–358.

Smith, R. C., & Eisenberg, E. M. (1987). Conflict at Disneyland: A root-metaphor analysis. *Communication Monographs, 54*(4), 367–380.

Srivastva, S., & Barrett, F. J. (1988). The transforming nature of metaphors in group development: A study in group theory. *Human Relations, 41*(1), 31–64.

Torlak, N. G. (2007). Analogical reasoning is the way to go beyond orthodoxy in formulating organisational problems: The use of an improved version of Morgan's metaphors revisited. *Sosyal Siyaset Konferansları Dergisi, 53*, 579–620.

Tsoukas, H. (1993). Analogical reasoning and knowledge generation in organization theory. *Organization Studies, 14*(3), 323–346.

Valentine, K. B., & Valentine, E. (1994). Metaphors in the university, or I never promised you an ivory tower. *Women and Language, 17*(2), 11–17.

Wegner, E., & Nückles, M. (2015). Knowledge acquisition or participation in communities of practice? Academics' metaphors of teaching and learning at the university. *Studies in Higher Education, 40*(4), 624–643.

Yanow, D. (2005, April). *Cognition meets action: Metaphors as models of and models for.* Paper prepared for the European Consortium for Political Research Workshop on Metaphors in Political Science, Granada, Spain. Retrieved from http://ecpr.eu/Filestore/PaperProposal/a8e7f41c-4522-4d25-8897-f9fb0174a5ca.pdf

5

Viewing Organizations as Enablers of Happiness

Vikas Rai Bhatnagar

Key Learning Points

- Appreciate the application of positive psychology in conceptualizing organizations.
- Understand the application of critical theory, a theory that attempts to achieve human emancipation in circumstances of domination and apprehension, in creating happiness in organizations.
- Understand and appreciate the conceptualization of happiness that converges the highest human aspiration with the expectations of stakeholders, including the organization.
- Gain awareness of the happiness equation and insights into applying it for creating happiness in one's self and in organizations.
- Understand the limitations of the prevailing neoclassical conceptualization of the human being as a rational economic man and appreciate a new conceptualization of the human being termed the "systemic economic man."
- Appreciate the concept of hyperspace or the science of higher dimensions of theoretical physics and understanding its application in organization science.
- Gain insights on the theory of creating happiness in organizations by understanding the new metaphor of organizations as "enablers of happiness."
- Gain insights into the limitations of the current performance management system (PMS) and on designing effective PMSs, grounded in the new metaphor of organizations as enablers of happiness and conceptualization of the human being as a "systemic economic man."

rganizations play an important role in shaping the future of people, society, and nations.[1] There is not a single global item for change understood outside of the role and functioning of organizations (Cooperrider & Dutton, 1999). Despite increasing material prosperity, business executives experience little satisfaction in their lives (Capra, 2003) and the dehumanizing effects of modern corporations limit the expression of an employee's true self (Kilmann, 2001). Increasing corporate scandals (Aven, 2015; Kish-Gephart, Harrison, & Treviño, 2010), higher instances of "meaninglessness" experienced by employees (Sarros, Tanewski, Winter, Santora, & Densten, 2002), higher instances of stress-related metabolic disorders, socioeconomically driven political upheavals, and growing ecological instability (Zohar & Marshall, 2004) indicate inadequacy in conceptualization and management of organizations. The concept of organization is elusive. Despite scholars' attempts to describe organizations, they remain enigmatic.

What are organizations? King, Felin, and Whetten (2010) posed this question and argued that organizations are a particular type of social actor capable of behaving in a purposeful and intentional manner. **Metaphors** are a device for embellishing discourse, and they are also a way of thinking, seeing, and perceiving reality (Morgan, 1986). They are the primal means by which we forge relationships with the world (Morgan, 1993). Metaphors help us to make sense of organizational events and influence actions. Sensemaking involves turning circumstances into a situation that we comprehend explicitly in words and serves as a springboard for actions (Weick, Sutcliffe, & Obstfeld, 2005). In order to make sense of the environment, we often draw on preexisting knowledge, which is exactly what metaphors do. Metaphors are an outcome of a cognitive process in which the literal meaning of a phrase or word applies to a new context in a figurative sense (Grant & Oswick, 1996). Because metaphors play an important role in conceptualizing organizations, understanding their nature and mechanism of operation provides huge opportunities for creating humanized organizations.

Since the dawn of industrialization, creating humanized organizations has been the dream of many organizational scholars. General agreements reached by scholars on key attributes of humanized organizations are as follows: employees are treated as the end and not as the means; employees are engaged in meaningful and challenging work; employees are encouraged to develop their unique human abilities fully; employees are treated justly and with dignity, placing them above the nonhuman aspects of organization; and employees are able to exert substantial control in making organizational decisions—particularly those that affect them directly (Nord, 1978). Notwithstanding the aspiration of creating humanized organizations, which facilitates self-actualization of employees, disengagement and alienation of employees is an organizational reality. Marx (2007) identifies four forms of human alienation: alienation from the product of his work, alienation from the act of producing, alienation from his fellow beings, and alienation from his own social nature or very essence of his self. With the global shift in employment from agriculture to industry and services, more people are increasingly forming part of organizations, posing challenges to organizational theory and practice for keeping employees engaged, happier, and on a path of self-actualization. The essence of Marx's view on alienation—a disorienting sense of exclusion and separation—is dissonance, divergence, and misalignment of the interests of capitalists and the working class. As an antithesis, a

convergence of interests provides hope and optimism for creating engaged and happier employees. Let us explore the concept of convergence.

The revolution of convergence is leading to global changes in products, organizations, technology, and industry. Convergence is the ability to connect ideas across cultures, knowledge, industry, and economic boundaries (Lee, Olson, & Trimi, 2010). Convergence of globalization and information technology has brought about a "flattening" of the world (Friedman, 2005) and cell phones represent a convergence of telecommunications, music, and photography. The uniqueness of this chapter lies in its providing convergence in the highest human aspiration and organizational purpose and eliminating the causes of alienation and meaninglessness experienced by employees, as alluded to by Marx (2007) and other scholars.

This chapter uses **critical theory** and scholarship of common sense in conceptualizing and proposing a new theory of organizations as being enablers of **happiness** (a feeling of joy, accompanied by higher levels of connectedness, love, compassion, and fairness). Critical theory attempts to achieve human emancipation in circumstances of domination and oppression (Horkheimer, 1982) and is concerned with radically improving human existence (Frost, 1980). Using critical theory, this chapter highlights limitations of Morgan's metaphors, leading to the crippling and dehumanizing effects experienced by employees. Without undermining the monumental contributions of Morgan in bringing the concept of metaphor from the literature to organizational science, I argue that outdated epistemologies such as the Cartesian–Newtonian deterministic worldview (Capra, 1975), the disease-based medical model (Frattaroli, 2001), and agency theory (Jensen & Mecking, 1976) ground few of Morgan's current metaphors. For instance, the Cartesian–Newtonian worldview, which undermines the role of human intentionality, purposefulness, and consciousness, informs the metaphors of machine, organism, and brain. The disease-based medical model, which aims to bridge deviations from established norms, embeds the metaphors of psychic prison and the metaphor of organizations as flux and transformation. The agency theory (the basic assumption of which is distrust between the employees and owners of a firm), explains the metaphors of political systems and instruments of domination. Pessimistic assumptions about human nature and organizations form the bedrock of most of Morgan's current metaphors, with the aim of social theory constrained to solving negative problems (Hirschman, 1970).

As methodology, this chapter integrates research evidence from **positive psychology** (the scientific study of optimal human functioning) and Plato's theory of forms, leading to the emergence of a new metaphor of "organizations as enablers of happiness." This chapter converges and subsumes Marxist communism within a holistic and benevolent capitalistic framework, aligns the assumed variances of interests of the owners of a firm and its employees (agency theory), and describes the possibility and promise of creating humanized organizations.

Dynamic Modeling of Morgan's Metaphors

Morgan suggests that it is not necessary for a single metaphor to explain the functioning of an organization and he uses the terms "dominant frames" and "supporting frames" for different metaphors of varying intensities operating in an organization. A bundle of metaphors, in varying proportions, enables comprehensive understanding of an organization. Critical thought seeks alternative modes of thought and behavior (Marcuse, 1964), reviewing the efficacy of current metaphors and opening up greater possibilities of employee happiness and organizational effectiveness. As broached earlier, because outdated epistemologies, models, and theory embed Morgan's current metaphors, the outcomes for an organization also tend to be crippled and suboptimal. To illustrate this point, I model the dynamic interactions of various Morgan's metaphors that operate in varying degrees in a hypothetical organization. The configuration of metaphors in the model is one of the many possibilities that may describe organizations. I choose to depict, highlight, and discuss the constrained nature in only one configuration of metaphors in Figure 5.1.

The model in Figure 5.1 depicts one possible configuration of metaphors that operate in organizations in varying proportions. The hypothetical organization depicted in Figure 5.1 is in a state of continuous flux and transformation, triggering generative processes and providing context in which events happen. Employers and employees have an innate tendency to dominate, while the mind's repressive, unconscious processes constrain perceptions and actions. Varying proportions of these attributes lead to the manifestation of four metaphors: bureaucratic and process focused (machine like), adaptive (organism like), capitalizing on the flow

FIGURE 5.1 ● A Configuration of Dynamic Interaction of Morgan's Metaphors

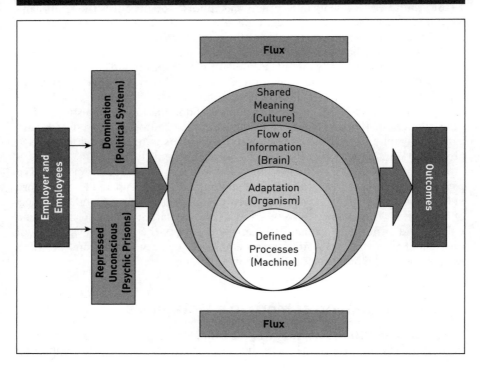

of information (brainlike), and performing by developing shared meaning (culture like). Growing corporate scandals, increasing meaninglessness, and alienation experienced by employees are outcomes of current metaphors shaping organizations. Hunt (2000) points out that devoting one's life to making ever more money for shareholders is ultimately not very inspiring. A metaphor grounded in positive psychology, which is the scientific study of human flourishing, holds promise for establishing humanized organizations and creating happiness by converging the highest aspirations of human beings and organizations' expectations for satisfying stakeholders.

Merleau-Ponty (1983) suggests that in order to see the world anew, we must break with our familiar acceptance of it. He indicates that our assumptions prevent us from seeing the puzzles and contradictions that fill our experiences, and he urges that we put aside our everyday assumptions and relearn to look at our experiences without prejudices. Morgan's approach to metaphors is primarily to understand an organization by using a different and familiar concept that has similarities to the realities of the organization. I draw out the mechanics of operationalization of metaphors in organizations. A metaphor is extracted from current organizational realities. Once isolated and understood, the metaphor contributes to shaping the future of an organization. Schein (1985) suggests that leaders impose their own values and assumptions, initiating the process of culture formation. Similarly, the metaphor playing in the minds of leaders contributes to the design of an organization. The cyclical process by which the metaphor operates can be described as follows: 1) a particular metaphor exists in the mind of the designer of the organization (it can be the promoter or a leader); 2) the metaphor is enacted in the organization and creates a reality, expressed in various artifacts (Schein, 1999); 3) the metaphor is extracted from artifacts, espoused values, and shared assumptions; and 4) conscious awareness of the extracted metaphor further shapes the organization. In the chain of causal events, the metaphor existing in the mind of the designer of the organization shapes reality. Figure 5.2 depicts this conceptualization and the mechanism by which a metaphor typically operates.

Metaphors are a product of mindsets. Dweck (2006) provides evidence and describes two types of mindsets: the fixed mindset and the growth mindset. Covey (1989) introduces the scarcity and abundance mindsets that shape people's outlook. Metaphors emerging from a growth or abundance mindset would be different from

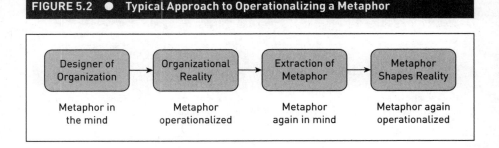

FIGURE 5.2 ● Typical Approach to Operationalizing a Metaphor

those originating from a fixed or scarcity mindset, and the outcomes in organizations will also vary from being marginal to optimal. Because the objective of critical theory is to enable human emancipation and do away with domination (Horkheimer, 1982), the alternate method utilizes the constructivist approach and generative capacity of a metaphor while designing the organization (Ortony, 1979). Drawing from Plato's theory of forms (Russell, 1946) and having understood the mechanism by which a metaphor in the mind of the designer translates to organizational realities, there is vast opportunity to make improvements in organizations by identifying metaphors of high potency. I describe a high-potency metaphor as one that has emancipative capacity and creates a high positive impact on operationalizing, and I propose the construction of one such metaphor by utilizing Plato's theory of forms. To appreciate construction of a high-potency metaphor, understanding Plato's theory of forms is essential. Plato believed that everything our senses perceive has a corresponding "form" or idea, which in the world of ideas is eternal and is a perfect reality of that thing (Landau, Szudek, & Tomley, 2011). The theory of forms serves the dual purpose of making us know the actual world of things and enabling us to evaluate, criticize, and thereby improve objective situations (Lavine, 1984). Plato (1997) used the metaphor of *shadows* for describing concrete, particular, and changing objects and *substance* for immutable, unchanging, unchangeable, and real objects. Tsoukas (1993) provides a hierarchical typology of metaphors as abstractions, analogies, literal similarities, mere appearances, and anomalies. He argued that abstractions are most effective for generating scientific knowledge because they operate at a high level of generality and reveal the generic properties of a variety of phenomena. I propose that a metaphor conceptualized and constructed based on the form and substance (as described by Plato) has enhanced generative potency for creating higher positive impact in organizations. I conceptualize an alternate method of creating high-potency metaphors by utilizing Plato's theory of forms. Figure 5.3 depicts this conceptualization, which was action researched successfully in an Indian cement company (Robbins, Judge, & Vohra, 2013).

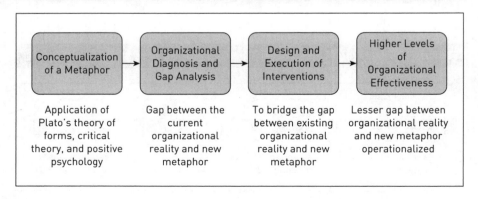

FIGURE 5.3 ● An Alternate Approach to Designing and Operationalizing a Metaphor

As seen in Figure 5.3 deploying Plato's theory of forms, critical theory aimed at attempting human emancipation and human flourishing (positive psychology), conceptualizes a high-potency metaphor. A distinct gap between current organizational reality and constructed metaphor is identified, leading to interventions for bridging the gaps and higher levels of organizational effectiveness.

Gaps in Basic Assumptions of Current Metaphors: Toward Enriching Them

At the root of artifacts and espoused values are basic assumptions that govern behavior (Schein, 1999). Exploring some of the basic assumptions of current metaphors provides insights into possible handicaps to creating humanized organizations and emancipating employees—the cherished goals of critical theory. I bring out gaps in basic assumptions in conceptualizing current metaphors by illustrating the metaphor of psychic prison. Because of space constraints, I am unable to discuss each metaphor; however, the basic assumptions and the accompanying gaps run across each of the current metaphors. Subsequently, I suggest and propose alternative assumptions, particularly those related to human beings that have emancipative characteristics.

Perceived Negative Aspects of Humans

The metaphor of organizations as psychic prisons emphasizes the darker side of human personality. I draw the analogy of complex and multifaceted human beings to the enigmatic nature of light, which exists as a potentiality of wave-particles and displays the behavior that an observer measures (Feynman, 1985). Just as the type of measurement yields a particular behavior of light (whether particle or wave), the perspective held by the observer reveals dimensions of multifaceted human beings. We may choose to perceive people as being trapped in Plato's cave or as cave dwellers who have seen reality beyond the current shadows, with the potential for self-awareness. At its heart lies our conceptualization of the human being. Jung (1969) argues that the extensiveness of human consciousness correlates with differentiated perceptions and emancipation from the collective rules, as the empirical freedom of will grows in proportion to the extension of consciousness. The metaphor of psychic prison emphasizes the limitations imposed by one's own ideas, thoughts, images, and actions. Morgan (1986) begins his chapter on organizations as psychic prisons by stating, "Human beings have a knack for getting trapped in webs of their own creation." Morgan draws from the allegory of cave dwellers used by Plato in his classic *Republic* (1997) and impresses how people in organizations become trapped in favored ways of thinking. Viewed from the constructivist perspective of critical theory, why should a favored way of thinking lead only to the "trapping" of people? Can it not lead to the liberating of anyone? Plato's cave allegory emphasizes the deplorable plight of cave dwellers who mistake shadows for reality. The allegory downplays the experience of one cave dweller who witnesses reality and ignores the possibility of getting trapped in the liberating experience that he witnesses. The trap of favored ways of thinking can have many deleterious effects, but it can also lead to many positive outcomes. Einstein's (1961) travel on a beam of light, which subsequently resulted in the special theory of relativity, was precisely an outcome of this trap of his thinking, leading to his revolutionizing of the concept of space, time, and reality.

As a zeitgeist, the current focus on fixing what is wrong attributes to what a leading postmodern philosopher, Foucault (1973), describes as the medical conceptual framework, which defines and also determines modes of human thought. Seligman and Csikszentmihalyi (2000) state that contemporary psychology's conceptualization of human beings rests on pathology, faults, and dysfunctions and is primarily a medical-oriented psychology. They argue that the focus needs to shift from managing deficiencies to optimizing the inherent potential of people for developing positive character traits or virtues. Positive psychology unites scattered and disparate lines of theory and research about what makes life worth living (Peterson & Park, 2003). This leads us to focus on our conceptualization of the human being and, more importantly, the efficacy of conceptualization for creating humanized organizations.

Conceptualization of Human Beings and Their Purpose

A review of human nature in general is important: No matter how limited economists or employers view an employee, the employee arrives in the organization as a holistic entity. The primary purpose of organizations is economic development, ordinarily conceived as a process involving greater capital formation for producing more goods and services (Tomer, 2001). The predominant conceptualization of the human being contributing to capital formation is the **rational economic man** (REM), a mechanistic conception of a human being that acts to maximize one's interests by evoking rational thinking, centered on cost-benefit analysis (Morgan, 2006). Five attributes characterize the REM: self-interest, rationality, separate, unchanging, and unreflective (Tomer, 2001). Neoclassical economics, based on objectivist ontology and positivist epistemology, has a mechanical view of humans, with robot-like unlimited rationality, negating the endowment of human nature that is irrational and has attributes such as empathy, compassion, resilience, optimism, and the like (Ketola, 2009). Zsolnai (2004) argues that the mechanistic and reductionist assumption of human nature is truncated, because human beings have evolved as sociable creatures with a strong ethical sense, for whom cooperation and security are essential. Tversky and Kahnemann (1982) demonstrated that rationality, as defined by economists, fails to hold in a number of situations. Developments in behavioral economics provide evidence that we live in more than one world of market realities. There is a social world characterized by social norms and another market world characterized by market exchanges. People apply different norms to different worlds. Applying market exchange norms in social situations will violate the social norm and hurt relationships (Ariely, 2008). German philosopher Arthur Schopenhauer (1973) held that rarely are people rational in their actions. According to Schopenhauer, people blindly pursue their petty and selfish desires, while they invoke reason to rationalize actions already performed on impulse. Sigmund Freud (2012) said that human actions stem from unconscious drivers and instincts and not from rationality, whereas German philosopher Friedrich Nietzsche was convinced that cosmic will and not human reason drives the world (Moore & Bruder, 2005). People are personally altruistic and managers do not behave as single-minded maximizers of profits (Selznick, 1957).

Wilber (1996) maps the entire range of human potential into three major categories (subconscious, self-conscious, and super-conscious) and ten stages of development. Wilber divides development stages into two arcs: The outward arc is the movement from subconscious to self-conscious and the inward arc is the movement from self-consciousness to super-consciousness. Self-assertion, individuation, and conquering outer worlds characterize the outward arc, and going within one's own self, transcending self, and achieving oneness characterize the inward arc. There is resonance of Wilber's model of human development with Maslow's (1971) hierarchy of needs (physiological, safety, belonging, self-esteem, self-actualization, and transcendence) and with Bhatnagar's (2012) conceptualization of an effective human being as someone optimizing physical, psychological, social, and spiritual capabilities.

Maslow (1971) highlights the limitations of the REM theory and derides it by stating that economists have made a "skilled, exact, technological application of a totally false theory of human needs and values, a theory that recognizes only the existence of lower needs or material needs." In terms of Wilber's model of human potential, the REM positions himself at the end of the outward arc and fails miserably for humans at significantly lower and higher levels of development. Far from being a self-actualized human being, the REM is simply a machine-like version of a person who has achieved a somewhat typical level of development in a modern capitalistic country (Tomer, 2001). The REM falls short of Bhatnagar's (2012) conceptualization of a human being as a spiritual-social-psychological-physical (S^2P^2) which operates not in a four-dimensional space-time but in a multidimensional and fused potentiality of the S^2P^2 field. Guided by self-interest, the REM at most utilizes his cognitive abilities to manipulate his emotional and social environment for the advancement of his interests, all the while failing to appreciate that separateness of humans (an essential attribute of the REM) alienates him in a world that is systemically interconnected.

Contrary to the neoclassical economists' view of the *homo rational economicus* or REM, the heterodox schools of thought conceptualize human beings as the *homo institutional economicus* or institutional economic man (IEM), *homo social economicus* or social economic man (SEM), *homo humanistic man* or humanistic economic man (HEM), and *homo socioeconomicus* or socioeconomic man (S-EM) (Tomer, 2001). The IEM acts in accordance with the values of institutions and learns from social and technical experiences (Hodgson, 1998). The SEM has two parallel attributes: an individual oriented toward economic betterment and a social being striving for belonging to communities and institutions (O'Boyle, 1994). The HEM conceptualizes man holistically, representing Maslow's hierarchy. It has a lower self that focuses on fulfilling material needs and a higher self that continually strives for self-realization (Lutz, 1985). The S-EM has two parts, the "I" and the "WE," which remain in conflict. "I" is akin to the REM, whereas the "WE" is oriented to others and is often moralistic in nature (Etzioni, 1998).

In the context of organizations, the concept of a human being suitable for creating humanized organizations and enabling human emancipation is an adaption from my conceptualization of physical, emotional, social, cognitive, cultural, and spiritual man (Bhatnagar, 2012). Although I place these in a hierarchy, with physical attributes at the bottom and spiritual attributes at the top, I extend the conceptualization by adding systemic nature to the interactions between various attributes. The physical, emotional, social, cognitive, cultural, and spiritual components in a human being, whereas forming a holarchy or a natural hierarchy of increasing wholeness (Wilber, 1996), are also systemically interconnected; the dynamic interactions of these components give rise to the uniqueness in human beings. The dynamic interactions between various components of a human being feed into each other while simultaneously maintaining a holarchy. I term this conceptualization of man as the *systemic homo economicus* or **systemic economic man** (SysEM), in which the physical, emotional, cognitive, social, cultural, and spiritual aspects of self are in systemic interactions, creating personal as well as economic capital. The SysEM concept is relevant in an organizational context because although it caters to the ultimate purpose of the HEM toward self-actualization, it also contributes to achieving organizational objectives. Extending and enriching my S^2P^2 conceptualization of the human being (Bhatnagar, 2012), Figure 5.4 depicts my conceptualization and modeling of SysEM.

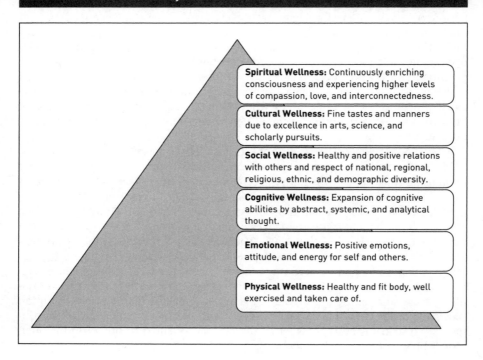

FIGURE 5.4   ●   Model of Systemic Economic Man

Spiritual Wellness: Continuously enriching consciousness and experiencing higher levels of compassion, love, and interconnectedness.

Cultural Wellness: Fine tastes and manners due to excellence in arts, science, and scholarly pursuits.

Social Wellness: Healthy and positive relations with others and respect of national, regional, religious, ethnic, and demographic diversity.

Cognitive Wellness: Expansion of cognitive abilities by abstract, systemic, and analytical thought.

Emotional Wellness: Positive emotions, attitude, and energy for self and others.

Physical Wellness: Healthy and fit body, well exercised and taken care of.

The model defines each dimension of wellness, which has the dual characteristic of forming a holarchy and having a systemic relationship. Of all of the conceptualized heterodox models of man, the SysEM includes consciousness, which, according to Bandura (2001), is the very substance constituting mental life, making life personally manageable and worth living.

The common denominator of comparative philosophy is the human being (Raju, 1995). However, none of Morgan's metaphors account for the fundamental purpose of human beings—the primary agents in an organization. Aristotle (1996) held that the fundamental purpose of a human being is to be happy. The essential element of Oriental mysticism is to experience all phenomena as manifestations of the same ultimate reality. Hindus term experiencing ultimate reality as *brahman*, Buddhists as *dharmakaya* or "body of being," and Taoists as *tathata* or "suchness" (Capra, 1975). Maslow's (1971) hierarchy of human needs, at the highest level, reflects humans' sole concern for the needs of self and a movement toward becoming concerned with others and ultimately becoming one with others as development progresses. Wilber's model of human development has, at its highest levels, the capacity for integrated thinking, connecting ideas, relating truths to one another, and integrating mind and body (Wilber, 1996). Schwartz (1995) describes the transpersonal stage as processes of consciousness subtler than everyday, outer-directed experiences and a movement toward experiencing ultimate unity or nonduality. The eight metaphors contributed by Morgan gloss over the primary purpose of the human being and ground the metaphors to the rational economic model of man that give primacy to the cognitive processes, while undermining the emotional, cultural, and spiritual aspects that influence behavior and thus fail to either optimize human potentiality or fulfill the purpose of human lives.

New Metaphor of Organizations as Enablers of Happiness

In proposing a new metaphor of "organizations as enablers of happiness," I experience sentiments similar to those of Kilmann (2001) when he wrote *Quantum Organizations: A New Paradigm for Achieving Organizational Success and Personal Meaning.* Kilmann talks about the prevailing research method in management science, in which a number of examples from business support a new theory or practice, lending the theory credibility. This form of knowledge validation is termed "the proof-is-in-the-pudding" approach, which Kilmann says suffers from the perplexing "newness" paradox. If many companies are already using a new theory or practice, it can hardly be *new*. The alternate approach that Kilmann subscribes to, which is also adopted in this chapter, is that of "the proof is in the experience." Using this approach, the proposed theory or metaphor must be judged based on logic, emotion, intuition, past experience, conviction, and some amount of faith. Because the metaphor is *new*, there would hardly be any organization practicing it. In the later part of this chapter, I will describe the execution of this happiness model in an Indian organization.

The initial trigger for developing organizations as enablers of happiness was an action research project that I carried out in a cement company. From an organizational development perspective, Jacobs and Heracleous (2006) suggest that change agents should take part in diagnosing the organization through an understanding of the language-based metaphors used by organizational actors. Excessive use of the word "happiness" by a few senior colleagues in the cement company led to operationalizing the concept in organizational processes, particularly substituting the performance management system (for which employees had expressed deep cynicism in a recently conducted engagement survey) with a newly conceptualized "happiness management system" (Bhatnagar & Singhi, 2013; Robbins et al., 2013). The development of a new metaphor of organizations as enablers of happiness utilized the systemic conceptualization of the human being, in which each of the faculties of a human being (e.g., physical, emotional, cultural, cognitive, and spiritual) are in dynamic interaction, each feeding into the other and lending purposefulness to the human being. In the action research carried out in the cement company, Plato's theory of forms was complemented with Cornelissen's (2005) domains-interaction model, in which metaphor involves the conjunction of whole semantic domains and a correspondence between terms or concepts is *constructed*, rather than deciphered, and the resulting meaning is *creative*, with important features being emergent. Because the rudimentary theory of organizations as enablers of happiness was developed while carrying out action research in the cement company, the concept has evolved from practice, is grounded in organizational realities, and thus is executable.

Aristotle (1996) states that the highest of all goods achievable by human actions is happiness. People seek happiness for its own sake, which is the final effect and not a cause of anything. Ryan and Deci (2001) explicate two distinct philosophies of well-being: the hedonic and the eudaimonic perspectives. The hedonic view focuses on preferences and pleasures of body and mind and on what makes experiences of life pleasant or unpleasant (Kahnemann, Diener, & Schwarz, 1999). The concept of eudaimonia is distinct from happiness and is defined as the feelings accompanying behavior in the direction of, and consistent with, one's true potential (Waterman, 1984). Within the hedonic view, Diener and Lucas (1999) describe subjective well-being (SWB) as having three components: life satisfaction, presence of positive mood, and absence of negative mood. Ryff and Keyes (1995), drawing from Aristotle, describe well-being as striving for perfection that represents the realization of one's true potential and psychological well-being (PWB), a construct distinct from SWB, as having six aspects for human actualization: autonomy, personal growth, self-acceptance, life purpose, mastery, and positive relatedness. Seligman (2011) had earlier equated the topic of positive psychology with happiness; his current interpretation of the topic of positive psychology is well-being and he argues that the gold standard for measuring well-being is "flourishing," with the goal of positive psychology to increase flourishing. He believes that the building blocks of flourishing consist of positive emotions, engagement, relationships, meaning, and accomplishment (termed PERMA). Csikszentmihalyi (1999) identifies four determinants of happiness: life satisfaction, affective experiences, good relationships, and experiencing meaning in work.

Lyubomirsky, Sheldon, and Schkade (2005) identified three determinants of happiness levels: set points, life circumstances, and intentional activity. The happiness set point is genetically determined, fixed and stable over time, and immune to influences and control. Life circumstances refer to incidental but relatively stable facts of one's life and include the national, geographical, and cultural region where one resides and demographic factors such as age, gender, marital status, ethnicity, and so forth. Intentional activity relates to the discrete actions or practices in which people engage, requiring the making of choices and some degree of effort in order to act. The set point contributes 50% to a person's happiness, life circumstances contribute 10%, and intentional activity contributes the remaining 40% (Lyubomirsky, 2007).

Leaders of organizations that organize the lives of employees around intrinsic values of a good life are happier compared with those who spend their lives in pursuit of material possessions and are extrinsically motivated by money-driven and consumer culture (Kasser, 2004). Values are desirable goals that vary in importance and serve as guiding principles in people's lives (Rokeach, 1973). Employees attain higher levels of well-being when they pursue healthy values and goals. Furthermore, if intrinsic reasons guide the attainment of goals and there is alignment between organizational goals and individual goals, then happiness and well-being are higher (Sagiv, Roccas, & Hazan, 2004). A growing body of research provides evidence that when people act mindfully, it promotes autonomous thoughts and behaviors and thus leads to better-informed decisions and improved psychological outcomes (Brown & Ryan, 2004).

In researching happiness at work, Fisher (2010) identifies constructs at three levels: transient, person, and unit. She emphasizes that there is little research on how individuals may voluntarily increase their own happiness at work, although general advice on increasing happiness can be applied to work settings. The extant literature and current practice lacks a comprehensive theory of how to increase happiness in an organization. Bradbury (2003) argues for taking a systems approach to building sustainable businesses by revitalizing ourselves within a revitalized economy that exists to serve, rather than exploit, natural and human/social systems. Positivist hypotheticodeductive approaches have identified determinants and consequences in isolation without an overarching conceptualizing of happiness in an organization by linking, as Bradbury (2003) invites, the internal worlds of employees and the external reality of organizations. The ability to connect ideas across cultures, disciplines, industries, and economic boundaries leads to new opportunities for value creation and development of robust business models (Lee et al., 2010). I explore a convergence of an employee's highest aspiration and organizational expectation while developing a systemic and holistic theory of creating happiness in organizations. The new metaphor of organizations as enablers of happiness emerges from and grounds itself in theory for creating happiness in organizations.

The conceptualization of happiness in organizations utilizes the SysEM discussed earlier in this chapter, intentional activity (Lyubomirsky et al., 2005), research evidence from extant literature on happiness, and the concept of **hyperspace** (defined as the science of higher dimensions or space that is multidimensional) from theoretical physics (Kaku, 1994). I propose the following equation for creating happiness in organizations:

Employee Wellness + Good Intentional Activity = Happiness

Employee wellness presupposes and assumes a concept of the human being. If organizations assume an REM, then the definition of health given by the World Health Organization (a state of complete physical, mental, and social well-being and not merely the absence of disease and infirmity) holds true. For creating economic capital, an employee should be disease free, have good cognitive abilities, and be socially adaptable in order to work efficiently in teams. I chose the SysEM in my conceptualization of employee wellness because of its comprehensive conceptualization of human faculties; the interconnection and interdependence of physical, emotional, cognitive, social, cultural, and spiritual aspects of self; and higher employee engagement by holistic deployment of human attributes at work (and not just physical, social, and mental). I define employee wellness as a state of physical, emotional, cognitive, social, cultural, and spiritual vibrancy, enabling performance of good intentional activities and thereby leading to higher states of happiness. Employee wellness operates at multiple levels, with each level systemically reinforcing the others.

As seen from the above equation, wellness alone will not lead to happiness. Drawing from Oriental traditions, the world is described as a realm of actions and activities (Radhakrishnan, 1948) in which performing actions is inevitable. Humans' very survival necessitates the performing of actions. Aristotle (1996) defines happiness as an expression of soul in considered actions. Locke (2014) defines good and evil actions in terms of the pleasure or pain that they bring. He explains that all good actions increase pleasure or decrease pain within us. King and Napa (1998) delineate the aspects of good life as the importance of having happiness, a sense of purpose, wisdom, creativity, philosophy of life, achievement, and experiencing love. Lyubomirsky (2007) describes good intentional activities as leading to an increase in happiness. If intentional activities are good, then they reinforce wellness and cause happiness. However, if intentional actions are not good, then they cause distress and reduce wellness and happiness. The current intent is to explain the happiness equation; subsequently, I will define specific good intentional activities that lead to happiness in the context of organizations.

The worthiness of pursuing the attainment of happiness as an ideal has evolved over time. Herodotus (1987) had a fatalistic view on happiness and believed that human agency was frustrated, human choices were contradictory, human suffering was inevitable; happiness, if it comes at all, happens largely by chance—humans have no control over it. The other end of thought on happiness is that good intentional activities improve levels of happiness (Sheldon & Lyubomirsky, 2004). The role of genetics in determining the level of happiness and fatalism associated with happiness is embedded in the old Cartesian–Newtonian paradigm, whereas volitional human actions determining the level of happiness are rooted in the quantum-psychophysical worldview (Kilmann, 2001).

Shifting the unit of analysis from organization to country, the U.S. Declaration of Independence promises the right of happiness to all its citizens. The Bhutan government (initiated by the fourth king of Bhutan, Jigme Singye Wangchuck) has measured the Gross National Happiness (GNH) of its citizens since 1972 and considers it more important than the Gross National Index (Bates, 2009). Article 9 of the Constitution of Bhutan states, "The state shall strive to promote those conditions that will enable the pursuit of Gross National Happiness." The Bhutan government measures GNH on the following nine dimensions: health, psychological well-being, culture and spirituality, time use, education, living standards, community vitality, environment, and governance. French president Nicholas Sarkozy constituted a committee including two Nobel laureates, Amartya Sen and Joseph E. Stigitz, to

FIGURE 5.5 ● The Happiness Model in an Organizational Context

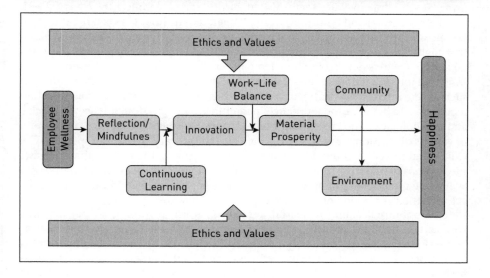

investigate the efficacy of gross national product as a measure of national progress and to suggest alternatives more relevant to the changing times. The committee suggested (Stiglitz, Sen, & Fitoussi, 2008) a shift from measuring economic production to measuring people's well-being and proposed measurement of the well-being of citizens on the following dimensions: material living standards (income, consumption, and wealth), health, education, personal activities (including work, political voice, and governance), social connections and relationships, environment (present and future conditions), and insecurity (of an economic and physical nature). If well-being and happiness have been conceptualized and executed successfully in Bhutan, and while other countries are attempting their implementation, attempts at conceptualizing happiness holistically in the context of organizations (a lower unit of analysis compared with a country) is a realistic progress of employee-related constructs, from satisfaction to engagement and, finally, to happiness.

As part of the action research that I carried out in the cement company and in testing operationalization of the new metaphor of organizations as enablers of happiness, I developed a model of happiness utilizing the above happiness equation and drawing heavily from extant literature on happiness, particularly in identifying good intentional activities. Figure 5.5 illustrates the happiness model, which utilizes the equation of happiness given above and draws from a review of extant literature on happiness.

The model follows the happiness equation that I shared earlier (Employee Wellness + Good Intentional Activity = Happiness) and utilizes the above-described SysEM model. Variables in gray depict good intentional activity in the model. I explain the model in brief and in sequence of the happiness equation: employee wellness, good intentional activity, and happiness.

Employee wellness is the overall, integrated outcome of physical, emotional, cognitive, social, cultural, and spiritual wellness. Gerdtham and Johannesson (2001), using Swedish micro data, identify that health status significantly covaries with well-being. Oswald and Powdthavee (2007) analyzed the links between hypertension (as measured by blood pressure) and body mass index (BMI) on well-being and found that higher blood pressure and BMI were associated with lower happiness and mental health. Fredrickson's (2004) broaden-and-build theory of positive emotions establishes the importance of emotional wellness. The theory states that positive emotions such as joy, interest, contentment, and love increase an individual's thought-action repertoire and build personal resources pertaining to the physical, intellectual, social, and psychological. The broaden-and-build theory reinforces the systemic interaction of various dimensions of wellness and validates the efficacy of the concept of SysEM. Gilkey and Kilts (2007) provide evidence of neurogenesis (the process that increases the neurons of important brain functions, such as motor behavior and memory, with age) strengthening and improving with choices people make and how people interact with their environment and gain experience. They posit that cognitive fitness—a state of optimized ability to reason, remember, learn, plan, and adapt—increases with certain attitudes, lifestyles, choices, and exercises, which enable people to make better decisions, solve problems, and deal with stress and change. Event construal, an important aspect of cognitive wellness, is strongly associated with happiness because research suggests that happy and unhappy people differ in the ways in which they interpret, remember, and experience events that serve to reinforce their respective affective disposition (Lyubomirsky & Tucker, 1998). Social wellness contributes to building social capital, which Putman (2000) defines as connections among individuals' social networks and the norms of reciprocity and trustworthiness that arise from them. Rath and Harter (2010), while discussing five essential elements for well-being, cite social well-being as one of the significant predictors of happiness. They remind us that our best moments occur at the intersection between two people and inform us that employees who have a best friend at work are seven times more likely to have higher well-being. Moberg (1979) defines spiritual well-being as wellness or health of the totality of the inner resources of people, the ultimate concerns around which all other values are focused, and as the central philosophy that guides conduct and the meaning-giving center of human life, influencing all individuals and social behavior. Aristotle (1996) defines the good of man as active exercise of the soul's faculties in conformity with excellence or virtue. Epictetus (1995) cautions that when we remember our aim as spiritual progress, we strive to be our best selves and thereby win happiness. Phenomenal and functional consciousness enables people to live meaningful lives and to form self-identity based upon how they live and reflect upon their lives (Bandura, 2001). Zohar and Marshall (2004) inform us that spiritual capital increases from serving deep meaning, from deriving a deep sense of purpose, and from serving fundamental human values. The different aspects of wellness discussed above have implications for designing organizations and providing forums for employees to exercise and excel in each dimension of wellness. A prerequisite for effective good intentional activity is wellness because a sick employee seldom carries out effective intentional actions.

I now discuss the good intentional activities that lead to reinforcement of employee wellness and thereby create happiness among employees. To reiterate, employee wellness alone does not lead to happiness. Work is inevitable; one cannot afford to not perform it (Radhakrishnan, 1948). Russell (1971) describes two types of activities that make work interesting: exercise of skills and construction. People are keen to exercise and demonstrate what they are good at, and creating something new makes work interesting. In the model of happiness in an organization, reflection and mindfulness are akin to meditation and abstract thought, which creates flow experiences (Csikszentmihalyi, 1990) and leads to gaining insights into a situation. Kabat-Zinn (2003) defines mindfulness as awareness that emerges through paying attention on purpose, in the present moment, and nonjudgmentally to the unfolding of experience moment by moment. Self-determined actions (experiencing of competence, autonomy, and relatedness; Ryan & Deci, 2000) and employee voice (Van Dyne & LePine, 1998) are implicit in the act of being mindful. Van Dyne and LePine (1998) define employee voice as making innovative suggestions for change and recommending modifications to standard procedures even when others disagree. Dolan and Metcalfe (2012) investigated the association between innovation and SWB and found them to be positively related. Csikszentmihalyi (1996) reports that when people across various professions were asked what they found most enjoyable, they responded with a common theme (i.e., designing or discovering something new). He provides evidence that people share the propensity to enjoy whatever they do, provided that it is new or they discover or design something new in doing it. Russell (1971) also alludes to work that constructs (final state of affairs embodying a purpose, emerging from an initial state that is comparatively haphazard) to be interesting. The work of construction for Russell is delightful to contemplate and is never so fully completed that there is nothing further to do about it. Continuous learning provides happiness; Russell mentions that work can be pleasurable provided the skill required is either variable or capable of infinite improvements. Research by Galor and Tsiddon (1997) clearly establishes an association between innovation and economic prosperity. Material prosperity is an essential aspect of happiness (Frijters, Shields, & Haisken-DeNew, 2004; Stevenson & Wolfers, 2008). Happiness intricately links with the creation of wealth—a necessity for carrying out many activities, including altruistic deeds. Money is a means to an end but is not an end in itself (King & Napa, 1998). Lamb (1992) reports that Plato, Aristotle, and Aquinas agreed that money pursued as an end in itself is dehumanizing. Although the association between work–life balance and well-being is well established, Gröpel and Kuhl (2009) investigated what leads to this effect and discovered that with additional time available, employees spend time satisfying their personal needs, which leads to higher levels of happiness. By helping others without an ulterior motive of expecting immediate returns, the giver signals a faith in a norm of collective care toward one another (Titmuss, 1970). Furthermore, when we indulge in prosocial behavior such as helping the community and taking care of the environment to enable sustainability, this improves well-being by displacing negative emotions (Moynihan, DeLeire, & Enami, 2015). When employees move up Maslow's hierarchy of needs, the focus tends to shift from self to others, leading to altruistic behavior. Ethics and values engulf all other variables of the happiness model. Plato (1997) argues that the just man is happy, the unjust man is miserable, and the best and most just character is the happiest. Similarly, Aristotle (1996) claims that happiness arises from a life of virtue and that behaving in a virtuous or ethical manner helps in acquiring virtue.

The model in Figure 5.5 conceptualizes happiness in an organizational context, converges the highest human aspirations with organizational expectations, and addresses the age-old agency problem of divergent goals of business owners (principals) and employees (agents). The pursuit of happiness becomes a common goal for principals as well as agents; however, they may have different roles to play in order to achieve happiness, with principals focusing on the design aspects of the organization and creating the optimal ecosystem for agents to achieve happiness (by delivering as per the above happiness equation and model).

I now evoke the concept of hyperspace from theoretical physics to bring about a convergence of happiness on yet another dimension. The concept of hyperspace or the science of higher dimensions enables the conceptualization of happiness as a single pursuit. The science of hyperspace informs us that laws of nature become simpler and elegant when expressed in higher dimensions (Kaku, 1994). Deploying the concept of hyperspace, happiness conceptualizes as the highest dimension that enfolds within itself multitudes of effects. From the perspective of hyperspace, all of the good intentional activities highlighted in Figure 5.5 and supported with the comprehensive literature review are enfolded as potentiality, which, over time and when external circumstances warrant, unfold as concrete activities. Figure 5.6 depicts

FIGURE 5.6 ● Convergence of Individual Aspiration and Organizational Expectations: Enfolding and Unfolding of Happiness

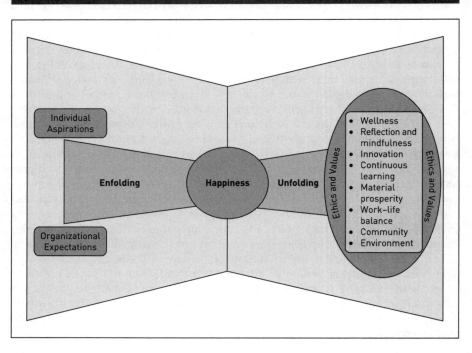

this conceptualization of happiness as the potentiality of good intentional activities that unfold over time. I conceptualized and developed this model as part of action research conducted in the cement company that I referred to earlier.

As seen in Figure 5.6, happiness is the highest dimension that converges individual aspirations and organizational aspirations and *en*folds them, which *un*folds when an organization and its processes are designed to facilitate employee self-determination and voice, continuous learning, innovations, material prosperity, work–life balance, and prosocial behaviors such as caring for the community and environment.

By deploying critical theory and adopting a constructivist approach to developing metaphors (including Plato's theory of forms, positive psychology, and the SysEM), the metaphor of organizations as enablers of happiness has great potential and vast applications in creating humanized organizations and making employees happier while simultaneously achieving multiple organizational objectives. The metaphor of organizations as enablers of happiness brings the employee to the center stage of the organization, removes multiple conceptual dissonances (e.g., divergent motives between principals and agents, theory and the practice of happiness and individual and organizational units of analysis pertaining to happiness), and, finally, offers opportunities for redesigning practices in organizations, leading to higher levels of employee happiness.

I cite the example of an Indian organization, where, as part of an action research project, we replaced the ineffective performance management system with a happiness management system (HMS), incorporating the SysEM model and having spiritual, social, cognitive, and psychological processes as essential elements (Bhatnagar & Singhi, 2013; Robbins et al., 2013). The HMS can be applied to overcome the limitations of the balanced scorecard approach to setting objectives (Kaplan & Norton, 1996). The balanced scorecard embeds in the REM model, where, ultimately, maximizing wealth by building capability, improving processes, and delighting customers is the implied objective. Setting holistic objectives for each of the dimensions of the happiness model (wellness, reflection, continuous learning, innovation, financial delivery, work–life balance, community, and environment) maximizes human happiness while simultaneously ensuring delivery of organizational objectives. Adopting a dual approach of setting objectives at the beginning of the year and documenting "as and when events occur" is a realistic alternative to the current practice of having objectives defined only at the beginning of the year. Serendipity associates with innovation and planning for innovation and foreseeing it is often not easy.

A major limitation of the new metaphor is that the extant literature on happiness considers it subjective (Diener, 1984) or psychological (Ryff, 1989), an aspect so deeply entrenched in the minds of scholars and practitioners that openness to the possibilities of actually creating happiness in an organization calls for a paradigmatic shift in mindsets.

I see the immediate direction of future research in testing the happiness model in the field in diverse cultural settings and then developing and validating an instrument around the happiness model for measuring happiness. Once the model for creating happiness is tested across geographies and cultures, refining the model by including and removing certain variables to bring the model in tune with the changing times will be a continuing effort.

Pursuing happiness as the sole objective of the individual and of the organization simplifies the objectives to the few that offer the greatest possibility for maximizing happiness and converges the highest aspirations of employees—their very purpose of being—with the cherished and stretched objectives of organizations. Increasing meaninglessness, bordering on alienation experienced by employees, must be reversed by grounding the current theories and practices in organizations on positive psychology and SysEM, which meaningfully engage with all faculties of the human being compared with the current focus of optimizing cognitive abilities. The cherished goal of organizational scholars for creating humanized organizations, and of critical theorists for emancipating human beings, can be realized by questioning basic assumptions pertaining to human beings, providing an alternate conceptualization, and deploying it in an organizational context.

Key Terms

Convergence	Metaphor
Critical theory	Positive psychology
Happiness	Rational economic man
Hyperspace	Systemic economic man

Notes

1. I am deeply indebted to Revered Prof. Prem Saran Satsangi (Chairman of the Advisory Committee on Education, Dayalbagh Educational Institute, Agra, India, and Spiritual Leader of the Radhasoami Faith) for constant and loving intuitive guidance, without which this chapter would not have seen the light of day.

I acknowledge Prof. Rajen Gupta, professor of Human Behavior and Organization Development at the Management Development Institute, Gurgaon, India, for giving me guidance at critical stages while I was writing this chapter and for providing me with rich insights and perspectives.

References

Ariely, D. (2008). *Predictably irrational.* London, England: HarperCollins.

Aristotle. (1996). *The nicomachean ethics.* Ware, England: Woodsworth Editions Limited.

Aven, B. L. (2015). The paradox of corrupt networks: An analysis of organizational crime at Enron. *Organization Science, 26*(4), 980–996.

Bandura, A. (2001). Social cognitive theory: An agentic perspective. *Annual Review of Psychology, 52*, 1–26.

Bates, W. (2009). Gross national happiness. *Asian-Pacific Economic Literature, 26*(2),1–16.

Bhatnagar, V. R. (2012). Blending Greek philosophy and oriental law of action: Towards a consciousness propelled leadership framework. In G. P. Prastacos, F. Wang, & K. E. Soderquist (Eds.), *Leadership through the classics: Learning management and leadership from ancient East and West philosophy* (pp. 161–180). Berlin, Germany: Springer.

Bhatnagar, V. R., & Singhi, M. (2013). From managing performance to creating future. In R. Chopra, S. Puri, J. Ranjan, & G. Malhotra (Eds.), *Beyond norms: Management for excellence* (pp. 180–189). New Delhi, India: Bloomsbury.

Bradbury, H. (2003). Sustaining inner and outer worlds: A whole-systems approach to developing sustainable business practices in management. *Journal of Management Education, 27*(2), 172–187.

Brown, K. W., & Ryan, R. M. (2004). Fostering healthy self-regulation from within and without: A self-determination theory perspective. In P. A. Linlay & S. Joseph (Eds.), *Positive psychology in practice* (pp. 105–124). Hoboken, NJ: John Wiley & Sons.

Capra, F. (1975). *The Tao of physics.* London, England: Flamingo.

Capra, F. (2003). *The hidden connections.* New Delhi, India: HarperCollins.

Cooperrider, D. L., & Dutton, J. E. (1999). *Organizational dimensions of global change: No limits to cooperation.* Thousand Oaks, CA: Sage.

Cornelissen, J. P. (2005). Beyond compare: Metaphor in organization theory. *Academy of Management Review, 30*(4), 751–764.

Covey, S. R. (1989). *7 habits of highly effective people.* London, England: Simon & Schuster.

Csikszentmihalyi, M. (1990). *Flow.* New York, NY: Harper & Row.

Csikszentmihalyi, M. (1996). *Creativity: Flow and the psychology of discovery and invention.* New York, NY: HarperCollins.

Csikszentmihalyi, M. (1999). If we are so rich, why aren't we happy? *American Psychologist, 54*(10), 821–827.

Diener, E. (1984). Subjective well-being. *Psychological Bulletin, 95*(3), 542–575.

Diener, E., & Lucas, R. E. (1999). Personality and subjective well-being. In D. Kahneman, E. Diener, & N. Schwarz (Eds.), *Well being: The foundations of hedonic psychology* (pp. 213–229). New York, NY: Russell Sage Foundation.

Dolan, P., & Metcalfe, R. (2012). The relationship between innovation and subjective wellbeing. *Research Policy, 41*(8), 1489–1498.

Dweck, C. S. (2006). *Mindset: How you can fulfil your potential.* London, England: Constable and Robinson.

Einstein, A. (1961). *Relativity.* New York, NY: Three Rivers Press.

Epictetus. (1995). *The art of living: The classical manual on virtue, happiness, and effectiveness.* New York, NY: Harper One.

Etzioni, A. (1998). *The moral dimension: Towards a new economics.* New York, NY: Free Press.

Feynman, R. (1985). *The strange theory of light and matter.* New York, NY: Princeton University Press.

Fisher, C. D. (2010). Happiness at work. *International Journal of Management Reviews, 12*(4), 384–412.

Foucault, M. (1973). *Birth of a clinic.* London, England: Tavistock.

Frattaroli, E. (2001). *Healing the soul in the age of the brain: Why medication isn't enough.* New York, NY: Penguin Books.

Fredrickson, B. L. (2004). The broaden-and-build theory of positive emotions. *Philosophical Transactions of the Royal Society, 359*(1449), 1367–1377.

Freud, S. (2012). *A general introduction to psychoanalysis.* Ware, England: Wordsworth Editions.

Friedman, T. L. (2005). *The world is flat: A brief history of the twenty-first century.* New York, NY: Farrar, Straus and Giroux.

Frijters, P., Shields, M. A., & Haisken-DeNew, J. P. (2004). Money does matter! Evidence from increasing real incomes in East Germany following reunification. *American Economic Review, 94*(3), 730–741.

Frost, P. (1980). Towards a radical framework for practicing organization science. *Academy of Management Review, 5*(4), 501–507.

Galor, O., & Tsiddon, D. (1997). Technological progress, mobility and economic growth. *American Economic Review, 87*(3), 363–382.

Gerdtham, U.-G., & Johannesson, M. (2001). The relationship between happiness, health, and socioeconomic factors: Results based on Swedish microdata. *Journal of Socio-Economics, 30*(6), 553–557.

Gilkey, R., & Kilts, C. (2007). Cognitive fitness: New research in neuroscience shows how to stay sharp by exercising your brain. *Harvard Business Review, 85*(11), 53–66.

Grant, D., & Oswick, C. (1996). Introduction: Getting the measure of metaphors. In D. Grant & C. Oswick (Eds.), *Metaphors and organizations* (pp. 1–20). London, England: Sage.

Gröpel, P., & Kuhl, J. (2009). Work–life balance and subjective wellbeing: The mediating role of need fulfilment. *British Journal of Psychology, 100*(2), 365–375.

Herodotus. (1987). *The history* (D. Grene, Ed.). Chicago, IL: Chicago University Press.

Hirschman, C. G. (1970). The search of paradigms as a hindrance to understanding. *World Politics, 22*(3), 329–343.

Hodgson, G. M. (1998). The approach of institutional economics. *Journal of Economic Literature, 36*(1), 166–192.

Horkheimer, M. (1982). *Critical theory.* New York, NY: Seabury Press.

Hunt, J. (27 September 2000). Leading with a magic twist. *Financial Times,* p. 24.

Jacobs, C. D., & Heracleous, L. T. (2006). Constructing shared understanding: The role of embodied metaphors in organization development. *Journal of Applied Behavioral Sciences, 42*(2), 207–226.

Jensen, M. C., & Mecking, W. H. (1976). Theory of the firm: Managerial behaviour, agency costs and ownership structure. *Journal of Financial Structure, 3*(4), 305–360.

Jung, C. G. (1969). *On the nature of the psyche.* New York, NY: Routledge.

Kabat-Zinn, J. (2003). Mindfulness-based interventions in context: Past, present and future. *Clinical Psychology: Science and Practice, 10*(2), 144–156.

Kahnemann, D., Diener, E., & Schwarz, N. (1999). *Well being: The foundations of hedonic psychology.* New York, NY: Russell Sage Foundation.

Kaku, M. (1994). *Hyperspace.* New York, NY: Oxford University Press.

Kaplan, R. S., & Norton, D. P. (1996). *The balanced scorecard.* Boston, MA: HBS Press.

Kasser, T. (2004). The good life or the goods life? Positive psychology and personal well-being in the culture of consumption. In P. A. Linley, & S. Joseph (Eds.), *Positive psychology in practice* (pp. 55–67). Hoboken, NJ: John Wiley & Sons.

Ketola, T. (2009). Pre-morphean paradigm: An alternative to modern and post-modern paradigms of corporate sustainability. *Sustainability Development, 17*(2), 114–126.

Kilmann, R. H. (2001). *Quantum organizations: A new paradigm for achieving organizational success and personal meaning.* Palo Alto, CA: Davies-Black.

King, B. G., Felin, T., & Whetten, D. A. (2010). Finding the organization in organizational theory: A meta-theory of the organization as a social actor. *Organization Science, 21*(1), 290–305.

King, L. A., & Napa, C. K. (1998). What makes a good life. *Journal of Personality and Social Psychology, 75*(1), 156–165.

Kish-Gephart, J., Harrison, D., & Treviño, L. (2010). Bad apples, bad cases, and bad barrels: Meta-analytic evidence about sources of unethical decisions at work. *Journal of Applied Psychology, 95*(1), 1–31.

Lamb, M. L. (1992). Theology and money: Rationality, religion and economics. *American Behavioral Scientist, 35*(6), 735–755.

Landau, C., Szudek, A., & Tomley, S. (2011). *The philosophy book.* London, England: Dorling Kindersley Limited.

Lavine, T. Z. (1984). *From Socrates to Sartre.* New York, NY: Bantam Books.

Lee, S. M., Olson, D. L., & Trimi, S. (2010). The impact of convergence on organizational innovation. *Organizational Dynamics, 39*(3), 218–225.

Locke, J. (2014). *An essay concerning human understanding.* Ware, England: Wordsworth Editions.

Lutz, M. A. (1985). Beyond economic man: Humanistics economics. In P. Koslowski (Ed.), *Economics and philosophy* (pp. 91–120). Tübingen, Germany: J.C.B. Mohr.

Lyubomirsky, S. (2007). *The how of happiness: A new approach to getting the life you want.* New York, NY: Penguin Books.

Lyubomirsky, S., Sheldon, K. M., & Schkade, D. (2005). Pursuing happiness: The architecture of sustainable change. *Review of General Psychology, 9*(2), 111–131.

Lyubomirsky, S., & Tucker, K. L. (1998). Implications of individual differences in subjective happiness for perceiving, interpreting, and thinking about life events. *Motivation and Emotions, 22*(2), 155–186.

Marcuse, H. (1964). *One-dimensional man.* London, England: Routledge & Kegan Paul.

Marx, K. (2007). *Economic and philosophic manuscripts of 1844*. New York, NY: Dover.

Maslow, A. H. (1971). *The farther reaches of human nature*. New York, NY: Penguin.

Merleau-Ponty, M. (1983). *The structure of behavior*. Pittsburgh, PA: Duquesne University Press.

Moberg, D. O. (1979). The development of social indicators for quality of life research. *Sociological Analysis, 40*(1), 11–26.

Moore, B. N., & Bruder, K. (2005). *Philosophy: The power of ideas*. New Delhi, India: Tata McGraw-Hill.

Morgan, G. (1986). *Images of organization*. Newbury Park, CA: Sage.

Morgan, G. (1993). *Imaginization: The art of creative management*. London, England: Sage.

Morgan, S. M. (2006). Economic man as model man: Ideal types, idealization and caricatures. *Journal of the History of Economic Thought, 28*(1), 1–27.

Moynihan, D. P., DeLeire, T., & Enami, K. (2015). A life worth living: Evidence on the relationship between prosocial values and happiness. *American Review of Public Administration, 45*(3), 311–326.

Nord, W. R. (1978). Dreams of humanization and the realities of power. *Academy of Management Review, 3*(3), 674–679.

O'Boyle, E. J. (1994). Homo socio-economicus: Foundations to social economics and the social economy. *Review of Social Economy, 52*(3), 286–313.

Ortony, A. (1979). Beyond literal similarity. *Psychological Review, 86*(3), 161–180.

Oswald, A., & Powdthavee, N. (2007). Obesity, unhappiness and the challenge of affluence. *Economic Journal, 117*(6), F441–F459.

Peterson, C., & Park, N. (2003). Positive psychology as the evenhanded positive psychologist views it. *Psychological Inquiry, 14*(2), 141–146.

Plato. (1997). *Republic*. Ware, England: Wordsworth Editions.

Putman, R. D. (2000). *Bowling alone: The collapse and revival of American community*. New York, NY: Simon & Schuster.

Radhakrishnan, S. (1948). *The Bhagavad Gita*. London, England: George Allen & Unwin.

Raju, P. T. (1995). Comparisons and reflections. In S. Radhakrishnan & P. T. Raju (Eds.), *The conception of man* (pp. 306–379). New Delhi, India: HarperCollins.

Rath, T., & Harter, J. (2010). *Well being*. New York, NY: Gallup Press.

Robbins, S. P., Judge, T. A., & Vohra, N. (2013). *Organizational behavior*. New Delhi, India: Pearson.

Rokeach, M. (1973). *The nature of human values*. New York, NY: Free Press.

Russell, B. (1946). *History of Western philosophy*. London, England: Routledge.

Russell, B. (1971). *The conquest of happiness*. New York, NY: Liveright.

Ryan, R. M., & Deci, E. L. (2000). Self-determination theory and the facilitation of intrinsic motivation, social development and well-being. *American Psychologist, 55*(1), 68–78.

Ryan, R. M., & Deci, E. L. (2001). On happiness and human potentials: A review of research on hedonic and eudaimonic well-being. *Annual Review of Psychology, 52*, 141–166.

Ryff, C. D. (1989). Happiness is everything, or is it? Exploration on the meaning of psychological well-being. *Journal of Personality and Social Psychology, 57*(6), 1069–1081.

Ryff, C. D., & Keyes, C. L. (1995). The structure of psychological well-being revisited. *Journal of Personality and Social Psychology, 69*(4), 719–727.

Sagiv, L., Roccas, S., & Hazan, O. (2004). Value pathways to well-being: Healthy values, valued goal attainment, and environmental congruence. In P. A. Linley & S. Joseph (Eds.), *Positive psychology in practice* (pp. 68–104). Hoboken, NJ: John Wiley & Sons.

Sarros, J. C., Tanewski, G. A., Winter, R. P., Santora, J. C., & Densten, I. L. (2002). Work alienation and organizational leadership. *British Journal of Management, 13*(4), 285–304.

Schein, E. H. (1985). *Organizational culture and leadership*. San Francisco, CA: Jossey-Bass.

Schein, E. H. (1999). *The corporate culture survival guide*. San Francisco, CA: John Wiley & Sons.

Schopenhauer, A. (1973). *Essays and aphorisms* (R. J. Hollingdale, Trans.). New York, NY: Penguin.

Schwartz, T. (1995). *What really matters: Searching for wisdom in America*. New York, NY: Bantam.

Seligman, M. (2011). *Flourish: A visionary new understanding of happiness and well-being*. New York, NY: Free Press.

Seligman, M. P., & Csikszentmihalyi, M. (2000). Positive psychology: An introduction. *American Psychologist, 55*(1), 5–14.

Selznick, P. (1957). *Leadership in administration*. Evanston, IL: Row, Peterson.

Sheldon, K. M., & Lyubomirsky, S. (2004). Achieving sustainable new happiness: Prospects, practices, and prescriptions. In P. A. Linlay & S. Joseph (Eds.), *Positive psychology in practice* (pp. 127–145). Hoboken, NJ: John Wiley & Sons.

Stevenson, B., & Wolfers, J. (2008). Economic growth and subjective wellbeing: Reassessing the Easterlin paradox. *Brookings Papers on Economic Activity, 39*(1), 1–87.

Stiglitz, J. E., Sen, A., & Fitoussi, J. P. (2008). Report by the Commission on the Measurement of Economic Performance and Social Progress. Retrieved from http://www.stiglitz-sen-fitoussi.fr

Titmuss, R. (1970). *The gift relationship: From human blood to social policy*. London, England: George Allen & Unwin.

Tomer, J. F. (2001). Economic man vs. heterodox men: The concepts of human nature in schools of economic thought. *Journal of Socio-Economics, 30*(4), 281–293.

Tsoukas, H. (1993). Analogical reasoning and knowledge generation in organizational theory. *Organization Studies, 14*(3), 323–346.

Tversky, A., & Kahnemann, D. (1982). The psychology of preference. *Scientific American, 246*(1), 160–173.

Van Dyne, L., & LePine, J. A. (1998). Helping and voice extra-role behaviors: Evidence of construct and predictive validity. *Academy of Management Journal, 41*(1), 108–119.

Waterman, A. S. (1984). *The psychology of individualism*. New York, NY: Praeger.

Weick, K. E., Sutcliffe, K. M., & Obstfeld, D. (2005). Organizing and the process of sensemaking. *Organization Science, 16*(4), 409–421.

Wilber, K. (1996). *A brief history of everything*. Boston, MA: Shambala.

Zohar, D., & Marshall, I. (2004). *Spiritual capital: Wealth we can live by*. London, England: Bloomsbury.

Zsolnai, L. (2004). The morality of economic man. *European Business Review, 16*(4), 449–454.

6

Combining Metaphors to Understand New Organizational Phenomena

Thomas Süße, Bernd-Friedrich Voigt, and Uta Wilkens

Key Learning Points

- Obtain a brief overview about Morgan's images and how they relate to organizational phenomena.
- Experience the value of Morgan's images for understanding organizational dynamics in general through a metaphor building process.
- Gain brief insights into the theory of metaphor in organization research.
- Gain an understanding of the challenges of a new trend in business called integrated product-service systems (IPSS) as the case of application in this chapter.
- Become familiar with how to analyze metaphors on a quantitative empirical basis referred to individual actions and behavior.
- Learn about the domains-interaction model as an approach to utilize metaphors in order to understand and create meaning of organizational phenomena.
- Experience the high value of Morgan's images as being applicable to understanding dynamics of organizing in IPSS.
- Learn how the perspective of an interdependent relationship of Morgan's images creates additional meaning for research and practice.

n this chapter, Morgan's images of organization are used as instruments for shaping the understanding of organizations and their phenomena. You will learn how Morgan's images, introduced about three decades ago, can still help to make sense of today's modern business trends and their dynamics in organizational life. With regard to using his images for specific cases of interest, Morgan himself demonstrates a practical application by comparing two organizations (Morgan, 2006, p. 345). He describes in an interpretive application process how managers, consultants, or other stakeholders may "read organizational life" through the lenses of his images. He argues that the interplay of multiple perspectives especially contributes to a meaningful process of reading organizations' inherent paradoxical nature. Thus, to create new meaning from reading and understanding organizations' dynamics, Morgan encourages the community to search for the application of multiple images as lenses of analysis. New meaning is essentially created by the interplay of various and partially contradicting perspectives (Figure 6.1).

This chapter addresses the suggested concept of using multiple images and lenses to read organizational life, as presented in Figure 6.1. A new style of **solution-oriented value proposition**, summarized as **integrated product-service systems (IPSS)**, is introduced as the modern case of application for Morgan's images (Davies, Brady, & Hobday, 2007). This recent trend in business shows specific dynamics of organizational phenomena that are interpreted throughout the chapter by applying Morgan's images.

As part of the application of Morgan's images, you will also learn more about how a selective process can be conducted to identify those images that may be more relevant than others when creating meaning of distinct organizational phenomena.

FIGURE 6.1 ● Multiple Ways of Understanding Organizational Phenomena

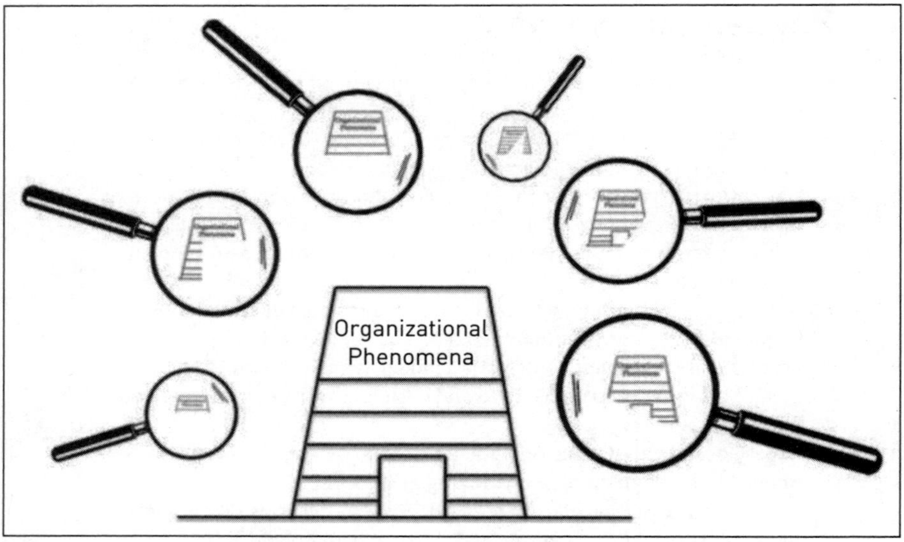

Source: Adapted from Morgan (2006, p. 341).

To provide you with a well-structured method of using Morgan's images, the process of analyzing, reading, and ultimately creating extended meaning of IPSS used here builds on Cornelissen's (2005) domains-interaction model. With the help of this recent model, you will learn how the use of Morgan's images leads to comprehensive meaning of IPSS as the example case of application. Insights about the organizational reality of IPSS are gained from empirical data of a survey among German engineers as an essential group of involved actors. The survey respondents reflected on the relevance of their actions and behaviors in IPSS. This creates an ambiguous picture that demands extensive interpretation in order to contribute to the understanding of the phenomenon among managers, employees, consultants, and researchers. This chapter closes with a reflection on Morgan's brain, organism, and flux and transformation images, which are the most relevant images to understanding IPSS.

The knowledge gained by reading this chapter may serve as future guidance when using Morgan's images, such as in your own projects in which you are aiming to understand and create meaning of organizational ambiguity or to introduce new perspectives to contribute to organizational change and development. In addition, this chapter also reflects on and reveals some limitations about using images of organization.

IPSS as the Case of Application

Increasing Relevance

This chapter refers to IPSS as a case of applying Morgan's images. IPSS are gaining increasing awareness in research and practice (Salonen, 2011). The concept is considered as a key driver for sustainable growth and competitiveness, especially for companies in the engineering sector (Mont, 2002; Tukker, 2004). The idea of IPSS is based on an integrated offering that became popular in the context of organizations shifting their strategies toward solution business. The IPSS as a type of **integrated value proposition (IVP)** of an organization builds on the mutual adjustment of products and services with the scope of delivering a highly individualized value-in-use for customers (Mont, 2002). Beuren, Gomes Ferreira, and Cauchick Miguel (2013, p. 224) provide some prominent examples of IPSS-oriented organizational offerings. They highlight the company Xerox International (http://www.xerox .com). Xerox offers customer-specific office solutions to help customers focus on their own relevant processes. The availability and functionality of hardware, software, and service is sold instead of the pure product or service itself.

Another example is Electrolux from Sweden (http://www.corporate.electrolux .com). This company sells functional solutions for consumers. They argue that instead of buying a washer or washing machine, people want to get clean and fresh clothes. Therefore, this company's approach is characterized by the business concept that consumers may not pay for owning a washing machine, but they simply pay per wash. As a consequence, consumers no longer buy the technical devices; rather, they buy the devices' usability or availability for specific purposes. Thus, they do not have to care about maintenance, replacement, or certain characteristics related to the product. They simply acquire the functionality of washing.

By considering these examples, the main concept of IPSS can be described as a complex system that demands the integration of products, services, and customer processes (Baines et al., 2007; Roy, Baines, Lightfoot, Benedettini, & Kay, 2009). It emphasizes a solution-oriented value proposition (Kowalkowski, 2010) and solves individual customer problems in order to gain sustainable competitive advantage. However, this depends on certain parameters, including technological, managerial, and institutional prerequisites (Martinez, Bastl, Kingston, & Evans, 2010; Oliva & Kallenberg, 2003).

Challenges of Transformation

Literature argues that an IVP, such as IPSS, is not only a challenge from an engineering or sales perspective (Davies et al., 2007; Oliva & Kallenberg, 2003; Roy et al., 2009). It calls for appropriate ways of organizing with respect to coordination, cooperation, and communication practices (Gebauer, 2007; Gebauer, Edvardsson, Gustafsson, & Witell, 2010; Gebauer & Friedli, 2005) as organizational language and beliefs (Neely, Benedettini, & Visnjic, 2011; Oliva & Kallenberg, 2003). The ad hoc provision of problem-solving capabilities to address customer-specific requirements is described as extremely challenging (Kowalkowski, 2010; Meier, Uhlmann, Völker, Geisert, & Stelzer, 2010; Schweitzer & Aurich, 2010).

Furthermore, the dynamic interplay of organizations' resources and customer demands creates potential misunderstandings and misconceptions not only among actors but also among researchers in this field (Nuutinen & Lappalainen, 2012). Thus, further interpretation and conceptualization of the phenomenon of IPSS seems crucially important, especially when it comes to the question of transforming rather traditional businesses to IPSS. A major obstacle of this transformation is perceived, for example, in the outstanding history of very successful traditional business models. These models are still, to a large extent, based on the concepts of industrialization and classical management approaches in terms of a bureaucratic or mechanistic way of managing and organizing (e.g., Burn & Stalker, 1961; Gummesson, Lusch, & Vargo, 2010; Morgan, 2006; Vargo & Lusch, 2008). The transformation required is generally characterized as a shift "from strong control and divisional (or function-based) optimization toward a more flexible, end-result and value-oriented way of managing" (Nuutinen & Lappalainen, 2012, p. 142; also see Vargo & Lusch, 2008). Furthermore, Nuutinen and Lappalainen (2012, p. 139) argue that IPSS require a transformation of "those deep, partly subconscious beliefs about an organization's purpose."

Challenges of Organizing

There is widespread agreement among researchers that a different way of organizing is an essential prerequisite for IPSS, especially to refocus on a deeper customer involvement into an organization's **value creation** processes. In IPSS, customers are considered more as a "resource" in order to understand their needs (Gummesson et al., 2010; Vargo & Lusch, 2004, 2008). This supports the recent trend in business in which the changing nature of customer demands pushes organizations toward a **value proposition** of mass customization (Da Silveira, Borenstein, & Fogliatto,

2001). It determines a specific field of ambiguity and uncertainty, especially for former traditional mass production–oriented organizations.

Thus, the literature argues that IPSS are considered as rather revolutionary and path breaking (Tukker, 2004). The success of IPSS is more crucially based on an ongoing reconfiguration of the organization itself (Baines et al., 2007; Oliva & Kallenberg, 2003; Roy et al., 2009; Vargo & Lusch, 2004, 2008). Based on a broad range of expert interviews, Brax (2005) also postulates that such businesses "require a different organizational setting" and are more "difficult to manage" (Gustafsson & Brax, 2005, p. 152). The literature argues that solution-oriented businesses, such as IPSS, can be characterized by their "perishable, complex and multifunctional nature" (Benade & Weeks, 2010, p. 406, with reference to Desmet, Van Looy, & Van Dierdock, 2003, p. 16; Fitzsimmons & Fitzsimmons, 2008, pp. 19–20; Gustafsson & Brax, 2005, p. 142). Value creation and delivery become more inseparable and highly interdependent (de Brentani, 1991; Vargo & Lusch, 2004). In addition, Normann (1991) supports this by arguing that customer-integrating businesses require not only a different management approach but also a new concept of organizing. This includes new configurations of processes, structures, and work practices (Externbrink, Wilkens, & Lienert, 2013; Gebauer & Fleisch, 2007) as well as capabilities (Ceci & Masini, 2011) and relationships with customers or suppliers (Evans, Partidário, & Lambert, 2007; Galbraith, 2002).

Furthermore, Cova and Salle (2007, pp. 142–143) identified four major obstacles in the concept of organizing for a solution-oriented offering. They highlight the challenges of changing the orientation of the firm, the need for different capabilities and skills, the transformation of structure and processes, and the implementation of the transformation processes within the firm. In line with this argument, Ulaga and Reinartz (2011) postulate significant challenges for organizational structures, processes, routines, and capabilities that are fundamentally distinctive. Neely et al. (2011) argue that organizations become more complex and contradictory, while coordination needs increase. More precisely, Shepherd and Ahmed (2000, p. 105) regard technical competence, integration competence, market or business knowledge competence, and customer partnering competence as the basis for integrated solution-oriented offerings.

Several authors emphasize the external orientation of IPSS organizations and thus their need for adaptability and flexibility to environmental changes (Galbraith, 2002; Gebauer & Friedl, 2005; Gremyr, Löfberg, & Witell, 2010; Martinez et al., 2010; Penttinen & Palmer, 2007; Vargo & Lusch, 2008). Neely et al. (2011) postulate that employees' and managers' capabilities of reflection on the traditional way of doing and thinking and letting the past go are crucial success drivers for IPSS. Biloslavo, Bagnoli, and Rusjan Figelj (2013, p. 426) mention certain dualities with regard to the organizational structure and the organizational behavior within IPSS businesses (also see Externbrink et al., 2013). As an example, they refer to the dualities of coexisting centralization versus decentralization, function orientation versus process orientation, and standardization versus mutual adjustment. Similarly, it is argued that for IPSS, the tension of efficiency versus effectiveness, which has traditionally been considered as an either/or decision, should be preserved as a duality (Dittrich, Jaspers, van der Valk, & Wynstra, 2006; Hakansson & Ford, 2002; Vargo & Lusch, 2004). In summary, as an increasing amount of recent literature shows, the phenomenon of IPSS is characterized by a high degree of dynamics and ambiguity across all levels of the organization.

However, an overarching concept is still missing. This raises further need to apply multiple perspectives (e.g., multiple images) to grasp the insights of this organizational context in order to contribute to the further interpretation and conceptualization of the IPSS phenomenon. Therefore, the concept of metaphors is introduced as an appropriate approach in the next chapter.

Metaphors as Frames for Understanding Organizational Phenomena

Metaphors can be defined as the mapping of entities, structures, and relations from a **source domain** onto a **target domain** (Cornelissen & Kafouros, 2008, p. 366; Lakoff, 1993; Morgan, 2006). The source domain can usually be an image (e.g., the brain) that researchers use to create extended meaning by connecting it with organizational phenomena. In that sense, organizations or organizational phenomena are considered the target domain. The resulting metaphors have the power to create extensive meaning, for example, by understanding phenomena of an organization under the lens of specific images (Morgan, 1983). Research has increasingly applied Morgan's images and provided additional and supplementary metaphorical conceptions of specific phenomena and characteristics of organization in order to contribute to further understanding and theory building (Boxenbaum & Rouleau, 2011; Cornelissen, 2005; Morgan, 2006). The literature especially in the field of organization research or education research makes use of the various images introduced by Morgan (see literature review by Cornelissen, Kafouros, & Lock, 2005).

Despite some criticisms, authors in organizational research emphasize the high value of metaphor, for example, to create extended meaning of empirical insights about organizations (Inns, 2002; Oswick, Keenoy, & Grant, 2002). Images of organization are discussed as fruitful perspectives that provide specific features shared among organizational researchers (Cornelissen, 2005). These images can serve as a framing concept for cognitions and interpretation processes of organizations (Foropon & McLachlin, 2013). Once these images are projected onto a specific target domain, they may trigger the generation of completely new ways of seeing, conceptualizing, and understanding organizations by means of the metaphorical representations that arise (Cornelissen, 2004, 2005; Cornelissen & Kafouros, 2008; Inns, 2002; Tsoukas, 1991, 1993). Cornelissen and Kafouros (2008, p. 367) define "the impact of a metaphor as forms of cognitive change in our theoretical framing and understanding of organizations."

However, as Morgan argues, taking the lens of an image always determines not only a way of seeing but also a way of not seeing and thus leaving other aspects unattended. Morgan (2006) describes this as a way of thinking and a way of seeing. When analyzing organizational phenomena, for example, with the help of his images, Morgan (2011) emphasizes the fact that the view toward certain contexts may not be limited to a single image but should be understood and analyzed by researchers' application and awareness of interdependent multiple images, as illustrated in Figure 6.1. In this sense, metaphors can combine multiple image projections in order to improve understanding of organizational dynamics and ambiguity (Cornelissen 2004, pp. 705–706). This creates a new meaning of an organizational reality.

Since Morgan (2006) encourages researchers to not only develop new metaphors but also use and apply existing ones, this chapter builds on the eight existing metaphors introduced in Table 6.1. This set of images sketches the way in which the concept of metaphor is applied to the case of IPSS in the following paragraphs. This

TABLE 6.1 ● Brief Summary of Morgan's Images of Organization	
Images of Organization	**Key Facets of Each Image of Organization**
Machine	Organization as being made up of interlocking parts, each part plays a clearly defined role in the functioning of the whole, considering organization's potential of being highly effective in certain circumstances
Organism	Attention on understanding and managing organizational needs in close relationship with the environment, types of different organizations as distinct species that emerge in specific environmental contexts and adapt to changing circumstances, e.g. on the basis of evolutionary patterns
Brain	Recognizing organization as information processing space where learning and intelligence are key characteristics of modern organization, e.g. the "learning organization"
Culture	Focusing on socially constructed and shared meaning like collective values, ideas, beliefs, norms, or rituals which serve as guiding principles or framing elements in organizational life
Political system	Consideration of organization as set of opposing interests, resulting conflicts, or power plays that are fundamentally shaping organizational activities
Psychic prison	Recognizing organization as a context where individual actors become trapped by their own thoughts, ideas, and beliefs or by their unconscious mind
Flux and transformation	Understanding organization under the lens of four metaphorical logics of change: self-producing systems (re)creating themselves, competing "attractor patterns," circular flows of positive and negative feedback, dialectic logics of opposite phenomena
Instrument of domination	Viewing organization as exploiting context using employees, host communities and/or the world economy to achieve own ends, e.g. by showing highly rational actions

Source: Adapted from Morgan (2006, p. 6 f.).

chapter refers to Morgan's images of organization as lenses of interpretation for the phenomenon of organizing in IPSS. A brief summary of Morgan's images of organization is illustrated in Table 6.1.

Domains-Interaction Model for Metaphor Development

To provide you with a well-structured framework that describes the interpretation process toward a metaphor about organizational reality, this chapter builds on the guiding methodology introduced by Cornelissen's (2005) **domains-interaction model** (see Figure 6.2). The domains-interaction model determines a three-step process of metaphor development, which can be customized for specific cases of application (Cornelissen, 2005, p. 758).

FIGURE 6.2 ● The Application of the Domains-Interaction Model of Metaphor Building in This Chapter

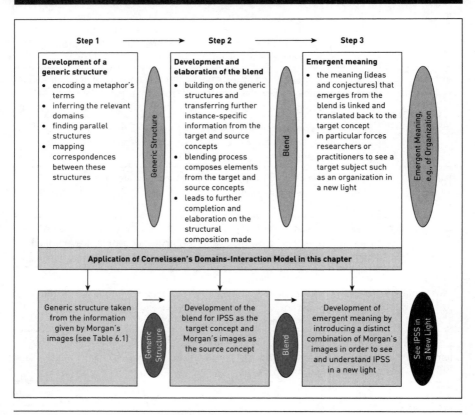

Source: Adapted from Cornelissen (2005, p. 758).

In the first step, the terms and meanings of possible metaphor(s) are encoded (see Step 1 of Figure 6.2). As the prominent example, you can refer to Morgan (2006), who has done this throughout his book by relating his images to organizational phenomena (see Table 6.1). By doing so, he developed the extended metaphorical meanings of organizational reality on the basis of his eight images. When reading his book, you will notice that Morgan identified parallel structures between the brain as an information processing entity and organizations, which aim to use information effectively for learning and development purposes. The result of this metaphorical connection is a **generic structure** that relates images to organizational phenomena and creates new meaning. Thus, Morgan's images can be seen as the highly regarded groundwork for this chapter, because they make up the starting point of the first step of the domains-interaction model.

Second, a composition is made on the basis of the generic structure of the first step. This results in a blend of the target concept (Morgan's images) and the source concept (IPSS). However, to build on distinct characteristics about IPSS as the target concept, the next sections introduce empirical data that have been gathered to generate more insights about this specific reality of IPSS. The empirical data are taken to develop the blend between IPSS and Morgan's images. The data provide distinct information about IPSS and they result from an engineering survey in this field of business. As such, the survey results provide the main input for the second step of the domains-interaction model. The developed blend indicates a combination of relevant images from Morgan that are seen as valuable for creating extended meaning of IPSS.

Finally, during the third step, this chapter outlines and discusses the generation of an emergent meaning by interpreting the results of the previous steps through an extended cognitive and creative process. This last step also reveals how the domains-interaction model contributes largely to the generation of emergent meaning of IPSS reality as a target concept by creating a specific metaphorical comprehension on the basis of Morgan's images.

Specifying Characteristics of Organizing in IPSS

Empirical Approach for Gathering Distinct Data

With reference to Morgan's *Images of Organization*, this chapter aims to develop a combined metaphor for IPSS to create emergent meaning of the related organizational phenomena. Thus far, most of the contributions in metaphor research have investigated narrative data. This means that they build on data from conversations among actors to reveal the presence of specific metaphors in organizations. Cornelissen, Oswick, Thoger Christensen, and Phillips (2008) have summarized multiple research approaches in this field. Despite the strong orientation toward using the written or spoken words of the actors involved for metaphorical investigation and development, it is important to note that Morgan himself also gives hints regarding the valuable source of information that can be drawn from observing, measuring, or reflecting about how work is actually performed (Morgan, 2006).

Inspired by Morgan's argumentation, this chapter aims to gather information about an IPSS-specific reality by building on quantitative measures from an engineering survey. The creation of a distinct IPSS reality in this chapter is based on an empirical analysis of quantitative data. Thus far, only a few cases in organizational research can be found that rely on other than narrative data of the written or spoken word for metaphorical conceptualizing and reflecting. In one example, Heracleous and Jacobs (2008) introduced an action-oriented approach. They built on "embodied metaphors" or "physical constructions that can be touched, moved, examined from various angles and serve as engaging occasions for sense making" (Heracleous & Jacobs, 2008, p. 309) to help employees understand and reflect on the dynamics of their workplace. In a similar way, the work provided by Garud and Kotha (1994) shows an early attempt to make use of existing images of organization as explicit cognitive frames to analyze and understand a prescribed organizational setup. Inspired by this approach, the study presented directs attention to characterizing the specific way of organizing in IPSS by individual work-related behaviors, team-oriented work practices, structural conditions, and perceived leadership. This target domain data shape a distinct impression of IPSS and can then be interpreted under the lens of multiple images.

Data presented in this study result from a survey among German-speaking engineers that was conducted in 2012 and 2013 across different industries and industrial services. The broad database allows searching for distinct ways of organizing beyond a single organization or branch, and more with respect to typical styles of value propositions. Engineers were selected for this study because their professions span a wide range of product- and/or service-related tasks. Moreover, this group comprises a highly interesting sample because it contains individuals who relate to a traditional way of doing business, to the new style of value proposition in IPSS, or to a subgroup that is currently involved in a transformation process from purer production-oriented to integrated ways of organizing. Since IPSS is not necessarily a organization-wide approach, but rather an emerging field in some work areas, the engineering survey across such different areas is most promising to conduct a comparative research. For brevity, this chapter summarizes only the most important overall results of the quantitative data evaluation. Sample characteristics and detailed information about statistical procedures are provided in Appendices A–G.

The sample contains 172 participants with representative gender and age distribution for this employee group. Further details are provided in Appendix A. The questionnaire applied includes 108 items (see Appendix H) with a seven-step Likert scale, where 1 means *I totally disagree* and 7 means *I totally agree*. The self-reported data are operationalized as scale-guided reflections about characteristics and their relevance in respondents' immediate work contexts. The set of items draws on established scales from evaluated instruments. Individual evaluations of job characteristics and work environment are based on the scale by Morgeson and Humphrey (2006); individual cognition, action, and team interaction relate to Wilkens and Gröschke (2008); and perceived leadership relies on both the Global **Transformational Leadership** Scale developed by Carless, Wearing, and Mann (2000) and the Multifactor Leadership Questionnaire developed by Bass and Avolio (1997). Furthermore, the questionnaire contains aspects of psychological and sociostructural **empowerment** from Spreitzer (1995, 1996). The setup of a value proposition is covered by a three-item scale from Cova and Salle (2007). This scale asks about the degree of combination of products and services, the interrelatedness of these fields, and the individualization in terms of customer-specific solutions. In this regard, the scale indicates different value proposition styles and allows the identification of discrete organizational setups along a continuum between standardization-driven and integration-driven offerings.

General Steps of Data Analysis and Evaluation

To develop a blend between IPSS and Morgan's images, it is crucial to first gather distinct information and data about IPSS. Building on the survey data, certain steps of data evaluation provide the statistical basis of narrowing down an IPSS-specific set of variables for further results interpretation. This set of variables is introduced in Table 6.2. Each variable expresses a specific content and meaning. In addition, the unique combination of these variables also expresses a specific content and meaning in organization. This distinct IPSS information serves as the base data for the metaphor building and combination process in the later sections of this chapter. The two main data evaluation steps to gather these variables are briefly introduced below.

The first basic step was designed to identify different styles of value proposition for a clustering of participants of the above-mentioned engineering sample. The clustering approach should identify a subgroup of the sample that can be attributed to an IPSS-oriented value proposition in contrast with other value propositions. Based on the items from the scale by Cova and Salle (2007), the statistical procedure builds on a hierarchical cluster analysis using Ward's method and estimations of squared Euclidian distances.

A second step was undertaken to search for all of the items in the questionnaire that are best suited to explain differences in the ways of organizing between the value proposition clusters identified by step 1 above. The data evaluation procedure builds on a multiple **discriminant analysis**. This analysis is grounded in a statistical procedure that aims to achieve the highest possible classification of cases (i.e., participants of the study) as predictors for categories of a dependent variable (i.e., styles of

TABLE 6.2 ● **Computed Canonical Coefficients of the Discriminant Vector (or Function)**

Variable	Function 1
I find it easy to discuss problems and challenges with people outside of the organization (e.g., suppliers, customers).	0.473
I usually try to learn from other people during daily work.	0.458
During daily work, I often communicate with people who are not employed at the same organization as me.	0.450
Our team is very good at using experiences of other groups for our own projects.	−0.270
The management inspires employees to solve problems and challenges in new ways.	0.183

value proposition) (Huberty & Olejnik, 2006). The classification logic finds a predictive set of items by means of item relatedness and closeness. The mathematical function that describes how these items align in order to attribute a participant to either one or another category of the value proposition is a synthetic vector (discriminant function or Eigenvector). It can be viewed as the representation of an underlying, latent or invisible dimension that results in the item-assembling observed. It is exactly this dimension that must be detected and interpreted on a qualitative basis for a full and meaningful utilization of the statistical data as such (Grimm & Yarnold, 1995; Stevens, 2002). In this chapter, the **latent dimension** is viewed as an indicator of those features that make up the difference between the ways of organizing under different styles of value proposition.

Results of Data Analysis and Evaluation

The above-mentioned data evaluation provides a set of variables that stands characteristically for IPSS. In other words, by focusing on these variables, one can rely on a valid predictor set that, if values are high, discriminates IPSS from other styles of value proposition. As such, the set of variables provides the necessary source of IPSS information for a blend with Morgan`s images of organization.

IPSS as a Distinct Style of IVP Participants in the study can be classified into three clusters by distinct styles of value proposition. The table in Appendix B shows the mean values, frequencies, and percentages of participants' cluster attributions. A total of 39.5% of participants ($n = 68$) fall into a value proposition that is rather IPSS oriented. Participants in this cluster reflect about their work context as being characterized by a value proposition with a high variety of highly interdependent product-service combinations, which are also highly individualized for customer needs. This style can be understood as a strong orientation toward an IPSS value proposition. It integrates customer needs, products, and services in a solution-oriented business concept. A total of 29.7% of participants ($n = 51$) reported that they are working within the context of an organization that represents a high degree of standardization or low degree of individualization. This value proposition style focuses on highly standardized combinations of products and services. It can be understood to comprise a product-driven way of organizing that entails supplementary services. Just under one-third (30.2%) of the participants ($n = 52$) relate their work to a value proposition that lacks an integration of products and services but is highly customized. It can be understood to make up a service-driven way of organizing that stems from a rather consulting-oriented business concept.

Distinct Variables of Organizing in IPSS Because the literature especially emphasizes the large differences between the ways of organizing under standardized and IPSS value propositions (Roy et al., 2009), this study aimed to identify the discriminant function and those variables that best separate these two clusters of the engineering sample. The upcoming paragraphs will refer to an IVP, whereas a **standardized value proposition** is indicated by the acronym SVP. Because of the refocus on IVP and SVP clusters, the third cluster ("customized services") was not further considered. A revised case analysis resulted in 117 valid cases for further computation in an IVP versus SVP cluster comparison. Five cases had to be removed from the samples due to missing data and the remaining cases fell into the "customized services" cluster. The final distribution of the sample used shows that 57.3% of participants ($n = 67$) judge their immediate work context as driven by an IVP, whereas 42.7% ($n = 50$) reported that they are working within the context of SVP.

For statistical data evaluation, Box testing results in a significance level of 0.110; eigenvalue computation and testing through the Wilks' Lambda statistic result in a significance level of 0.000 (see Appendix C–E). The function is 0.491 for the centroid of the IVP cluster and –0.658 for the centroid of the SVP cluster. The discriminant vector is represented in a five-dimensional order, which was attained through forward stepwise analysis, while reducing Wilks' Lambda from 0.931 to 0.753 (see Appendix F). This result shows that there are considerable differences between an IVP and an SVP with respect to five characteristics from the entire set of variables in the questionnaire. Based on the discriminant vector achieved, a computation of correctness was conducted for original and cross-validated classifications. The discriminant analysis correctly classifies 75.2% of all cases (cross-validated 70.9%), 85.1% of the IVP (cross-validated 80.6%), and 62% of SVP cluster cases (cross-validated 58%), which can be viewed as a very satisfactory degree of correctness (see Appendix G for absolute numbers and the percentage for each category of the classification analysis). Table 6.2 shows the resulting variables and their absolute value of correlation between the discriminant variable and standardized canonical discriminant function. Thus, Table 6.2 provides important information for later content-related qualitative interpretation.

By analyzing the discriminant function, it can be noticed that the variable "I find it easy to discuss problems and challenges with people outside of the organization (e.g., suppliers, customers)" has a major influence on the discriminant function (0.473), whereas the variable "The management inspires employees to solve problems and challenges in new ways" has a low influence (0.183). The latent dimension (discriminant function) created is based highly on variables that indicate an external orientation for problem solving, learning, and communication. The content and order of the variables in the discriminant function provide the statistical information about those characteristics of the way of organizing for IVP that make up the difference when contrasted with the way of organizing for SVP. In the remainder of this chapter, the way of organizing for IVP and SVP is referred to as the **integrating way of organizing** (IWO) and the **standardizing way of organizing** (SWO), respectively.

The following three conclusions can be summarized related to the results of the statistical data evaluation. First, the initial predictors (item battery assembled for this questionnaire) formed one statistically significant discriminant vector for contrasting IVP with SVP clusters. Second, based on this vector, a discriminant function was built through an algebraic linear combination of five predictor variables. In comparing the IVP with the SVP, these variables represent an assembling dimension that can be considered as a higher-order variable (e.g., quality of outwardly oriented information processing procedures). Third, the most important IWO predictor is the item "I usually try to learn from other people during daily work" (see Table 6.2). Moreover, it is interesting to note that experience-based learning (see variable 4 in Table 6.2) characterizes an SWO feature as its function and has a negative value for IVP, whereas outward orientation, communication, and inspiring leadership are key features for IWO (see Table 6.2). The IWO features are considered as IPSS indicators in the next section.

Applying Morgan's Images to the Set of IPSS Variables

As presented above, a distinct pattern of IPSS-related characteristics and dynamics of organizing could be specified on the basis of the empirical data. However, these empirical results need further interpretation and generation of extended meaning in order to foster the understanding about IPSS and a related way of organizing. This data interpretation process is conducted throughout this section by applying three steps of the domains-interaction model: developing a generic structure, developing and elaborating the blend, and creating emergent meaning of IPSS specific phenomena (see Figure 6.2 for further explanation).

Developing a Generic Structure as Basis for the Blend

As suggested by the domains-interaction model, the interpretation processes starts with the development of a generic structure. Parallel features of the source (Morgan's images) and target domain (IPSS characteristics) are identified and connected. As a result, a generic structure emerges that connects IPSS with a set of Morgan's images. As illustrated in Figure 6.2, connections between the source and the target domain can be established by explorative identification and finding processes. These processes contribute to the development of **parallel structures** and mapping of both domains (Cornelissen, 2005, p. 758). By identifying parallel meanings and mapping IPSS variables (Table 6.2) with characteristics of Morgan's images (Table 6.1), the explorative interpretation process results in a specific generic structure. This generic structure places special emphasis on the mapping of IPSS with Morgan's images of the brain, organism, and flux and transformation. Table 6.3 provides the results of this mapping process. The specific mapping is based on the following interpretation scheme of IPSS indicators from Table 6.2 with regard to Morgan's images.

The first indicator ("I find it easy to discuss problems and challenges with people outside of the organization [e.g., suppliers, customers]"), emphasizes an external orientation of information processing and evaluating, such as constructively processing stimuli from external partners or customers of the organization. This relates the indicator's meaning to the characteristics of the organism and the brain. The second indicator ("During daily work, I often communicate with people who are not employed at the same organization as me.") relates rather to communicative interactions with external actors. Thus, this indicator has been related to the organism, as it shows a strong orientation toward the interactions with the external environment. The third indicator ("I usually try to learn from other people during daily work.") creates a picture of a rather strong orientation toward learning as well as facets of self-improvement and the reallocation of knowledge. This indicator can be mainly connected to the learning features of the brain. With the brain, Morgan especially emphasizes effective problem solving and learning mechanisms of organizations. The fourth indicator ("Our team has challenges at using experiences of other groups for our own projects.") indicates difficulties in exploiting knowledge from others, as knowledge may be reconfigured steadily in IPSS. This is considered as a characteristic that potentially occurs in very fast-changing environments in which the half-life of knowledge can be extremely short. Thus, it can be an indicator for organization that shows a high degree of transformation and reconfiguration. This strongly connects to Morgan's flux and transformation image.

Finally, the fifth indicator ("The management inspires employees to solve problems and challenges in new ways.") points toward a purposeful and framed reconfiguration of routines in order to achieve adapted or transformed outcomes (e.g., for customers). Because of the reconfiguring characteristic and its target-oriented feature, it has been connected not only to Morgan's flux and transformation but also to his brain image. In addition, it can also be argued that this indicator addresses challenges that are also connected to the fourth indicator, thus revealing that actors struggle in the process of using former experiences that may no longer lead to appropriate problem solutions. These images seem to create a high level of correspondence to the IPSS-specific variable revealed from the statistical analysis. Table 6.3 presents the resulting generic structure by allocating the IPSS indicators to related images introduced by Morgan.

Developing and Elaborating the Blend

The blending process was conducted on the basis of the generic structure. The researchers reflected about each IPSS indicator as well as their distinct combination with respect to Morgan's organism, flux and transformation, and brain images. As such, this blending process interrelated IPSS and each of Morgan's images. In doing so, a collective search for a meaningful representation of the generic structure from the previous step resulted in the labeling of three overarching blend dimensions related to Teece (2007): A ("sensing the environment"), B ("transforming knowledge"), and C ("reconfiguring routines"). Most interestingly, these dimensions form a vertical blend to connect the IPSS indicators as well as a horizontal blend across Morgan's images (see Table 6.3). As a result, it can be argued that each of the dimensions represents a core function of IPSS, such as focusing on the integration of customer knowledge into the organization's resource base in order to find solutions for new and highly individual customer problems.

In addition, this blend (as shown in Table 6.3) also connects complementary functions of Morgan's images. For example, the dimension "sensing the environment" connects the external orientation of the organism with the information processing capabilities of the brain in order to gain and utilize appropriate information. As a result, through their inherent meaning, the three dimensions strengthen the mapping of the IPSS indicators with the general structure created to the three images from Morgan. Table 6.3 shows the overall results of the blend between the source concept (Morgan's images) and the target concept (IPSS).

Creating Emergent Meaning

The third and final step of the domains-interaction model of metaphor is the creation of emergent meaning by linking the blend to the initial target and source concepts (see Figure 6.2). By doing so, it becomes apparent that there is a meaningful connection between the above-introduced dimensions "sensing the environment," "transforming knowledge," and "reconfiguring routines" with Morgan's three images of organism, flux and transformation, and brain. Even more interestingly, it

TABLE 6.3 ● Generic Structure and Blend of the Metaphor Development Process for IPSS

IPSS Indicators		Machine structure of interlocking parts	Organism coping with the environment	Flux and transformation logic of change for ongoing (re)creation	Brain effective problem solving and learning	Culture socially constructed realities based on communication and cognition	Psychic prison self-constructed realities based on unconscious preoccupations	Political system cooperation mechanisms and power plays	Instrument of domination exploitation mechanisms to achieve own ends
A. Sensing the environment	1. I find it easy to discuss problems and challenges with people outside of the organization (e.g., suppliers, customers).								
	2. During daily work, I often communicate with people who are not employed at the same organization as me.								
B. Transforming knowledge	3. I usually try to learn from other people during daily work.								
C. Reconfiguring routines	4. Our team has challenges at using experiences of other groups for our own projects.								
	5. The management inspires employees to solve problems and challenges in new ways.								

Morgan's images

Blending

Generic Structure

turns out that the resulting metaphor for IPSS is based on the interplay of Morgan's brain, flux and transformation, and organism images (see Figure 6.3).

It can be argued that IPSS can be regarded as an organism-oriented context of organization that has the capability for self-inspiration and self-transformation through brain-oriented cognitive routines of information evaluating, fast and sustainable problem solving, and learning. For this purpose, the brain makes sense of external stimuli and recognizes an ongoing need for learning and adaption triggered by the experiences of its organic counterpart. At the same time, it is important in IPSS to remain self-critical about achievements already accomplished in order to ensure that the organization is in flux. Based on the concept of a triangle of the suggested images, which are supposed to mutually enforce each other, a hierarchical ordering of the images is suggested as a structuring element of the metaphorical representation. This puts the brain in the center, as the empirical results show the highest relevance for IPSS by the item "I find it easy to discuss problems and challenges with people outside of the organization (e.g., suppliers, customers)" (see Table 6.2). These characterizations of IPSS and the attitude

FIGURE 6.3 ● Application of IPSS-Specific Work Practice to Morgan's Metaphors With the Help of the Domains-Interaction Model

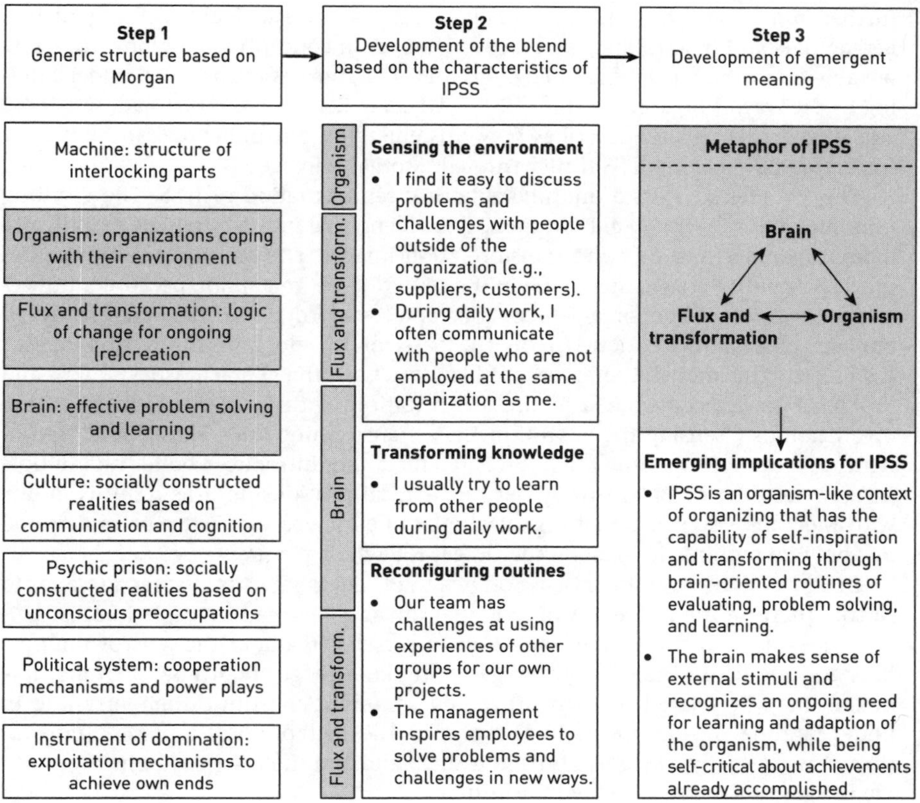

toward a balancing of information and knowledge in order to find solutions for problems can be especially, but not exclusively, allocated to Morgan's brain image.

In this regard the brain image specifically helps in detecting and understanding facets of efficient information management as a dominant characteristic of organizing in IPSS. Thus, it is suggested that one of the important design principles of an IPSS-oriented way of organizing might be to always frame and keep the connectivity and information flows to the environment "up and running." An additional insight of interest is the observation that, despite the strong orientation toward external stimuli, there is still a clear distinction about what determines the internal context of the organization and what is allocated to the external environment but considered as a resourceful element for interaction. As the overall result of the metaphor building process for IPSS, a triangle metaphor with a hierarchical structuring is suggested. The suggested triangle metaphor puts the brain in the center (see Figure 6.3). The brain is considered as the central information processing entity utilizing external and internal stimuli initiated from features of the organism and dynamics of flux and transformation.

Conclusions

IPSS is a newly emerging phenomenon in business. This phenomenon calls for further understanding and theorizing about its specific reality of organizing. Researchers and practitioners still face challenges in conceptualizing how this style of value proposition can be assured by means of an integration-oriented understanding of the way of organizing (Brax, 2005; Ulaga & Reinartz, 2011). To address these challenges, this chapter describes how this emerging phenomenon can be further understood by reading IPSS reality through Morgan's images.

This chapter suggests a multimetaphorical representation of IPSS. The resulting multimetaphor for IPSS builds on the specific blend that makes a triangle of Morgan's brain, organism, and flux and transformation images. The brain as an information processing entity is suggested to be in the center of this metaphor, because it utilizes and frames stimuli from organism and flux and transformation. The metaphor development process was conducted on the basis of the domains-interaction model. Inspired by this model, the process of blending both the characteristics of IPSS and Morgan's images contributed to the identification of three core activities for IPSS organizations ("sensing the environment," "transforming knowledge," and "reconfiguring routines"). Because the IPSS-related metaphor introduced builds on multiple images and their complementary but hierarchical relationship, this result is in line with Morgan, who states that organizational phenomena can better be understood by applying multiple images in order to get the whole picture.

In addition, through the discussion of a multimetaphor, this chapter also aims to further increase the awareness of potential linkages between multiple images. This even goes beyond the understanding of organizations under the lens of multiple images. It points to the direction of gathering knowledge about how such multiple images may be related to each other and mutually constitute their meaning in understanding organizations. In the case of the metaphorical representation for IPSS, it is especially the reflection about the blend and the interplay between multiple images that create extended meaning.

Thus, it can be concluded that the genuine complementarity between Morgan's images of brain, organism, and flux and transformation seems to pollinate a semantic representation that mirrors the pivotal contribution of exchange between multiple perspectives within this emerging way of organizing.

From a methodical perspective, it must be noted that the analytical procedure applied is a rather new approach in metaphor research and is based on a standardized questionnaire gathering individuals' estimation about the relevance of different individual problem-solving behaviors, intra- and intergroup cooperative practices, structural conditions, and perceived leadership.

Nonetheless, the purposeful design of the study proved its utility for the following reasons. When members of an organization face a rather new concept, such as IPSS, they might find it difficult to verbalize the characteristics of a very new way of organizing. In such cases, it would be difficult to legitimize which share of an image can be denoted to which way of organizing. This is of particular importance when researchers are interested in determining how a newly emerging way of organizing is different or distinct from, for example, former ways of organizing, because narrative data may be inevitably infected by inherited representations from earlier ways of organizing or current highly salient information. Consequently, the empirical investigation of the case presented builds on the standardized inquiry of individuals' reflections about problem-solving behaviors, intra- and intergroup coordination practices, leadership, and general structural conditions in their immediate work context. Based on a statistical data evaluation, a characteristic pattern of indicator variables was uncovered, which created a "profile" of IPSS. Only by relating the reflective processes of the researchers themselves to this profile can it be argued that the understanding of the target domain was based on clearly salient and shared evidence.

However, the definition of necessary dimensions used for the quantitative survey can also be considered as a limitation of a possible holistic and unbiased understanding of the "particular new." It must be acknowledged that quantitative research is also biased by traditional operationalization and work conceptions that would only prove insufficient or less unfruitful under a more qualitative perspective on target data.

In summary, this chapter makes two main contributions to understanding metaphor research and Morgan's images by shaping the understanding of an IPSS way of organizing. First, this chapter applies Morgan's images of organization to a distinct style of value proposition with the help of the domains-interaction model. Both the case of research and the utilization of the domains-interaction model to interpret IPSS-specific quantitative data form a unique combination of applying Morgan's images to this newly emerging organizational phenomenon. This procedure proves high relevance in order to better understand the characteristics of the way of organizing in IPSS.

Second, the chapter introduces a methodological perspective that goes beyond analyzing narrative case study information. By introducing a quantitative approach of gathering and processing cross-sectional engineering data, the analysis of the target domain presented embraces a scope of possible nuances under the umbrella of an IVP style. This makes the description and understanding of an emerging organizational phenomenon less contingent on single case influences.

Finally, by introducing a new multimetaphorical lens on IPSS, this chapter aims to encourage the community to search for further in-depth applications of Morgan's and other possible images of organization to this or other fields of emerging relevance. It can be argued that this chapter supports the high relevance of Morgan's images and contributes to the development of a well-structured way in which they are applied to organizational reality. Despite the fact that they were introduced almost three decades ago, these images still serve as a fruitful and guiding cognitive framework toward an extended understanding of newly emerging contexts of organizing.

Key Terms

Discriminant analysis

Domains-interaction model

Eigenvalue

Empowerment

Generic structure

Integrated product-service systems (IPSS)

Integrating value proposition (IVP)

Integrated way of organizing (IWO)

Parallel structures

Solution-oriented value proposition

Source domain

Standardized value proposition (SVP)

Standardizing way of organizing (SWO)

Target domain

Transformational leadership

Value creation

Value proposition

References

Baines, T. S., Lightfoot, H. W., Evans, S., Neely, A., Greenough, R., Peppard, J., . . . Wilson, H. (2007). State-of-the-art in product-service systems. *Proceedings of the Institution of Mechanical Engineers, Part B: Journal of Engineering Manufacture, 221*(10), 1543–1552.

Bass, B. M., & Avolio, B. J. (1997). *Full range leadership development: Manual for the multifactor leadership questionnaire.* Palo Alto, CA: Mind Garden.

Benade, S., & Weeks, R. V. (2010). The formulation and implementation of a servitization strategy: Factors that ought to be taken into consideration. *Journal of Contemporary Management, 7*, 402–419.

Beuren, F. H., Gomes Ferreira, M. G., & Cauchick Miguel, P. A. (2013). Product-service systems: A literature review on integrated products and services. *Journal of Cleaner Production, 47*, 222–231.

Biloslavo, R., Bagnoli, C., & Rusjan Figelj, R. (2013). Managing dualities for efficiency and effectiveness of organisations. *Industrial Management & Data Systems, 113*(3), 423–442.

Boxenbaum, E., & Rouleau, L. (2011). New knowledge products as bricolage: Metaphors and scripts in organizational theory. *Academy of Management Review, 36*(2), 272–296.

Brax, S. (2005). A manufacturer becoming service provider: Challenges and a paradox. *Managing Service Quality: An International Journal, 15*(2), 142–155.

Burn, T., & Stalker, G. M. (1961). *The management of innovation.* London, England: Tavistock.

Carless, S. A., Wearing, A. J., & Mann, L. (2000). A short measure of transformational leadership. *Journal of Business and Psychology, 14*(3), 389–405.

Catoiu, I., Èšichindelean, M., & Vinerean, S. (2013). Using discriminant analysis in relationship marketing. *Annales Universitatis Apulensis Series Oeconomica, 2*(15), 727–736.

Ceci, F., & Masini, A. (2011). Balancing specialized and generic capabilities in the provision of integrated solutions. *Industrial and Corporate Change, 20*(1), 91–131.

Cornelissen, J. P. (2004). What are we playing at? Theatre, organization, and the use of metaphor. *Organization Studies, 25*(5), 705–726.

Cornelissen, J. P. (2005). Beyond compare: Metaphor in organization theory. *Academy of Management Review, 30*(4), 751–764.

Cornelissen, J. P., & Kafouros, M. (2008). Metaphors and theory building in organization theory: What determines the impact of a metaphor on theory? *British Journal of Management, 19*(4), 365–379.

Cornelissen, J. P., Kafouros, M., & Lock, A. R. (2005). Metaphorical images of organization: How organizational researchers develop and select organizational metaphors. *Human Relations, 58*(12), 1545–1578.

Cornelissen, J. P., Oswick, C., Thoger Christensen, L., & Phillips, N. (2008). Metaphor in organizational research: Context, modalities and implications for research introduction. *Organization Studies, 29*(1), 7–22.

Cova, B., & Salle, R. (2007). Introduction to the IMM special issue on "Project marketing and the marketing of solutions": A comprehensive approach to project marketing and the marketing of solutions. *Industrial Marketing Management, 36*(2), 138–146.

Da Silveira, G., Borenstein, D., & Fogliatto, F. S. (2001). Mass customization: Literature review and research directions. *International Journal of Production Economics, 72*(1), 1–13.

Davies, A., Brady, T., & Hobday, M. (2007). Organizing for solutions: Systems seller vs. systems integrator. *Industrial Marketing Management, 36*(2), 183–193.

de Brentani, U. (1991). Success factors in developing new business services. *European Journal of Marketing, 25*(2), 33–59.

Desmet, S., Van Looy, B., & Van Dierdock, R. (2003). The nature of services. In B. Van Looy, P. Gemmel, & R. Van Dierdonck (Eds.), *Services management: An integrated approach* (2nd ed, pp. 3–26). Harlow, England: Pearson Education.

Dittrich, K., Jaspers, F., van der Valk, W., & Wynstra, F. (2006). Dealing with dualities. *Industrial Marketing Management, 35*(7), 792–796.

Evans, S., Partidário, P. J., & Lambert, J. (2007). Industrialization as a key element of sustainable product-service solutions. *International Journal of Production Research, 45*(18–19), 4225–4246.

Externbrink, K., Wilkens, U., & Lienert, A. (2013). Antecedents to the successful coordination of IPS2 Networks: A dynamic capability perspective on complex work systems in the engineering sector. In Y. Shimomura & K. Kimita (Eds.), *The philosopher's stone for sustainability* (pp. 103–108). Berlin, Germany: Springer.

Fitzsimmons, J. A., & Fitzsimmons, M. J. (2008). *Services management: Operations, strategy, information technology.* London, England: McGraw-Hill.

Foropon, C., & McLachlin, R. (2013). Metaphors in operations management theory building. *International Journal of Operations & Production Management, 33*(2), 181–196.

Galbraith, J. R. (2002). Organizing to deliver solutions. *Organizational Dynamics, 31*(2), 194–207.

Garud, R., & Kotha, S. (1994). Using the brain as a metaphor to model flexible production systems. *Academy of Management Review, 19*(4), 671–698.

Gebauer, H. (2007). An investigation of antecedents for the development of customer support services in manufacturing companies. *Journal of Business-to-Business Marketing, 14*(3), 59–96.

Gebauer, H., Edvardsson, B., Gustafsson, A., & Witell, L. (2010). Match or mismatch: Strategy-structure configurations in the service business of manufacturing companies. *Journal of Service Research, 13*(2), 198–215.

Gebauer, H., & Friedli, T. (2005). Behavioural implications of the transition process from products to services. *Journal of Business & Industrial Marketing, 20*(2), 70–80.

Gebauer, H., & Fleisch, E. (2007). An investigation of the relationship between behavioral processes, motivation, investments in the service business and service revenue. *Industrial Marketing Management, 36*(3), 337–348.

Gremyr, I., Löfberg, N., & Witell, L. (2010). Service innovations in manufacturing firms. *Managing Service Quality: An International Journal, 20*(2), 161–175.

Grimm, L. G., & Yarnold, P. R. (1995). *Reading and understanding multivariate statistics.* Washington, DC: American Psychological Association.

Gummesson, E., Lusch, R. F., & Vargo, S. L. (2010). Transitioning from service management to service-dominant logic: Observations and recommendations. *International Journal of Quality and Service Sciences, 2*(1), 8–22.

Gustafsson, A., & Brax, S. (2005). A manufacturer becoming service provider: Challenges and a paradox. *Managing Service Quality: An International Journal, 15*(2), 142–155.

Håkansson, H., & Ford, D. (2002). How should companies interact in business networks? *Journal of Business Research, 55*(2), 133–139.

Heracleous, L., & Jacobs, C. D. (2008). Crafting strategy: The role of embodied metaphors. *Long Range Planning, 41*(3), 309–325.

Huberty, C. J., & Olejnik, S. (2006). *Applied MANOVA and discriminant analysis.* Hoboken, NJ: John Wiley & Sons.

Inns, D. (2002). Metaphor in the literature of organizational analysis: A preliminary taxonomy and a glimpse at a humanities-based perspective. *Organization, 9*(2), 305–330.

Kowalkowski, C. (2010). What does a service-dominant logic really mean for manufacturing firms? *CIRP Journal of Manufacturing Science and Technology, 3*(4), 285–292.

Lakoff, G. (1993). The contemporary theory of metaphor. *Metaphor and Thought, 2,* 202–251.

Martinez, V., Bastl, M., Kingston, J., & Evans, S. (2010). Challenges in transforming manufacturing organisations into product-service providers. *Journal of Manufacturing Technology Management, 21*(4), 449–469.

Meier, H., Uhlmann, E., Völker, O., Geisert, C., & Stelzer, C. (2010). Reference architecture for dynamical organization of IPS² service supply chains in the delivery phase. In *Proceedings of the 2nd CIRP IPS² Conference, Linköping* (pp. 331–338).

Mont, O. K. (2002). Clarifying the concept of product-service system. *Journal of Cleaner Production, 10*(3), 237–245.

Morgan, G. (1983). More on metaphor: Why we cannot control tropes in administrative science. *Administrative Science Quarterly, 27*(4), 601–607.

Morgan, G. (1986). *Images of organization.* Newbury Park, CA: SAGE.

Morgan, G. (2006). *Images of organization.* London, England: SAGE.

Morgan, G. (2011). Reflections on images of organization and its implications for organization and environment. *Organization & Environment, 24*(4), 459–478.

Morgeson, F. P., & Humphrey, S. E. (2006). The work design questionnaire (WDQ): Developing and validating a comprehensive measure for assessing job design and the nature of work. *Journal of Applied Psychology, 91*(6), 1321–1339.

Neely, A., Benedettini, O., & Visnjic, I. (2011). *The servitization of manufacturing: Further evidence.* Proceedings of the European Operations Management Association Conference, Cambridge, England: University of Cambridge.

Normann, R. (1991). *Service management, strategy and leadership in service business* (2nd ed.). New York, NY: John Wiley & Sons.

Nuutinen, M., & Lappalainen, I. (2012). Towards service-oriented organisational culture in manufacturing companies. *International Journal of Quality and Service Sciences, 4*(2), 137–155.

Oliva, R., & Kallenberg, R. (2003). Managing the transition from products to services. *International Journal of Service Industry Management, 14*(2), 1–10.

Oswick, C., Keenoy, T., & Grant, D. (2002). Note: Metaphor and analogical reasoning in organization theory: Beyond orthodoxy. *Academy of Management Review, 27*(2), 294–303.

Penttinen, E., & Palmer, J. (2007). Improving firm positioning through enhanced offerings and buyer-seller relationships. *Industrial Marketing Management, 36*(5), 552–564.

Roy, R., Baines, T. S., Lightfoot, H. W., Benedettini, O., & Kay, J. M. (2009). The servitization of manufacturing. *Journal of Manufacturing Technology Management, 20*(5), 547–567.

Salonen, A. (2011). Service transition strategies of industrial manufacturers. *Industrial Marketing Management, 40*(5), 683–690.

Schweitzer, E., & Aurich, J. C. (2010). Continuous improvement of industrial product-service systems. *CIRP Journal of Manufacturing Science and Technology*, *3*(2), 158–164.

Shepherd, C., & Ahmed, P. K. (2000). From product innovation to solutions innovation: A new paradigm for competitive advantage. *European Journal of Innovation Management*, *3*(2), 100–106.

Spreitzer, G. M. (1995). Psychological empowerment in the workplace: Dimensions, measurement, and validation. *Academy of Management Journal*, *38*(5), 1442–1465.

Spreitzer, G. M. (1996). Social structural characteristics of psychological empowerment. *Academy of Management Journal*, *39*(2), 483–504.

Stevens, J. P. (2002). *Applied multivariate statistics for the social sciences* (4th ed.). Mahwah, NJ: Lawrence Erlbaum.

Teece, D. J. (2007). Explicating dynamic capabilities: The nature and microfoundations of (sustainable) enterprise performance. *Strategic Management Journal, 28*(13), 1319-1350.

Tsoukas, H. (1991). The missing link: A transformational view of metaphors in organizational science. *Academy of Management Review, 16*(3), 566–585.

Tsoukas, H. (1993). Analogical reasoning and knowledge generation in organization theory. *Organization Studies, 14*(3), 323–346.

Tukker, A. (2004). Eight types of product-service system: Eight ways to sustainability? Experiences from SusProNet. *Business Strategy and the Environment, 13*(4), 246–260.

Ulaga, W., & Reinartz, W. J. (2011). Hybrid offerings: How manufacturing firms combine goods and services successfully. *Journal of Marketing, 75*(6), 5–23.

Vargo, S. L., & Lusch, R. F. (2004). Evolving to a new dominant logic for marketing. *Journal of Marketing, 68*(1), 1–17.

Vargo, S. L., & Lusch, R. F. (2008). From goods to service(s): Divergences and convergences of logics. *Industrial Marketing Management, 37*(3), 254–259.

Wilkens, U., & Gröschke, D. (2008). *Measuring the leverage effect between individual and collective competence.* Conference of the Strategic Management Society, Cologne, October 13–14, 2008.

Appendix A: Sample Structure Based on Sociodemographic Variables

Age				
≤**29**	30–39	40–49	50–59	≥60
42 (24.4%)	57 (33.1%)	42 (24.4%)	24 (14.0%)	7 (4.1%)

Education		
PhD	University/Advanced Technical College	University of Applied Science
15 (8.7 %)	151 (87.8 %)	6 (3.5%)

Work Experience (Years)							
≤**5**	6–10	11–15	16–20	21–25	26–30	≥31	Not Specified
64 (37.2%)	23 (13.4%)	19 (11.0%)	16 (9.3%)	20 (11.6%)	17 (9.9%)	11 (6.4%)	2 (1.2%)

Appendix B Three Styles of Value Propositions

Value Proposition	Combination of Products and Services (Mean Value)	Interrelatedness of Products and Services (Mean Value)	Individualization of Products and Services (Mean Value)	Frequency	Percent
1. IPSS	6.15	6.30	6.03	68	39.5
2. Standardized products and services	5.20	4.80	3.30	51	29.7
3. Customized services	2.20	2.75	5.00	52	30.2
Not specified				1	0.6
Total				172	100

Appendix C Results of the Box Test

Box-M		**23.026**
F	Approximated	1.461
	df1	15
	df2	44591.970
	Significance level	0.110

Predictors' variance and covariance were calculated for both categories of the factor considered (value proposition). Variance-covariance equality was tested by applying the Box test, which verifies the null hypothesis that the variance-covariance matrix does not differ throughout the factor categories. A significance level of 0.110 determines the acceptance of the null hypothesis.

Appendix D Computed Eigenvalue for the Discriminant Function

Function	Eigenvalue	% of Variation	Cumulated Variation	Canonical Correlation
1	0.329	100.0	100.0	0.497

For every eigenvector, there is an eigenvalue that mathematically represents a resizing of the discriminant vector and, statistically, the intensity in which the discriminant vector differentiates the factor categories (Catoiu, Èšichindelean, & Vinerean, 2013). Appendix D shows the results of eigenvalue computation. The statistical significance of the eigenvalues computed is tested through the Wilks' lambda statistic, which is based on the χ^2 distribution. Based on the significance level, this discriminant function can be taken into further consideration.

Appendix E Results of Wilks' Lambda Test

Testing of the Discriminant Function	Wilks-Lambda	Chi-Square	df	Significance Level
1	0.753	31.956	5	.000

Appendix F Summarized Results of the Discriminant Analysis (Integrated – Standardized)

Step	Variable	Wilks` Lambda	F	Standardized Canonical Coefficients
1	I find it easy to discuss problems and challenges with people outside of the organization (e.g., suppliers, customers).	0.931	8.459**	0.410
2	During daily work, I often communicate with people who are not employed at the same organization as me.	0.877	8.016**	0.455
3	Our team is very good at using experiences of other groups for our own projects.	0.839	7.253**	−0.673
4	The management inspires employees to solve problems and challenges in new ways.	0.789	7.469**	0.574
5	I usually try to learn from other people during daily work.	0.753	8.016**	0.688

After the canonical coefficients have been multiplied by the standard deviations of the predictors, the values of the standardized canonical coefficients are obtained. The table displays these values for the variables in the order of their stepwise inclusion in the analysis. The table also shows respective Wilks' lambda for each step and resulting F value and level of significance.

Appendix G Results of Classification Analysis

			Predicted Group		
		Ward Method	IPSS	Standardized	Total
Original	Number	IPSS	57	10	67
		Standardized	19	31	50
		Unclassified cases	31	19	50
	%	IPSS	85.1	14.9	100.0
		Standardized	38.0	62.0	100.0
		Unclassified cases	62.0	38.0	100.0
Cross-validated	Number	IPSS	54	13	67
		Standardized	21	29	50
	%	Integrated	80.6	19.4	100.0
		Standardized	42.0	58.0	100.0

Appendix H Sample Items of the Questionnaire

Dimension	Level (No. of Items)	Sample Items
Work Characteristics		
Organizational offering	Individual (5)	*"I work on highly individualized solutions."*
	Organization (5)	*"Our offering is made of combined and harmonized products and services."*
Job demands	Individual (14)	*"In my daily work I often communicate with people that are not employed by my organization."*
Competencies		
Dealing with complexity	Individual (11)	*"In a complex situation it is difficult for me to identify the core of the problem."*
	Team (5)	*"In our team we purposefully filter available information."*

Dimension	Level (No. of Items)	Sample Items
	Organization (5)	"In our organization we systematically analyse environmental conditions."
Self-reflection	Individual (5)	"I actively seek feedback from others in order to increase my performance."
	Team (6)	"In our team we regularly reflect on our approach to team work."
	Organization (5)	"In our organization, we regularly reflect on ways to improve our processes."
Combination	Individual (6)	"In order to develop new solutions to problems I often make use of creative approaches."
	Team (4)	"In our team we creatively use our experiences to solve new problems."
	Organization (5)	"In our organization we succeed in using existing know-how to solve new problems."
Cooperation	Individual (11)	"I usually reach consensus in conflict."
	Team (7)	"Our team succeeds in working together with external partners constructively."
	Organization (6)	"Our organization successfully enters fruitful collaborations."
Leadership and Empowerment		
Social-structural Empowerment	Not specified (10)	"I have access to the strategic information I need to do my job well."
Psychological empowerment	Not specified (12)	"I have significant autonomy in determining how I do my job."
Transformational leadership style	Not specified (7)	"My boss encourages thinking about problems in new ways and questions assumptions."
Transactional leadership style	Not specified (11)	"My boss has transparent evaluation criteria for my achievements."
Laissez-faire (inversely coded)	Not specified (3)	"My boss is always there when needed."
Self-efficacy	Individual (10)	"I can find a solution for any problem that occurs at work."

Exploring Metaphors of Leadership

Turo Virtanen

Key Learning Points

- Understand that all colorful expressions are not metaphoric.
- Know how metaphors of organization and leadership are linked to each other.
- Recognize that quantitative methods are helpful when we want to know how people relate individual metaphors to each other without intentional discretion and how these connections constitute underlying leadership culture.
- Understand that the reactions of organizational members to positive as well as negative metaphors of leadership show the nature and degree of the legitimacy of organizational leadership.
- Understand that metaphorical behavior of organizational members may contribute to both the self-understanding of individual leaders and attempts to develop the effectiveness of their leadership communication.
- Recognize that the underlying structure of organic, human relations type of leadership metaphors implies the existence of leadership duality: charismatic leadership and leadership based on solidarity.
- Know that political leadership can be distinguished conceptually from other leadership styles, but people tend to link positive political metaphors of leadership to human relations leadership and negative metaphors to bureaucratic leadership.
- Understand that analysis of metaphors helps to integrate studies of organizations and studies of leadership, because metaphors are linked to deeper understanding of order, change, and culture.

Thanks to the seminal work of Gareth Morgan (1986), metaphors and images have become common conceptual instruments in organizational research. Their use is related to the boom in organizational culture studies and qualitative methodology in the social sciences in general. The role of metaphors in the theory building of organizational research has also emerged as a research theme (Cornelissen, Kafouros, & Lock, 2005; Cornelissen, Oswick, Christensen, & Phillips 2008). Between 2001 and 2003 (Cornelissen et al., 2005), the dominant root metaphors in the articles published in 23 leading scientific journals of organization and management studies were machine (design, structure, control, size), animated being (learning, self, success, ability, knowledge, behavior), culture (culture), warfare (strategy), system (environment, fit), and linkage (network, networked), with the machine and animated being forming the overwhelming majority of the metaphors.

Weick (1989) contends that representations such as metaphors are inevitable in theory building, given the complexity of the subject matter of organization studies. Because the role of metaphors is understood to be crucial for human thinking and communication in general (Lackoff & Johnson, 1980; Ortony, 1993), it is obvious that leadership can be analyzed in relation to metaphors and that there are many metaphors in both scientific and other literature on leadership and in the practice of leadership. The main idea underlying the study of this chapter is that metaphors of organization and leadership may be linked to each other in human thinking. Metaphors of organization may differ in their assumptions about boundaries or main styles of leadership behavior and metaphors of leadership may differ in their assumptions about the organizational structures and environment in which the metaphorical leadership behaviors take place. A sort of evidence for this linkage is that in the classical study of administration (e.g., Fayol, 1916/1949; Gulick & Urwick, 1937; Weber, 1922/2013), there is no clear distinction among the concepts of organization, management, and leadership. The divergence and differentiation of research into public administration, organization, and management (and organizational) leadership studies emerged only later as part of disciplinary evolution. However, this does not prove that these fields would not share some conceptual ideas, such as those of order, direction, goals, change, motivation, group, and so forth, with partly different interpretations.

There seems to be more research on metaphors of organizations (e.g., Cornelissen et al., 2008; Grant & Oswick, 1996; Mangham & Overington, 1987; Morgan, 1986; Putnam, Phillips, & Chapman, 1996; Terry, 1997) than on metaphors of leadership (Alvesson & Spicer, 2011; Buchanan, Cladwell, Meyer, Storey, & Wainwright, 2007; Dreachslin, Kobrinski, & Passen, 1994; Grisham, 2006). This may only be apparently true because there are, for example, studies on metaphorical reasoning within the context of organizational change (Palmer & Dunford, 1996; Sementelli & Abell, 2007), organizational development (Jacobs & Heracleous, 2006), and strategic thinking (Heracleous & Jacobs, 2011) that come close to organizational leadership. Bolman and Deal (1997) use image-like expressions to frame structural, human resource, political, and symbolic aspects of leadership. In addition, there are many typologies of leaders and leadership styles that are expressed in metaphor-like terminology.

As an example, Reddin (1970) distinguishes among compromisers, developers, missionaries, and autocrats. Moreover, Hodgkinson (1983) formulates four archetypes of leaders that articulate different values, corresponding more or less to the need hierarchy of Maslow (1954) and Herzberg (1966): the careerist, the politician, the technician, and the poet. Chen and Meindl (1991) have shown how leadership is constructed with images and metaphors such as preacher, parent, father, maverick, builder, entrepreneur, Mr. Peanut, Spartan, visionary, wizard, whiz, and competitor. Fenley (1998) analyzes different styles of management of discipline using the metaphors of lion, buffalo, elephant, and zebra. Alvesson and Spicer (2011) introduce metaphors of leaders as saints, gardeners, buddies, commanders, cyborgs, and bullies. Leadership literature offers metaphors of war, game and sports, art, machine, and the religious/spiritual (Oberlechner & Mayer-Schönberger, 2003). These types of metaphors are also found in politics. Mumby (1983) discovered three principal metaphors in an analysis of political stories on television news: politics as war, as a game, and as a drama. There seems to be some overlap between the metaphors of organization, leadership, and politics; this is to be expected because all three are related to power as a social activity. The possible overlap demonstrates that metaphorical thinking may contribute to the parsimony of theoretical constructs and may provide an avenue for more informative theoretical constructs à la Occam's razor.

There are some resemblances between metaphors of organization and leadership, but there is no research about the nature of this relationship, so there are no key debates or research literature to start with. In this situation, there are two basic ways to analyze the relationship: conceptual analysis and empirical analysis. Conceptual analysis of the meanings that researchers attach to their expressive words would lead to detailed textual analysis. The conclusions would be more or less introspective speculation about intentional and nonintentional meanings that writers may have in their minds or "semiotical" meanings originating from the language itself. Of course, there are also other strategies for conceptual study. In this chapter, we have chosen an empirical approach: a survey in which organizational members use metaphorical expressions in describing the leadership in working-life organizations. The analysis of the resulting connections between hundreds of responses may show something interesting about the metaphorical thinking about leadership in an organizational context.

Need for Quantitative Analysis

Metaphorical analysis is often qualitative (e.g., David & Graham, 1997; Gibson & Zellmer-Bruhn, 2002). Brink (1993) even believes that such analysis can only be qualitative if the research is based on the data about metaphors produced by those being researched. Quantitative research of metaphors is rare (e.g., McCorkle & Gayle, 2003; Schlesinger & Lau, 2000), but it can help us to understand their descriptive nature and also contributes to the cultural analysis of leadership. What is lacking is a quantitative empirical study employing a plenitude of metaphors to describe the variation of organizational leadership in working-life organizations. What is also lacking is an understanding of how metaphors of organization relate to metaphors of leadership in the minds of organizational members. When the research design is built on using Morgan's organization metaphors as a classification and source of leadership metaphors, there is also an opportunity to observe how members of organizations actually link different leadership metaphors to each other and whether the leadership metaphors finally group together approaching the initial classification of metaphors. Because Morgan's metaphors reflect (as a big picture) the major schools of organization and management theory, the potential connections also show to what extent there is a kind of bridge between organization and leadership on a very general level of metaphorical thinking. Any evidence deriving from a large survey would be stronger than that of qualitative studies based on the analysis of a few metaphors and a small sample.

This chapter takes up this challenge. The power of metaphors is employed as a measurement instrument of leadership culture in a quantitative research design. The research is based on a larger study in which a set of leadership metaphors was constructed and used to measure leadership culture in 17 agencies of the Finnish state government. The metaphors were part of a questionnaire in which the majority of the questions were about attitudes related to superior–subordinate relations. Metaphors were included because their capability of measuring the deeply felt experience of leadership, understood as latent meaning structures of leadership, was expected to be better than ordinary questions with attitudinal assertions. Previous research on metaphors suggests that they are capable of describing the valence of leadership behavior as subordinates interpret it. This is based on the iconic sign that metaphors are capable of introducing (see below). Individual metaphors can reveal something about the positive and negative aspects of leadership culture because leadership metaphors do not tend to be neutral but rather highly descriptive in terms of valuation and emotions. The idea of bridging organization and leadership thinking was not the original objective of the survey, but its design provided an additional opportunity to explore this aspect of the power of metaphors with certain limits.

The purpose of the study is to explore the descriptive power of leadership metaphors in relation to the main schools of organization and management studies by employing a plenitude of metaphors, a large sample, and quantitative analysis. With this goal and these data, an attempt is made to answer the following research questions:

1) What are the latent meaning structures of leadership culture as measured by metaphors?
2) To what extent are these meaning structures capable of expressing the major orientations of organizational leadership as inspired by Morgan's metaphors of organization?

Before moving on to the empirical part of the study, we need to know more about the concept of metaphor. Not all colorful expressions are metaphors.

What Are Metaphors?

According to Beardsley (1972), a metaphor is a transfer in meaning both in intension and extension. "Metaphorical" is often contrasted with "literal." In every metaphor, there is a **modifier** and a subject. In the metaphor "the river of time," "river" is the modifier, "time" is the subject in the metaphor, and time, as the referent, is the subject-thing. In other words, together with the subject, the modifier creates the particular meaning of the subject-thing. One may also say that the modifier recontextualizes the subject in the metaphor.

Beardsley (1972) finds two cognitive roles for the use of metaphors outside of the aesthetic aspects that belong to rhetoric and poetics. First, metaphor extends the resources of language because it creates novel senses of words for particular purposes and occasions. Second, metaphor is condensed shorthand by which a great many properties can be attributed to an object all at once. Although metaphors are not capable of verification in the sense of logical positivism, they are intelligible, not nonsense phrases. They are similar to comparisons in which "like" or "as" has been omitted (time is like a river) but in which a particular tension is built into the comparison. This tension involves a double semantic relationship: The modifier is not to be interpreted literally, but rather it refers to something that is proposed as an iconic sign of the subject-thing (certain notable features of rivers are ascribed to time, for example, the one-dimensional directionality). The potential meanings of this iconic sign constitute a potentiality for metaphorical meaning, providing novel senses of the subject-thing. Metaphors are used in science when terms are taken from ordinary language (e.g., "field" or "force") but, in time, scientific metaphors are either reduced to literalness (dead metaphors) or replaced by technical neologisms.

Following this stream of thinking as the framework of this study, is the content of the above examples of leadership metaphors metaphorical? A sign-function arises when an expression is correlated with a content (Eco, 1976), but metaphorical sign-function is not the only function that exists. For example, "developer" sounds more **metonymical** than metaphorical. Not all of the names of leadership styles or leader types are metaphorical, but many are. The central condition is that the leadership has to be linked to familiar words, albeit with new expressions as modifiers, in order to provide a contextual source of new meanings. This means that good metaphors are "familiar words in the wrong places." There has to be enough tension to make the imagination work. On the other hand, the tension will not last forever. Some words begin to feel at home in their new environment and lose their ability to arouse novel meanings. This has effects on both the formulation of new knowledge and the possibilities for rich communication.

Many of these basic distinctions of metaphor can be found in organizational research on metaphors. In referring to previous research, Putnam et al. (1996, p. 377) characterize metaphors as "a way of seeing a thing as if it were something else" and as "a particular linguistic expression that provides a cognitive bridge between two dissimilar domains." These characterizations remind us of comparisons with meaning transfer. Furthermore, for some theorists, metaphors "link abstract constructs to concrete things," whereas for others, metaphors "tie the familiar to the unknown." These are specifications of the modifier and the subject of the metaphor. However, in the context of organizational research, there are elements in understanding metaphors that are absent in Beardsley's distinctions. Metaphors "legitimate actions, set goals, and guide behaviors" and are "constitutive in that they facilitate the creation and interpretation of social reality"—they "shape how we see and make sense of the world by orienting our perceptions, conceptualizations, and understanding of one thing in light of another" (Putnam et al., 1996, p. 377).

All of these meanings are related to the constitutive nature of metaphors, which are mostly understood in terms of social constructivism. They also apply to organizational leadership. However, the constitutive nature of metaphors may be the same as the idea of Beardsley's dead metaphors because both can be understood to be latently effective in the interpretation of situations. Dead metaphors also remind us of metonymical modes of understanding that Morgan (1996) relates to traditional science, as opposed to science that reveals the metaphors behind the metonymical constructs. It is the constitutive nature of metaphors that makes them instrumental in exploring cultural aspects of leadership.

The Formulation of Leadership Metaphors and Data Generation

Morgan's (1986) metaphors of organization were used as a source for developing leadership metaphors. The goal was to use the most concrete and familiar everyday words of ordinary language as modifiers for leadership. Five metaphors of organization were used as the source of inspiration and six metaphors of leadership were formulated for each of them. Not all metaphors were used because not all of them were considered easily applicable to ideas of leadership and there were space limitations within the questionnaire. Culture, psychic prison, flux and transformation, and domination were left out.

The metaphors of leadership were not deduced mechanically from Morgan's textual descriptions, but certain key ideas related to each metaphor of organization were included in the formulation of leadership metaphors. Machine-like or **bureaucratic leadership** refers to centrality of rules, hierarchical power, and active supervision. Organism-like or **human relations leadership** is about social relationships that are actively nurtured and used (i.e., about group dynamics but not environment). **Political leadership** is built around power: competing for positions, orthodox ideologies, agitation, negotiations, and victories. Brains-like or **network leadership** is concentrated on connections that make leadership dynamic, being dependent on other people and unexpected circumstances. However, laissez-faire metaphors were also included, although they are not based on Morgan's metaphors of organization. This was justified by the fact that laissez-faire is a classical style of leadership (Lewin, Lippitt, & White, 1939) and, in a way, an antithesis of creating order, a key idea behind the concept of organization. **Laissez-faire leadership** refers to an absence of active leadership. It may be ignorance, neglect, laziness, even innocence, at best reactive but definitely not proactive. Without laissez-faire metaphors, organizational leadership would not have covered an essential part of organizational practice.

The actual names of the metaphors of leadership were based on the key ideas (above) and the linguistic imagination of the author inspired by the meaning-generating power of Morgan's metaphors. In this way, the formulation relied on the generative nature of the very concept of metaphor. The philosophical basis for this comes from Popper's (1968) general instruction to create brave conjectures in the formulation of hypotheses. Falsifiability and the passing of empirical tests is a sufficient condition for their scientific quality.

The survey provided an opportunity for testing whether the respondents' reactions to 30 different metaphors of leadership can produce the original five groups, each based on a different metaphor of organization, and with laissez-faire leadership as the sixth group. The metaphors developed are presented in Table 7.1 by their assumed link to organizational leadership styles based on metaphors of organization. In fact, the grouping constitutes a hypothesis about the most obvious connections of different metaphors in people's minds. The metaphors in Table 7.1 have been translated from Finnish into English. Literal translation, even if possible, is certainly incomplete with metaphors because they are bound to their linguistic culture.

TABLE 7.1 ● Leadership Metaphors by Their Assumed Links to Leadership Styles and Morgan's Metaphors of Organization	
Metaphors (in the questionnaire, in alphabetical order, without grouping by style)	**Description given in the questionnaire**
Laissez-faire	
Draught animal	Lugs a heavy load unwillingly, without help.
Driftwood	Floats with the tide, no will of his or her own.
Figurehead	Needed only for external visibility.
Fixture	Always there, but doesn't get a move on anything.
Hermit	Seeks solitude, shuns subordinates.
Monologist	Holds on speaking even when no one is listening.
Bureaucratic (Machine)	
Border guard	Watches over his or her territory, "Don't cross the border!"
Careerist	His or her own career is all that matters.
Prosecutor	Looks for errors and violations everywhere, trusts nobody.
Sergeant-major	"I'm the boss here!"
Spy	Snoops around, lurks, covers up his or her tracks.
Squire	Assumes respect, arouses fear.
Human Relations (Organism)	
Coach	Encourages, trains, corrects.
Confessor	Listens to your sorrows, confidentially.

Metaphors (in the questionnaire, in alphabetical order, without grouping by style)	Description given in the questionnaire
Gardener	Nurtures everyone, supports the growth of all of us.
Goodwill ambassador	Warm, empathetic, finds no one evil.
Master of ceremonies	Creates the right atmosphere, entertains, keeps company.
Theater producer	Finds an important role for everyone, even many roles.
Political (Political System)	
Arbitrator	Calms down the surfs, settles the situation.
Counsel	Helps you when people keep charging you.
Preacher	Leads the way to the future, agitates.
Sectarian fundamentalist	Does not approve of heretics.
Super salesman	Capable of making people believe anything.
War hero	Victorious and prestigious fighter.
Network (Brains)	
Addicted visitor	Makes new acquaintances everywhere, knows everybody.
Adventurer	Bounces here and there, takes risks.
Fixer	Has a good grasp of the backstage networking.
Magician	Copes with impossible situations.
Rusher	Hustles and bustles around everything, sometimes hitting on new solutions.
Travel guide	Conducts the party to new landscapes.

Table 7.1 also includes brief definitions of the metaphors. Definitions were considered necessary because the author's previous research had revealed that, in interview situations, metaphors can be understood in so many ways that the analysis of voluminous data with survey methodology is not valid without specifying meanings to some extent. A qualitative methodology would have enabled the search for different interpretations of one and the same metaphor, a valuable outcome if the goal is to find different interpretations. In this study, the goal was to look for the interaction of different metaphors in a larger population, which is less valid if the interpretations of one and the same metaphor vary to a great extent. The definitions of metaphors were brief because their role was only to show the

main perspective that was referred to (e.g., the positive meanings of gardener, not the negative ones). The purpose was not the closure of the signification process but rather to give it a start.

The data were collected from a sample from 17 public agencies with the Finnish state government in 1997. The agencies included both relatively large organizations (the number of staff varying from 195 to 8,228) and relatively small organizations (50 to 129 staff members). The selection criteria of the agencies were organizational size (measured by the number of staff) and the nature of their organizational output (measured by standardization of output following a typology of main outputs: goods, norms, knowledge, and customer service). The sample is meant to be theoretically, not statistically, representative (there was no probability sampling), covering different contexts of leadership in public organizations. The assumption was that leadership differs partly due to the size of the organization and partly due to the nature of its organizational work. The nature of organizational work is dependent on the nature of its output. For example, leadership in producing knowledge is different from leadership in producing goods. Consequently, the statistical significance is tested only to control random effects, not to make generalizations about the population of Finnish public servants. The research is of more of an exploratory and descriptive nature. Can public servants actually reproduce the assumed organizational–metaphorical links of leadership metaphors generated by the author's theoretical imagination à la Popper?

A self-administered questionnaire was sent to the whole staff of the 17 public agencies in the Finnish state government. Each respondent received a personal letter through the internal mail (for more details on the research procedure, see Virtanen, 1997). The 30 metaphors were not presented to respondents as grouped by organizational metaphor, but rather were mixed in alphabetical order. All respondents were also asked to use all 30 metaphors (see the relevant part of the questionnaire in Appendix A). The study analyzes the respondents' answers to a closed question that was composed of 30 leadership metaphors, each defined in a few words. Respondents were asked to describe the leadership behavior of two superiors within their agency, Superior A and Superior B, by circling one figure between 1 and 7, with 1 indicating that the metaphor describes the superior very badly or not at all, 7 indicating that the metaphor describes the superior very well, and 4 indicating undecided. Either A or B was to be the respondent's closest superior, but the respondents were asked not to identify which. The reason for this formulation was to encourage respondents to give honest answers. In this way, researchers were unable to say which assessment was related to which superior. On the level of agency, the answers were balanced because the profiles of Superiors A and B were nearly the same in each agency. The similarity of the profiles is probably based on a more or less random selection of A or B to represent one's closest superior. The analysis is based on the responses to questions about Superior A. A total of 1,932 respondents answered all items concerning Superior A (1,808 respondents answered all items concerning both Superiors A and B), with the total response rate to the survey being 50% (varying between 35% and 80% by agency). A total of 24.1% of respondents held a position as a superior (on different organizational levels) and 75.9% were employees with no subordinates.

Overview of the Distribution of Metaphors

Metaphors that are most often considered descriptive of superiors in group A (as measured by the mean of each metaphor shown in Figure 7.1) are "fixer" (N), "confessor" (H), "coach" (H), "arbitrator" (P), "counsel" (P), and "addicted visitor" (N). Letters in parentheses refer to the assumed (hypothetical) leadership style of the metaphor as follows: B = bureaucratic, H = human relations, L = laissez-faire, N = network, and P = political. The metaphors that are least often considered descriptive are "prosecutor" (B), "fixture" (L), "hermit" (L), "driftwood" (L), and "draught animal" (L). The general built-in tone of these metaphors implies that the top descriptive metaphors are positive, whereas the bottom descriptive metaphors are negative. The most obvious conclusion is that respondents are more often contented with their superiors than discontented. The positive/negative ratio also seems to hold in each assumed leadership style: the most common metaphor is more positive than the least common (in network style, the distinction is not so clear). In the assumed bureaucratic leadership style, "border guard" is the most common and "prosecutor" is the least common. "Confessor" is the most common in the assumed human relations style and "master of the ceremonies" is the least common. In the assumed network style, the most prevalent metaphor is "fixer" and the least prevalent is "theater producer." "Arbitrator" is the most common and "super salesman" is the least common in the assumed style of political leadership. In the laissez-faire style, "monologist" is in the top position, whereas "fixture" is at the bottom.

If we compare the distribution of metaphors in group A with the distribution of metaphors in group B, we find that many group B metaphors are more common than group A metaphors and they tend to be mostly negative. It seems that respondents often chose Superior B to represent a "bad leader" and Superior A a "good leader." This reminds us of the dark side of metaphors (Alvesson & Spicer, 2011). Most differences between the values of the A and B pairs of metaphors are statistically significant. Apparently, respondents chose A and B to be relatively distant rather than close to each other, creating a situation of contrasting images.

Considering the assumed links of leadership metaphors to metaphors of organization (Table 7.1), the metaphor of organism (or human relations style) seems to be more prevalent in terms of its frequency (Figure 7.1) than the others, with machine (or bureaucratic style) taking the last position before laissez-faire style (not being based on metaphors of organization). However, metaphors assumed to be connected to brains (network style) and political system (political style) are, in relative terms, more scattered in terms of their frequencies. The distribution of leadership metaphors indicates that there are some tighter and looser links between leadership metaphors and their assumed relationships with metaphors of organization. Therefore, we need additional tools to go deeper into the interactions between different leadership metaphors.

The Latent Meaning Structures of Leadership Culture

Metaphors can be used to describe the leadership culture of agencies, but the variation also reveals how people can link different metaphors together and indicate the

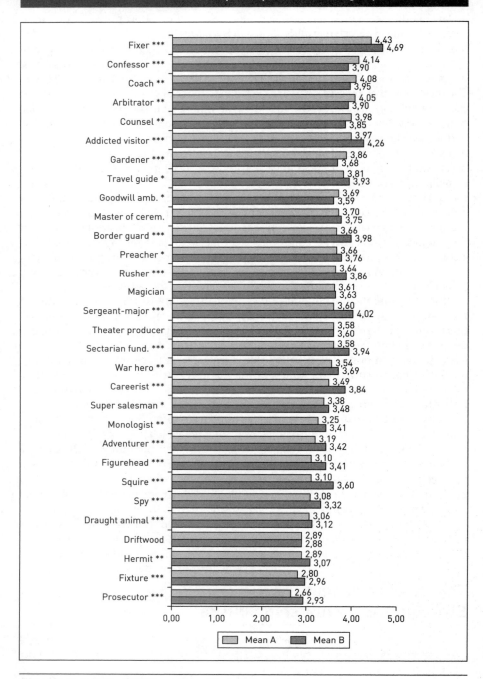

FIGURE 7.1 ● Means of Leadership Metaphors Describing Superiors A and B

*** p<.001, ** p<.01, * p<.05 Wilcoxon Signed Ranks Test; N=1,808.

existence of certain metaphorical styles of leadership on a more general level. For this purpose, it is interesting to see what the latent relationships are between the variables. Latent relationships can be interpreted as latent meaning structures. They "are there" even if no one intends to relate the meanings of different metaphors to each other in certain ways. Being latent, they are more culture like than manifest or outspoken meanings of single metaphors. The assessed importance of the metaphors reflects the meaning structures of leadership culture. In this sense, the latent meaning structures may reflect the assumed "meta-metaphors" originating from Morgan's (1986) seminal work. **Meta-metaphors** are metaphors of metaphors. For example, machine can be understood as a meta-metaphor of leadership metaphors that constitute bureaucratic leadership culture.

When we talk about leadership culture based on metaphorical meaning structures latently shared by members of organization, the concept of culture may be interpreted along the lines of Morgan's (1986) metaphor of culture. He also talks about leadership styles in the context of organization as culture. However, we are not interested in single organizational cultures in this study, although the data of metaphors can be used for comparing the cultures of the 17 agencies involved in the study. Our focus is on the latent relationships between leadership metaphors and how the shared nature of these relationships refers to broader metaphorical meanings of organization. The shared nature of these meanings is understood here as a cultural construct because the latent meanings are something the members of organizations (respondents) do not choose intentionally. Furthermore, as noted earlier, Morgan's metaphor of culture was not used in the generation of the metaphors of leadership.

A common technique for analyzing these kinds of latent relationships between leadership metaphors is factor analysis, which reduces the variation of 30 metaphors to a few dimensions. The metaphors that belong together constitute their own factor to the extent that they are independent of other metaphors. The interpretation of factors is based only on the researcher's theoretical sensitivity. Factor analysis with Varimax rotation produces the factor matrix shown in Table 7.2. Principal component analysis was used as a factor extraction method to form uncorrelated linear combinations of the observed variables.

Four factors result without specifying the number of factors (if the minimum eigenvalue, the amount of variance in the original pool of variables explained by the factor, is set to 1, as is customary). The extraction of five factors creates a factor structure in which only two variables have relatively high loadings with the fifth factor. The interpretation of the four-factor solution is quite easy. The fourth factor is clearly the factor of laissez-faire leadership. Five of the six metaphors in the assumed style of laissez-faire leadership belong to this factor. The third factor reflects the network orientation (inspired by the metaphor of brains): four of the six network metaphors have high loadings and "master of ceremonies," assumed to be related to human relations (inspired by the metaphor of organism), is the fifth variable. Entertaining and keeping company in the context of ceremonies is probably seen to have more in common with "connections" than with "group." The second factor has all six metaphors from the assumed bureaucratic style (inspired by the metaphor of machine), one from political style (inspired by the metaphor of political system), and one from human relations style (with negative loading, "goodwill

TABLE 7.2 ● Varimax Rotated Factor Matrix Based on the Correlations Among Leadership Metaphors

	Factor 1	Factor 2	Factor 3	Factor 4
Human relations (Organism)				
H – Coach	**.71**	−.33	−.03	−.22
N – Magician	**.71**	−.04	.10	−.24
H – Gardener	**.70**	−.45	−.03	−.14
P – War hero	**.67**	.18	.09	−.29
P – Counsel	**.65**	−.38	−.08	−.13
P – Preacher	**.65**	−.11	.29	−.27
H – Confessor	**.63**	−.45	−.10	.03
H – Theater producer	**.63**	−.02	.29	−.02
P – Arbitrator	**.63**	−.50	−.13	.03
N – Travel guide	**.56**	−.13	.38	−.27
P – Super salesman	**.51**	.14	.45	−.14
Bureaucratic (Machine)				
B – Sergeant-major	−.12	**.82**	.12	.06
B – Squire	.01	**.81**	.08	.01
B – Border guard	−.08	**.71**	.03	.21
B – Prosecutor	−.24	**.71**	.12	.25
P – Sectarian fundam.	−.11	**.64**	.18	.18
H – Goodwill amb.	.44	**−.56**	.01	.20
B – Spy	−.18	**.56**	.27	.33
B – Careerist	−.34	**.51**	.30	.37
L – Monologist	−.19	**.45**	.32	.34
Network (Brains)				
N – Addicted visitor	.09	.09	**.71**	.03
N – Rusher	−.01	.17	**.71**	.04

	Factor 1	Factor 2	Factor 3	Factor 4
N – Adventurer	.03	.22	*.69*	.06
H – Master of cerem.	.39	−.21	*.56*	−.04
N – Fixer	.14	.27	*.46*	−.14
Laissez-faire				
L – Driftwood	−.30	−.09	.08	*.78*
L – Fixture	−.26	.10	−.04	*.74*
L – Draught animal	−.01	.29	−.14	*.64*
L – Hermit	−.17	.35	−.27	*.53*
L – Figurehead	−.10	.31	.31	*.52*

Factor	Eigenvalue	% of Var.	Cum %
1	8.97	29.9	29.9
2	4.46	14.9	44.7
3	2.02	6.7	51.5
4	1.50	5.0	56.4

Note: Metaphors are marked by their assumed link to leadership styles and metaphors of organization in the following way: B = Bureaucratic (machine), H = Human relations (organism), L = Laissez-faire, N = Network (brains), P = Political (political system).

ambassador" consequently becoming "badwill ambassador"). There is clearly a negative tone built into this factor resulting from the respondents' tendency to link these metaphors together.

In the first factor, the strongest loadings are produced by five political metaphors, four human relations metaphors, and two network metaphors (see Table 7.2). The tone reflected by these metaphors is positive, oriented more to human relations than to politics. All of this seems to imply that political leadership style has no identity in the minds of the respondents: The positive elements of the assumed political style seem to belong to human relations and the negative elements to the bureaucratic dimension. The metaphors of the assumed bureaucratic style all prove to be negative, whereas most metaphors of the assumed political style prove to be positive. This may be a mistake in the generation of the metaphors. On the other hand, it may imply that the identity of political style in leadership is genuinely obscure. Positive political style overlaps human relations style and negative political style overlaps bureaucratic style. When positive political style is understood as legitimate power, a distinction between human relations style and political style is probably almost impossible in the everyday signification of leadership activities.

Factor analysis leads us to conclude that only four dimensions in leadership culture are relatively independent. If we have five styles of leadership in theory or in the intended behavior of leaders and in the reactions of their followers, then people can "truly" make a difference only between four styles. The latent styles would be latent meaning structures of leadership. As latent regularities, they constitute the crucial meaning structures of leadership and function as latent frameworks of everyday interpretation of superior–subordinate relations. However, we should not rely on only one technique of data analysis. Multidimensional scaling (MDS) and hierarchical cluster analysis (HCA) are also useful whenever there is a need to find a structure in voluminous quantitative data.

MDS is a technique in which the locations of objects are estimated from matrices of distances or similarities between pairs of objects (Kruskall & Wish, 1986). In this case, the objects are leadership metaphors. There are different methods for measuring the distances between the objects, but the computation of Euclidean distance is perhaps the most common. Euclidean distance refers to a dissimilarity or distance measure for continuous data. The difference between two items is the square root of the sum of the squared differences in values for each variable. A badness-of-fit measure used in multidimensional scaling is s-stress. A value of 0 indicates perfect fit and 1 indicates complete lack of fit. A value below 0.200 is normally considered acceptable. s-stress represents the square root of the differences between the optimally transformed data and the squared distances as a proportion of the total sum of squares.

In Figure 7.2, an MDS plot of leadership metaphors is shown. The distances are computed between pairs of variables in a matrix of 30 × 30 metaphors. The mutual location of metaphors reflects how far or close they are to each other in the same way that towns are shown on a map. The analyst can determine the number of dimensions, but more than two or three dimensions is usually beyond fruitful theoretical interpretation.

The dimensions have to be interpreted by the analyst. In this case, there are two dimensions that are interpreted as the *strength of power orientation* and *formal orientation* between superior and subordinates. If the power and formal orientations are strong, then a suitable interpretation of the metaphors of this quadrant is bureaucratic culture or machine metaphor. The opposite of this is human relations culture or metaphor of organism: Both power orientation and formal orientation are weak. If power orientation is weak but formal orientation is strong, then a laissez-faire culture is present. The opposite of this is network culture or the metaphor of brains, in which power orientation is strong but formal orientation is weak.

The locations of metaphors clearly reflect the factor loadings of different metaphors in the factor analysis. The four metaphors of laissez-faire quadrants are the same as the key variables of factor four. "Prosecutor" is closer to the quadrant of bureaucratic culture than that of laissez-faire culture. The borders of the quadrants do not mean either/or distinctions because the scales of the axes are optional; their modification does not change the proportions of the distances, as is the case with

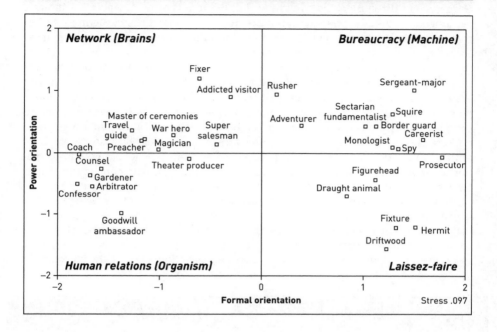

FIGURE 7.2 ● An Interpretation of a Multidimensional Scaling Plot of Leadership Meta-Euclidean Distance

geographical maps. With the exception of "adventurer" and "rusher" in the quadrant of bureaucratic culture and the "badwill ambassador" in factor two, the quadrant and the factor include the same metaphors. The metaphors in the quadrants of network culture and human relations culture come rather close to each other. The composition of factors one and three does not correspond directly to those of the two quadrants even though they are similar. However, hierarchical cluster analysis (HCA) seems to be capable of making the variation more understandable.

HCA is a procedure that attempts to identify relatively homogeneous groups of cases (or variables) based on selected characteristics using an algorithm that starts with each case (or variable) in a separate cluster and combines clusters until only one is left (Aldenderfer & Blashfield, 1987). There are different cluster methods, of which the between-groups linkage method is used here. It combines clusters to minimize the average distance between all pairs of items in which one member of the pair is from each of the clusters. This method uses information about all pairs of distances, not just the nearest or the farthest. Also here, the Euclidean distance is used to measure the difference between two items and, in clustering, distances are computed between variables, not cases, because we are interested in the differences in metaphors, not the differences in individual respondents. HCA is used here only to make the result of MDS more crystallized. HCA is normally used in conjunction with other procedures because different cluster algorithms produce different results and there are no rules for how many clusters we should accept. Theoretical sensitivity comes into the picture once again.

Figure 7.3 shows the previous MDS plot with five circles of metaphors. These circles represent the clusters that we can find in the results of HCA. Figure 7.4 shows a dendrogram, a visual representation of the steps in a hierarchical clustering solution that shows the clusters being combined and the values of the distance coefficients at each step. Connected vertical lines designate joined cases. The dendrogram rescales the actual distances to numbers between 0 and 25, preserving the ratio of the distances between steps. The circles of Figure 7.3 can be found in the dendrogram. The laissez-faire and bureaucratic clusters are easy to find, but what was previously interpreted either as network culture or human relations culture now seems to be more complex. There are actually three clusters, from which one can be interpreted as a network cluster, one as a charismatic cluster, and one as a solidarity cluster. Metaphors of the charismatic cluster are clearly more related to characteristics of individual superiority (Bryman, 1992) than those of the solidarity cluster. The latter are, in turn, more clearly related to reactions to "bottom-up" processes generated by group dynamics.

The clusters of charisma and solidarity are new in the sense that they were not anticipated during the generation of metaphors. Dimensions of charismatic behavior or group maintenance were not consciously present. Charismatic cluster and solidarity cluster are combined in the later step of the clustering process. This cluster can easily be interpreted as a human relations cluster. In this way, there are, again, four clusters: the bureaucratic

FIGURE 7.3 ● An Interpretation of a Multidimensional Scaling Plot and Clusters of Leadership Euclidean Distance

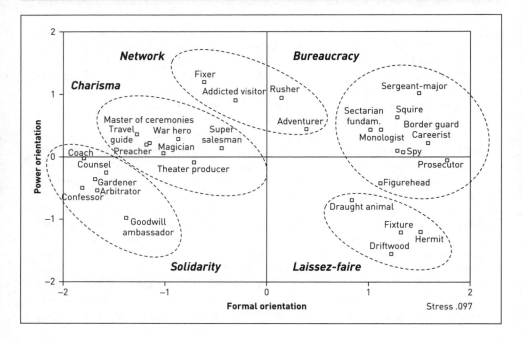

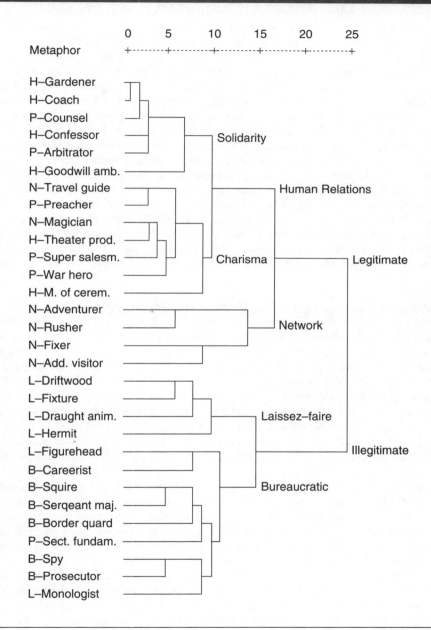

FIGURE 7.4 ● Dendrogram of Leadership Metaphors and the Interpretation of Clusters (Average Linkage Between Groups)

Note: Metaphors are marked by their assumed link to leadership styles and metaphors of organization in the following way: B = Bureaucratic (machine), H = Human relations (organism), L = Laissez-faire, N = Network (brains), P = Political (political system).

cluster, the laissez-faire cluster, the network cluster, and the human relations cluster. When these clusters are understood as latent meaning structures, then the new result compared with the results of factor analysis and MDS is that the meaning structure of human relations derives basically from the meanings of charisma and solidarity.

The final step of clustering produces two clusters, one reflecting a positive and one a negative tone of leadership. They can be called "good leadership" and "bad leadership" or, as is done here, legitimate leadership and illegitimate leadership. The concept of legitimacy is used because good and bad leadership may also refer to effectiveness of leadership, which is not at stake here. Both legitimate and illegitimate leadership can be effective, albeit not necessarily equally. If we believe in the contingency theory of leadership (starting from Fiedler, 1964), then illegitimate leadership, which actually equates to the nonexistence of leadership and the existence of illegitimate management, can also be effective in some situations if management is able to maintain subordinates' compliance to managerial norms. The basic rupture of leadership culture in superior and subordinate relations seems to be between bureaucratic culture and laissez-faire culture on the one hand and between network culture and human relations culture on the other. To understand the logic behind this rupture, we have to look more closely at these clusters of culture. However, it is surprising that the covariation of metaphors fits so well with the basic distinctions made between schools of scholarly thought about metaphors of organization even though the assumed links to leadership styles proved to be partly wrong.

Results Compared With Previous Research

Since the 1990s, a few empirical studies have been made of metaphors or images of leadership or management. For example, Gaziel (2003) employed Bolman and Deal's (1984) model and identified the corresponding four different metaphorical ways used by school principals in describing the workings of their organizations: the structural model (organizations as machines), the human resource model (organizations as organisms), the political model (organizations as political systems), and the symbolic model (organizations as cultural patterns and clusters of myths and symbols). In other studies (e.g., David & Graham, 1997; Fenley, 1998; Gibson & Zellmer-Bruhn, 2002; McGorkle & Gayle, 2003), the scope and approach are too different for meaningful comparison.

Bolman and Deal (1997) reframe leadership by resorting to the same four frames with which they frame organizations. The authors use images in describing the dimensions of leadership, but they do not actually base their study on metaphors. Neither do the images come from empirical studies. In any case, some images bear resemblance to the four factors found in our research, which provides an opportunity to assess and learn from Bolman and Deal's distinctions.

The frame of human resource leadership has the most striking overlap as "catalyst" and "servant" with processes of supporting empowerment that are close to metaphors of human relations in our study. However, in our study, war hero, counsel, preacher, arbitrator, and super salesman have the strongest loadings on the human resource factor, although we assumed them to be part of the political factor. These metaphors have quite a strong resemblance with "advocate" and "negotiator," which belong to Bolman and Deal's frame of political leadership. Although our empirical study could not retain the assumed political style, the question is whether a corresponding study based on Bolman and Deal's model would retain it in empirical tests. Gaziel's (2003) study shows that political and human resource orientations can form factors of their own, but the research design is different. Quantitative studies of the metaphorical behavior of members of an organization may not retain all theoretical distinctions based on images or metaphors.

Human resource and political leadership can be distinguished theoretically, but our study implies that people may not be able to distinguish between the positive elements of human resource and political leadership. Our study does not systematically differentiate between positive and negative (or effective and ineffective) metaphors of each leadership style. Empirically at least, as perceived by the respondents in our study, most negatively toned metaphors clump with bureaucratic and laissez-faire leadership (see Table 7.2). These metaphors overlap with the meanings of abdication, manipulation, and fraud, the ineffective side of the political frame in Bolman and Deal's model. There is also overlap with management by detail and fiat and "petty tyrant," ineffective contents of the structural leadership, as well as the fanatic and mirage of the ineffective sides of the symbolic frame.

The results of the factor analysis and HCA imply that people are able to distinguish between at least two negative styles: bureaucratic leadership and laissez-faire leadership. The analyst and architect with the processes of analysis and design, characteristic of the effective leadership in the structural frame of Bolman and Deal's model, do not correspond to any metaphors in our study. Our list of metaphors clearly lacks these kinds of meanings. In this respect, the generation of metaphors may be considered flawed: in our study, there are no metaphors for rational calculation, analysis, or design. However, these are more related to management than to leadership, which is the focus of this chapter.

Conclusions

Metaphors of leadership are strong instruments for describing the culture of leadership in organizations. Their descriptive power is based on their inherently evaluative content. Single metaphors can illustrate many dimensions of culture and they are an efficient communication tool. In the data for this study, the metaphors of "fixer," "confessor," "coach," "arbitrator," "counsel," and "addicted visitor" were the most common, whereas the metaphors of "prosecutor," "fixture," "hermit," "driftwood," and "draught animal" were the least common. The top descriptive metaphors have a tone of positive meaning and the bottom ones have a tone of negative meaning, simply in the sense of how these words sound in connection to leadership. The structure of the latent relationships of metaphor implies that metaphors are capable of expressing orientations of organizational leadership, with the exception of political style.

The qualitative analysis of single metaphors or their latent relationships can reveal many dimensions of leadership culture, but such analysis is not capable of describing leadership culture in a large population of organizations. Quantitative analysis of a set of metaphors enables efficient procedures for the specification of the latent relationships among metaphors even when the number of cases and metaphors is voluminous. The latent relationships can be understood as meaning structures of leadership culture that affect the interpretation of everyday actions between superiors and subordinates. The results show that all of the assumed five leadership styles inspired by Morgan's (1986) metaphors of organization, except the political style, could be retained in the analysis of the data. The mere fact that this took place is somewhat surprising and needs an explanation, which is, however, quite difficult to offer. Almost all of the metaphors of the assumed political leadership style (Morgan's metaphor of political system) proved to belong to the latent meaning structure of human relations (Morgan's organism), with only one belonging to the bureaucratic meaning structure of leadership (Morgan's machine). It seems that the tone of the power-related metaphors was so positive in the minds of respondents that they were unable to make the expected distinctions. This implies that there is no identity for political leadership in organizations if both the positive and negative aspects of power are upheld. In this sense, Morgan's distinction between metaphors of political system and domination is understandable and is also supported by our study.

Closer analysis of the meaning structure of human relations reveals that the structure is produced by two clusters of metaphors that can be called clusters of charismatic leadership and solidarity leadership. HCA indicates that laissez-faire leadership and bureaucratic leadership can be understood to reflect the meanings of illegitimate leadership. Human relations leadership proves to be part of the meanings of legitimate leadership, but network leadership is ambivalent. It is related to both but is closer to legitimate leadership. The respondents' reactions to leadership metaphors indicate that it might be interesting to also conduct empirical research on the legitimacy of different metaphors of organization among the members of organizations.

For adequate measurement of different aspects of organizational leadership, one might think that each orientation or style of leadership should include both positive and negative metaphors. However, based on the results of this study, respondents' latent meaning structures seem to keep positive and negative elements as separate factors. This leads us to a more general conclusion: A single metaphor of leadership cannot have a strong loading with both a positive and a negative factor (representing a meta-metaphor) in a large sample of respondents. Perhaps metaphorical meanings tend to be either/or. Metaphors may seem to generate meanings without any control, but not without any "causal" background. For example, depending on one's personal experiences related to garden, the metaphor of gardener may launch meanings of creation and nurture of natural beauty or elimination of the "wrong" plants while weeding flower beds. This uncontrollability may be true only about the first emerging meanings because metaphorical thinking can also be analytic, being based on contemplation of different emerging meanings and following a path of reasoning chosen beforehand. The flow of everyday organizational life may be strongly affected by leadership metaphors if no moments of contemplation occur. Behavior generated by the use of metaphors in organizational and leadership communication opens an avenue for research into metaphorical behavior related to organizations and leadership.

Although studies of organizational symbolism were frequent during the 1980s and 1990s (e.g., Pondy, Frost, Morgan, & Dandridge, 1983; and later writers) and symbolic or cultural leadership (e.g., Deal & Kennedy, 1982; Sergiovanni, 1984; and later writers) is a well-known area of research and consultation, the role of metaphors, qualitatively different from those of material artifacts as symbols, has not been given sufficient attention in the study of organizational leadership. Deeper understanding of meta-phorical behavior may contribute both to the self-understanding of individual leaders and attempts to develop the effectiveness of their leadership communication operat-ing more and more over digital networks. This also includes the metaphorical role of images (still or in motion) in leadership communication. The role of metaphors can easily be extended to visual identity management and brand management (e.g., Grunig, 1993; Wheeler, 2006), but leadership metaphors may cover only a minor part of that type of metaphorical communication.

All in all, the latent regularities of respondents' reactions to numerous leadership metaphors inspired by Morgan's (1986) metaphors of organization show that leader-ship metaphors and metaphors of organization have interesting commonalities. This indicates the existence of a dormant bridge between organization theory and leader-ship theory on the level of metaphors—a challenge for further research. There is a need for original research, especially on the side of management studies that has been characterized (Alvesson & Sandberg, 2013) as concentrating on "incremental" and "gap-spotting" research without new theoretical openings. Utilization of meta-phors may contribute to the theoretical development of leadership and management studies and build links to organizational research, which has a longer history in metaphorical understanding of organizational phenomena. Overlapping areas are, for example, concepts and phenomena of order, direction, and change because they are created, maintained, and transformed by interactive mechanisms of organiza-tion, management, and leadership. Constructing convergent bonds between streams of research is working against the "natural law" of diversification in the evolution of academic research. Perhaps metaphors can play a role there, along the lines of Weick's (1989) idea of the inevitable role of metaphors in theory building.

Key Terms

Bureaucratic leadership	Metonymy
Human relations leadership	Modifier
Laissez-faire leadership	Network leadership
Meta-metaphor	Political leadership
Metonymical	

References

Aldenderfer, M. S., & Blashfield, R. K. (1987). *Cluster analysis*. Beverly Hills, CA: Sage.

Alvesson, M., & Sandberg, J. (2013). Has management studies lost its way? Ideas for more imaginative and innovative research. *Journal of Management Studies*, *50*(1), 128–151.

Alvesson, M., & Spicer, A. (Eds.). (2011). *Metaphors we lead by: Understanding leadership in the real world.* New York, NY: Routledge.

Beardsley, M. C. (1972). Metaphor. In P. Edwards (Ed.), *The encyclopedia of philosophy* (Vol. 5, pp. 284–289). New York, NY: Macmillan.

Bolman, L. G., & Deal, T. E. (1984). *Modern approaches to understanding and managing organizations.* San Francisco, CA: Jossey-Bass.

Bolman, L. G., & Deal, T. E. (1997). *Reframing organization: Artistry, choice, and leadership* (2nd ed.). San Francisco, CA: Jossey-Bass.

Brink, T. L. (1993). Metaphor as data in the study of organizations. *Journal of Management Inquiry, 2*(4), 366–371.

Bryman, A. (1992). *Charisma and leadership in organizations.* London, England: Sage.

Buchanan, D., Cladwell, R., Meyer, J., Storey, J., & Wainwright, C. (2007). Leadership transmission: A muddled metaphor? *Journal of Health Organization and Management, 21*(3), 246–258.

Chen, C. C., & Meindl, J. R. (1991). The construction of leadership images in the popular press: The case of Donald Burr and People Express. *Administrative Science Quarterly, 36*(4), 521–551.

Cornelissen, J. P., Kafouros, M., & Lock, A. R. (2005). Metaphorical images of organization: How organizational researchers develop and select organizational metaphors. *Human Relation, 58*(12), 1545–1578.

Cornelissen, J. P., Oswick, C., Christensen, L. T., & Phillips, N. (2008). Metaphor in organizational research: Context, modalities and implications for research—Introduction. *Organization Studies, 29*(7), 7–22.

David, C., & Graham, M. B. (1997). Conflicting values: Team management portrayed in epic metaphors. *Journal of Business and Technical Communication, 11*(1), 24–48.

Deal, T. E., & Kennedy, A. A. (1982). *Corporate cultures: The rites and rituals of corporate life.* Reading, MA: Addison-Wesley.

Dreachslin, J. L., Kobrinski, E. J., & Passen, A. J. (1994). The boundary path of exchange: A new metaphor for leadership. *Leadership & Organization Development Journal, 15*(6), 16–23.

Eco, U. (1976). *A theory of semiotics.* Bloomington, IN: Indiana University Press.

Fayol, H. (1949). General and industrial management (C. Storrs, Trans). London, England: Sir Isaac Pitman & Sons. (Original work published in French 1916)

Fenley, A. (1998). Models, styles and metaphors: Understanding the management of discipline. *Employee Relations, 20*(4), 349–364.

Fiedler, F. E. (1964). A contingency model and leader effectiveness. In L. Berkowitz (Ed.), *Advances in experimental social psychology* (Vol. 1, pp. 149–190). New York, NY: Academic Press.

Gaziel, H. (2003). Images of leadership and their effect upon school principals' performance. *International Review of Education, 49*(5), 475–486.

Gibson, C. B., & Zellmer-Bruhn, M. E. (2002). Minding your metaphors: Applying the concept of teamwork metaphors to the management of teams in multicultural contexts. *Organizational Dynamics, 31*(2), 101–116.

Grant, D., & Oswick, C. (Eds.). (1996). *Metaphor and organizations.* London, England: Sage.

Grisham, T. (2006). Metaphor, poetry, storytelling and cross-cultural leadership. *Management Decision, 44*(4), 486–503.

Grunig, L. A. (1993). Image and symbolic leadership: Using focus group research to bridge gaps. *Journal of Public Relations Research, 5*(2), 95–125.

Gulick, L. H., & Urwick, L. F. (Eds.). (1937). *Papers on the science of administration.* New York, NY: Institute of Public Administration, Columbia University.

Heracleous, L., & Jacobs, C. D. (2011). *Crafting strategy: Embodied metaphors in practice.* Cambridge, England: Cambridge University Press.

Herzberg, F. (1966). *Work and the nature of man.* Cleveland, OH: World.

Hodgkinson, C. (1983). *The philosophy of leadership.* Oxford, England: Basil Blackwell.

Jacobs, C. D., & Heracleous, L. T. (2006). Constructing shared understanding: The role of embodied metaphors in organizational development. *Journal of Applied Behavioral Science, 42*(2), 207–226.

Kruskall, J. B., & Wish, M. (1986). *Multidimensional scaling.* Beverly Hills, CA: Sage.

Lakoff, G., & Johnson, M. (1980). *Metaphors we live by.* Chicago, IL: University of Chicago Press.

Lewin, L., Lippitt, R., & White, R. K. (1939). Patterns of aggressive behavior in experimentally created "social climates." *Journal of Social Psychology, 10,* 271–299.

Mangham, I., & Overington, M. A. (1987). *Organizations as theatre: A social psychology of dramatic appearances.* Chichester, England: Wiley.

Maslow, A. (1954). *Motivation and personality.* New York, NY: Harper.

McCorkle, S., & Gayle, B. M. (2003). Conflict management metaphors: Assessing everyday problem communication. *Social Science Journal, 40*(1), 137–142.

Morgan, G. (1986). *Images of organization.* Beverly Hills, CA: Sage.

Morgan, G. (1996). An afterword: Is there anything more to be said about metaphor? In D. Grant & C. Oswick (Eds.), *Metaphor and organizations* (pp. 227–240). London, England: Sage.

Mumby, D. K. (1983). Ideology and television news: A metaphoric analysis of political stories. *Central States Speech Journal, 34*(3), 162–171.

Oberlechner, T., & Mayer-Schönberger, V. (2003). *Through their own words: Towards a new understanding of leadership through metaphors.* (Working Papers, Center for Public Leadership). Cambridge, MA: Harvard University.

Ortony, A. (Ed.). (1993). *Metaphor and thought* (2nd ed.). Cambridge, England: Cambridge University Press.

Palmer, I., & Dunford, R. (1996). Conflicting uses of metaphors: Reconceptualizing their use in the field of organizational change. *Academy of Managerial Review, 21*(3), 691–717.

Pondy, L. R., Frost, P. J., Morgan, G., & Dandridge, T. C. (Eds.). (1983). *Organizational symbolism.* Greenwich, CT: JAI Press.

Popper, K. R. (1968). *Conjectures and refutations: The growth of scientific knowledge.* New York, NY: Harper & Row.

Putnam, L. L., Phillips, N., & Chapman, P. (1996). Metaphors of communication and organization. In S. R. Clegg, C. Hardy, & W. R. Nord (Eds.), *Handbook of organization studies* (pp. 375–408). London, England: Sage.

Reddin, W. J. (1970). *Managerial effectiveness.* New York, NY: McGraw-Hill.

Schlesinger, M., & Lau, R. R. (2000). The meaning and measure of policy metaphors. *American Political Science Review, 94*(3), 611–626.

Sementelli, A. J., & Abel, C. F. (2007). Metaphor, cultural imagery, and the study of change in public organizations. *Journal of Organizational Change Management, 20*(5), 652–670.

Sergiovanni, T. J. (1984). Leadership and excellence in schooling. *Educational Leadership, 41*(5), 4–13.

Terry, L. (1997). Public administration and the theatre metaphor: The public administrator as villain, hero, and innocent victim. *Public Administration Review, 57*(1), 53–62.

Virtanen, T. (1997). *Johtamiskulttuurin muutos ja tuloksellisuus. Valtionhallinnon uudistumisen seurantatutkimus 1995–1998. Ensimmäinen väliraportti.* Helsinki, Finland: Valtiovarainministeriö, hallinnon kehittämisosasto.

Weber, M. (1922/2013). *Economy and society.* Berkeley, CA: University of California Press.

Weick, K. E. (1989). Theory construction as disciplined imagination. *Academy of Management Review, 14*(4), 516–531.

Wheeler, A. (2006). *Designing brand identity: A complete guide to creating, building, and maintaining strong brands.* Hoboken, NJ: John Wiley & Sons.

Appendix A: The Question of Leadership Metaphors

1 = Very badly or not at all	3 = Somewhat badly	6 = Well
	4 = Undecided	7 = Very well
2 = Badly	5 = To some extent	

Many aspects of leadership can be expressed figuratively, in the language of metaphors. In the following, there is a set of metaphors. We ask you to evaluate how well they describe the activities of TWO managers working currently in your Agency. When you answer, please keep in mind your own superior and some other manager who affects your work. One of these is A and the other B, but we do not need to know which one is your own superior. Below you can find quite many metaphors just to make it sure that as many sides of leadership are covered as possible. Some of the metaphors may seem too negative. As they are metaphors, they indeed may be fulsome and playful. One cannot draw any direct conclusions about the quality of leadership on the basis of this survey, but the results will tell all of us something important. When you answer, please answer **first the column A, then column B,** so that both superiors are given a "full body shot." The Agency's supreme leader selects two managers who report to him or her.	THE METAPHOR DESCRIBES **SUPERIOR A** Circle one figure	THE METAPHOR DESCRIBES **SUPERIOR B** Circle one figure
Addicted visitor - Makes new acquaintances everywhere, knows everybody.	1 2 3 4 5 6 7	1 2 3 4 5 6 7
Adventurer - Bounces here and there, takes risks.	1 2 3 4 5 6 7	1 2 3 4 5 6 7
Arbitrator - Calms down the surfs, settles the situation.	1 2 3 4 5 6 7	1 2 3 4 5 6 7
Border guard - Watches over his or her territory, "Don't cross the border!"	1 2 3 4 5 6 7	1 2 3 4 5 6 7
Careerist - His or her own career is all that matters.	1 2 3 4 5 6 7	1 2 3 4 5 6 7
Coach - Encourages, trains, corrects.	1 2 3 4 5 6 7	1 2 3 4 5 6 7

Note: This appendix is part of the original Finnish questionnaire translated into English.

Confessor - Listens to your sorrows, confidentially.	1 2 3 4 5 6 7	1 2 3 4 5 6 7
Counsel - Helps you when people keep charging you.	1 2 3 4 5 6 7	1 2 3 4 5 6 7
Draught animal - Lugs a heavy load unwillingly, without help.	1 2 3 4 5 6 7	1 2 3 4 5 6 7
Driftwood - Floats with the tide, no will of his or her own.	1 2 3 4 5 6 7	1 2 3 4 5 6 7
Figurehead - Needed only for external visibility.	1 2 3 4 5 6 7	1 2 3 4 5 6 7
Fixer - Has a good grasp of the backstage networking.	1 2 3 4 5 6 7	1 2 3 4 5 6 7
Fixture - Always there, but doesn't get a move on anything.	1 2 3 4 5 6 7	1 2 3 4 5 6 7
Gardener - Nurtures everyone, supports the growth of all of us.	1 2 3 4 5 6 7	1 2 3 4 5 6 7
Goodwill ambassador - Warm, empathetic, finds no one evil.	1 2 3 4 5 6 7	1 2 3 4 5 6 7
Hermit - Seeks solitude, shuns subordinates.	1 2 3 4 5 6 7	1 2 3 4 5 6 7
Magician - Copes with impossible situations.	1 2 3 4 5 6 7	1 2 3 4 5 6 7
Master of ceremonies - Creates the right atmosphere, entertains, keeps company.	1 2 3 4 5 6 7	1 2 3 4 5 6 7
Monologist - Holds on speaking even when no one is listening.	1 2 3 4 5 6 7	1 2 3 4 5 6 7
Preacher - Leads the way to the future, agitates.	1 2 3 4 5 6 7	1 2 3 4 5 6 7
Prosecutor - Looks for errors and violations everywhere, trusts nobody.	1 2 3 4 5 6 7	1 2 3 4 5 6 7
Rusher - Hustles and bustles around everything, sometimes hitting on new solutions.	1 2 3 4 5 6 7	1 2 3 4 5 6 7
Sectarian fundamentalist - Does not approve of heretics.	1 2 3 4 5 6 7	1 2 3 4 5 6 7
Sergeant-major - "I'm the boss here!"	1 2 3 4 5 6 7	1 2 3 4 5 6 7

Spy - Snoops around, lurks, covers up his or her tracks.	1 2 3 4 5 6 7	1 2 3 4 5 6 7
Squire - Assumes respect, arouses fear.	1 2 3 4 5 6 7	1 2 3 4 5 6 7
Super salesman - Capable of making people believe anything.	1 2 3 4 5 6 7	1 2 3 4 5 6 7
Theater producer - Finds an important role for everyone, even many roles.	1 2 3 4 5 6 7	1 2 3 4 5 6 7
Travel guide - Conducts the party to new landscapes.	1 2 3 4 5 6 7	1 2 3 4 5 6 7
War hero - Victorious and prestigious fighter.	1 2 3 4 5 6 7	1 2 3 4 5 6 7

8

Developing Metaphors in Light of the Visual and Digital Turns in Organizational Studies

Toward a Methodological Framework

Ron Kerr, Sarah K. Robinson, and Carole Elliott

Key Learning Points

- Understand that the increasing complexity of some 21st century organizations and forms of organizing may need, in addition to Morgan's existing metaphors, new metaphors as a means of understanding how these organizations operate.
- Recognize that the visual and digital turns in organizational research reflect the importance that contemporary organizations place on their visual and digital projections: New metaphors may be needed to demonstrate how contemporary organizations use these media.
- Know that Morgan's proposed methodology is a good starting point for identifying further metaphors; however, the complexity of the visual/digital age calls for a more systematic approach to organizational analysis. A shift from *reading* organizations to *actively viewing* them is suggested.

- See that a hermeneutic framework is in keeping with Morgan's existing methodology and allows researchers of organizations to examine organizational projections through different cycles of analysis.
- Understand that when actively viewing organizations' visual and digital projections, what *cannot* be seen is as important as what can be seen.
- Know that a full understanding of how an organization operates cannot be gained solely from analysis of the organization's websites. However, the digital age affords organizational researchers the means to research an organization widely and develop appropriate metaphors from reading and actively viewing the organization's representations of itself and researching what other entities project about the organization.

This chapter considers how Gareth Morgan's (1986) seminal work can be applied and complemented given developments in organizations and forms of organizing in the 30 years since the original publication of *Images of Organization*. It takes Morgan's original metaphor-based methodology as a starting point and develops a methodological framework for "reading" (Morgan, 2006) the increasingly complex and **dis-integrated organizations** emerging in the late 20th and early 21st centuries. The chapter is framed within two interrelated "turns" understood as shifts in organizational emphasis and associated shifts in epistemological and methodological concern within the field of organization studies: the **visual turn** and the **digital turn**. These turns, it could be argued, are attempts to capture changes in organizing that relate to the increasingly image-rich and digitized nature of contemporary organizations.

In proposing a further development of Morgan's metaphors, given these changes in organizing and in the study of organizations, this chapter asks:

1) What can we learn about changes in organizing over the past 30 years through studying visual and digital projections of organizations (the two "turns")?

2) How might we develop a methodology for engaging with and examining in depth this new level of organizational reality? This question leads to the following:

3) Which of Morgan's metaphors are helpful in understanding these complex, image-rich organizations and what new organizational metaphors might emerge from this analysis?

This chapter presents an empirical case, that of a contemporary form of a transnational corporation, and provides an in-depth description of its visual and digital presence. Morgan's images of organization are then applied through the development of a **hermeneutic** approach that demonstrates the continued relevance of Morgan's metaphors in understanding this new form of organization. An additional metaphor that captures the organization's use of its digital presence to reveal and conceal specific aspects of its structure is also suggested. In so doing, we propose a methodological framework that can be adapted by other organizational researchers and students of organizations in working with Morgan's metaphors and developing their own metaphors for studying diverse and multifaceted contemporary organizations.

Extending Morgan's work in this way to examine what is visible and what is not provides a means of reconceptualizing and researching how some contemporary corporations organize themselves and present themselves to the outside world. It also provides an approach that allows the researcher to gain an understanding of the organization that evades the organization's attempts to control its visual and digital projections. The theoretical and methodological background to this chapter is now given through outlining the development of the visual and digital turns in organizational studies.

The Visual and Digital Turns in Organizational Studies

As previously mentioned, this chapter draws on the development of two interrelated "turns" in organizational studies, the visual and the digital, which both, in different ways, reflect attempts to understand the increasing importance of image and identity for contemporary organizations. An earlier turn, the linguistic turn, was described by Alvesson and Kärreman (2000, p. 136) as an increased interest in and focus on language. For the purposes of this chapter, we consider the visual and digital turns to be an increased academic interest and focus in the visual and digital elements of organizing and organizations. More specifically, the "visual turn" (Meyer, Höllerer, Jancsary, & van Leeuwen, 2013; Warren, 2009) places particular emphasis on the significance of relatively static visual projections of organizations such as branding and advertising. In technological terms, we might associate these phenomena with the concept of Web 1.0, which is understood as the visually static and noninteractive nature of the web before the mid-1990s. The related, but more recent, "digital turn" (Elliott & Robinson, 2014) focuses more on the development of interactive websites, viral marketing, digital entrepreneurship, and attempts to capture the quick-changing digital projections of organizations. These mobile and interactive phenomena align, we argue, with the concept of Web 2.0 (O'Reilly, 2007).

The Visual Turn in Organizational Studies

Over the past 20 years, there has been an increasing number of studies using visual approaches to study organizations (Bell, Warren, & Schroeder, 2014; Meyer et al., 2014). Such studies include, for example, research on the function of photographs and other images in organizational documentation such as company reports (Anderson & Imperia, 1992; Benschop & Meihuizen, 2002; Campbell, McPhail, & Slack, 2009; Davison, 2009; Dougherty & Kunda, 1991; Preston & Young, 2000; Warren, 2005). That is, images have come to be used as a basis for reading "clues" about the organization that presents them (Warren, 2009, p. 568).

The visual turn both challenges and is in some way a reaction to the earlier linguistic turn, which, originating in critiques of representationalism ("language represents reality") (Alvesson & Kärreman, 2000, p. 137), examines how organizations are constructed through discursive practices (Bell et al., 2014, pp. 2–3). However, as Fairhurst and Putnam (2004, p. 8) note, discourse-based approaches include both those that focus primarily on texts and other approaches that draw on, for example, Foucault, to look at discourses that are powerful beyond the text.

Nevertheless, according to Bell et al., (2014) "the linguistic turn . . . may have gone too far in asserting the primacy of language in the constitution of socially constructed organizational realities," with the consequence that "visuality and vision have remained under-explored and under-theorised in the organizational literature" and, therefore, that "a focus on the visual . . . potentially opens up areas which have been less explored by management researchers" (pp. 2–3). Proponents of a visual turn therefore argue that "organizations and individuals inhabit (and generate) a visually saturated culture where visual communication, based on showing, or mimesis, has come to occupy a parallel status to verbal communication based on telling, or diegesis" (Bell et al., 2014, pp. 2–3), with a strategic focus on the visual dimension of goods, services, and brands that are "constructed through corporate livery, logos, etc." (Warren, 2009, p. 567), including the design of monumental buildings intended to project corporate identity (e.g., General Foods corporate headquarters; Kerr & Robinson, 2015; Pelkonen, 2011). This turn to the visual has encouraged a concomitant search for appropriate methodologies from, for example, art historians such as Panofsky (1939/1976; also see Davison & Warren, 2009), visual culture, and, in light of the interactions between text and visuals, from multimodal methods (Kress & van Leeuwen, 2006).

Such research interests have also, over the past few years, been extended to the examination of organizations' web pages and other forms of digital projection, thus connecting to a more nascent turn in organizational studies, the digital turn.

The Digital Turn in Organizational Studies

The concept of the digital turn aims at capturing the move from the static pages of Web 1.0 to the more interactive Web 2.0 (O'Reilly, 2007), which incorporates phenomena such as blogging, wikis, and social media (Bell & McArthur, 2014; Leonard, 2014); communication and mobile technologies (Eriksson-Zetterquist, Lindberg, & Styhre, 2009; Matusik & Mickel, 2011); and digital entrepreneurship (Davidson & Vaast, 2010). This last phenomenon translates as "Enterprise 2.0" in (idealized) business terms, loosely defined as the use of social media to corporate ends (Bughin, 2008). In this context, the study of the use of digital technologies in and by organizations is increasingly wide-ranging, focusing on how organizations use these technologies and how employees and other stakeholders experience their use (Bell et al., 2014; Schultz & Hernes, 2013) and on their role in organizational change (Volkoff, Strong, & Elmes, 2007; Zammuto, Griffith, Majchrzak, Dougherty, & Faraj, 2007). In relation to the present study, what particularly interests us is what comes at the intersection of these two turns (i.e., where the visual and digital intersect in the study of organizational websites). These phenomena are interesting in this context in that they are not solely visual media, but they also contain many digital elements (blogs, interactive fora, hyperlinks) in addition to pictures, video, and text (Pink, 2006).

However, although the study of the role of organizational websites within organizational studies is still relatively new and constantly evolving, the importance of websites, especially in terms of communication of corporate identity, must not be underestimated. For example, many of an organization's potential stakeholders first encounter an organization through its webpages (Coupland & Brown, 2004; Pablo & Hardy, 2009). Therefore, websites provide stakeholders with information and are a means of transmitting (Segars & Kohut, 2001), and sometimes of responding to, high-level management messages (Coupland & Brown, 2004), and projecting the wider "look and feel" of an organization (Pablo & Hardy, 2009). Websites are therefore complex organizational projections that have evolved from largely mimicking text-based documentation (Coupland & Brown, 2004) to sophisticated combinations of visual, textual, and interactive media.

Given the strategic importance of websites as global communication tools, calls have been made to gain a deeper understanding of their role as a component part of corporate identity, especially in terms of communicating messages and shaping perceptions of organizations (Melewar & Karaosmanoglu, 2006; Warren, 2009). The concept of corporate visual identity (CVI; see Melewar, 1993) has developed through the visual turn into a methodological approach, which focuses on how a company name, symbol or logotype, typography, color, and slogan "reflect the company culture and values and . . . create physical recognition for the organization" (Simões et al., 2005, p. 158; see also Bartholme & Melewar, 2011; Melewar & Akel, 2005).

CVI provides a useful first step in considering the effect of organizations' visual projections on their stakeholders. However, given the increasing interactivity of Web 2.0 generation websites, Elliott and Robinson (2014) question the ability of CVI to make sense of the full complexity of web identity, suggesting that it is not fully able to capture the importance of corporate web presence and its relationship to the form and purpose of the organization. This is because websites are part of a wider digital domain that cannot be controlled by the organization. Websites are multimodal and, as such, their role in engaging with an organization's diverse stakeholders and shaping their perceptions of the organization (Melewar & Karaosmanoglu, 2006, p. 853) goes beyond reflecting, transmitting, and protecting visual identity (Elliott & Robinson, 2014).

Elliott and Robinson (2014) therefore examined existing work on the nature, role, and purpose of organizational websites and identified five major features of contemporary corporate websites that, it could be argued, constitute or help to establish an emergent corporate web identity (CWI), focusing on the visitor's experience and interaction with the website. Such an approach helps the organizational theorist to develop a methodology of actively engaging with websites as organizational artifacts: analyzing what the corporation wants to show to its viewers and how it wants them to experience the "visit," but also helping the analyst to identify what is perhaps inadvertently shown and what is not shown.

It has been argued that the philosophical rejection of representationalism (e.g., by Herder and later by Wittgenstein) involved a rejection of the epistemological authority of the visual as a dominant and dominating form (see Jay, 1994). We might suggest that this rejection coincided with, and helped to open the way for, the methodologies of the hermeneutics of suspicion (Ricoeur, 1970) by means of which contradictions can be identified between appearance and reality, either between the conscious and the repressed unconscious (as with Freud), or between the "the hidden haunts of production" and the commodity form (as with Marx, 1867/1981, pp. 138–139). This Marxian approach to commodification—which was further developed by, *inter alia*, Lukacs (1923/1971), Polanyi (1936), Benjamin

(1999), and Korsch (1938/1963)—culminated in Debord's (1967/1992) "society of the spectacle," in which "the real world is transformed into mere images then mere images are transformed into real beings" (Jappe, 1993/1999, p. 107). Ultimately, however, for the post-Marxist Baudrillard and the later Debord (see Jay, 1994), there is no longer an "outside" to the spectacle or simulacrum created by late or postmodern capitalism and the hermeneutics of suspicion must fall silent. However, distrust of what is visible—of "taking at face value"—might, we argue, be returning to the forefront as a concern given the developments associated with **Web 3.0** (Berners-Lee, Hendler, & Lassila, 2001), by means of which the web becomes "smarter, is getting to know you better . . . and [is] automatically delivering content to you that is relevant" (Macmillan Dictionary, 2014) through technologies of hidden surveillance such as tracking systems or cookies placed by corporate interests.

The digital turn therefore renews our focus not only on what we see (or what we are shown) but also on what we do not see (or what we are not shown), and this, we argue, calls for a methodological response from organizational studies. That is, how can this combination of the visual and digital turns be applied to *actively view* contemporary organizations (understood as a combination of reading the text and seeing the visual) and then analyzing what this unearths about organizational forms such as the transnational corporation? We suggest that this can be done through Morgan's approach of applying metaphors of organizations (Collinson & Morgan, 2009) and through an interpretation process that requires the analyst to draw on other resources that exist in the digital domain. This means getting "outside" what is directed at the viewer by the corporation in order to get *behind* the corporation's own digitally displayed construction of its identity. Following Morgan's approach, then, is a way of identifying differing or conflicting perspectives in which metaphor can be used as a bridge or conduit, a means of taking us out to the wider picture, and then perhaps bringing us back in again.

Given that we are looking for contradictions *within* a website and contradictions *between* what is shown and what is not and for conflicting perspectives, and given that this builds on Morgan's own approach, which, as he explains, "has a good deal in common with the hermeneutic approach to social analysis that views social life as a 'text' that has to be interpreted and 'read'" (Morgan, 2006, p. 417), we believe that critical hermeneutic analysis is an appropriate methodology to adopt (Prasad & Mir, 2002; Robinson & Kerr, 2009, 2015). This is because although hermeneutics has its origins in the study of written texts, it has been adopted or adapted to the study of the visual in art history by, in particular, Panofsky, as argued in Panofsky (1932) and developed as a three-cycle approach to visual analysis (Panofsky, 1939/1976). This approach has more recently been used to analyze websites (e.g., see Elliott & Robinson, 2012). In the following section, we present a "visual-digital" case study in which we initially approach a contemporary organization through its website using a three-stage hermeneutic process of analysis.

The Case: Mondelēz International

Stake (1995) identifies three types of case studies: intrinsic, instrumental, and collective. This study is, in Stake's terms, an instrumental case study because it aims to provide insight into an issue or problem. For an example of this, see Myers (1994), who uses a single case to address wider social and organizational issues. In this type of analysis, understanding the complexities of the case is secondary to understanding wider organization phenomena.

Our study therefore focuses on one organization because 1) its website provides a wealth and depth of data, both visual and textual, that allow us to identify some of the characteristics of the contemporary transnational corporation and 2) the company has a long history, although it is in some senses new (it was founded in 2012), as will be explained below. Drawing on Ovide (2011), a brief overview of the corporation's origins and development is also provided below.

So what or who is Mondelēz International? On its corporate website and in its publicity material, Mondelēz International (2012) is presented as a "reimagined company . . . with a single focus in mind: 'create delicious moments of joy.'" It is "a whole new company" with a newly fabricated name intended to represent a "delicious world" (on the basis of *monde + delice*; Mondelēz International, 2012). However, in order to understand more thoroughly what Mondelēz International is as an entity and its relationship to the food giant Kraft, we need first to track its history (for more details on its prehistory, see Ovide, 2011).

In 2010, Kraft took over the U.K. chocolate maker Cadbury in a £11.5 billion hostile bid. Later, in 2012, Kraft Foods Inc. demerged into two companies: Kraft Foods Group Inc., with a North American grocery focus, and Mondelēz International, with a "snacking" focus (Mondelēz brands include Oreo, Cadbury Dairy Milk, and Chiclets). Mondelēz International, the demerged company, has its head office in Northfield, Illinois, and its shares are quoted on the NASDAQ securities exchange market in New York. The company's operations are global but strategically focused on "emerging markets," with new or expanded manufacturing centers in Brazil, China, Mexico, India, and Russia, in addition to older centers in the United Kingdom, United States, Canada, and North Africa. Many changes continue to take place within the organization that are not documented on their website, such as the closing down of factories in Kenya and the moving of operations to Bahrain and the coffee business spun off in 2014 to form a joint venture controlled by Douwe Egberts (Gasparro & Calia, 2014). This information is available online from specialist resources such as *Confectionery News* (http://www.confectionerynews.com), *Marketing Week* (http://www.marketingweek.co.uk), Oxfam (http://policy-practice.oxfam.org.uk), the *Wall Street Journal* (http://www.wsj.com), and the International Union of Food, Agricultural, Hotel, Restaurant, Catering, Tobacco and Allied Workers' Associations (IUF; http://www.iuf.org). The next section discusses how we can research and understand the nature of this new organization through a focus on its most visible and accessible external projection, its corporate website. This move to the digital requires a move by the researcher from "reading" the organization to "active viewing" that involves an engagement that, starting from the website, moves beyond and behind to try to understand the full complexity of the organization.

Actively Viewing Mondelēz International:
A Methodological Framework

Given that Mondelēz International is a new corporate entity with a new web presence, we were able to follow the evolution of its website from its beginning in

2012, capturing changes at regular periods (every 3 months or so since the website's launch). We then examined the website using a three-stage hermeneutic approach, which includes 1) informal analysis: our first impressions and description of what we see; 2) formal analysis: using the framework of CWI (Elliott & Robinson, 2014); and 3) synthesis: in which the two forms of analysis are brought together through a critical application of metaphor (Morgan's original metaphors leading to the development of our own emergent metaphor; see Table 8.1).

Our multilayered critical hermeneutic approach (Elliott & Robinson, 2012; Phillips & Brown, 1993; Prasad & Mir, 2002; Robinson & Kerr, 2009, 2015; Thompson, 1981) is in keeping with Morgan's own methodological approach (as noted above; see Morgan, 2006). In discussing his approach, Morgan (2006, p. 417) explains: "Taking the domain of organizational theory as a reference point, it shows how we can open the way to different modes of understanding by using different metaphors to bring organizations into focus in different ways."

Again, following Morgan, we do not see these applications of metaphor as "a regimented approach," but rather "the aim is to use understanding of metaphor to create a sensitivity for the competing dimensions of a situation, so that we can proceed with our interpretations in a flexible manner" (Morgan, 2006, p. 419). What we add is a framework for organizational researchers to systematically consider what the organization is visually and digitally projecting (and what it is not) and thus to develop appropriate metaphors accordingly. This framework is outlined below.

TABLE 8.1 ● Analytical Framework for Website Case Analysis

Stage of analysis	Type of analysis	Findings
First cycle (informal)	Our first impressions and description of what we see.	Dominance of brands. Distanced management and family of "founders."
Second cycle (formal)	Corporate web identity (CWI): *mobility, accessibility, visuality, interactivity, customisation* Evaluates visitor's encounter with the website.	Dominance of brand images. Bands active and mobile. Lack of opportunity for the viewer to interact with the site. Customization policy unclear to the viewer.
Third cycle (synthesis)	Applying images—bringing the outside in. Active viewing—identifying different perspectives. Application of images: brain, flux, instrument of domination. Creation of new metaphor: trompe l'oeil.	Dominant corporate perspective. What is visible: brands, "founders," management. What is not shown: workers, history of corporate predation. Apotheosis of the brands, invisibility of the workers.

Hermeneutic Cycle 1: Informal, Our First Impressions

In this first section of analysis, we describe what we as active viewers see on accessing the Mondelēz International website (accessed November 18, 2014). For ease of description, we go through the different constituent panels or blocks that constitute the home page, as shown in Figure 8.1.

On the Mondelēz home page, in panel 1, the corporate name appears spelled out in a purple, cursive font with small, red teardrops on each end and the word "International" underneath. In panel 2, we find the continuously updated share price tracker. Panel 7 is the "Investor Center," which hyperlinks to information on the company's financial position, including reports, announcements, statements to analysts, and so forth. Panel 8 ("News Center") links to press releases. Panel 6 is "Well Being," which links to information on "mindful snacking" aimed at "empowering" the consumer, who needs snacks to "treat, fuel, boost" the machine-like body. There is no nutritional information here nor are there warnings or recommendations about snacking responsibly, so it unclear to us how this "mindful snacking" can be achieved.

On panel 4, "About Us" links to the management team, pictured celebrating at the corporation's public opening in New York. The chief executive officer (CEO), Irene Rosenfeld, is at the center of the group, surrounded by the rest of the team, which includes one person dressed as an Oreo cookie and another dressed as a Milka cow (both Mondelēz International brands). Members of the management are all applauding and smiling for the camera, so there is an informal snapshot feeling to the photo. There is no information identifying individual team members (e.g., names, background, and experience).

The "About Us" box also links to a "Heritage" page that shows pictures and "Our Founders" as one of the headings. We are surprised that this new organization could claim to have 19th and 20th century founders, and also that the history of so many historic companies and their products (Cadbury, Suchard) is reduced to "great men" (and one woman).

Then, in the "Our Values, Our Manifesto" section (also accessed from "About Us"), we find the corporate manifesto, which evokes: "A world full of differences," "Different lives . . . But really, we're all the same . . . We all seek joy." We find ourselves not exactly disagreeing with this statement but reflecting on its relevance and relationship to the products presented here. Panel 10, the main display panel on the front page, presents a purple and white globe (*le monde*) that opens up so that named and animated brands can explode out, appearing, rising, falling, disappearing. These

FIGURE 8.1 ● Mondelēz International Home Page as of October 2012, Formal Analysis

(1) Corporate Name/Logo	(2) Share Price Tracker				(3) Search Function
(4) About Us	(5) Brand Family	(6) Well Being	(7) Investor Center	(8) News Center	(9) Join Us
(10) Front Page Illustration					

brands are the *delice* in "Mondelēz." We are again surprised to see that what we term "the bouncing brands" are the most animated "beings" on the website. We now move on from our first impressions to a more structured analysis.

Hermeneutic Cycle 2: Formal Analysis

The digital turn, as we argued above, calls for a multimodal analysis of text plus image but extends this to include Web 2.0 features such as interactivity, accessibility, mobility, visuality, and customization. In this context, *mobility* refers to the movement both of the site itself and how visitors can navigate freely around it. In the Mondelēz website, the animation and lively colors of the brands simulate the "joy" proclaimed as the overarching corporate value. However, there is much less sign of the mobility of human agents, with very little in the way of videos or talking heads. *Accessibility* relates to how visitors are able to navigate through a mass of information and how they receive, react to, and make sense of the information and messages. Here, the Mondelēz site is quite clearly signposted and easy to follow. A lot of information is readily available (e.g., financial), but there is also quite a bit missing, in particular, where are the major sites of production?

The visual function of a website is significant in its own right: we use the term *visuality*, or what can be seen by the eye, to refer to this element. The main visual feature on the Mondelēz homepage is the very prominent purple globe that opens, allowing the global brands to leap out. The role of the colorful teardrops that accompany the brands is unclear, although they may be intended as a visual expression of "joy."

A potential role played by the website visitor is that of *interactivity*, or engagement in dialogue with the corporation, often facilitated through multiple channels of communication such as blogs and discussion fora. We note here that such features are missing from this site, although we note that there is considerable *customization*, or variation between different regional sites, depending on which brands are being strongly marketed in different contexts; examples would be dark chocolate and coffee in Ukraine.

Hermeneutic Cycle 3: Synthesis, the Critical Cycle

So where are we so far? From our analysis above, what emerges as significant about the visual and digital projections of this organization? We note the following aspects that we find worthy of more critical investigation: 1) the dominance and personification of the brands, 2) the importance of the foundational history, 3) the lack of human presence, and 4) the lack of opportunity for the viewer to interact with human beings, in particular with Mondelēz employees, and ask questions.

In addressing these four issues through the use of metaphor, we note that Morgan's images emerge from engagement *within* organizations and therefore do not deal with the organization's visual or digitally projected identity—although certain images, in particular the *brain, flux,* and *instrument of domination,* do resonate from behind the screen of commodification, allowing us to capture contradictions between the corporation's and other, different, perspectives. On the other hand, the image of the *organism* with its origins in biology obscures, we think, the role of human agency, as does the image of the Taylorist *machine*, which reduces the human agents to calculable numbers, while *culture* suggests a natural and total way of life. No doubt the corporation is in some senses a *political system*, but this is nowhere visible on the website; the *psychic prison* evokes a psychological rather than a visual or material perspective.

From an external perspective, then, we note the need to legitimate the object as "brand" through the mobilization of "history" to guarantee the continuity of the brand even though the "founder's" business as such no longer exists. Although the organization can be seen as being in a condition of *flux and transformation* (Morgan, 2006), with its acquisitions, divestments, and changes of name, a corporate version of history is used to provide an illusion of permanence—an enduring identity as a "family" of brands and founders that is presented to the viewer as a defined, enduring entity. As organizational researchers, we know this is not unusual as a means of establishing organizational legitimacy; however, we note that, as applied to an apparently "new" organization, it provides an interesting internal contradiction: "A whole new company that's been reimagined with a single focus in mind: Create joy." Within the website, corporate history is also reduced to a succession of "great men" (and one woman) and to the production of brands ("Our Founders" and "Historic Brands") that are co-opted into the new corporate history. This presents (i.e., makes visible) a fictitious continuity or genealogy, one that might be contradicted by a not visible alternative history of corporate predation.

From the Mondelēz website we learn about the brands, their activities and histories, and how they have been gathered into Mondelēz as a "brand family" or "house of brands." We also learn about the constantly updated share price: part of the corporate website is designed primarily to communicate with investors. This is consistent with the concept of a "house of brands" in that the Mondelēz identity gives a unifying umbrella under which the brands can "live." Although there are, as we have noted, visuality, mobility, accessibility, and customization, there is no form of interaction on the website; it is a spectacle of investment and consumption controlled by a corporate brain (Morgan 2006).

In **actively viewing** the website, we might ask: Where does the manufacture of the products take place? How and by whom are the material objects, the material basis of the brands and the profits they produce, themselves produced? In fact, the production workers either are invisible on the website or appear only as fungible financial "costs." To learn about them, we must turn to a parody website, Screamdelēz International (http://screamdelez.org), which was set up by the IUF as part of a campaign to support trade unionists in Mondelēz's geographically distant manufacturing centers. The Screamdelēz website was designed to bring to light the widely dispersed struggles of the production workers, who are absent both visually and textually from the Mondelēz corporate website.

The IUF's parody website replicates the Mondelēz website, but with significant differences, in that recognizable aspects of the original's form are retained but the content is replaced. On the home page, panel 1 contains the website's name, "Screamdelēz," exactly replicating the "Mondelēz International" logo, while panel 2 (top center) replaces Mondelēz International's share price tracker with the CEO's "executive compensation this year" ($28 million as of October 2013).

However, the main focus of the IUF's campaign is to reinstate sacked union organizers in Mondelēz's production plants in Egypt and Tunisia, textually expressed as "Mondelēz International workers scream for justice." Immediately below the top line, there is a row of headings that are almost identical to those on the Mondelēz website. These are panel 4 ("About the campaign"), in which the history of the workers' struggles, not only in Tunisia and Egypt but also in Pakistan, the United States, and Canada, replaces the spectral "Founders," thus connecting local antiunion activities by Mondelēz into a global narrative. Panel 10, the dominant panel in size, presents a color photograph of workers demonstrating against Mondelēz in Egypt. This takes the place of the brands on the Mondelēz front page, thus making visible the corporeally embodied human agents involved in challenging the employment practices of Mondelēz, which can be understood here in Morgan's terms as an instrument of domination.

Finally, returning to Mondelēz, although the website contains little that is evidently interactive or indeed mobile (only the brands and the share price are animated), our analysis does tell us something about changes in how corporate power interacts with us, developments that are captured in the concept of Web 3.0 (in Morgan's terms, the organization as brain), with Mondelēz's plans to collaborate with Google, Twitter, and Facebook in directing tailored advertising to consumers through digital technology (Joseph, 2014).

Discussion: Evolving a New Image Through Our Digital Methodology

For the situated observer, contradictions and conflicts are discernible both within the website and outside in the digital and material world. By utilizing what Jay (1994) identifies as a generalized suspicion of the visual, we can say that, from the corporation's perspective, the workers (as producers) are invisible behind a veil of commodification, whereas the products (as commodities) are made visible, mobile, and active to consumers and the changing share price is made visible to investors. So, like the shadows cast on the walls of Plato's cave that the prisoners view as reality (Morgan's psychic prison; Morgan, 2006), the website presents the active viewer with a distorted view of the corporation: a world turned upside down that can be interpreted as an allegory of contemporary capitalism (Marx's *camera obscura*; see Marx & Engels, 1845) with its visible and animated commodities that "take on a semblance of life . . . seem to be masters of their own destiny" (Polanyi, 1936, p. 349), whereas the producers are invisible or hidden.

Although, as we explain below, we feel that it is necessary to develop a new metaphor to capture what our analysis has revealed of this organization, this is not to argue that Morgan's images no longer have a firm grip on contemporary corporations. Indeed, for us, engaging with Mondelēz as a psychic prison, brain, or flux has been particularly fruitful in understanding contemporary dis-integrated transnational corporations. However, we believe that, in order to capture what digital and visual corporate identity shows and what it hides, a further image is needed. What we are looking for is an image that will capture our suspicion of what these images present. Here, we suggest that, from the perspective of a corporeally embodied spectator placed in front of a computer screen, the organization presents a ***trompe l'oeil*** or "the actual tricking of the eye into assuming that a painted object is real" (Kitson, 1966, p. 33). *Trompe l'oeil* painting is based on the manipulation of perspective to create an illusion of bodies in space (Jay, 1994), as in Late Baroque ceiling paintings on the interior vaults of church domes that are only coherent to the spectator from one fixed position.

The key example we are thinking of is Andrea Pozzo's *Allegory of the Missionary Work of the Jesuits* (c. 1685–1694), also known as *Apotheosis of St. Ignatius,* painted on the vault of Sant'Ignazio, the Jesuit church in Rome (Figure 8.2). Here, *trompe l'oeil* architecture and painting exploit theories of linear perspective to present a soaring vision of the saint ascending into heaven. It has been argued (e.g., by Buci-Glucksmann; see Turner, 1996) that Late Baroque art is paradigmatically art in the service of religious or secular power. In Sant'Ignazio, the aim of the *trompe l'oeil* painting is to glorify the power of a particular religious organization, the Jesuits, through the apotheosis of the Order's founder, St. Ignatius. By contrast, on the Mondelēz home page, the exploding world of commodities presents an apotheosis of the brands, ascending out of the world and returning to it bringing "joy" to consumers, but it is also an assertion of the power of the corporation that has collected all of these brands into its "family."

FIGURE 8.2 ● *Trompe l'oeil*: Pozzo's Allegory of the Missionary Work of the Jesuits (c. 1685–1694)

However, Pozzo's *Allegory* can only be seen as a coherent vision from one spot immediately below the vault. When you as the spectator move, the illusion collapses and you begin to see how it is fabricated. Such an approach, we argue, helps us to ask: Wait a minute, what is going on here? What is not being shown? In this, we take our cue from Morgan, who introduced the idea of multiple perspectives on organizations and that no image of an organization is neutral. So with the corporation's website, the corporation is visible as a coherent organization of history and brands from one perspective only. From the alternative perspective of the IUF, we can see beyond the *trompe l'oeil* of commodification to the embodied material existence of workers whose local struggles are widely separated in geographical terms but who can come together and be known in digital space, making these local yet connected disputes globally visible.

In addition, from our present analysis but also moving into the future, we gain the sense of *something* behind the presented corporate identity: not just the hidden producers and the employees, but also something active that wants to learn about us (who we are, where we live), and that wants to change the way we behave (see Harvey, 1990, pp. 285–286). The brands, and therefore the corporation that owns them, have material effects through the reconstruction of everyday life, particularly in the "emerging markets" around a "fast" and "vibrant" yet solitary lifestyle—by producing the neoliberal subject—"got to get to work" . . . no time for breakfast? Have a breakfast bar. Running out of energy? "Refuel" at your desk. Hooked on incessant activity . . . as Mondelēz's brand consultants explain: "Mondelēz International brands came together, ready to move forward into the future, inviting people to live vibrantly" (http://www.attik.com/case_study/Mondelēz-visual-identity/).

These comparatively recent developments, which we have associated with Web 3.0 as used for corporate ends, present further theoretical and methodological challenges for organizational researchers: We suggest that further images and metaphors, again taking inspiration from Morgan's work, will be needed to meet these challenges.

Conclusions: Contributions of This Chapter and Ways Forward For Organizational Studies

In this chapter, we set out first to illustrate how Morgan's metaphors from *Images of Organization* might be used in research, teaching, and practice. Next, we offer insights into different ways of using Morgan's metaphors (providing guidelines for how to use them in practice) and, finally, we present innovations and new developments in the application of Morgan's metaphors.

To do this, we asked three questions:

1) What can we learn about changes in organizing over the past 30 years through studying visual and digital projections of organizations (the two "turns")?

2) How might we develop a methodology for engaging with and examining in depth this new level of organizational reality? This question leads to the following:

3) Which of Morgan's metaphors are helpful in understanding these complex, image-rich organizations and what new organizational metaphors might emerge from this analysis?

In answering these questions, we have shown how new ways of actively viewing arising from the digital turn and employing new images and methodological frameworks can be used to analyze how corporate identities are projected, thus helping us to understand the historical evolution of organizations and organizing.

This has also allowed us to demonstrate the continuing relevance of Morgan's work as extended to the understanding of contemporary organizations. In particular, our analysis has uncovered changes in organizing that can be understood through Morgan's images of the brain, flux, and domination. However, we also suggest that, in order to understand more fully a transnational corporation such as Mondelēz International and its visual and digital projections, we need to introduce a new metaphor, the one that we have chosen here: the *trompe l'oeil*. We argue that, in presenting the spectator with a picture of a family of vibrant brands while hiding the story of the embodied workers on whose labor Mondelēz's corporate profits are based, the website operates as a *trompe l'oeil*. This metaphor could therefore be used further to interrogate such practices and, following Morgan, could help in developing "an organization theory *for* the exploited" (Morgan, 2006, p. 30), thus giving this methodology a practical application.

This visual–digital case study therefore helps us to understand the recent evolutions of organizing as reflected through a corporation's visual and digital projections, capturing how, through active viewing, we might see behind and beyond the perspective of the corporate center, an approach that provides great purchase in researching 21st-century forms of organization.

Key Terms

Actively viewing
Digital turn
Dis-integrated
    organizations

Hermeneutics
Trompe l'oeil
Visual turn
Web 3.0

References

Alvesson, M, & Kärreman, D. (2000). Taking the linguistic turn in organizational research: Challenges, responses, consequences. *Journal of Applied Behavioral Science, 36*(2), 136–156.

Anderson, C. J., & Imperia, G. (1992). The corporate annual report: A photo analysis of male and female portrayals. *Journal of Business Communication, 29*(2), 113–128.

Bartholme, R. H., & Melewar, T. C. (2011). Remodelling the corporate visual identity construct: A reference to the sensory and auditory dimension. *Corporate Communications: An International Journal, 16*(1), 53–64.

Bell, E., & McArthur. (2014). Visual authenticity and organizational sustainability. In E. Bell, S. Warren, & J. Schroeder (Eds.), *The Routledge companion to visual organization* (pp. 365–374). London, England: Routledge.

Bell, E., Warren, S., & Schroeder, J. (2014). Introduction: The visual organization. In E. Bell, S. Warren, & J. Schroeder (Eds.), *The Routledge companion to visual organization* (pp. 1–16). London, England: Routledge.

Benjamin, W. (1999). *The arcades project.* Cambridge, MA: Harvard University Press.

Benschop, Y., & Meihuizen, H. E. (2002). Keeping up gendered appearances: Representations of gender in financial annual reports. *Accounting, Organizations and Society, 27*(7), 611–636.

Berners-Lee, T., Hendler, J., & Lassila, O. (2001). The semantic web. *Scientific American, 284,* 35–43.

Buci-Glucksmann, C. (1996). *Baroque reason: The aesthetics of modernity.* London, England: Sage.

Bughin, J. (2008). The rise of enterprise 2.0. *Journal of Direct, Data and Digital Marketing Practice, 9,* 251–259.

Campbell, D., McPhail, K., & Slack, R. (2009). Face work in annual reports: A study of the management of encounter through annual reports, informed by Levinas and Bauman. *Accounting, Auditing & Accountability Journal, 22*(6), 907–932.

Collinson, S., & Morgan, G. (2009). Images of the multinational firm. In S. Collinson & G. Morgan (Eds.), *The multinational firm* (pp. 2–4). Oxford, England: Wiley-Blackwell.

Coupland, C., & Brown, A. (2004). Constructing organizational identities on the web: A case study of Royal Dutch/Shell. *Journal of Management Studies, 41*(8), 1325–1347.

Davidson, E., & Vaast, E. (2010). Digital entrepreneurship and its sociomaterial enactment. In *Proceedings of the 43rd International Conference on System Sciences, Honolulu, Hawaii, January 5–8, 2010.* Washington, DC: IEEE Computer Society.

Davison, J. (2009). [In]visible [in]tangibles: Visual portraits of the business élite. *Accounting, Organizations and Society, 35*(2), 165–183.

Davison, J., & Warren, S. (2009). Imag[in]ing accounting and accountability. *Accounting, Auditing & Accountability Journal, 22*(6), 845–857.

Debord, G. (1967/1992). *La société du spectacle [The Society of the Spectacle]* (3rd ed.). Paris, France: Gallimard.

Dougherty, D., & Kunda, G. (1991). Photography analysis: A method to capture organizational belief systems. In P. Gagliardi (Ed.), *Symbols and artifacts: Views of the corporate landscape* (pp. 185–206). Edison, NJ: Transaction.

Elliott, C., & Robinson, S. (2012). MBA imaginaries: Projections of internationalisation. *Management Learning, 43*(2), 157–181.

Elliott, C., & Robinson, S. (2014). Towards and understanding of corporate web identity. In E. Bell, S. Warren, & J. Schroeder (Eds.), *The Routledge companion to visual organization* (pp. 273–288). London, England: Routledge.

Eriksson-Zetterquist, U., Lindberg, K., & Styhre, A. (2009). When the good times are over: Professionals encountering new technology. *Human Relations, 62*(8), 1145–1170.

Fairhurst, G. T., & Putnam, L. (2004). Organizations as discursive constructions. *Communication Theory, 14*(1), 5–26.

Gagliardi, P. (2006). Exploring the aesthetic side of organizational life. In S. R. Clegg, C. Hardy, T. B. Lawrence, & W. R. Nord (Eds.), *Handbook of organization studies* (pp. 701–724). London, England: Sage.

Gasparro, A., & Calia, M. (2014, May 7). Mondelēz, D.E. Master Blenders combine coffee companies. *Wall Street Journal.* Retrieved from http://online.wsj.com/news/articles/SB10001424052702304655304579547440661257808?mod=wsjcfo_hp_midLatest&mg=reno64-wsj

Harvey, D. (1990). *The condition of postmodernity.* Oxford, England: Blackwell.

Jappe, A. (1993/1999). *Guy Debord*. Berkley: University of California Press.
Jay, M. (1994). *Downcast eyes: The denigration of vision in twentieth century French thought*. Berkeley: University of California Press.
Joseph, S. (2014). Mondelez pens "biggest" global video ad deal with Google. *Marketing Week*. Retrieved from https://www.marketingweek.com/2014/10/01/mondelez-pens-biggest-global-video-ad-deal-with-google/
Kerr, R., & Robinson, S. (2015). Architecture, symbolic capital and elite mobilizations: The case of the Royal Bank of Scotland Corporate Campus. *Organization*. Advance online publication. doi: 10.1177/1350508415606988
Kitson, M. (1966). *The age of the Baroque*. London, England: Paul Hamlyn.
Korsch, K. (1938/1963). *Karl Marx*. Retrieved from http://marxists.anu.edu.au/archive/korsch/1938/karl-marx/index.htm
Kress, G., & van Leeuwen, T. (2006). *Reading images: The grammar of visual design* (2nd ed.). London, England: Routledge.
Leonard, P. (2014). Social media and organizations. In E. Bell, S. Warren, & J. Schroeder (Eds.), *The Routledge companion to visual organization* (pp. 322–334). London, England: Routledge.
Lukacs, G. (1923/1971). *History and class consciousness*. Cambridge, MA: MIT Press.
Macmillan Dictionary. (2014). Web 3.0. Retrieved from http://www.macmillandictionary.com/buzzword/entries/web3.html
Marx, K. (1867/1981). *Capital: Volume 1: A critique of political economy*. London: Penguin Books.
Marx, K., & Engels, F. (1845). *The German ideology*. Retrieved from https://www.marxists.org/archive/marx/works/1845/german-ideology/
Matusik, S., & Mickel, A. (2011). Embracing or embattled by converged mobile devices? Users' experiences with a contemporary connectivity technology. *Human Relations, 64*(8), 1001–1030.
Melewar, T. C. (1993). Determinants of the corporate identity concept: A review of literature. *Journal of Marketing Communications, 9*(4), 195–220.
Melewar, T. C., & Akel, S. (2005). The role of corporate identity in the higher education sector: A case study. *Corporate Communications: An International Journal, 10*(1), 41–57.
Melewar, T. C., & Karaosmanoglu, E. (2006). Seven dimensions of corporate identity: A categorisation from the practitioners' perspective. *European Journal of Marketing, 40*(7/8), 846–869.
Meyer, R.E., Höllerer, M.A., Jancsary, D., & van Leeuwen, T. (2014). The visual dimension in organizing and organizational research: Core ideas, current developments, and promising avenues. *Academy of Management Annals, 7*(1), 489–555.
Mondelēz International. (2012). *Mondelēz International fact sheet*. Chicago, IL: Mondelēz International.
Morgan, G. (1986). *Images of organization*. Beverly Hills, CA: Sage.
Morgan, G. (2006). *Images of organization* (3rd ed.). London, England: Sage.
Myers, M. D. (1994). A disaster for everyone to see: An interpretive analysis of a failed IS project. *Accounting, Management and Information Technology, 4*(4), 185–201.
O'Reilly, T. (2007). What is Web 2.0: Design patterns and business models for the next generation of software. *Communications & Strategies, 65*(1), 17–38.
Ovide, S. (2011, August 4). The long, strange history of Kraft Foods. *Wall Street Journal*. Retrieved from http://blogs.wsj.com/deals/2011/08/04/the-long-strange-history-of-kraft-foods/
Pablo, Z., & Hardy, C. (2009). Merging, masquerading and morphing: Metaphors and the World Wide Web. *Organization Studies, 30*(8), 1–23.
Panofsky, E. (1932). Zum problem der beschreibung und inhaltsdeutung von werken der bildenden kunst. *Logos, 21*, 103–119.
Panofsky, E. (1939/1976). *Studies in iconology: Humanistic themes in the art of the renaissance*. New York, NY: Harper & Row.

Pelkonen, E.-L. (2011). *Kevin Roche: Architecture as environment.* New Haven, CT: Yale University Press.

Phillips, N., & Brown, J. L. (1993). Analyzing communication in and around organizations: A critical hermeneutic approach. *Academy of Management Journal, 36*(6), 1547–1576.

Pink, S. (2006). *The future of visual anthropology.* London, England: Routledge.

Polanyi, K. (1936). The essence of fascism. In K. Polanyi, J. Lewis, & D. K. Kitchin (Eds.), *Christianity and the social revolution* (pp. 349–354). London, England: Victor Gollancz.

Polanyi, K., Lewis, J., & Kitchin, D. K. (Eds.). (2006). *Christianity and the social revolution.* London, England: Victor Gollancz.

Prasad, A., & Mir, R. (2002). Digging deep for meaning: A critical hermeneutic analysis of CEO letters to shareholders in the oil industry. *Journal of Business Communication, 39*(1), 92–116.

Preston, A., & Young, J. (2000). Constructing the global corporation and corporate constructions of the global: A picture essay. *Accounting, Organizations and Society, 25*(4–5), 427–449.

Ricoeur, P. (1970). *Freud and philosophy.* New Haven, CT: Yale University Press.

Robinson, S., & Kerr, R. (2009). The symbolic violence of leadership: A critical hermeneutic study of leadership and succession in a British international organization in the post-Soviet context. *Human Relations, 62*(6), 877–905.

Robinson, S., & Kerr, R. (2015). Reflexive conversations: Constructing hermeneutic designs for qualitative management research. *British Journal of Management, 26*(4), 777–790.

Schultz, M., & Hernes, T. A (2013). Temporal perspective on organizational identity. *Organization Science, 24*(1), 1–21.

Segars, A. H., & Kohut, G. F. (2001). Strategic communication through the World Wide Web: An empirical model of effectiveness in the CEO's letters to stakeholders. *Journal of Management Studies, 38*(4), 535–557.

Simoës, C., Dibb, S., & Fisk, R.P. (2005). Managing corporate identity: An internal perspective. *Journal of the Academy of Marketing Science, 33*(2), 153–168.

Stake, R. E. (1995). *The art of case study research.* Thousand Oaks, CA: Sage.

Thompson, J. B. (1981). *Critical hermeneutics: A study in the thought of Paul Ricoeur and Jürgen Habermas.* Cambridge, England: Cambridge University.

Turner, B. S. (1996). Introduction. In C. Buci-Glucksmann (Ed.), *Baroque reason: The aesthetics of modernity* (pp. 1–36). London, England: Sage.

Volkoff, O., Strong, D. M., & Elmes, M. B. (2007). Technological embeddedness and organizational change. *Organization Science, 18*(5), 832–848.

Warren, S. (2005). Photography and voice in critical qualitative management research. *Accounting, Auditing & Accountability Journal, 18*(6), 861–882.

Warren, S. (2009). Visual methods in organizational research. In D. A. Buchanan & A. Bryman (Eds.), *The Sage handbook of organizational research methods* (pp. 566–582). London, England: Sage.

Zammuto, R. F., Griffith, T. L., Majchrzak, A., Dougherty, D. J., & Faraj, S. (2007). Information technology and the changing fabric of organization. *Organization Science, 18*(5), 749–762.

Reflections, Commentaries, and Constructive Critique

Imagination and the Political Use of Images

Vitor Hugo Klein Jr. and Christian Huber

Key Learning Points

- Learn that imagination is a resource that actors use to sustain, elicit, or impose ways of organizing through images.
- Learn that understanding imagination is important to examine how images are used in organizations.
- Learn that imagination is at the center of political struggles over the meanings of images.
- Examine four assumptions about how imagination and images can affect organizations.
- Identify the (hidden) interests behind four assumptions about the uses of images and imagination in organizations.
- Understand that images comprise more than just metaphors.
- Acknowledge the multiple imaginations in processes of organizing through images.
- Understand that politics is an inherent feature of the use of images in organizations.

Published 30 years ago, the groundbreaking *Images of Organization* (Morgan, 1986) remains a rich source for managers and students of organizations. Its creative rhetorical style and cogent explanations of the root metaphors that underpin organization theory made it a classic. However, despite the many insights that the book still offers, something seems to have escaped the attention of students of metaphors. While on the one side Morgan has shown that the way people see and act on organizations very much depends on how they imagine them, on the other side, we still know little about the role of imagination in organizations (Komporozos-Athanasiou & Fotaki, 2015). Thus, although **imagination** is pivotal to understanding the political use of **images** in organizations, it has been largely overlooked by studies of metaphors (Cornelissen & Clarke, 2010; Cornelissen, Holt, & Zundel, 2011; Inns, 2002; Oswick, Keenoy, & Grant, 2002; Pablo & Hardy, 2009; Sackmann, 1989; Tsoukas, 1991). To fill this gap, this chapter shows that imagination lies at the center of competing views of the role of images. Based on this, the chapter fleshes out four ways of how imagination affects organizations through images: images can mobilize the imagination of organizational actors in order to legitimate, reproduce, challenge, or deceive organizations. In this view, images are subject to struggles, disputes, or impositions underpinned by people's imaginations. Here a caveat is necessary. By using the term "image" instead of "metaphor," this chapter defines images as both the metaphors used to understand organizations as well as the expectations, interests, values, and beliefs shaping organizations through imagination. More specifically, the chapter focuses on the political significance of imagination and argues that politics is inherent to the very use of images in organizations.

It is worth noting that Morgan views imagination, at least implicitly, as a useful, mostly positive resource for organizational analysis, a view that although correct leaves the nuances of imagination untapped. Imagination appears in his concept of **imaginization** at the end of *Images of Organization* (1986) and later in his book titled *Imaginization: New Mindsets for Seeing, Organizing, and Managing* (Morgan, 1993). While in the former Morgan describes images as useful resources to generate insights about organizations and how to manage them, *Imaginization* is his more explicit call for scholars, students, and practitioners to consider the possibility of drawing on images in order to create new ways of seeing and organizing. Imaginization amounts, therefore, to organizing through images. Underpinning both books, however, is the idea that people can use imagination to analyze organizations and to organize them in different, innovative, and more efficient ways. Morgan (1986, p. 350) illustrates this point with the Multicom case, in which eight interpretations based on different **root metaphors** offer practical insights to examine and act on Multicom from the point of view of a management consultant, a social critic, and a policy analyst. The case shows the analytical usefulness of images. However, it leaves one without knowing how people mobilize other people's imagination in organizations to promote a particular way of organizing and how, in this process, different forms of imagination clash. That is, although hinting at the important role of imagination in the creation and use of images for organizational analysis, Morgan stops short of developing a full theory of imagination that accounts for how images are used politically in organizations.

In this chapter, a closer examination of imagination will show how actors in organizations might use images for political aims. Research findings have already shown that imagination is key to decision making and action because it underpins actors' values and beliefs (e.g., see Anderson, Lepper, & Ross, 1980; Carrol, 1978; Oettingen, Schnetter, & Pak, 2001; Tversky & Kahneman, 1973). Furthermore, because values and beliefs are open to contradictions, imagination often leads to conflicting interpretations of images. Imagination is defined accordingly as a resource with which actors sustain, elicit, or impose ways of organizing through images. In contrast with Morgan's view of imagination — as a resource managers and scholars can count on for organizational analysis and theorization — imagination is described here as the often conflicting interpretations that people put into effect to pursue their interests and values in the process of organizing. Images are, in the view proposed in this chapter, rhetorical instruments of persuasion that are mobilized through imagination according to different interests and competing views.

To provide a comprehensive view of the role of imagination in the political use of images, the chapter builds on the works of Paul Ricoeur and Cornelius Castoriadis. Ricoeur's (1994) work opens up new possibilities for understanding the consequences that different forms of imagination have for organizational behavior. Castoriadis (1987) provides a way of seeing images and imagination as an inherent part of relations of power. By helping to clarify how the political struggles around images are opened up by different types of imagination, the chapter addresses past critiques claiming that Morgan's work has underplayed the sociopolitical implications and material aspects involved in the use of metaphors (Reed, 1990; Tinker, 1986). The main goal here, however, is not to argue for a controlled use of tropes (Morgan, 1983; Pinder & Bourgeois, 1982), but rather to advance a deeper understanding of the relationship between imagination and images. It is argued that, without a theory of imagination that explains how individuals engage with images, it is difficult to judge whether metaphors are used to hide vested interests (Tinker, 1986, p. 363) or to promote creative and "different ways of thinking" (Tsoukas, 1991).

The chapter pays greater attention to how imagination influences **power relations** in organizations. It enriches the reading of *Images of Organization* by advancing a view of images both as analytical resources that draw on imagination to create "powerful insights" (Morgan, 1986, p. 5) and as resources that are at the heart of political struggles over meanings. Such an explanation will be pursued in three steps. First, the next section will show how different forms of imagination underlie competing views on the role of images and will explain the consequences of each of them for organizational behavior. The section after that will shed light on why imagination makes every use of images in organizations inevitably political. The final section will discuss some implications of a political account of imagination for organizational research and practice.

Assumptions About Images and Imagination

Drawing on Paul Ricoeur's (1994) work on imagination, this section explains how competing views of what imagination means result in different interpretations of the role of images in organizations. Based on that, the section fleshes out four sets of assumptions about how imagination affects organizations through images; images can **mobilize the imagination** of organizational actors in order to legitimate, reproduce, challenge, or deceive organizations. These assumptions point to the political underpinnings of the use of images in organizations.

Paul Ricoeur was a philosopher deeply involved with the study of metaphors, imagination, and, more generally, language. According to him, imagination has been addressed by past research in at least four different ways. First, imagination can be seen as the process of bringing to mind "things" that are absent but which were experienced in the past (Ricoeur, 1994, p. 119). Second, imagination can be understood as the processes of transferring events into images, diagrams, and models (e.g., Puyo et al., 2012). Third, imagination can also refer to the creative process of establishing unusual relations, a process closely related to the realm of fiction and dreams. Finally, imagination can indicate some sort of illusion that people become trapped in. Based on these different and competing views, Ricoeur groups the main theories of imagination along two axes.

The first axis concerns the object of imagination, namely, the image. Understandings vary in this respect according to whether imagination simply repeats something that has been experienced in the past or produces something new. On the one end of this axis are theories in which imagination works merely as a mechanism of the repetition of past experiences. The image is, in this view, what Ricoeur calls a weakened form of **perception** which imagination is merely responsible for reliving in one's head. Morgan's focus on similarity, contiguity, and contrast enabled by the combination of words (e.g., organization as machines, as organisms, as brains, etc.) shares, in part, the idea that images are echoes of perception because all of the eight images are part of shared experiences. In other words, for Morgan, images are not assessed directly by the senses (i.e., an organization is not an actual, physical brain), but are activated by the repetition in the mind of mental perceptions (i.e., an organization is perceived through its brain-like characteristics). In this case, the object of imagination is an image of some "thing" (e.g., culture, politics, brains, etc.) or characteristics of this "thing" that imagination brings into consciousness. In summary, at the one end of this first axis, images result from past experiences and imagination is responsible for replicating in one's head such weakened echoes of experience.

At the other end of the first axis, Ricoeur groups theories referring to the image as a result of a productive type of imagination. **Productive imagination** refers to conceptualizations suggesting that people can imagine entirely new things and not just a combination of things that already exist in the world. Productive imagination is common in works of fiction, portraits, and dreams (Ricoeur, 1994, p. 120). Within this tradition, imagination is not only responsible for reliving in the mind weakened echoes of experience, but it is also "the faculty of *deforming* the images offered by perception, of freeing ourselves from the immediate images; it is especially the faculty of *changing* images" (Bachelard, 1969, p. 19, italics in original). The view of imagination as an active rather than passive force assumes that the human mind can actually produce something new, a new image and meaning, without the need to have experienced them before in some way.

Along the first axis are thus two diametrically opposed theories of imagination and the image (see Figure 9.1). On the one side rests imagination as responsible for reliving in the mind the images of past experiences. On the other side, imagination is seen as a productive force that can create, distort, or forge images beyond what has been experienced.

However, theories of imagination can also be grouped, Ricoeur argues, along a second axis: the axis concerning the subject of imagination. On this axis, the question is

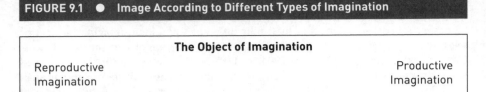

FIGURE 9.1 ● Image According to Different Types of Imagination

The Object of Imagination

Reproductive
Imagination

Productive
Imagination

Images are echoes
of experience

Images go beyond
experience

Source: The authors.

whether the individual is capable of distinguishing between real and fictional images. Answers to this question vary according to the role attributed to imagination. The spectrum ranges from what Ricoeur calls the fascinated consciousness, when one is completely unaware of the **socially constructed** aspects of the image, to the critical consciousness of the subject, when one is aware that the image is just a partial view of reality (see Figure 9.2).

In the fascinated consciousness mode, individuals lack critical awareness of the role of their imagination in the creation and reproduction of images. In this case, individuals passively believe in images that are taken for the "real." In the critical consciousness mode, individuals have some form of critical distance between themselves and the images that they share (Ricoeur, 1994, p. 120). Therefore, instead of assuming that images mirror some form of "reality," individuals tend to address images through **reflexive thinking** and practice (Cunliffe, 2004). By helping to explain the underlying assumptions of organizational theory, *Images of Organization* contributes to reflexive thinking in organizations (Morgan, 1986). However, Morgan stops short of explaining how images affect organizations differently depending on the type of imagination in which people engage. The rest of this section will explain how different views on imagination underpin different assumptions about the role of images in organizations (see Figure 9.3).

Figure 9.3 shows four sets of assumptions about how imagination affects organizations. According to these assumptions, the influence of images on organizations depends on how reflexively (or not) organizational actor engage with images. More specifically, the figure shows that imagination can be used by people in order to legitimate, reproduce, disrupt, or deceive organizations.

Note that the four quadrants present four different sets of assumptions about imagination, each offering different outcomes regarding organizational behavior and actions. Most traditional approaches to understanding imagination can be grouped into these four quadrants. Each set has strengths and weaknesses and their usefulness will depend on the specific challenges that organizations face. For example, Morgan's *Images of Organization* can be closely associated with quadrant one to the extent that it explains that images are often taken for granted; however, his book *Imaginization*

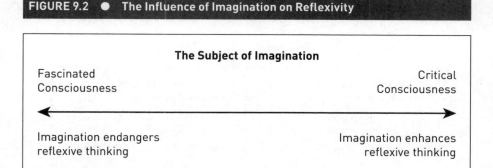

FIGURE 9.2 ● The Influence of Imagination on Reflexivity

The Subject of Imagination

Fascinated   Critical
Consciousness   Consciousness

←――――――――――――――――――――――――――――――――→

Imagination endangers   Imagination enhances
reflexive thinking   reflexive thinking

Source: The authors.

can be situated in quadrant two. In the later parts of this chapter, however, we will present a concept of imagination that goes beyond the four quadrants.

Quadrant 1: Imagination Legitimates Organizations

Images of Organization (Morgan, 1986) exposed the root metaphors at the heart of organization theory and practice. Each of the eight metaphorical images described by Morgan (machine, organism, brain, culture, political system, psychic prison, flux and transformation, and instrument of domination) brings advantages and limitations to both theory and practice because a metaphor is a way of both seeing and of not see-ing. The main assumption of the book is that images support patterns of seeing, thinking, and organizing. Most of the time, however, images reproduce specific ways of seeing and organizing because they remain hidden in discourse and action and are therefore taken for granted.

The assumption underlying this view is that imagination reproduces an estab-lished order. Imagination brings forth images that are familiar and used to prompt routine organizational behavior. Accordingly, images based on experiences work as analytical devices "to understand one element of experience in terms of another" (Morgan, 1986, p. 4). Morgan's concept of *imaginization* shares, at least in part, this view because imaginization is not just about producing new images, but it is also about using images already familiar to people. As the book *Imaginization* (Morgan, 1993) illustrates, similar metaphors can be drawn upon in different contexts and the organizations in Morgan's cases can all eventually be summarized as belonging to one or several of the root images. From this view, when deeply embedded in organizational culture and language, images legitimize practices. Imagination is, in this view, closely related to dominant images taken as "the reality" that individuals share but which have implications and limitations that remain unknown.

One example here is the war metaphor at the root of organizational practices, such as strategy. The war or military metaphor can be easily recognized in managerial speeches, documents, and language of private organizations (Weick, 1979) and

FIGURE 9.3 ● Assumptions About Imagination and Images

Critical Consciousness

2 **Imagination reproduces organizations**

- Images are used to read and shape organizations.
- Imagination recombines sets of characteristics from a repertoire of metaphors to promote change or stability (*imagination functions here as repetition*).
- Politics:
  - o A small number of actors use images to change organizations according to their interests.
  - o Divergent and conflicting images are disregarded.

3 **Imagination disrupts organizations**

- Images are highly ambiguous and open to questioning.
- Imagination challenges ways of seeing and organizing by creating novel and unusal connections (*imagination works here as invention*).
- Politics:
  - o Because individuals address images critically, interpretative processes in organizations are highly contested.
  - o Yet political struggles over the meaning of images may result in the creation of new frames of understanding (new categories, images, etc.).

1 **Imagination legitimates organizations**

- People in organizations follow images fed from the top of the organization blindly.
- Imagination reinforces accepted norms of conduct and routines.
- Politics:
  - o Imagination is mobilized to maintain the status quo.
  - o Conflicting interpretations of images exist, but remain unsaid.

4 **Imagination deceives organizations**

- Images are followed blindly yet underpin a mismatch between ways of seeing and organizing.
- Imagination limits organizational capacity to interpret events.
- Politics:
  - o Images are used to deceive and elude.
  - o Sometimes entire organizations get trapped in misleading images.

Reproductive Imagination

Productive Imagination

Fascinated Consciousness

despite having a rather different purpose than private organizations, it has already infiltrated public organizations as well. The point to stress here is that such an image is not illusory; on the contrary, organizations do compete with each other, but the image of organization as a search for survival in a war reinforces specific patterns of organizational behavior exactly because the image is taken for real. Therefore, when most organizational participants take images for granted, imagination is used to retain existing perspectives inside of the organization and to legitimate them. In such circumstances, people are not fully aware of the influence an image may have on their thoughts and actions. For example, when people use the metaphor of war to visualize a new strategy, they will likely frame competitors as enemies rather than potential partners. Such a view may promote actions that an organization may need in certain situations. However, whereas these situations are not openly political, politics is always on a symbolic level part of organizations. The political remains hidden from the organizational agenda either in higher-ranking employees, who do not fully comprehend the implications of the images they use and impose on the organization, or from the lower-ranking employees, who, by taking images for granted, reinforce patterns of behavior.

The assumption that people's imaginations are mostly concerned with the reproduction of images that are taken for granted overlooks the fact that conflicting interpretations of images exist in everyday organizational life. Practitioners and students may, in fact, use images to see organizations in a new light, for example, during a workshop, where a consultant or a team member tries to highlight through different images certain aspects of the organization that are not entirely clear to the group. At this point, by making people aware of the influence of metaphors on organizational practices, another set of assumptions and subsequent actions becomes evident: imagination can also *reproduce* organizations according to different images.

Quadrant 2: Imagination Reproduces Organizations

Images of Organization also points to the potential of metaphors for organizational change, something Morgan addresses more explicitly in his book *Imaginization* (1993). According to this view, images not only legitimate organizations but can be also used to create different forms of organizing. That is, through imaginization, as Morgan calls it, people can think of different images to interpret and overcome organizational problems. Here, scholars, students, managers, or consultants become aware of the role of images and use their imagination for designing organizations. However, used to highlight aspects of an organization by bringing it in contrast with other domains of experience, the image is still understood here as a weakened form of perception. Concepts of imagination belonging to quadrant 2 are more flexible than those in quadrant 1, but still rely on existing images. Morgan's imaginization is an example of a flexible approach to images that is still rooted in existing (but not yet fully established) images.

In this view, imagination is seen as something that must be activated through metaphorical language and that can be used to change organizations when needed. It is worth noting that, despite some actors becoming aware of the role of metaphors, these actors are mainly consultants and managers interested in change. In other words, only a limited number of people are aware of the power of images, a view assuming that imagination occurs in a rather restricted way. Most of the time, the majority of people in organizations are passive recipients of the images fed to them by top management or consultants. For those aiming at change, images are used to transform organizations according to their interests. From this perspective, images support either stability or change, but not both simultaneously. An organization can be a machine, and too much machine-like thinking can be a danger to the organization's survival. Problems emerge when the image is almost too stable in the face of uncertain challenges and then comes the management team, which imagines a different conception of organization based on the characteristics of a different metaphor. This new, and hopefully better, future is an organization based on a different image that is more appropriate for the challenges at hand. Imagination is thus mobilized so that management can substitute an unfit metaphor for a new one. More generally, this view ties imagination to a specific image because most members of organizations do not use their imagination actively for criticizing or shaping organizations.

Imagination is therefore restricted to specific moments (e.g., change) and people (e.g., top management) who try to shape the future of the organization. Imagination remains something to be trained and tamed in order to prompt specific forms of organizational behavior. However, the scope and complexity involved in the relation between imagination and images are narrowed down. Marginal and deviant interpretations of a particular image, as well as the ambiguities of images explored politically in organizations, remain unappreciated.

Quadrant 3: Imagination Disrupts Organizations

A little-explored aspect in *Images of Organization* refers to the ambiguities and the conflicting interpretations of images (e.g., see Cornelissen, 2006; Inns, 2002; Milne, Kearins, & Walton, 2002). The assumption underlying this view is that imagination produces more than one single meaning of a particular image. Addressing how a single metaphor can be interpreted differently by groups depending on contextual elements, Cornelissen (2006) presents a case study of the identity metaphor used within organizational research communities. The case shows that the identity metaphor has been understood in "very different ways as different communities work from very different conceptions" of organization (Cornelissen, 2006, p. 683). To say that communities of research have different conceptions of organization is, however, another way of saying that researchers have different interests and values to which the identity metaphor might be adapted. At the heart of such creative appropriation lies imagination, calling into question the legitimacy of images according to different stances. Therefore, through ongoing and often competing interpretations, images are constantly reworked and expanded and are not simply the repetition of a set of characteristics of past experiences.

The main assumption underlying this view is that imagination is responsible for both the formation and change of images. By using images in organizations, people produce new meanings through imagination and do not simply recombine an existing set of characteristics taken from experiences of different domains. This view is consistent with studies highlighting the ambiguities involved in the use of organizational images (Brown, Stacey, & Nandhakumar, 2008; Cornelissen, 2006; Milne et al., 2002). Such studies also elaborate on the importance of different forms of language for creative action (Cornelissen et al., 2011; Oswick et al., 2002). In short, as an active element in the struggles around the meaning of images in practice, imagination potentially disrupts organizations. However, when imagination is reflexively engaged by different members of the organizations, images are unlikely to present one single, unanimously shared view of a situation. On the contrary, images will likely involve creative interpretations and conflicting views common to a highly political situation, in which the clashes of interests might lead to new and unexpected meanings.

Quadrant 4: Imagination Deceives Organizations

The productive type of imagination can also produce harmful consequences to organizations, especially when it hinders critical thinking. In this respect, Morgan has explicitly stressed that images can make life in organizations difficult (i.e., as ways of not seeing). However, he stops short of tackling the dark side of imagination. The idea that creativity might be bad for management is an assumption largely missing in *Images of Organization*. In practice, imagination can underpin deceptive images (Weick, 2005), making people fall for particular images that are inconsistent with unfolding events in organizations. *Images of Organization* neglects this aspect because metaphors are seen as predominantly helpful for analyzing and managing organizations. However, the use of images as a form of deception is a rather common practice in organizations.

An example of how images can be used against meaningful ways of managing organizations is "bullshitting." Writing about the role of bullshit in organizations, Spicer (2013) argues that most talk and text in organizations is produced with little regard for the truth. Consider, for example, how politicians employ seductive rhetoric to appease their potential voters or how CEOs misuse concepts and ideas to justify top management decisions. In the field of branding, Naomi Klein (2000) provides countless examples of how images are used as a form of deception, such as the idea of the Internet as an expression of freedom conveyed by the portmanteau *netizens* ("net" and "citizens") crafted by America Online or the ideals of economic progress associated with the proliferation of export-processing zones. These images, as Klein cogently shows, misrepresent the practices to which they refer. Many people, nonetheless, share them blindly.

To a certain degree, *Images of Organization* has discussed the role of the dark side of imagination through the image of organizations as psychic prisons. The point to stress here, however, is the negative impact that images may have in organizations when people use imagination without critical distance. In such mode, organizations become trapped in misleading images because imagination is impoverished to the extent that it turns into **fancy**, "the power of inventing the novel and unreal by recombining the elements found in reality" (Merriam-Webster, 1984, p. 415, in Weick, 2006, p. 447). Weick describes that when people in organizations engage in fancy rather than imagination, they tend to combine elements of reality that do not match with actual situations. Fancy, however, is different from the reproductive type of imagination of quadrants 1 and 2 because it tends to produce misspecifications, mis-estimations, and misunderstandings in organization's images (Weick, 2005). To illustrate the impact of poor imagination on organizations, Weick analyzes the *Columbia* shuttle disaster. In the events preceding the accident of the *Columbia* shuttle, Weick shows, managers had bracketed unusual problems, which should have been classified as "out-of-family" problems and led to different actions, into established frames of thinking (i.e., as "in-family" problems). Therefore, instead of reflecting about these new and unusual problems to better understand what was happening, by engaging in fancy or poor imagination, managers were misled by an image (in-family problems) that did not reflect the reality that they were experiencing. Reflexive thinking is thus key to "surfacing the taken for granted rules underlying organizational decisions" (Cunliffe, 2004; Cunliffe & Jun, 2005, p. 227). When people lack the critical type of awareness concerning imagination, organizations can become trapped in misleading images shared by their members (e.g., Sievers, 1999, 2003, 2008).

An in-depth account of imagination helps us to see images beyond straightforward "good" management practice to analyze organizations from multiple perspectives. As this chapter has been arguing, imagination is part of the relations of power that are at the center of politics in organizations. The next section will push this reasoning further by exploring a conception of imagination based on the writings of Cornelius Castoriadis.

From Images *of* Toward Imagination *in* Organization

Images of Organization pays little attention to imagination and therefore marginalizes the political uses of images *in* organizations. By drawing on Ricoeur's work, the previous section showed, however, that images can mobilize the imagination of organizational actors in order to legitimate, reproduce, challenge, or deceive organizations. These four assumptions offer a framework that helps in identifying when and how metaphors can hide interests (Tinker, 1986, p. 363), promote creative ways of thinking (Tsoukas, 1991), or simply deceive organizations. Images can hide interests when they are taken for granted (quadrant 1) or when change through a new image is promoted by a small number of actors (quadrant 2); images promote creative ways of thinking when people engage with imagination reflexively (quadrants 2 and 3); and images are highly deceptive because, when taken for granted, they set serious limitations to interpretation in organizations (quadrants 3 and 4). This section focuses on explaining how politics is always part of the use of images in organizations. With that, the section presents an alternative understanding of images and imagination as it is offered by Cornelius Castoriadis (1987). For him, imagination plays a powerful role in struggles over meaning through which images emerge, disappear, or are continuously transformed. Applying Castoriadis's perspective to revisit Morgan's images of organizations will help us to understand politics as an inherent, and inevitable, feature of the use of images in organizations.

The first point of a Castoriadian view on imagination is that, in contrast with Morgan's concept of imaginization, Castoriadis addresses imagination as a collective endeavor. For him, imagination is always part of power relations because the images that society relies upon go beyond the materiality of things. Consider, for instance, the ideas of democracy, justice, and progress. These are all images with a force that depends largely on the practices to which they refer, such as elections, trials, or social movements, but that cannot be limited to these very practices. Castoriadis calls these images that go beyond the materiality of things "**social imaginary significations**." They are imaginary because they are instituted through creation and do not correspond to "real" or "rational" referents (Castoriadis, 1987, p. 230) and they are social because they only exist while shared by a society, a group, or, indeed, an organization.

Castoriadis's view contributes a novel understanding of images because, in contrast with Morgan's focus on metaphors, imaginary significations include political struggles over the question of what certain images mean in practice. Consider, once again, the example of "democracy." To realize the image of democracy, that is, to put it into effect, a particular society needs continuous debates, parliaments, and politicians who not only "do" democracy but also change the idea of democracy itself, for example, through an update of electoral rules or the inclusion of issues held as relevant to the democratic debate. Democracy is therefore an image, an imaginary signification, larger than any existing legal code or practice. It is the imaginary that triggers actions that change the very nature of what democracy is. However, the concept of imaginary significations involves more than just positive-laden values such as democracy. Take, for instance, risk; as an image underpinning many organizational practices, the idea of risk calls for ongoing interpretation of facts, situations, and events in order to define what counts as risk (Hilgartner, 1992; V. H. Klein, 2015). Risk is imaginary because it is never real until the moment it materializes—the moment when it stops being a risk and becomes damage (Huber & Scheytt, 2013). Because dangers are always "selected for public concern according to the strength and direction of social criticism" (Douglas & Wildavsky, 1982, p. 7), they have first to be imagined and talked about; however, the image of risk as danger remains.

The concept of imaginary significations broadens the understanding of the role of images because images in this case are not necessarily constrained to "things in the world." The imaginary is "not an image *of*, [rather], it is the unceasing and essentially *undetermined* (social-historical and psychical) creation of figures/forms/images" (Castoriadis, 1987, p. 3). The images that concern Castoriadis are not "ways of seeing" an organization. They are instead what enable objects and practices to be made sense of according to particular interests. In such practical situations, people must cope with questions involving imaginary significations, such as "Progress and freedom to whom?," "Democracy according to which criteria and defined by whom?," "Who defines which risks are priorities to act upon?," and "Why are these priorities?" When people interact to answer such questions, they struggle to pursue particular preferences and interests. This process can be understood as a political struggle around meanings that often involves conflicting interpretations of images or imaginary significations.

Imaginary significations are, therefore, points of access to broader ways of seeing and organizing in which imagination stands for the spontaneity and heterogeneity of the interpretations of images and the creation of new content (Urribarri, 2002). Such images have at their core political debates that try to settle their meaning in practice. In the following box, the recent nuclear accident in Fukushima provides a useful illustration to contrast this view of images with that of Morgan.

CASE

NUCLEAR POWER IN GERMANY AFTER FUKUSHIMA

On March 11, 2011, as a consequence of the tragedy of the strongest earthquake in recent Japanese history, nuclear meltdowns occurred in three of the six blocks of the Fukushima nuclear power plant. This had been the most severe accident at a nuclear power plant since the Chernobyl disaster in 1986. Beyond the immediate and long-term impact on the people and environment of Japan, the Fukushima disaster had multiple consequences.

As an indirect but linked consequence, Germany made a resolution to stop investing in nuclear energy and the government decided to completely exit nuclear power by the end of 2022. This decision was greeted with much public support in Germany.

Following Morgan, one could argue that the image underpinning the organization of a nuclear power had changed. Traditionally, the machine might have been the appropriate metaphor to understand this type of organization because nuclear power, one of the great achievements of modernity, was perceived as something highly reliable and in which work took place relatively mechanically. This image changed after the events in Fukushima and images of flux and transformation became more fitting metaphors for nuclear power, as a quick review of the newspapers of that time indicates. In the understandings of the wider public, it became an organization less predictable and less controllable despite appearing deceptively stable. Although representing the big picture well, such a diagnosis would underestimate the political struggles that were in play in Germany at the time.

The general consensus that nuclear energy was too dangerous was founded on a long tradition of the green movement in Germany, evident in the strong Green Party (Bündnis 90/Die Grünen). Followers of this tradition had promoted the image of nuclear energy as dangerous for a long time. They had argued, in strong terms, that nuclear energy was something evil. The conservative party (CDU/CSU), on the other hand, had been much more reluctant in its damnation of nuclear power and had painted the image of an interim solution (German: Brückentechnologie, which is translated as "bridging technology"). Several public groups such as political parties or nongovernmental organizations had used different images when referring to nuclear power, from "necessary evil" to "eco-friendly alternative to fossil fuel." It is not difficult to see the political elements in these struggles for the appropriate image of nuclear power (Downer, 2014a, 2014b). Economic interests with powerful lobbies of traditional or renewable energy in the background motivated the struggle. After Fukushima, mobilizing an appropriate image was also important for political parties to secure votes in elections. In particular, the conservative parties leading the government had to change their appearance from reluctant proponents of nuclear power to forceful change agents. The opposing parties (especially the Green Party) were quick to point out any delays in the exit strategy that could somehow be associated with the conservative party. Thereby, the Green

Party could use the image of dangerous nuclear power to show how the Green Party reflected public opinion whereas the Conservatives were reluctant to do so.

With time, the struggle had shifted from whether to exit nuclear power to what the time horizon of an exit was. This debate is still ongoing at the time of writing and gives an indication that general agreement does not necessarily rest on the same interpretations of an image at multiple local levels. In each case, imagination involves both representations of what nuclear power is and political and ideological debates of what it can become. This is evident in the fact that Germany was, at least as a reaction to the disaster in Fukushima, the only country worldwide that abandoned nuclear power production.

This small vignette of the consequences of the Fukushima nuclear accident shows how imagination can be understood from different perspectives. Following Morgan's view, imagination relates to the metaphors people choose as fitting for analyzing and organizing nuclear power. Following Castoriadis's view, imagination is about the continuous struggle about how an image is used in practice for politics; that is, creating and maintaining a particular image of nuclear power is about which interests and actions become politically dominant through a mobilization of imagination. In this regard, Castoriadis (1987, 1994) offers two more concepts that help to describe the forces involved in such political struggles over meanings: the instituted and the instituting imaginary.

The instituted imaginary refers not to what Tsoukas (1991) describes as dead metaphors, but rather to the ongoing attempts of people to maintain some significations consistent with certain forms of doing things. Consider, for instance, the attempts to shape organizations according to culturally established preferences; for example, when advocates of the organization as a machine reaffirm their preferences continuously by defining lines of what distinguishes good from bad organizational practice, such as efficiency is good, inefficiency is bad, lines of authority are good, no authority is bad. It is not the case that such practices are unimportant; the point is that these preferences are sustained by practices and the imaginary alike. The instituted imaginary thus supports forms of organizing by providing an entire network of significations that are defended and hard to change.[1]

The instituted imaginary, however dominant it may be, is always open to questioning. Castoriadis calls the emerging changes within the social imaginary the **instituting imaginary**. The instituting imaginary refers to emerging values, beliefs, and actions that potentially endanger the instituted imaginary in order to create new meanings and ways of organizing. Such meanings arise, accordingly, from the inside of societies and organizations, operating through a radical form of imagination. The dynamic between instituted and instituting imaginary underscores society's and an organization's capacity to invent itself through images. These images might emerge in the form of a need to establish or renew values, beliefs, and expectations, for example, after a global financial crisis that leads people to call for greater accountability of banks or a nuclear catastrophe that leads to a revaluation of environmental risk. Such a process is always, and at the same time, a creative and political process. The concepts developed by Castoriadis highlight the politics inherent in the use of images in organizations. The concepts bring forth the conflicting interpretations of images through which people talk and act in order to control the imaginary in organizations. The ideas advanced in this section help us to understand that images are not only tools that analysts use to read and shape organizations from multiple perspectives (i.e., imaginization); images in the broader sense of imaginary significations are also constructs over which actors struggle to make sense and shape the future of organizations.

Discussion and Conclusions

This chapter has elaborated a view of images of organization in which imagination has a privileged role. More specifically, the chapter highlights the political significance of imagination in processes of organizing. In this respect, two aspects of imagination became clear. First, a Ricoeur-inspired account of imagination helps to show that organizational behavior varies depending on the understanding of images one takes and how reflexively people engage with them. However, this shows that different forms of imagination lead to competing roles of images in organizations. Second, the works of Castoriadis provide a conceptualization of the social aspects of imagination and image. A Castoriadian perspective underscores the political role of images and imagination in social interactions. Images are, in this view, not only metaphors enabling different "ways of seeing," but also loci of conflicting interpretations, interests, and values. This final section outlines the consequences of this latter view for organizational research and practice. It first compares Morgan's (implicit) concept of imagination with the one proposed in this chapter and then discusses the ethical implications of a politically informed understanding of imagination.

A Comprehensive Concept of Imagination

By bringing imagination and images into relation, this chapter helps to show how images can mobilize the imagination of organizational actors in order to legitimate, reproduce, challenge, or deceive organizations. Each set of assumptions results in different outcomes regarding organizational behavior and action. It is worth noting that, despite being described in mutually exclusive terms, these sets may coexist in organizations. Accordingly, images very much depend on individual imagination and how different people's imaginations are in conflict with each other. Applying Ricoeur's (1994) framework to Morgan's *Images of Organization*, Morgan mostly assumes that individuals are fascinated by images and passive either because they take images for granted or because only a small elite group uses images for organizational analysis and change (e.g., see quadrant 1, imagination legitimates organizations). However, one finds traces of other assumptions about imagination in Morgan's work because people sometimes become more active in imagining their own organization. Especially in Morgan's book *Imaginization*, people take a more active stance toward images. Although they do not produce new ones, they engage in using them (e.g., see quadrant 2, imagination reproduces organization). It is interesting to see *Images of Organization* and *Imaginization* as two sides of a coin because the sets of assumptions about imagination identified in the matrix appeared to be, as Ricoeur implied, mutually exclusive. The answer to this puzzle is politics.

The political stance underlying Morgan's assumption about image and imagination become more evident in the book *Imaginization*. In that book, the images of organization are put to use to help management creatively find new ways of seeing and organizing. It is helpful to look at that book in addition to *Images of Organization* because it claims that images can be used for helping organizations. In *Images of Organization*, Morgan advocates for a mostly descriptive view of metaphor because people can use different images to interpret organization ("reading the organization"); in *Imaginization*, he assumes a normative stance in the sense that images are important for "writing the organization."

In the book *Imaginization*, the story usually goes that an organization corresponds to a certain image and then the management imagines a different image and the organization is changed for the better. Here prevails a form of discrimination with regard to who has what kind of imagination. Managers have active imagination and can exercise it creatively in order to change the organization; employees in turn will only reproduce a dominant image. In the Ricoeur-inspired matrix, the set of assumptions in quadrant 2 (imagination reproduces organization) applies here because only some have the power to use images; for others, imagination is an instrument of domination. As this chapter argues, this is a deeply politicized view in which politics refers to who can force which interests on whom. In this sense, top management holds power because of its better position to impose particular images on the other parts of the organization. Any political struggle, say, of a trade union, would then also be a political struggle around the dominant image coming from multiple imaginations. Morgan's stance toward organizational change, creativity, and imagination is, in this view, deeply political because it reinforces a widespread stereotype in organizational studies of creativity unanimously leading to better performance.

Imaginary Struggles for Power

The good news for the powerless (and the bad for the powerful) is that if images are deeply political, at least in principle, then the image-based political structures can always change. Symbolic struggles about images are one way of upsetting the balance of power. However, major changes to the balance of power in organizations happen only occasionally. Consistent with this, most people in an organization agree to the diagnosis of one specific core metaphor being dominant. With respect to Morgan's work, the question can be asked: If images are political and yet could be changed, then why are they seen as fairly stable?

By building on the works of Cornelius Castoriadis, two points help to explain why images of organization are political yet fairly stable. First, for Castoriadis, imagination is something that a whole society achieves together. It is not only individuals who imagine something, but rather what all collectively imagine that makes a difference. The social imaginary significations, as Castoriadis calls them, cannot be easily changed by an individual because they are a collective product. That means that individual imagination makes a difference to the extent that it politically influences how imaginary significations are put into practice. In an organization, this might be easier for powerful top managers than for lowly ranked employees; however, images set by top management are not free from contradiction coming from alternative imaginations.

The second point helping to explain why images are political yet fairly stable is that the content of imagination matters. Although some ideas defend and reproduce an already established image, others challenge and add to this image. Castoriadis calls these two aspects of collectively imagining the instituted and the instituting imaginary. These imaginations influence each other (see Figure 9.4), which means that images are principally open to the creation of new meanings. Images can be undermined, bent, or used to justify practices and aspects that favor one particular point of view and interest. Struggles around the meaning of images are therefore at the heart of politics. Sometimes, these struggles are settled by compromise built on a practical definition of an image; at other times, struggles around meanings are settled by imposition or coercion.

The political struggles over images can make organizations conservative and hard to change, but they also may eventually lead to new ideas and unexpected ways of organizing. However, what an image actually does will depend on the totality of individuals' who are interpreting the images and acts on them. Coming back to *Images of Organization*, an example would be if an image of an organization as a psychic prisons serves the discourse of a minority who feel oppressed, then they will likely use this image to undermine any competing image of the organization, say, as a big family. The dominant group in turn may use this image for its own ends, saying that they are working on many projects to better the organization. Whether change in the organization will happen depends on which group has more power of persuasion or how compromise will be achieved. In short, because political struggles take place whenever people try to interpret and give meaning to images in practice, every use of images in organizations is a political act.

FIGURE 9.4 ● The Instituted and Instituting Imaginary

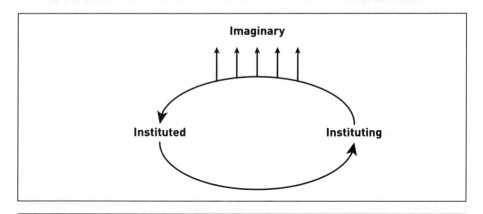

Source: Adapted from V. H. Klein (2015).

The Ethics of Imagination

An important set of implications for organizational studies and practice concerns the ethics underpinning the use of images and imagination in organizations. In Morgan's works, imagination is seen as something that most of the time produces positive outcomes, especially when individuals use imagination to change the images through which they understand (their) organizations. From this view, organizations can gain potential for innovation, reduce internal struggles, or find a new reflexivity, enabling them to improve important organizational capabilities. However, the comprehensive account of imagination presented in this chapter emphasizes that creativity is not necessarily good for organizations. On the contrary, imagination may sometimes lead to terrible consequences, especially when it hinders critical thinking, the Nazi regime and all of its symbolism being a most villainous example (Castoriadis, 1997). More mundanely, the many forms of "bullshitting" in organizations are an example of how imagination can jeopardize organizational culture through deceptive or plainly nonsensical images (Frankfurt, 2005; Spicer, 2013). Imagination must be accounted for in its role in the creation and maintenance of mischievous, ridiculing, or misguiding images of organization. It is, therefore, very important to address the role of positive and negative outcomes of imagination when images are used in organizations.

In conclusion, this chapter has argued that an in-depth study of imagination opens new windows into understanding the politics of organizing. Not fully theorized in *Images of Organization*, this chapter has proposed a concept of imagination based on the works of Paul Ricoeur (1994) and Cornelius Castoriadis (1987, 1994). Imagination is defined, accordingly, as a key resource with which organizational actors sustain, elicit, or impose ways of organizing through images. Future work will be needed to empirically study the political significance of imagination in organizational practice. Part of this inquiry will concern the fact that, without a theory of imagination, it is difficult to judge whether metaphors are used to hide vested interests (Tinker, 1986, p. 363) or to promote creative and different ways of thinking (Tsoukas, 1991). Consistent with Morgan's approach, this chapter suggests that students, practitioners, and researchers alike are capable of realizing the potential that images and imagination have for meaningful organizing.

Key Terms

Fancy

Image

Imagination

Imagining

Imaginization

Instituting imaginary

Mobilize the imagination

Perception

Power relations

Productive
  imagination

Reflective thinking

Root metaphor

Social constructionism
  and socially
  constructed

Social imaginary
  signification

Acknowledgment

We would like to thank an anonymous reviewer and Anders Örtenblad for their valuable suggestions. Likewise, we are thankful to Avelar Fortunato for designing the figures in the chapter.

Note

1. For a more complete account on the relation between the imaginary, logics, and institution, see V. H. Klein, 2015).

References

Anderson, C. A., Lepper, M. R., & Ross, L. (1980). Perseverance of social theories: The role of explanation in the persistence of discredited information. *Journal of Personality and Social Psychology, 39*(6), 1037–1049.

Bachelard, G. (1969). *On poetic imagination and reverie*. Hartford, CT: Spring.

Brown, A., Stacey, P., & Nandhakumar, J. (2008). Making sense of sensemaking narratives. *Human Relations,* 61(8), 1035–1062.

Carrol, J. S. (1978). The effect of imagining an event on expectations for the event: An interpretation in terms of the availability heuristic. *Journal of Experimental Social Psychology, 14*(1), 88–96.

Castoriadis, C. (1987). *The imaginary institution of society*. Cambridge, MA: MIT Press.

Castoriadis, C. (1994). Radical imagination and the social instituting imaginary. In G. Robinson & J. Rundell (Eds.), *Rethinking imagination: Culture and creativity* (pp. 136–154). London, England: Routledge.

Castoriadis, C. (1997). Done and to be done. In D. A. Curtis (Ed.), *The Castoriadis reader* (pp. 361–417). Oxford, England: Oxford University Press.

Cornelissen, J. (2006). Metaphor and the dynamics of knowledge in organization theory: A case study of the organizational identity metaphor. *Journal of Management Studies, 43*(4), 683–709.

Cornelissen, J., & Clarke, J. (2010). Imagining and rationalizing opportunities: Inductive reasoning and the creation and justification of new ventures. *Academy of Management Review,* 35(4), 539–557.

Cornelissen, J., Holt, R., & Zundel, M. (2011). The role of analogy and metaphor in the framing and legitimization of strategic change. *Organization Studies, 32*(12), 1701–1716.

Cunliffe, A. L. (2004). On becoming a critically reflexive practitioner. *Journal of Management Education, 28*(4), 407–426.

Cunliffe, A. L., & Jun, J. S. (2005). The need for reflexivity in public administration. *Administration & Society, 37*(2), 225–242.

Douglas, M., & Wildavsky, A. (1982). *Risk and culture: An essay on the selection of technological and environmental dangers*. Berkeley: University of California Press.

Downer, J. (2014a). *In the shadow of Tomioka: On the institutional invisibility of nuclear disaster*. London, England: London School of Economics Centre for Analysis of Risk and Regulation.

Downer, J. (2014b). Rationalising the meltdown. In P. Ladkin, C. Goeker, & B. Sieker (Eds.), *The Fukushima Dai-Ichi accident* (pp. 79–96). Munster, Germany: LIT Verlag.

Frankfurt, H. (2005). *On bullshit*. Princeton, NJ: Princeton University Press.

Hilgartner, S. (1992). The social construction of risk objects: Or, how to pry open networks of risk. In J. F. Short & L. Clarke (Eds.), *Organizations, uncertainties, and risk* (pp. 39–53). Boulder, CO: Westview Press.

Huber, C., & Scheytt, T. (2013) The dispositif of risk management: Reconstructing risk management after the financial crisis. *Management Accounting Research, 24*(2), 88–99.

Inns, D. (2002). Metaphor in the literature of organizational analysis: A preliminary taxonomy and a glimpse at a humanities-based perspective. *Organization, 9*(2), 305–330.

Klein, N. (2000). *No logo*. New York, NY: Knopf.

Klein, V. H., Jr. (2015). Bringing values back in: The limitations of institutional logics and the relevance of dialectical phenomenology. *Organization, 22*(3), 326–350.

Merriam-Webster. (1984). *Webster's New Dictionary of Synonyms*. Springfield, MA: Author.

Milne, M. J., Kearins, K., & Walton, S. (2002). Creating adventures in wonderland: The journey metaphor and environmental sustainability. *Organization, 27*(2), 294–303.

Morgan, G. (1983). More on metaphor: Why we cannot control tropes in administrative science. *Administrative Science Quarterly, 28*(4), 601–607.

Morgan, G. (1986). *Images of organization*. Beverly Hills, CA: Sage.

Morgan, G. (1993). *Imaginization: New mindsets for seeing, organizing and managing*. London, England: Sage.

Oettingen, G., Schnetter, K., & Pak, H.-J. (2001). Self-regulation of goal setting: Turning free fantasies about the future into binding goals. *Journal of Personality and Social Psychology, 80*(5), 736–753.

Oswick, C., Keenoy, T., & Grant, D. (2002). Metaphor and analogical reasoning in organization theory: Beyond orthodoxy. *Academy of Management Review, 27*(2), 294–303.

Pablo, Z., & Hardy, C. (2009). Merging, masquerading and morphing: Metaphors and the World Wide Web. *Organization Studies, 30*(8), 821–843.

Pinder, C., & Bourgeois, V. W. (1982). Controlling tropes in administrative science. *Administrative Science Quarterly, 27,* 641–652.

Puyo, F.-R., Quattrone, P., McLean, C., & Thrift, N. (2012). *Imagining organizations: Performative imagery in business and beyond*. New York, NY: Routledge.

Reed, M. (1990). From paradigms to images: The paradigm warrior turns post-modernist guru. *Personnel Review, 19*(3), 35–40.

Ricoeur, P. (1994). Imagination in discourse and in action. In G. Robinson & J. Rundell (Eds.), *Rethinking imagination* (pp. 118–135). London, England: Routledge.

Sackmann, S. (1989). The role of metaphors in organisation transformation. *Human Relations, 42*(6), 463–485.

Sievers, B. (1999). Psychotic organization as a metaphoric frame for the socioanalysis of organizational and interorganizational dynamics. *Administration & Society, 31*(5), 588–615.

Sievers, B. (2003). Your money or your life? Psychotic implications of the pension fund system: Towards a socio-analysis of the financial services revolution. *Human Relations, 56*(2), 187–210.

Sievers, B. (2008). The psychotic university. *Ephemera, 8*(3), 238–257.

Spicer, A. (2013). Shooting the shit: The role of bullshit in organisations. *M@n@gement, 16*(5), 653–666.

Tinker, T. (1986). Metaphor or reification: Are radical humanists really libertarian anarchists? *Journal of Management Studies, 23*(4), 363–384.

Tsoukas, H. (1991). The missing link: A transformational view of metaphors in organizational science. *Academy of Management Review, 16*(3), 566–585.

Tversky, A., & Kahneman, D. (1973). Availability: A heuristic for judging frequency and probability. *Cognitive Psychology, 5*, 207–232.

Urribarri, F. (2002). Castoriadis: The radical imagination and the post-Lacanian unconscious. *Thesis Eleven, 7*(1), 40–51.

Weick, K. (1979). *The social psychology of organizing*. Reading, MA: Addison-Wesley.

Weick, K. E. (2005). Organizing and failures of imagination. *International Public Management Journal, 8*(3), 425–438.

Weick, K. E. (2006). The role of imagination in the organizing of knowledge. *European Journal of Information Systems, 15*(5), 446–452.

Organization as Affect

Moving on Metaphorically

David Grant and Cliff Oswick

Key Learning Points

- Understand the value of the existing body of work on metaphor and organization.
- Appreciate the challenges posed to the application and value of metaphor to the study of organization by new forms of organization and ways of organizing.
- Understand future directions in the use of metaphor as a vehicle for studying organizations, including critically engaging with Morgan's development of new metaphors of organization.
- Understand the metaphor of "affect" in the study of organization, specifically in relation to new forms of organization and ways of organizing.

Some 20 years ago, we reflected on the use and value of metaphor in the field of organization studies and asked: "Where are we and where do we go from here?" (Oswick & Grant, 1996b). In doing so, we drew on an observation made by George Lakoff and Mark Johnson (1980) in their seminal work *Metaphors We Live By*. These scholars noted how the metaphor of a journey seems to apply to all walks of life. It is, for example, apparent where we consider life as a journey or purposes as destinations (Lakoff, 1987).

Revisiting the Metaphor
and Organization Journey

To us, writing in the mid-1990s, the metaphor of a journey also seemed highly applicable within the field of organization studies; we noted it being used to portray approaches and practices such as human resource management or organization development and change as either an ongoing or discrete journey (Grant, 1996; Marshak, 1993; Oswick & Grant, 1996a). We also argued that the idea of a journey could be used as a means by which to consider and explore the application of metaphor to organizations and organization theory. Accordingly, we presented an interpretation of where, at that point in time, metaphor-focused research in organization studies was in its journey and proposed some alternative ways forward for researchers involved in the journey's next stages.

Our review led us to suggest that the work undertaken thus far as part of the metaphor and organization journey had been of considerable value. It had involved the successful translation of concepts taken from disciplines such as philosophy, linguistics, and cognitive psychology and their application to organization theory. This, in turn, had contributed to the popularization of metaphor-related research in organization studies and the generation of new understanding about the significance of metaphor to the study of organization among organization theorists.

Although we welcomed these developments, we went on to argue that existing approaches to the study of metaphor would not, by and large, yield further fresh insight and understanding. We cautioned that, in effect, the journey that we were describing was in danger of reaching a dead end. To resolve this, we highlighted three possible new avenues of research:

1). More **applied research** on metaphor in organization theory and analysis
2). Using metaphor as a **vehicle** for, rather than a target of, research
3). Greater exploration of other **tropes** (**synecdoche**, **irony**, and **metonymy**) closely related to metaphor

Our sense is that the last 20 years has yielded much research across these three areas, as evidenced by contributions in this edited volume. There have been significant applied studies of metaphor and a greater emphasis on using metaphor as a vehicle for studying organization (Amernic, Craig, & Tourish, 2007; Cornelissen, Holt, & Zundel, 2012; Fleming, 2005; Hatch & Yanow, 2008; Heracleous & Jacobs, 2008; Latusek & Vlaar, 2015; Oswick & Montgomery, 1999; Pablo & Hardy, 2009). Similarly, there have been several studies that have sought to examine the **generative value** of tropes associated with metaphor (Alcadipani, Westwood, & Rosa, 2015; Cornelissen, Kafouros, & Lock, 2005; Hamilton, 2003; Musson & Tietze, 2004; Oswick, Keenoy, & Grant, 2002; Oswick, Putnam, & Keenoy, 2004).

It seems, then, that the metaphor and organization journey has continued along the lines that we argued for in our 1996 chapter—and with some success. Metaphor-based studies continue to appear regularly in the organization studies literature and many have, in our opinion, made the kind of meaningful contributions that we were hoping for.

A New Challenge

Now, however, the value of metaphor to the study of organization is once again being challenged and, with it, the progression of the metaphor and organization journey. On this occasion, the challenge is not self-inflicted in the way that it was 20 years ago; that is, it does not emanate from the way that researchers are studying or applying metaphor per se. Rather the challenge emanates from the changes that are taking place in the way that people think about and perform organization and organizing. The difficulties now being encountered are not so much concerned with "deploying the wrong metaphors" (i.e., a **figurative vehicle problem**) as much as they are with "the wrong conceptualization of organizations" (i.e., a **literal target problem**).

The emergence of new forms of organization and ways of organizing means that those involved in their study must find new ways to explain and understand these phenomena. This applies as much to researchers interested in applying metaphor to the study of organizations as it does to researchers who use other approaches. Specifically, it means that those using metaphor-based approaches are struggling to generate insight into new organizational forms that have emerged as a result of new social and economic structures and the rapid advances in technology that have fuelled the digital disruption and transformation of the way that organizations interact with their stakeholders (e.g., customers, employees, shareholders, the wider community, etc.) and each other.

These changes have challenged prevailing thinking about the application and value of metaphor to the study of organization to the extent that even the salience of the eight metaphors identified in Gareth Morgan's (1986) now seminal work, *Images of Organization*, might be called into question. **Metaphorical analysis** should concentrate primarily on the similarities between the metaphor (commonly referred to as the "source" or "base" domain) and the subject or object onto which it is projected (the "target" domain) (Lakoff & Johnson, 1980; Ortony, 1993; Tsoukas, 1991). Meaningful insights arise in situations in which the **source domain** shares an optimum level of overlap (i.e., moderate similarities) with the **target domain**. In the case of Morgan's eight metaphors (organizations as machines, organisms, brains, cultures, political systems, psychic prisons, systems of change and flux, and instruments of domination), these seem, as source domains, unable to provide sufficient overlap with a target domain characterized by new organizational forms and behaviors that are now a prevalent part of our everyday social and working lives. Indeed, in a recent interview with us, Morgan himself reflected that although they might act as highly effective but "relatively static reflections" (i.e., provide a history of organization theory), their capacity to act as "relatively dynamic projections" (i.e., to help stimulate the formulation of further organizational images) in the present context is uncertain (Oswick & Grant, 2015).

During the interview, Morgan went on to discuss the potential for new organizational metaphors to address this challenge and highlighted two specific metaphors that he thought offered interesting possibilities. These were the "global brain" and the "organization as media," which build upon the earlier work of McLuhan (1964) who is credited with predicting the advent of the Internet and who talks about such technological innovation creating a "global village." Both metaphors go a considerable way in helping us to understand recent developments in organization. In the case of the global brain, Morgan observes that, clearly, this is a variation on his brain metaphor, but that "it goes way beyond this" in that it helps us to understand the significance of the Internet and to grapple with the emerging importance of **"Big Data"** and the **"knowledge economy"** (Oswick & Grant, 2015, pp. 2–3). In the case of the organization as media metaphor, Morgan suggests that this opens up new understandings of what we mean by literacy (i.e., it goes beyond our thinking of literacy as just being associated with the written word) and that it can help us better comprehend the digital revolution and shift to electronic-mediated, multisensory modes of understanding and communication, all of which are occurring at levels of intensity that we have not experienced before (Oswick & Grant, 2015, pp. 3–4).

Morgan's new metaphors offer valuable ways of thinking about the role of technology in driving new forms of organization and organizing. However, as helpful as these two new metaphors may be, our sense is that they are partial representations insofar as they rely heavily on "technology" as the primary mechanism for capturing what is happening to contemporary organization and organizing. In short, we wonder whether privileging a "technology lens" may unduly overshadow or obscure other metaphors that can generate alternative ways of thinking.

The "global brain" and "media" metaphors may also unintentionally reinforce a widely held perception that new forms of organization and organizing result in, and are confined to, nontraditional organizations or particular sectors of the economy. Examples of such organizations might include UK-based Agora, which seeks to foster social innovation by developing initiatives and projects that are based on maximizing cooperation and trust and minimizing hierarchy (Agora, 2015), and US-based Zappos, a mail order firm that adopted "holacracy," a form of governance and organization under which CEOs formally relinquish their authority to a constitution and reorganize everyone into decentralized teams that choose their own roles and goals (Zappos, 2015).

To us, then, it would seem that although the metaphors proposed by Morgan are helpful, they do not sufficiently capture and express the impact and extent of the radical, even paradigmatic, shifts in organization and organizing that have permeated all sectors of the economy and wider society. These shifts are epitomized by, for example, an increased focus on new network structures (Enjolras, Steen-Johnsen, & Wollebæk, 2013; Mao & Shen, 2015; Waters, Burnett, Lamm, & Lucas, 2009), the social role of the organization (Earl, 2015; Huag, 2013; Rao et al., 2000), interorganization collaboration (Hardy, Lawrence, & Grant, 2005; Newell & Swann, 2000; Vangen & Huxam, 2003), continuous organizational change (Brown & Eisenhardt, 1997; Marshak, 2002; Pettigrew, Woodman, & Cameron, 2001), stakeholder-focused organizations (Sloan & Oliver, 2013; Weitzner & Deutsch, 2015; Yu, 2012), connectivity (Kolb, Caza, & Collins, 2012; MacCormick, Dery, & Kolb, 2012; Matusik & Mickel, 2011), and a greater differentiation between leadership and management (Alvesson & Sveningsson, 2003; Carroll & Levy, 2008; Kotterman, 2006).

Organization as Affect

We contend that a more expansive and productive metaphor, one that might better cope with developments in organization and organizing, is that of **affect**. To us, it seems that underlying the many changes that we have seen in organization and organizing is the capacity for organizations to perform in ways that can only be described as affective. Affect is more than just emotion. Emotion relates to an individual's internal state. More specifically, and for organizational scholars, affect takes us beyond the idea of emotional labor (Hochschild, 1983). **Emotional labor** focuses on how workers feel when they are required to develop interpersonal and decision-making skills previously reserved for managers and, in doing so, to come up with outcomes and changes that respond to a need for more flexible work processes, ongoing restructuring, and improvement and the search for product uniqueness (Barley & Kunda, 2001; Castells, 2004). Affect, in contrast, is a focus on how people interact socially and connect with one another. It is **"trans-personal"** in that it manifests as a socialized impulse, driving particular ways of being and doing. Therefore, it is something that is seemingly illogical and unpredictable and cannot easily be captured by language (Brennan, 2004; Deleuze, 1997; Massumi, 2002).

We are aware that some have already looked at affect in organizations in the literal sense; that is, they have examined how affect manifests itself among, and impacts upon, the interactions and behaviors of individual organizational members. Here, however, we are applying affect as a metaphor at the organizational level as a means by which to generate alternative understanding and meanings attached to new forms of organization and organizing that arise from the interactions and behaviors of organizations.

As a metaphor for developments in contemporary organizations and organizing, affect offers some interesting possibilities. We offer a few short illustrations. The metaphor might, for example, help us to explain the new forms of organization and organizing that we have witnessed in the online and digital space and to understand the impact of digital disruption. This could include its encouraging new ways of thinking about and new ways of seeing the emergence, mobilization, and representation, often via the use of social media, of key stakeholders and interest groups and the expectation of instantaneous responses from organizations to their demands. (Think, for example, of the recent backlash, much of it via social media, to Volkswagen [VW] having misled customers and regulatory agencies about emissions from diesel vehicles and how, in order to contain damage to its reputation and brand, the company immediately responded using social media.[1]) More specifically, it could include the metaphor generating fresh insight into the emergence of, for example, virtual forms of organization (Chalofsky, 2010; Gilson, Maynard, Jones Young, Vartiainen, & Hakonen, 2015; Verona, Prandelli, & Sawhney, 2006; Wilson, Boyer O'Leary, Metiu, & Jett et al., 2008) and the advent of crowd-sourcing techniques used to organize social action or to secure funding and support for entrepreneurial activities (Bauer & Gegenhuber, 2015; Brabham, 2012; Howe, 2008; Wexler, 2011).

The organization as affect metaphor might also be helpful in explaining Morgan's observation (referred to earlier when we discussed his "organization as media" metaphor) that we are no longer tied to literal (written) forms of media and that we can express ourselves more freely and spontaneously, often using technology such as social media and using visual cues such as emojis (Oswick & Grant, 2015). Related to this, affect is recognized to be a very time-efficient way of transmitting a large amount of information (Thrift, 2004). As Iedema and Grant (2013, p. 67) observe, "We can communicate more in the split-second that we hold someone else's gaze than in the report that took us a week to craft." Furthermore, the nature of affect means that there can be an involuntary instant response to such affective behavior. In summary, affect is something that can manifest and spread in a very short period of time and can communicate a large amount of information. Again, these attributes seem commensurate with the many forms of organization and organizing that take place in the digital and online spaces. Applied through a metaphor-based lens, they help us to understand and explain the now taken-for-granted and expected immediacy of organizational conduct and outcomes.

A further attribute of the organization as affect metaphor is that it helps to address an important point that we made above: That much of the attention paid to new forms of organization and organizing has focused on "nontraditional" organizations or, in particular, often new sectors of the economy such as those pertaining to information and communication technology, digitalization, and innovation. However, when we look at new forms of organizing and organization, these are not, of course, confined to the nontraditional and include a focus on changes that affect all sectors of the economy. By way of example, there has been a dramatic rise in **"knowledge work"** and, with it, ways of organizing that center on the generation, dissemination, and application of data and information as quickly as possible across all sectors. These ways of organizing have, in turn, resulted in a knowledge-based economy characterized by "informationalisation, networking, and globalisation" (Castells, 2004). Scholars have created the term **fast capitalism** to describe the rapidity with which these dynamics are played out (Gee & Lankshear, 1995). To survive it, and in order to keep apace with their competitors, organizations must be more innovative and creative and instantly respond to the latest developments in their fields: "Change has become 'the name of the game.' Organizations old and new, irrespective of sector, now engage in change because this has become the norm: not changing is no longer a viable business option" (Iedema & Grant, 2013, p. 66).

This need to change cannot be put down to simple explanations such as products becoming obsolete faster than ever before or that competitors are able to revise their production and service streams thanks to advances in technology. Rather, change is now viewed as a resource in and of itself and as a way of the organization "asserting . . . vitality" (Iedema & Grant, 2013, p. 66). What is intriguing about this change is that it is not simply being driven by a need for improvement, but instead by a perceived need to establish new kinds of economic and social credibility (Thrift, 2004) among key organizational stakeholders (employees, customers, the public, shareholders, etc.). Obtaining this credibility relies on being temporary and always becoming different. It has led to modern organizations increasingly exhibiting "unstable interaction systems" among themselves and with these various stakeholders. In short and consistent with the way that affect plays out for the contemporary organization, the unexpected is an increasingly expected and accepted way of doing things. There is a perceived value attached to uncertainty and such uncertainty is obtained via practices, services, and products being subject to constant reinvention (Iedema & Grant, 2008, pp. 66–67). Achieving this requires a reorientation away from structures that predetermine or regulate an organization's actions and a move toward processes and interactions that, as with affect, enable it to innovate the present (Spinosa, Flores, & Dreyfus, 1997). As a result, in responding to its stakeholder needs, the organization is immediately able to capitalize on the interaction taking place in innovative and often unexpected ways and is adept at quickly identifying new opportunities and solutions.

Conclusions

In this chapter, we have sought to find a way in which to progress the metaphor and organization journey. Our concern has been that, at present, there appear to have been few, if any, studies that have offered a metaphor or metaphors that sufficiently resonate with, and thereafter help us to understand and make sense of, the new forms of organization and organizing that have emerged recently. This dearth of studies represents an impasse on the journey. Our suggested solution has been to propose a new metaphor: that of organization as affect.

We appreciate that, as with many metaphors, ours may not work for everyone and its effectiveness will rest on its interpretation by the individual (Davidson, 1978). For some, the metaphor will have its limitations. These might, for example, emanate from a belief that there is insufficient overlap between the source and target domains or that the metaphor is too superficial to yield any meaningful insight. In other instances, the limitation might reflect concerns about the purchase and value of a metaphor that seemingly **reifies** organization (Døving, 1996; Tinker, 1986).

Our response to these concerns is twofold. First, we believe that our proposed metaphor should only be seen as *a* metaphor for examining new forms of organization and organizing and that it should not been seen as *the* metaphor for doing so. Our aim has been to identify and apply a metaphor that can be used as an effective vehicle for analyzing contemporary organization. This aim, an **applied metaphor approach** in which metaphor is a vehicle by which to analyze organizational phenomena, is consistent with two of the three approaches that we suggested for progressing the metaphor and organization journey in our 1996 chapter (Oswick & Grant, 1996b). The third approach was to explore and use other tropes associated with metaphor. We would welcome studies that use other metaphors as alternatives to ours, adopt any or all of these three approaches, and shed further light on the organizational phenomena that we have discussed.

Second, this chapter has merely proposed the metaphor of affect as a way of addressing a challenge currently faced by organization scholars and, specifically, those interested in the application of metaphor to organization. Aside from the illustrations used to demonstrate some key points, the chapter does not seek to apply the metaphor in any great detail. Instead, our intention has been to use it as an opportunity to provoke discussion about the metaphor and to highlight its potential. We hope that our doing so encourages others to test the metaphor's veracity. Moreover, we anticipate that placing it under such scrutiny will lead to its being developed further and in ways that demonstrate its value, thereby addressing the concerns and possible limitations that we have highlighted.

Ortony (1975, p. 45) contended that "vividness," "compactness," and the "ability to convey the inexpressible" are qualities that make metaphor a valuable aid to learning. These are qualities that have the potential to enhance research. First, the **compactness** and **vividness** of metaphor can help to ensure that manageable amounts of valid information and data are generated. Second, metaphors can provide a means of accessing the aspects of organization and organizing that we would otherwise find difficult to articulate in literal terms (Oswick & Grant, 1996b). The new forms of organization and organizing that we have discussed in this chapter have far-reaching social and economic implications. We therefore hope that the organization as affect metaphor is proven to have these qualities and that it becomes a valuable medium with which to develop new insights into these important organizational phenomena.

Key Terms

Affect	Knowledge work
Applied metaphor approach	Literal target problem
Applied research	Metaphorical analysis
Big Data	Metonymy
Compactness	Reifies
Emotional labor	Source domain
Fast capitalism	Synecdoche
Figurative vehicle	Target domain
problem	Trans-personal
Generative value	Tropes
Irony	Vehicle
Knowledge economy	Vividness

Note

1. After investigation in the United States, VW admitted in September 2015 that it had manipulated software in diesel engines in up to 11 million vehicles sold worldwide by its VW, Audi, Skoda, and SEAT brands. There was a significant public outcry and customer criticism, much of it conveyed via social media. In the days after the initial revelations, VW's stock lost around a third of its value (US$29 billion), suggesting serious investor concern (VW went on to post a 2015 €1.73 billion (US$1.9 billion) third-quarter net loss and issued a full-year profit warning) (Boston, 2015). In response to the scandal, the company CEO Martin Winterkorn and other senior executives either stepped down or were suspended as part of a management reorganization. At the same time, VW sought to quickly and robustly address the crisis by monitoring sentiment on social media and launching a campaign to show that it was acting immediately and decisively not only to fix the problems but also to tell people that it was doing so. The campaign itself was generally regarded as having contained some of the damage to the company's reputation and brand value and, in so doing, to have increased VW's chances of long-term survival (Coleman, 2015).

References

Agora. (2015). Agora. Retrieved from http://www.agora.uk.com/

Alcadipani, R., Westwood, R., & Rosa, A. (2015). The politics of identity in organizational ethnographic research: Ethnicity and tropicalist intrusions. *Human Relations, 68*(1), 79–106.

Alvesson M., & Sveningsson. S. (2003). Managers doing leadership: The extra-ordinarization of the mundane. *Human Relations, 56*(12), 1435–1459.

Amernic, J., Craig, R., & Tourish, D. (2007). The transformational leader as pedagogue, physician, architect, commander, and saint: Five root metaphors in Jack Welch's letters to stockholders of General Electric. *Human Relations, 60*(12), 1839–1872.

Barley, S., & Kunda, G. (2001). Bringing work back in. *Organization Science, 12*(1), 76–95.

Bauer R. M., & Gegenhuber, T. (2015). Crowdsourcing: Global search and the twisted roles of consumers and producers. *Organization, 22*(5), 661–681.

Boston. W. (2015, October 28). Volkswagen posts loss as emissions scandal bites. *Wall Street Journal*. Retrieved from http://www.wsj.com/articles/volkswagen-posts-loss-as-emissions-scandal-bites-1446021802?mod=pls_whats_news_us_business_f

Brabham, D. C. (2012). Crowdsourcing: A model for leveraging online communities. In A. Henderson & J. Delwiche (Eds.), *The Routledge handbook of participatory culture* (pp. 120–141). New York, NY: Routledge.

Brennan, T. (2004). *The transmission of affect*. Ithaca, NY: Cornell University Press.

Brown, S., & Eisenhardt, K. (1997). The art of continuous change: Linking complexity theory and time-paced evolution in relentlessly shifting organizations. *Administrative Science Quarterly, 42*(1), 1–34.

Carroll, B., & Levy, L. (2008). Defaulting to management: Leadership defined by what it is not. *Organization, 15*(1), 75–96.

Castells, M. (2004). *The power of identity (the information age: Economy, society and culture* Vol. 2, 2nd ed.). Oxford, England: Blackwell.

Chalofsky, N. E. (2010). *Meaningful workplaces: Reframing how and where we work*. San Francisco, CA: Jossey-Bass.

Coleman, A. (2015, October 23). Saving your reputation when a PR scandal hits. *The Guardian*. Retrieved from http://www.theguardian.com/small-business-network/2015/oct/23/save-reputation-pr-scandal-media-brand

Cornelissen, J. P., Holt, R., & Zundel, M. (2012). The role of analogy and metaphor in the framing and legitimization of strategic change. *Organization Studies, 32*(2), 1701–1716.

Cornelissen, J. P., Kafouros, M., & Lock, A. R. (2005). Metaphorical images of organization: How organizational researchers develop and select organizational metaphors. *Human Relations, 58*(12), 1545–1578.

Davidson, D. (1978). What metaphors mean. In S. Sacks (Ed.), *On metaphor* (pp. 29–46). Chicago, IL: Chicago University Press.

Deleuze, G. (1997). *Essays critical and clinical* (D. W. Smith & M. A. Greco, Trans.). Minneapolis: University of Minnesota Press.

Døving, E. (1996). In the image of man: Organizational action, competence and learning. In D. Grant & C. Oswick (Eds.), *Metaphor and organizations* (pp. 185–199). London, England: Sage.

Earl, J. (2015). The future of social movement organizations: The waning dominance of SMOs online. *American Behavioral Scientist, 59*(1), 35–52.

Enjolras, B., Steen-Johnsen, K., & Wollebæk, D. (2013). Social media and mobilization to offline demonstrations: Transcending participatory divides? *New Media & Society, 15*(6), 890–908.

Fleming, P. (2005). Metaphors of resistance. *Management Communication Quarterly, 19*(1), 145–166.

Gee, J., & Lankshear, C. (1995). The new work order: Critical language awareness and fast capitalism. *Discourse: Studies in the Cultural Politics of Education, 16*(1), 5–19.

Gilson, L. L., Travis Maynard, M., Jones Young, N. C., Vartiainen, M., & Hakonen, M. (2015). Virtual teams research: 10 years, 10 themes, and 10 opportunities. *Journal of Management, 41*(5), 1313–1337.

Grant, D. (1996). Metaphors, HRM and control. In C. Oswick & D. Grant (Eds.), *Organisation development: Metaphorical explorations* (pp. 193–208). London, England: Pitman.

Hamilton, P. M. (2003). The saliency of synecdoche: The part and the whole of employment relations. *Journal of Management Studies, 40*(7), 1569–1585.

Hardy, C., Lawrence, T., & Grant, D. (2005). Discourse and collaboration: The role of conversations and collective identity. *Academy of Management Review, 30*(1), 58–77.

Hatch, M. J., & Yanow, D. (2008). Methodology by metaphor: Ways of seeing in painting and research. *Organization Studies, 29*(1), 23–44.

Haug, C. (2013). Organizing spaces: Meeting arenas as a social movement infrastructure between organization, network, and institution. *Organization Studies, 34*(5–6), 705–732.

Heracleous, L., & Jacobs. C. (2008). Understanding organizations through embodied metaphors. *Organization Studies, 29*(1), 45–78.

Hochschild, A. R. (1983). *The managed heart: Commercialisation of human feeling.* Berkeley: University of California Press.

Howe, J. (2008). *Crowdsourcing: Why the power of the crowd is driving the future of business.* New York, NY: Three Rivers.

Iedema, R., & Grant, D. (2013). Feeling and affect in the contemporary workplace. *European Business Review, 4,* 66–74.

Kolb, D. G., Caza, A., & Collins, P. D. (2012). States of connectivity: New questions and new directions. *Organization Studies, 33*(2), 267–273.

Kotterman, J. (2006). Leadership versus management: What's the difference? *Journal for Quality and Participation, 29*(2), 13–17.

Lakoff, G., & Johnson, M. (1980). *Metaphors we live by.* Chicago, IL: University of Chicago Press.

Latusek, D., & Vlaar, P. W. L. (2015). Exploring managerial talk through metaphor: An opportunity to bridge rigour and relevance? *Management Learning, 46*(2), 211–232.

MacCormick, J., Dery, K., & Kolb, D. (2012). Engaged or just connected? Smartphones and employee engagement. *Organizational Dynamics, 41*(3), 194–201.

Mao, J., & Shen, Y. (2015). Cultural identity change in expatriates: A social network perspective. *Human Relations, 68*(10), 1533–1556.

Marshak, R. J. (1993). Managing the metaphors of change. *Organizational Dynamics, 22*(1), 44–56.

Marshak, R. J. (2002). Changing the language of change: How new contexts and concepts are challenging the ways we think and talk about organizational change. *Strategic Change, 11*(5), 279–286.

Massumi, B. (2002). *Parables for the virtual: Movement, affect, sensation.* Durham, NC: Duke University Press.

Matusik, S. F., & Mickel, A. E. (2011). Embracing or embattled by converged mobile devices? Users' experiences with a contemporary connectivity technology. *Human Relations, 64*(8), 1001–1030.

McLuhan, M. (1964). *Understanding media: The extensions of man.* New York, NY: McGraw-Hill.

Morgan, G. (1986). *Images of organization.* Beverly Hills, CA: Sage.

Musson, G., & Tietze, S. (2004). Places and spaces: The role of metonymy in organizational talk. *Journal of Management Studies, 41*(8), 1301–1323.

Newell, S., & Swan, J. (2000). Trust and inter-organizational networking. *Human Relations, 53*(10), 1287–1328.

Ortony, A. (1975). Why metaphors are necessary and not just nice. *Educational Theory, 25*(1), 45–53.

Ortony, A. (1993). Metaphor, language and thought. In A. Ortony (Ed.), *Metaphor and thought* (2nd ed., pp. 1–16). Cambridge, England: Cambridge University Press.

Oswick, C., & Grant, D. (1996a). Organisation development and metaphors: Mapping the territory. In C. Oswick & D. Grant (Eds.), *Organisation development: Metaphorical explorations* (pp. 1–4). London, England: Pitman.

Oswick, C., & Grant, D. (1996b). The organization of metaphors and the metaphors of organization: Where are we and where do we go from here? In D. Grant & C. Oswick (Eds.), *Metaphor and organizations* (pp. 213–226). London, England: Sage.

Oswick, C., & Grant, D. (2015). Re-imagining images of organization: A conversation with Gareth Morgan. *Journal of Management Inquiry.* Advance online publication. doi: 10.1177/1056492615591854

Oswick, C., Keenoy, T., & Grant, D. (2002). Metaphors and analogical reasoning in organization theory: Beyond orthodoxy. *Academy of Management Review, 27*(2), 294–303.

Oswick, C., & Montgomery, J. (1999). Images of an organization: The use of metaphor in a multinational company. *Journal of Organizational Change Management, 12*(6), 501–523.

Oswick, C., Putnam, L., & Keenoy, T. (2004). Tropes, discourse and organizing. In C. Hardy, D. Grant, C. Oswick, & L. Putnam (Ed.), *Handbook of organizational discourse* (pp. 105–128). London, England: Sage.

Pablo, Z., & Hardy, C. (2009). Merging, masquerading and morphing: Metaphors and the world wide web. *Organization Studies, 30*(8), 821–843.

Pettigrew, A. M., Woodman, R. W., & Cameron, K. S. (2001). Studying organizational change and development: Challenges for future research. *Academy of Management Journal, 44*(4), 697–713.

Rao, H., Morrill, C., & Zald, M. (2000). Power plays: How social movements and collective action create new organizational forms. *Research in Organizational Behavior, 22*, 237–281.

Sloan, P., & Oliver, D. (2013). Building trust in multi-stakeholder partnerships: Critical emotional incidents and practices of engagement. *Organization Studies, 34*(12), 1835–1868.

Spinosa, C., Flores, F., & Dreyfus, H. (1997). *Disclosing new worlds: Entrepreneurship, democratic action and the cultivation of solidarity.* Cambridge, MA: MIT Press.

Thrift, N. (2004). Thick time. *Organization, 11*(6), 873–880.

Tinker, T. (1986). Metaphor or reification: Are radical humanists really libertarian anarchists? *Journal of Management Studies, 25*(4), 363–384.

Tsoukas, H. (1991). The missing link: A transformational view of metaphors in organizational science. *Academy of Management Review, 16*(3), 566–585.

Vangen, S., & Huxham, C. (2003). Nurturing collaborative relations: Building trust in interorganizational collaboration. *Journal of Applied Behavioral Science, 39*(1), 5–31.

Verona, G., Prandelli, E., & Sawhney, M. (2006). Innovation and virtual environments: Towards virtual knowledge brokers. *Organization Studies, 27*(6), 765–788.

Waters, R. D., Burnett, E., Lamm, A., & Lucas, J. (2009). Engaging stakeholders through social networking: How nonprofit organizations are using Facebook. *Public Relations Review, 35*(2), 102–106.

Weitzner, D., & Deutsch, Y. (2015). Understanding motivation and social influence in stakeholder prioritization. *Organization Studies, 36*(10), 1337–1360.

Wexler M. N. (2011). Reconfiguring the sociology of the crowd: Exploring crowdsourcing. *International Journal of Sociology and Social Policy, 31*(1–2), 6–20.

Wilson, J. M., Boyer O'Leary, M., Metiu, A., & Jett, Q. R. (2008). Perceived proximity in virtual work: Explaining the paradox of far-but-close. *Organization Studies, 29*(7), 979–1002.

Yu, K. (2012). Formal organizations and identity groups in social movements. *Human Relations, 65*(6), 753–776.

Zappos. (2015). *Life at Zappos.* Retrieved from https://jobs.zappos.com/life-at-zappos

11

The "Metaphor" Metaphor

Educating Practitioners for Reflective Judgment

Haridimos Tsoukas

Key Learning Points

- Know that the world does not speak; only people do.
- Realize that we have no direct access to reality except through language.
- Understand that metaphors structure human experience and are an essential ingredient of all imaginative thinking.
- Recognize that *Images of Organization* makes the reader think reflectively.
- Know that metaphorical thinking encourages perspectivism—different understandings of reality.
- Understand that metaphorical thinking sharpens perception and, thus, reflective judgment.

I have no doubt that *Images of Organization* (hereafter: *Images*) is the best textbook that has been written so far in organization studies (Morgan, 1986). It is not only Morgan's prose that makes it attractive and a pleasure to read. Gareth Morgan is certainly a very good writer; he knows how to motivate the reader, explain abstract ideas, and tell a good story. More than that, however, *Images* is a *reflectively* written textbook. Its author wants to make the reader *think* rather than simply impart information to him. Why do I say this? Let me put it this way: If **reflective thinking**, as Dewey (1910/1997, p. 13) noted long ago, "involves willingness to endure a condition of mental unrest and disturbance," then this is exactly what the reader (especially the student and the practitioner) will likely experience upon reading *Images*.

Reflective Thinking

Viewing organizations through the lenses of different (and often incompatible) metaphors not only informs, but also generates "mental unrest." When used in a particular situation, which metaphor is better suited? How are the diverse insights of several metaphors to be synthesized? It is not easy to tell, at least immediately. Doubt creeps in. In embracing doubt, reflective thinking involves movement: a state of perplexity *and* an active search for the basis upon which a belief may be adopted. We reflect when, prompted by some obstruction, dilemma, or ambiguity, we go beyond the comfort of received wisdom, "the inertia that inclines one to accept suggestions at their face value" (Dewey, 1910/1997, p. 13), in search of a clearer view of a situation.

Mental inertia may come from a variety of sources: our socialization within particular discursive practices or communities, which makes us adopt dominant definitions, norms, and standards of evaluation; imitation, doing what others do in pursuit of legitimacy or out of sheer laziness; or stress, which forces us to revert to familiar forms of thinking. To think reflectively, notes Dewey (1910/1997, p. 13), means to acquire "the attitude of suspended conclusion" and keep searching for better candidates of belief.

This is exactly what Morgan invites the reader to do with his *Images*. Any situation may be seen from a variety of perspectives and none of them is inherently better than any other. Even the most mechanistic organization may be seen through lenses other than the mechanistic metaphor; culture, politics, and psychoanalytical considerations, to name a few, are also relevant. Insights generated from each of these perspectives can illuminate the situation at hand. Working with diverse insights creates "mental unrest." How can I better understand the situation? How should I act? Insofar as the reader of *Images* begins to think this way, she has entered a reflective mode; Morgan will have managed to have instilled movement in her mind. The reader searches actively for a better understanding for the sake of effective action. She will no longer act out of sheer impulse or habit, but rather is stimulated to act reflectively and with **reflective judgment**. Notice that Morgan does not tell the reader how to decide. There is a **phronetic** spirit in *Images* that, while inviting the reader to engage in reflective thinking, leaves action open-ended. The actor bears responsibility for his actions.

In addition to good writing and an invitation for reflective thinking, there is a third feature of *Images* that makes it a great textbook. Whereas most textbooks organize their material thematically (namely, in terms of the received categories that make up the core of a discipline; e.g., motivation, structure, culture, decision making, etc.), Morgan does so *meta*-thematically: What is important for him is not so much the several field topics per se as much as what the topics reveal if approached from different perspectives. In other words, he shifts the reader's attention from the "reality" of organizations to what that "reality" is made out to be if seen through different lenses. Morgan's lenses are metaphorical descriptions: through them, organizations kaleidoscopically present different aspects to the viewer; there is no single lens to reveal what organizations are really about. What you see depends on how you turn the kaleidoscope.

If the "metaphor" metaphor does not strike us as particularly novel today, it is a testimony to its astonishing intellectual success, to which Morgan's *Images* was the most important contributor in organizational studies. Having become normalized (an almost dead metaphor), the "metaphor" metaphor has enabled us to ask new and interesting questions, which we could not do before (Gascoigne, 2008, p. 157). The most important new question that we can now ask, without hackles being raised, is as simple as this: "Whose interpretation is this?" If we believe that reality does not speak and that numbers do not tell a story, then we are impelled to wonder about the interpretations that are always already embedded in the way that humans conduct themselves and query them.

When *Images* was first published in the mid-1980s, organizational studies was a different field: Anxious in the post–World War II years to be recognized as a "science," it had been dominated by the onto-epistemology of scientific rationality (Sandberg & Tsoukas, 2011). The echo of the linguistic turn, however, which was already occurring in philosophy (Rorty, 1980, 1992), reverberated across the social sciences, including organizational studies. Morgan was the strongest amplifier of that echo in the field. His idea that theories are grounded on metaphorical descriptions was novel, although not entirely surprising because he had already nodded in that direction in his seminal *Sociological Paradigms and Organizational Analysis* with Gibson Burrell (Burrell & Morgan, 1979).

Images enabled Morgan to achieve two things at once: on the one hand to re-tell, in a nonplatitudinal way, the story of organization studies for a broad audience and, on the other, to address his fellow scholars, suggesting a new way of viewing theory development as well as the relationship between theory and praxis. In short, Morgan showed that metaphors matter for both practitioners/students and scholars. This is what made *Images* a genuinely interesting book: It partially refuted our hitherto expectations about what a good textbook is *and* its key organizing principle and narrative line enabled it to attract diverse audiences. Murray Davis (1971) would have found *Images* a perfect illustration of what makes a piece of writing "interesting"!

Metaphor

What makes metaphors so special to give them as high a status as Morgan does? **Metaphor** is about the transference of relations across semantic fields (Kittay, 1997, p. 387), for example, "this company is a family," "the country has become a jail," "austerity is asphyxiating." Because concepts designate categories, through metaphorical description, we aim at reclassifying category membership for the sake of better understanding or creating new meaning.

Meaningfulness arises from structuring experience. Some preconceptual experience is structured the way it is because of the way the world is and the way our bodies are constituted. However, as Lakoff (1987, p. 303) argues, "in domains where there is no clearly discernible preconceptual structure to our experience, we import such structure via metaphor. Metaphor provides us with a means for comprehending domains of experience that do not have a preconceptual structure of their own." Abstract thought is imaginative in that, because it is not grounded directly on experience, it does not reflect external reality like a mirror, but rather seeks to grasp it through mental imagery. It is metaphorical descriptions that enable the making of conceptual knowledge.

To say, for example, as the Greek minister of immigration recently did (referring to thousands of refugees from the Middle East being trapped in Greece, unable to move on to central and northern Europe), "it is outrageous that Greece will become Europe's jail" (TVXS, 2016) is to assign a country (Greece) to the category of jail. When this happens, the category used (the metaphor vehicle, "jail") functions as an attributive category; it attributes new properties to the metaphor topic ("Greece") (Glucksberg, Manfredi, & McGlone, 1997, p. 347). The metaphorical statement is a class membership assertion. A new category has been created ("Greece as a prison") to express a new experience. Notice that such a reclassification does not disclose an antecedent similarity (there is nothing inherently similar between a country and a prison), but rather *creates* a similarity. Metaphors do so "by dislodging some items from familiar classifications and regrouping them with items that normally belong to different, even disjoint categories. So dislodging and regrouping items or subclassifications not only creates a new category, but also disrupts normal classifications" (Kittay, 1997, p. 389).

Metaphor, as Davidson (2001, p. 245) aptly remarked, is "the dreamwork of language." Because metaphors do not disclose an antecedently existing meaning, but rather make links between bits of reality, thus asserting the meaning of a particular experience, they may change the way we think. The re-reclassifications asserted are ways of world-making rather than world-representing (Gascoigne, 2008, p. 155). Such a view of metaphors underlines the irreducible *contingency* of language (Kolenda, 1990, pp. 12–13; Rorty, 1989, pp. 3–22). There is no necessity in describing the world in a particular vocabulary; rather, we describe bits of the world in ways that we find useful in coping with the world at particular points in time. Classical Greek *demokratia* (democracy), Jesus's *agape* (love), and Newton's *gravitas* (gravity) are not so much representations of the world as much as they are tools for doing things in the world that suit particular purposes. As Rorty (1989, p. 17) remarks, new vocabularies are like tools "for doing things which could not even have been envisaged before these tools were available." The distinction between the literal and the metaphorical is not a distinction between two kinds of interpretation, but rather a distinction between familiar and unfamiliar uses of language. Recognizing the metaphorical roots of all meaning-making and interpretation means becoming aware of the contingency of language and, thus, of the possibility of reconceiving what we already know and care about. This is where *Images* comes in so handy.

Perception

Morgan does not say that you can describe organizations in any way you like, that anything goes, or that any interpretation is as good as any other. His message is more subtle than that. The question "which perspective gets it right?" arises only if metaphorically structured perspectives are considered in isolation from a context of action. To be precise, the question concerning the evaluation of metaphorically generated concepts arises only when a practical situation is bracketed so that different concepts are removed from the world of practice and inserted instead into the world of *theoria* (e.g., see Cornelissen, 2005; Dreyfus, 2000, p. 317; Oswick, Keenoy, & Grant, 2002; Tsoukas, 1991, 2015, pp. 65–66). In the scholarly world of theory, questions of the validity of respective knowledge claims are generated and this is what keeps us academics busy (and employed!).

Morgan, however, has another context in mind. Although his approach is sufficiently novel to appeal to both scholars and practitioners, he writes primarily for people who want to either learn or improve the practice of management in organizations. He wants his readers to appreciate what all of his *images* of organization have to offer. In the world of practice (or, to be precise, of "practical coping"; Sandberg & Tsoukas, 2011, p. 343; Tsoukas, 2015, p. 64), metaphors generate insights and sharpen a practitioner's perceptual understanding. As Morgan (1997, p. 5) remarks: "In recognizing theory as metaphor, we quickly appreciate that no single theory will ever give us a perfect or all-purpose point of view. We realize that the challenge is to become skilled in the art of using metaphor: to find fresh ways of seeing, understanding, and shaping the situations that we have to organize and manage."

Sharpening practitioners' perception is what *Images* is mainly about: to see with greater perspicacity, to make more refined distinctions, to "complicate" one's understanding (Tsoukas, 2005; Weick, 1979, p. 261). We should stop asking, Morgan suggests, what organizations *are* and instead think about the ways that we describe them and what those descriptions enable us to do. If there is no Olympian summit from which we may obtain a definitive view of organizations, all we are left with are partial descriptions, with each one pointing to a particular aspect of organizational life. If all perspectives are incomplete and biased, then we need to be aware that we are always potentially missing something and should therefore keep searching for an ever-clearer view. There are clear echoes of Bateson's (1979, pp. 73–74) "double description" in Morgan's approach: The juxtaposing and synthesis of different descriptions creates extra informational depth. Another way of putting it is to see in double description evidence of reflective thinking: "to maintain the state of doubt and to carry on systematic and protracted inquiry" (Dewey, 1910/1997, p. 13). It is the attitude of "suspended conclusion" that Dewey marks out as the most important characteristic of reflective thinking. Similarly, it is the attitude of "suspended conclusion" that Morgan urges his readers to adopt by noting the paradoxical character of metaphors: "Metaphor is inherently paradoxical. It can create powerful insights that also become distortions, as the way of seeing created through metaphor become a way of *not* seeing" (Morgan, 1997, p. 5). To take notice of the language that you use to cope with organizational reality is to begin to be aware of what your language reveals and obscures and to keep striving to further refine it.

Morgan's view of metaphors has strong echoes of Bohr's "complementarity principle" (Plotnitsky, 2002, pp. 1–28). Indeed, at one point, he draws a parallel between the nature of light as both a particle and a wave, noting that "both tendencies of qualities co-exist" (Morgan, 1997, p. 349) with the multifaceted nature of organizations in which, similarly, "different qualities can coexist." Writes Morgan (1997, pp. 349–350): "Think 'structure' and you'll see structure. Think 'culture' and you'll see all kinds of cultural dimensions. Think 'politics' and you'll find politics. Think in terms of system patterns and loops and you'll find a whole range of them. . . . In using different perspectives to create different modes of engagement we are able to tap into these and understand the same situation in many ways."

Organizations as Texts

Morgan's (1997) "metaphor" metaphor draws on philosophical **hermeneutics**. His plea for managers to engage in "the art of using metaphors" (p. 6) and thus become sophisticated "readers" of organizational life (p. 350) is grounded on the metaphor of organizations as texts. Viewed as texts, organizations are imbued with *self-difference* (rather than self-identity). Self-difference is the notion that "something can become different from itself whilst remaining itself instead of becoming something else" (Bortoft, 2012, p. 71). Just as a multiperspectival figure like a duck/rabbit (see Figure 11.1) does not consist of a duck *and* a rabbit, but, rather, each figure, respectively, is complete in itself without being the only possibility, so the multiple interpretations of organization-as-text belong to the possibility of the text: Each interpretation is not external to the text.

There is a virtuality of meaning in texts, which is actualized in the event of understanding. This is what Morgan (1997, p. 350) means in noting that "reality has a tendency to reveal itself in accordance with the perspectives through which it is engaged." What is critical to emphasize, because it is often misunderstood, is that the different insights generated by viewing an organizational situation through different metaphorical lenses belong to the situation itself; they are not merely subjective readings. Although we certainly bring our reflective open-mindedness and creativity to bear on our reading of organizations, our interpretations bring into existence what is already inherent in the situation: its multiplicity (like the duck/rabbit image in Figure 11.1).

In the world of practice, the multiple insights created are not so much intellectually evaluated by practitioners as they are used as tools to do things. Some insights may turn out to be powerful insofar as they resonate with people's experience of the situation at hand, whereas others might appear weak. Therefore, to take Morgan's (1997, p. 349) example, if the view has prevailed that a particular structure is anachronistic and therefore in need of change,

FIGURE 11.1 ● Duck/Rabbit

then a reflective practitioner, alongside a new organization design, will also think of the cultural, autopoietic, political, and psychological implications of structural change. It is not a question of which metaphorical insight is better suited to account for the situation at hand (this is a question for the academic world of scholarship, not the world of organizational practice; Sandberg & Tsoukas, 2011), but rather which one enables a manager to cope effectively in the given context and manage the complexities of the unfolding change.

Therefore, the insight that a particular structure, albeit now inefficient, may have become a defense against anxiety, enables a reflective manager to be more sensitive to reactions, more perceptive in looking for subtle behavioral cues, and more capable of attending to the big picture than he would otherwise be. A change of structure is not a mere replacement of an organizational chart with another (a mechanistic view), but rather is imbued with meaning, which is never complete but always coming into being through understanding over time. Although a particular metaphorical insight may initiate action, the latter, once beginning to unfold, will likely create a new context that may bring forward a new possibility. Some metaphorical insights may become more salient than others over time.

If, say, the corporate board expects a new strategy to be implemented in order to increase growth and a new structure to be enacted to realize the strategy (McNulty, 2002), then the mechanistic metaphor may inform the design of a new structure because, in an institutionalized environment, it produces visible action for all parties concerned. However, in the unfolding of change, other issues may gain importance: the organization may resist the new structure protecting its autopoietic identity; culture may have invested the old structure with positive symbolism and is now upset with the change; politics, previously subdued, may now become important; or the stability generated by the old structure may be threatened, inducing anxiety. It is not necessarily the case that diverse metaphorical insights are all equally relevant at the same time, but in the course of a dynamically evolving, context-dependent, interactive behavioral phenomenon, some insights may become more revealing and useful than others. In other words, although, in theory, there may be a myriad of conflicting interpretations of a situation, in practice, "it is what 'makes a difference' that matters, not the abstract possibilities of difference (or *différance*) as such" (Solomon, 2003, p. 41) and what makes a difference depends on context and time— it is a matter of phronetic judgment (Shotter & Tsoukas, 2014a, 2014b).

Refined Understanding

When I use *Images* in MBA classes, I find that it tends to generate a shift in students' thinking, especially those trained in the sciences and engineering. Whether using the case of "Eagle Smelting" (in which repairing an unexpected breakdown in a loco-motive not only goes badly, but also brings forth all sorts of organizational problems; Morgan, 1988) or "Welcome aboard" (in which a capable, forward-looking, new CEO of an old and successful company initiates change, at the behest of the board, only to find out the senior management rebelling and the change leading nowhere, threaten-ing her position; McNulty, 2002), the result is similar: Typically, MBA students begin with applying a quasi-mechanistic frame to the case at hand, focusing on structure and rational thinking. It is enlightening for them to see the insights generated by alternative metaphors: The same organization is manifested differently through different metaphors. This is the beauty of *Images*: It encourages students to practice and value interpretation in making sense of organizational problems. Rather than being handed "the" answer, students are encouraged to search for answers and are initiated into the art of becoming phronetic practitioners who must simultaneously maintain "a state of doubt" while searching for better candidates of belief.

The whole point of viewing organizations through metaphor is to make practitioners *refine* their ordinary practices of understanding (Tsoukas, 1994). Faced with a difficulty, they tend to bring a prereflective reading to a situation (typically, having been socialized into modern institutions, a rationalistic, quasi-mechanistic one). Theories-as-metaphors provide the conceptual means for a reflective *rearticulation* that attempts to improve upon the original, prereflective reading. Notice that the purpose of this hermeneutical engagement is not to break with the original prereflective understanding, but rather to refine it—to obtain a more perspicuous, insightful account (Smith, 1997, p. 66). This is possible insofar as prereflective understanding is grounded on the taken-for-granted categories and beliefs that people incorporate into their practical coping with the world. Through further articulation, people refine their commonsensical understanding by becoming aware of the categories that they employ and the taken-for-granted mental habits that they may be following in searching for new understandings.

If this strikes you as unexceptional today, it is because the "metaphor" metaphor has now become normalized in the 30 years following the astonishing success of *Images*. We now have a well-established vocabulary to be able to appreciate interpretative diversity, reflect on the language we use and the diverse purposes we put it to, and realize that whatever is said is said by someone; numbers, organizations, science, and the world do not speak; only people do. Gareth Morgan deserves the credit for convincing us to see the merits of such a suggestive vocabulary and for providing huge impetus to the conversation. We must keep it going.

Key Terms

Hermeneutics	Reflective
Metaphor	judgment
Phronesis	Reflective thinking

References

Bateson, G. (1979). *Mind and nature*. Toronto, ON, Canada: Bantam Books.

Bortfoft, H. (2012). *Taking appearances seriously*. Edinburgh, Scotland: Floris Books.

Burrell, G., & Morgan, G. (1979). *Sociological paradigms and organizational analysis*, London, England: Heinemann.

Cornelissen, J. (2005). Beyond compare: Metaphor in organization theory. *Academy of Management Review, 30*(4), 751–764.

Davidson, D. (2001). *Inquiries into truth and interpretation*. Oxford, England: Oxford University Press.

Davis, M. (1971). That's interesting! Towards a phenomenology of sociology and a sociology of phenomenology. *Philosophy of the Social Sciences, 1*(4), 309–344.

Dewey, J. (1910/1997). *How we think*. Mineola, NY: Dover.

Dreyfus, H. (2000). Responses. In M. A. Wrathall & J. Malpas (Eds.), *Heidegger, coping, and cognitive science* (pp. 313–349). Cambridge, MA: MIT Press.

Gascoigne, N. (2008). *Richard Rorty*. Cambridge, England: Cambridge University Press.

Glucksberg, S., Manfredi, D. A., & McGlone, M. S. (1997). Metaphor comprehension: How metaphors create new categories. In T. B. Ward, S. M. Smith , & J. Vaid (Eds.), *Creative thought* (pp. 327–350). Washington, DC: American Psychological Association.

Kittay, E. F. (1997). Of "men" and metaphors: Shakespeare, embodiment, and filing cabinets. In T. B. Ward, S. M. Smith, & J. Vaid (Eds.), *Creative thought* (pp. 375–402). Washington, DC: American Psychological Association.

Kolenda, K. (1990). *Rorty's humanistic pragmatism*. Tampa: University of South Florida Press.

Lakoff, G. (1987). *Women, fire, and dangerous things*. Chicago, IL: University of Chicago Press.

McNulty, E. (2002, October). Case study: "Welcome aboard (but don't change a thing)." *Harvard Business Review*, pp. 32–35.

Morgan, G. (1986). *Images of organization*. Beverly Hills, CA: Sage.

Morgan, G. (1988). Teaching MBAs transformational thinking. In R. E. Quinn & K. S. Cameron (Eds.), *Paradox and transformation* (pp. 237–248). Cambridge, MA: Ballinger.

Morgan, G. (1997). *Images of organization* (2nd ed.). Thousand Oaks, CA: Sage.

Oswick, C., Keenoy, T., & Grant, D. (2002). Metaphor and analogical reasoning in organization theory. *Academy of Management Review, 27*(2), 294–303.

Plotnitsky, A. (2002). *The knowable and the unknowable*. Ann Arbor: University of Michigan Press.

Rorty, R. (1980). *Philosophy and the mirror of nature*. Oxford, England: Blackwell.

Rorty, R. (1989). *Contingency, irony, and solidarity*. Cambridge, England: Cambridge University Press.

Rorty, R. (1992). *The linguistic turn*. Chicago, IL: Chicago University Press.

Sandberg, J., & Tsoukas, H. (2011). Grasping the logic of practice: Theorizing through practical rationality. *Academy of Management Review, 36*(2), 338–360.

Shotter, J., & Tsoukas, H. (2014a). In search of phronesis: Leadership and the art of judgment. *Academy of Management Learning & Education, 13*(2), 224–243.

Shotter, J., & Tsoukas, H. (2014b). Performing phronesis: On the way to engaged judgment. *Management Learning, 45*(4), 377–396.

Smith, N. H. (1997). *Strong hermeneutics*. London, England: Routledge.

Solomon, R. C. (2003). *Living with Nietzsche*. New York, NY: Oxford University Press.

Tsoukas, J. (1991). The missing link: A transformational view of metaphors in organizational science. *Academy of Management Review, 16*(3), 566–585.

Tsoukas, H. (1994). Refining common sense: Types of knowledge in management studies. *Journal of Management Studies, 31*(6), 761–780.

Tsoukas, H. (2005). *Complex knowledge: studies in organizational epistemology*. Oxford, England: Oxford University Press.

Tsoukas, H. (2015). Making strategy: Meta-theoretical insights from Heideggerian phenomenology. In D. Golsorkhi, L. Rouleau, D. Seidl, & E. Vaara (Eds.), *Cambridge handbook of strategy as practice* (2nd ed., pp. 58–77). Cambridge, England: Cambridge University Press.

TVXS. (2016, January 26). Mouzalas: We were asked to make camp for 400,000 refugees in Athens: The challenge. Retrieved from http://tvxs.gr/news/ellada/moyzalas-mas-zitisan-na-ftiaksoyme-stratopedo-gia-400000-prosfyges

Weick, K. E. (1979). *The social psychology of organizing* (2nd ed.). Reading, MA: Addison-Wesley.

Of Tropes, Totems, and Taboos

Reflections on Morgan's *Images* From a Cross-Cultural Perspective

Peter Case, Hugo Gaggiotti, Jonathan Gosling, and Mikael Holmgren Caicedo

---

Key Learning Points

- Recognize that *Images of Organization* occupies the cusp of modern and postmodern organization theory.
- Understand that metaphors fulfil a community-forming function in much the same way as totems are seen to operate in both classical and contemporary anthropology. In this way, *Images* presents a theory of organization that is at once dematerialized, iconic, and narratively embedded—foreseeing the narrative turn in organization theory.
- Take into account the *translational* implications of using *Images* as a training resource when working with participants in non-Anglophone settings.
- Realize that although there may be cultural patterns that inform a given national group's interpretation of organizational images, international students appear to respond to Morgan's metaphors openly and make varying semantic associations with them.

- Understand that the international organizational theory teacher must acquire and maintain a kind of ethnographic sensibility that allows and, indeed, encourages space for multiethnic interpretation, pedagogical flexibility, and genuine educational encounter.
- Recognize that Morgan's metaphors are not really "Morgan's" per se but, instead, are appropriated by readers whose differing ethnicities mediate and modulate their meaning and application.

There can be little doubt that *Images of Organization* (hereafter *Images*) is one of the most important and iconic contributions to organizational theory in recent decades. Several generations of organization studies academics, students, and practitioners owe a great debt to Gareth Morgan for the intellectual work presented in *Images* and it is entirely apposite to take this opportunity, some 30 years after the first edition (Morgan, 1986) to acknowledge and celebrate this volume. As scholars who favor **social constructionist** and **interpretative approaches** to the study of organization, we can testify personally to the impact that the emergence of *Images* had intellectually, pedagogically, and practically.[1] Here was a volume that, at once,

- served to consolidate and summarize social scientific thinking about organizations;
- gave due emphasis to the relativity of perspective;
- offered new ways of *seeing* and *interpreting organizational conduct* through a series of highly suggestive metaphors;
- enabled new forms of social and organizational critique; and
- served as an impressively comprehensive yet accessible and student-friendly teaching resource.

In short, *Images*, in all of its incarnations (Morgan, 1986, 1997, 2006), is nothing short of an organizational theory *tour de force*, and yet, this encyclopedic work is unquestionably a product of its time. We will argue that *Images* is the last **modern** organizational theory text and also one of the first **postmodern** texts. Its impact derives at least in part from its timely combination of comprehensive scope and accessibility. It is an all-embracing theory of the provisional, perfectly fitting the moment at which we wanted to know how to approach our discipline in a way that is at once postmodern and authoritative. Furthermore, because *Images* proposed that organizations might be studied through the lenses of specific metaphors, it sensitizes us to the fact that, regardless of whether we are explicit or conscious of it, we inevitably study organizations in metaphorical terms. It follows, therefore, that our own discipline and methods are subject to the same remove from representational truth. Since Morgan's epic contribution, moreover, there has been no all-encompassing reformulation of organizational theory.

As Morgan (2011) reflects, *Images* began life as notes for an undergraduate course he taught as a visiting fellow at Pennsylvania State University, in the United States, in the early 1980s. The thinking in the first edition was, as Morgan himself acknowledges, greatly influenced by the collaborative work that he undertook with Gibson Burrell at the University of Lancaster's Department of Behaviour in Organizations on *Sociological Paradigms and Organizational Analysis* (hereafter *Sociological Paradigms*) (Burrell & Morgan, 1979). He and Burrell were still doctoral students when they wrote this volume in part as an exercise in making sense of the sociological and philosophical literature and various perspectives that they were working through (Morgan, 2011). Like *Images*, *Sociological Paradigms* is a work of categorization in which organizational analysis is mapped into competing paradigmatic domains according to meta-theoretical assumptions informing the groupings of theory.

Although both influential and controversial, Morgan was ultimately dissatisfied with *Sociological Paradigms* primarily because of its relative inaccessibility and intellectually demanding style. For example, few colleagues or students were familiar with the seminal work of science historian Thomas Kuhn (1962, 1970) on scientific paradigms. Driven by the demands of undergraduate teaching, Morgan wanted to translate *Sociological Paradigms* into a work that would appeal not only to academics and students of organization but also to practitioners. In pursuit of this aim, he alighted upon what we might characterize as a **super-metaphor**: the idea that "all theories are metaphorical." Working intensively in the University of Lancaster library in the early 1980s to review organization and management theory as comprehensively as possible, within a few short years, Morgan explored the relationships among paradigm, metaphor, and problem solving in organizational theory (Morgan, 1980), considered some of the methodological implications of his thinking (Morgan, 1983; Morgan & Smircich, 1980), and had begun serious work on drafting the first edition of *Images* (see Morgan, 2011, p. 461).

However, for all of its many merits, Morgan's work has not escaped critical gaze. Positivists have challenged the **ontological relativism** of *Images*, for example, whereas left-leaning detractors question its **ethical relativism** and unwillingness to commit politically to either a Marxist or a post-Marxist critique of organizational theory and activism. Others are unhappy with the abstracted *analytical* position of Morgan's predominantly **ocular view** of organizations, arguing that it gives insufficient attention to embodied engagement with organizing practices. Although Morgan (2006, 2011) has produced robust rejoinders to these forms of critique, we want to shift discussion to other grounds for thinking critically yet constructively about his work. By so doing, we also want to suggest ways of moving "beyond" organizational theory as the (reflexive) deployment of metaphor.

We have selected two specific movements in organizational theory through which to deepen our critical appreciation and pedagogical application of *Images*: the language turn (Czarniawska, 2011; Tietze, Cohen, & Musson, 2003; Westwood & Linstead, 2002) and the cultural turn (Martin, 1992; Morrill, 2008; Smircich, 1983; Trice & Beyer, 1993; Willmott, 1993). In exploring these territories, we focus on how *Images* functions, asking how the metaphor (as deployed in *Images*) works as a **cultural artefact** of organizational theory. We suggest that these metaphors operate as **totems** in the organizational theory community and we analyze their functions in a manner similar to Taussig's (2003) treatment of the totemic figures of the Cuna. Furthermore, we suggest that a deeper understanding of *Images'* efficacy in teaching organizational theory might be derived from the totemic status of metaphor in international classroom settings.

Our aim is primarily to develop insight into how *Images* embodies a specific set of cultural assumptions and to reflect on its use in non-Anglophone settings. The rationale for pursuing this line of argument is that we see the eight metaphors as tending to establish eight patterns of self-referential discourse that carry the danger of communicating an **ethnocentric** view of organization and organizing. Furthermore, because of their totemic functions, there can be a strong temptation to reify Morgan's eight metaphors and engage with them in relatively static terms.

The volume has acquired "orthodox textbook" status for many academics teaching organizational theory and organizational analysis courses in universities across Europe and the United States (both undergraduate and postgraduate). Ironically, to accept the eight metaphors as a form of orthodoxy, we suggest, is to risk sucking the very life from the concept of *metaphor* and its "**connotational field**." Indeed, it risks broaching a point where metaphor is no longer metaphor in any meaningful sense (i.e., once lively images descend into "**dead metaphors**"). If there is a core meaning to metaphor, it is one that invokes **movement** in both psychic and material terms. To augment and make Morgan's work useful to the contemporary world of organization studies, we need to be more reflexive in using **totemic metaphors**; to understand their *ethical* implications, to recognize the moral jeopardy that they can invoke, and to be sensitive to their use in differing cultural/linguistic contexts.

This chapter begins by setting up a **reflexive social anthropological stance** from which to explore the **mimetic qualities** and possibilities of Morgan's images. It then proceeds to consider the pedagogical implications of this theoretical reinterpretation of his work by offering some reflections on the use of *Images* in contemporary international teaching contexts, which is the empirical basis for our argument in this chapter. This chapter thus seeks to extend Morgan's work by moving further along the linguistic/postmodern and cultural turns taken by Morgan himself by introducing an anthropological sensibility offered by the concept of totem and by exploring some experiential illustrations of the challenges posed by linguistic and cultural *translations* of images in non-Anglophone settings.

Understanding Tropes, Totems, and Taboos

Morgan (2006, p. 340) suggested that metaphor can be used creatively to rethink and reshape organizational theory and practice. As such, it is a way of imagining and theorizing the world that can both stimulate and obscure our understanding of organizing. Alvesson and Deetz (2000, p. 43) frame this issue graphically when posing the question: "What are we able to see or think about if we talk about it in this way rather than that?" Case and Gaggiotti (2014, p. 4), for example, point out the dangers of deploying reductive economic metaphors in organization analysis: "While metaphor operates ubiquitously within both everyday and specialist discourses (Lakoff and Johnson 1980), the relative value of its usage varies considerably." Although Morgan is aware of the propensity of metaphor to act simultaneously to mask aspects of reality as much as reveal them, he is less explicit about his own reflexive position as a white Anglo-Saxon man espousing predominantly Western forms of organization and social theory. Image construction becomes problematic when it is the product of materials and ideas hailing from a restricted societal and linguistic standpoint and for reasons other than the ethical relativism admitted when other tropes are excluded. In this section, we examine the cultural significance of images, perhaps the most important yet also the most *hidden* of metaphors in *Images*.

The title of the book, *Images*, selects specifically ocular references for Morgan's metaphors. Although Morgan points out that metaphors influence both what we see and how we look, his use of image remains somewhat implicit. Why not choose, for example, *Feelings of Organization, Tastes of Organization*, or *Sounds of Organization*? Limiting ourselves to only one of our senses in everyday life—the use of only ocular images—reduces possibilities exclusively to what Taussig (2003, p. 57) refers to as the production of "visual means":

> Medicinally triggered visions ministered by healers in the Upper Amazon . . . are surely effective not only because of visual imagery, but also on account of non visual [*sic*] imagery . . . the senses cross over and translate into each other. You feel redness. You see music. Thus non visual imagery may evoke visual means.

The following analysis seeks to challenge Morgan's way of working with images as metaphors from the point of view of its nascent ethnocentric and (subconsciously) colonial disposition. Although it may not be possible to avoid ethnocentricity entirely in organizational analysis, we would like to emphasize the importance of remaining reflexively open to plural modes of representation and rhetoric. This is a point whose salience we try to illustrate later in the chapter when discussing our experiences of teaching in international settings.

Images as Natural and Not Cultural Totems

The identification and uses of metaphorical classes or patterns by Morgan could be understood from an anthropological standpoint as an exercise in **totemic selection**, operating with the **homologous logic** of objects linking the natural and the social. In other words, each of Morgan's eight metaphorical patterns has **totemic characteristics**. Like totems, the eight images simultaneously include *and* exclude. Morgan (2006, p. 67) refers to this propensity of metaphor **epigrammatically** by pointing out that "a way of seeing is a way of not seeing."

Both totemism and metaphor presuppose translation and movement between objects which are re-presented (presented again) in another form (**animate or inanimate** things or words). Although metaphors have unquestionably been more popular in organizational theory (e.g., Alvesson & Spicer, 2011), some authors have recognized the potential of totemism as a way of understanding how organizational classifications and meanings are constructed, in particular, with respect to organizational identity (Burgi & Roos, 2001). Likewise, Letiche (2004, p. 159) suggests that "narratives are totems—mythic structures that mirror the natural and the social, the individual and the universal."

The practice of totemism is based on the notion that the human soul and human thoughts pass into a class of animal, plant, or other objects. Discussing totemism, the anthropological pioneer Tylor (1898, p. 143) refers to "the tendency of mankind to classify out the universe" by personifications and by making associations of people (or thoughts) with certain *selective classes* of animate or inanimate things, **mimetic objects**, or natural species. Totems operate by representationally imbuing an object with a distinctive quality or power-through-association with which a cultural grouping can readily identify. By offering the possibility of identification, totems thus serve to create group ties and a sense of the collective. Durkheim (1976) explains how emblems and coats of arms, for example, work as modern totems by identifying people (family names) with particular images. In his organizational ethnography of teamwork in a Kenyan firm, Kamoche (1995, p. 371) noticed that "organizational members combine language and ritual to construct an organizational phenomenon in the form of a totem," which, by offering a common way of imagining, creates ties that reinforce differences between the included and excluded. By excluding, including, and differentiating between those who imagine in the accepted way and those who imagine "differently," totems represent the **taboos** that need to be avoided by the members of a group or clan (Freud, 1913/1918).

We suggest that Morgan's metaphors can usefully be positioned as totemic images that define the taboos that those who imagine in a particular way need to avoid. For those who imagine organizations around the mechanistic totem, for example, to be unconventional is a taboo:

> Mechanistic organization discourages initiative, encouraging people to obey orders and keep their place rather than to take an interest in, and question what they are doing. People in a bureaucracy who question the wisdom of conventional practice are viewed more often than not as troublemakers. (Morgan, 2006, p. 30)

The organismic totem invokes the taboo of avoiding being pluralistic and retaining individual freedom:

> The organismic metaphor has had a subtle yet important impact on our general thinking by encouraging us to believe in a state of unity where everyone is pulling together. (Morgan, 2006, p. 68)

Interpreted from this perspective, Morgan's images seem to follow the pattern of Malinowski and Radcliffe-Brown's functionalist approach to totemism, in which cultural representations resonate with biological needs. As Burgi and Roos (2001, p. 8) observe:

> Totemism in this way tends to see the most important meaning in the "totem" or sacralized element itself, believing that the specific choice of species attempts to magically transfer properties of the species to the human group.

Each of Morgan's totem images (machine, organism, brain, culture, etc.) has the propensity, *through forms of identification*, to transfer its properties to the group; that is, the group appropriates for itself the (mechanistic, naturalistic, intelligible, cultural, etc.) qualities of the totem image. As Morgan (2006, p. 143) notes, for example, "Under the influence of the culture metaphor, leaders and managers come to see themselves as people who ultimately help to create and shape the meanings that are to guide organized action." The totemic organizational image thus has the potential to construct and render the individual reader—an academic, an organizational theorist, a manager, a student, a practitioner—subject to the power of images. As we have argued above, if not reflective and circumspect, readers of *Images* risk becoming captured by univocal representations that serve to reify organizational possibilities because the selection and reduction upon which totem images are based, the "as if" quality of their existence, is forgotten or not even noticed.

Evans-Pritchard (1951) and, later, Lévi-Strauss (1962/1963) argued that being captured by a totem is equivalent to being defined by association with it and thus satisfies needs to belong. The reason for totemism is not so much revelatory as it is existential; it is a manifestation of how groups distinguish among them. For Lévi-Strauss, the motivation of totemic identification is to understand, relate, and situate one's group in relation to other groups: "Natural species are chosen [as totems] not because they are 'good to eat' but because they are 'good to think'" (Lévi-Strauss, 1962/1963, p. 89). The Lévi-Straussian concept of totemic phenomena (as opposed to "totemism") places emphasis on the relation between groups and totems rather than the individual power of each totem within each group. The machines, brains, organisms, and so forth that are viewed as totems are also functional for social groups (e.g., academics, leaders, managers) who need to represent themselves and the organizations that they study or work for. Even if it might seem to an impartial observer that these are magical metaphors with the power to facilitate understanding of the world (Morgan, 2006, p. 367), their significance exceeds sheer conceptual comprehension, instead possessing the capacity to colonize subjectivities and shape organizational acts.

The Power of Images to Effect Action

A central topic discussed among ethnographers is how mimetic objects—replicas—afford this associative and relational power and help communities find explanations that motivate individual and collective action. Describing the curing figurines of Cuna culture in Panama, for instance, Taussig (1993) refers to the seductive power of **multifaceted replication**. The Cuna developed a practice of modeling figurines as a way of responding to physical and mental ailments that they encountered. The Cuna created these figurines to replicate an individual who was sick, with the belief that such ritual mimesis would have curative effects. Although the primary purpose may have been to cure, Taussig points out that the figurine replicas came to serve a much wider purpose: to understand and make sense of self and other, in particular, the colonist in relation to the Cuna. The mimetic figurines not only represent qualities from one referent to another by similarity, but they also function to transform social relations:

Note the magical, the soulful power that derives from replication. For this is where we must begin; with the magical power of replication, the image affecting what it is in an image of, wherein the representation shares in or takes power from the represented. (Taussig, 1993, p. 2)

The way that the Cuna treat illness with the figurines has interesting resonances with the way that we use metaphor. According to Taussig, the Cuna base cure on the creation of a set of social meanings surrounding the illness. The "other" as figurine becomes an agent that enables everybody to associate with the meaning of the illness, including the person represented, and by so doing to contribute collectively to the cure. To "cure" in this context does not necessarily imply a state of "perfect health," but rather a state of health that is consonant with shared expectations of what it is to have that ailment. (In an analogous way, in Western society, the meaning of "having cancer" is different from that of "having Alzheimer's disease." A diagnosis of either emerges as a figure representing much more than the pathology of the disease.)

The metaphors in *Images* function much as the Cuna figurines: images that obtain an apparent sense-making agency. That the Cuna figurines are replicas of European white men is of particular note; neither the Cuna nor other local ethnic groups are represented. However, curiously, the Cuna themselves deny any connection between the two. This may express an unconscious (but quite reasonable) association of illness with foreignness. However, the fact that they claim not to recognize this association alerts us to the possibility that we may not recognize associations vested in the metaphors of *Images*. As Taussig (1993, p. 8) says, reflecting on the model of him made by the Cuna:

What magic lies in this, my wooden self, sung to power in a language I cannot understand? Who is this self, objectified without my knowledge, that I am hell-bent on analyzing as object-over-there fanned by sea breezes and the smoke of burning cocoa nibs enchanting the shaman's singing?

It might be appropriate, therefore, to conclude this section with a reflection on *our* authorial engagement with the images of *Images*. We might usefully ask: "Who are we, organization theorists hell-bent on analysing Morgan's metaphors as objects-over-there?" In the following section, we begin to form an answer to this question by reflecting on our experience of *using* Morgan's book in non-Anglophone teaching settings and pointing to the quasi-colonial and postcolonial challenges of encouraging international students to *see their world* through totemic organizational images originating in modern Anglo-Saxon culture.

Totems, Images, and Replicas in International Encounters

As we indicated in the previous section, Taussig points out that the Cuna figurines resemble white colonists. However, paradoxically, the Cuna themselves deny any connection between the two. This creates an epistemic dilemma in anthropology that, we suggest, is similar to dilemmas that we potentially face when using *Images* as a teaching resource: Something that appears obvious to Anglo-Saxon organizational academics using Morgan's text might not be so obvious for non–Anglo-Saxon students and/or for those for whom English is not a first language. In this section, we recall and reflect on our own experiences of using Morgan's text while teaching in other countries and in other languages. Our overall point is that, in teaching organizational analysis in different cultural contexts and/or using different languages, one must remain as sensitive as possible to the diverse *interpretative responses* of students to the images being mobilized. From our experiential observations, as we endeavor to point out, tropes function differently in varying cultural and linguistic contexts. In what follows, we connect Taussig's observations regarding mimesis to the accounts that doctoral and MBA students we have taught in the Nordic region, the Balkans, South America, Catalonia, and Southeast Asia offer when explaining the meaning of Morgan's images. It must be acknowledged that we did not set out systematically to research "uses of Morgan's metaphors" in non-Anglophone countries, so the countries represented here simply reflect the somewhat contingent experiences and linguistic capacities of the authorial team. Nonetheless, our observations do encompass an intercontinental spread of countries and range of both non-Indo-European (Finnish, Malay) and Indo-European (Albanian, Spanish, and Catalan) languages.

Finnish

While lecturing in Finland, one of the authors interviewed a Finnish business school colleague about the challenges of teaching Morgan's metaphors to Finnish students. One interesting point made was in reference to his experience of explaining Morgan's (2006, p. 34) organismic metaphor and, specifically, "the idea that individuals and groups, like biological organisms, operate most effectively when their needs are satisfied." The colleague mentioned how the students struggled to imagine "organisms as living systems existing in a wider environment" (Morgan, 2006, p. 33) because the word for "organism" (*organismi*) in Finnish can be used to denote more than one thing: a nonliving being, a compound of parts of something, or, for example, a multifaceted instrument like a church organ. The metaphor did not work as an image, not because of its lack of capacity of being a good copy (*antigraphos*), but because of its limitations when inducing complexity to the imagination and multiplying functions for the same image, a possibility inhibited if the word *organismi* is used. Working on the nature of the Cuna replicas, Taussig mentioned the multiplicity of the functions that the figurines (putative images) had and described at least four different uses of the same figurine.

The work with our Finnish colleague when using Morgan's *Images* also resonates with Taussig's reflections of how the self is constructed by others and how the image *constructs the metaphor*. Explaining the contradictory feelings experienced when translating into Finnish Morgan's words for images, our colleague remarked:

> I remembered that I actually used a different Finnish word to denote organism in Morgan: *eliö*. *Eliö* has its roots in *elävä*, *elämä*, meaning "living, life."

Sometimes I also offer a related concept, *olio* (creature, thing) to complement *eliö*. I use *eliö* because *organismi* in Finnish has this connotation of referring to systems or institutions in a more general sense that I want to avoid [i.e., referring to "organized systems" or "organized wholes"].

Our Finnish colleague suggested that when copies are not just copies but *replicas*, not only does the metaphor construct the image, but the inverse also applies: The image constructs the metaphor. As we noted in the previous section, this "magic of mimesis," when the replica constructs the original, is also acknowledged by Taussig in his reflections on how a wooden Cuna figurine became an objectification of himself. Taussig (1993, p. 121) also mentions the power of the replicas to construct holistic explanations of the cure when spiritual and substantial levels of reality are conjoined and seen by the Cuna "as distinct yet complementary." Similarly, our Finnish colleague found himself having to engage in considerable translational work, a kind of magical transubstantiation, with Morgan's original *organismic* image to construct meaningful metaphors for his students that, in effect, were distinct yet complementary to that original.

Albanian

Using *Images* when teaching a doctoral course in Pristina, Kosovo, one of the authors made specific reference to Morgan's "organizations as brains" metaphor. He noticed that students seemed to struggle to "get" either the root metaphor or explanations of the point being made. Changing the pedagogical tack, the colleague asked students for examples of what came to their mind when the words for "brain" and "organization" were linked. In response, they said it was difficult to explain in English and that the best way of understanding the connection was with another metaphorical construction. They made reference to an Albanian proverb: *Qingji I but I thithë dy nëna* ("A soft lamb sucks from two mothers").

The students said they used this phrase to refer to someone who is competent, sensible, and capable of engaging others in an organizational context, someone who is capable of "being" with more than one person or engaging in more than one activity. Simultaneously, it denotes someone who is very young, inexperienced, and yet is aware enough to see the sense in being able to adapt to more than one organizational situation.

The "brain" that Albano-Kosovar students imagined was not aligned with what we might, through our theoretical lens, see as Morgan's functionalist approach to totemism (one magic object, a brain, with one transformational image, a learning organization). Instead, they *translated* and recovered the totem in a way that resembles a Lévi-Straussian idea of totemic phenomena: one that emphasizes the social sensibility around the "totem" brain; one that invoked connotations of "learning from others," "humility," "modesty born of inexperience," "openness to learning," and "capacity to *be with* more than one person." This is a rich constellation of meaning that is quite different from that which we might expect as teachers working with students, for example, in the United Kingdom or United States.

Spanish

As Taussig (1993, p. 57) observes when discussing the magic induced by mimesis, "a first step here is to insist on breaking away from the tyranny of the visual notion of image." When consulting *Images*, readers might be tempted to construct a single and "positive" image of, for example, a brain that is infinitely capable of learning. However, discussing the "organizations as brains" metaphor once again, but this time while teaching postgraduate research students in Buenos Aires, Argentina, one of the authors encountered yet more revealing challenges of trans-cultural uses of Morgan's work. Having been introduced to the brain metaphor, instead of invoking a positive image of "individual and organizational learning," students interpreted it in an entirely opposite way. This image was taken to express an incapability rather than the capability to learn. Asked for examples, they expressed their interpretation of the metaphor through a proverb: *No ve dos en un burro* ("She/he doesn't see two people [riding] on a donkey"). The students said this proverb represents an individual's incapacity to learn. It can refer to someone who is incapable of understanding anything that is socially or organizationally complex; that is, someone who lacks sensitivity and is rather simplistic in their outlook, someone who, moreover, is only capable of linear and unidimensional thinking. This is quite a contrast, once again, to the interpretation of the brain image that one might expect in an Anglophone teaching context.

Catalan

Taussig describes how there are many different wooden replicas of turtles among the Cuna, among them turtles for medical practice and turtles for hunting. The turtles, even though they have the same name and are made with the same material (wood), are essentially different. Following a parallel with the Cuna turtles, the "same" metaphor rooted in the "same" analogy can evoke very different images. For example, during a discussion in Catalan of "organizations as psychic prison" in a university in Barcelona, Spain, doctoral students indicated that this image prompted multiple associations with the idea that social practices constrain, like prison walls, mental and emotional possibilities. The same *physical* place evokes differing *symbolic* spaces. Asked for examples, one link that they made was to the meaning of the Catalan word *can* (place). This is a term that can be used **synecdochically** to refer to the "same" organization but with a connotation that is different according to circumstances and depending on who inhabits the organization. *Can* is the same metaphor represented by the same word but, like the turtle replicas, it has different meanings and uses. *Can Barça*, for instance, could be used as a **dysphemism** to refer to executives of the soccer club "Barcelona," but also as an **approbative** to refer to club players. In Catalan, the metaphor of prison as *a place* evokes the question "whose side am I on?" As an image, it is neither purely descriptive nor objective any more than the turtle totems of the Cuna.

Malaysian

As noted above, even if we accept Morgan's suggestion that the creative uses of metaphor can help rethink and reshape organizations, we must also acknowledge, following Alvesson and Deetz (2000), that metaphors can obscure our understanding of them. We have experienced the obscuration effect in three ways when introducing the mechanistic metaphor to Malaysian MBA students.

The first was when students indicated that they not only have difficulties imagining organizations through the mechanistic metaphor but, in particular, are unable even to imagine what "a machine" in Morgan's sense is. Morgan's "machine" was perceived to constrain and limit students' imagination. The image of a machine represented for them a more complex and hybridized blend of images, one that simultaneously invoked *inter alia* brains, politics, and culture. This resonates to some extent with our earlier claim that Morgan's eight metaphors, however unintentionally, seem to operate as modern Western totems, each separated out and treated in a reified way. Asked for examples of what they meant by "machine," the Malaysian students came back with a range of possibilities, including robots, cell phones, search engines, computer/phone apps, satellite navigation systems (satnavs), and others. One of our students commented:

> With reference to the Malay language, if you say something like *organisasi adalah seperti mesin* (organizations are like machines), this suggests the organization is something like a robot. (Student 4)

One nonculturally specific explanation of this interpretation would be that images of "a machine" and "mechanistic relations" have changed significantly in the 30 years since Morgan first suggested the machine as an organizational metaphor. However, we have used the metaphor extensively with mainland European and British students (as well as non-European internationals students in the United Kingdom) and, in doing so, have not been presented with similar responses. The following is a field note made by one of the authors on the day that the machine metaphor was introduced to the Malaysian students:

> When discussing Morgan's mechanistic metaphor, students came back with examples of apps, mobile phones, robots, or even cyborgs, humanoids and "machines" that they referred to as "more related with the social, the environment . . . "; like a political party, a school. They described emotional relations between machines and humans, or between humans and machines. *Manga* comics, the relationship between machines and people in Kurosawa's filmography and Šabanović's (2014) ethnography on the Humanoid Robotics project and the relationship between culture and "kansei robotics" in Japan, came to my assistance later [as I took the discussion further].

As can be seen, students came up with the image of a machine in terms of what **actor-network theorists** might take to be *hybrid objects* and *quasi-objects* (Callon, 1986; Czarniawska & Hernes, 2005), for which sociomaterial elements combine in an alembic of the human, cultural, material, and environmental to make up "a machine." Unlike in the Anglophone context, there is no easy separation between the human and nonhuman in the Malay conception of a "mechanistic view." When this issue was discussed with the students, their responses revealed a very different kind of understanding than might be expected in Anglophone classes. In place of independent, isolated, and autonomous conception of machines, we find a far more hybridized sensibility:

I have the impression that Morgan is thinking of isolated machines, with no humans, and not part of the world. Let's assume that the machine is a sailing ship. As such, the following can be related as a metaphor to an organization: the sail—organizational direction; the engine—USP [unique selling point] of an organization; the captain—the leader or CEO [chief executive officer] of an organization; the sailors—an organization's objectives; the waves in the ocean—the challenges that an organization faces on a day to day basis; the oars in a sailing ship—the tools used by an organization to move forward; the hull of the ship—the financial security and stability of the company to keep it afloat and prevent it from sinking. . . . The whole is the machine, but is not only "mechanical." (Student 3)

The second experience of obscuration relates back to what we said earlier about Taussig's concept of "visual means" and the reductionist dangers of exclusively using *ocular* images. Students came with a range of imagining through senses other than the visual. Here is an illustrative example as represented in the field notes of one of the authors:

In the morning, I visited with the students the factory of an Asian carmaker, a semiautomatic robotic factory based on Japanese Mitsubishi design during the late 1980s in KL [Kuala Lumpur]. The students came to the class in the afternoon and when discussing the mechanistic image they described making references not only to what we saw—order, machines, processes—but to electric beeps, intermittent tuba-like horns and odours of brand-new plastics, tyres and coffee (from the coffee machines situated in some corners of the factory where the workers have breaks). This is not really what came to my mind when imagining the "well-oiled engine" or "nuts and bolts" machine of Morgan's *Images*.

The third obscuration effect reflected in this experience of teaching Malaysian students relates to our suggestion that Morgan's metaphors operate as totemic images that simultaneously define *taboos* to be avoided by those doing the **"imaginization."** This taboo aspect of the image was, in fact, one of the main concerns of our Malaysian students. As already pointed out, the machine metaphor excludes those who imagine unconventionally, yet for the Malaysian students, this image seemed to have quite the opposite effect. For them, to be unconventional is not a taboo to be avoided if someone imagines organizing mechanistically. As one of the students commented:

The machine liberates you. By working mechanistically you can suggest improvements, innovate, discover other ways. The employees at Proton can suggest improvements precisely because they work mechanistically. It is like Chinese calligraphy: to repeat, liberates you.

The notion that mechanistic work can liberate the imagination is something quite alien to the Western mind. Marx, Marcuse, Braverman, et alia would be utterly appalled! However, this student's words act as a potent illustration of just the kind of challenge faced in using Morgan's book when teaching in international settings or, indeed, international students more generally. As with the other teaching experiences related above, this encounter serves as a cautionary tale to those who would otherwise take for granted the semantic fields and forces that any one of Morgan's eight metaphors might be *expected* or *presumed* to evoke.

Conclusions

In this chapter, we have considered the culture-making ways in which Morgan's images function as totems and have also reflected experientially on their uses in teaching organizational theory in international settings. The chapter opened with the suggestion that *Images* occupies the cusp of modern and postmodern organizational theory. Advocating multiple perspectives on organizing and disclosing the conditional subjectivity of each perspective, Morgan invites his readers to invent whichever new metaphors they choose. Our discussion considers the sociocultural function of the metaphors; specifically how, as images, they provide means for collective identification in much the same way as totems are seen to in both classical and contemporary anthropology. By analogy with the totemic figures of the Cuna, as studied by Taussig (1993), we draw attention to the way in which Morgan's metaphors have come to represent the pathologies of organizational theory, cast in the likeness of the organizations that must be "other" to us, constituting ourselves as organization theorists and teachers. Morgan's metaphors have become the totems of organizational theory. Therefore, the first part of the chapter contributes an interpretation of the community-forming functions of *Images*.

We then proceeded to consider the *translational* implications of using *Images* as a teaching resource when working with students in non-Anglophone settings. Having taught *Images* in languages other than English and in non-Western cultures, we draw on our experience of the differing ways in which images of machine, brain, organism, and so forth are constructed, evoke diverse associations, and afford varying possibilities for organization theorization and interpretative analysis. We offered a series of lessons and cautionary tales deriving from our postgraduate teaching experiences in Finland, Albania, Argentina, Spain, and Malaysia. If pushed to derive a general conclusion from these diverse encounters, it would be that Morgan's metaphors uniformly resist any single, univocal, or unequivocal interpretation. Although there may be cultural patterns that inform a given national group's interpretation of the images, international students appear to respond to Morgan's metaphors openly and to make varying semantic associations with them. This equates metaphorically to a kind of postmodern pedagogical unraveling of the modern theoretical tapestry to be found in *Images*. The associations and identifications made by international students have often been surprising and unexpected to us as organizational theory teachers.

The key lesson that we forge from this is that Morgan's metaphors cannot be interpreted or valued free from context. Furthermore, anyone who uses Morgan's metaphors in an international setting (e.g., whether in international collaboration on research, business, education, or anything else or in international teaching, consultancy, or research) must acquire and maintain a kind of anthropological sensibility that allows and, indeed, encourages space for multiethnic interpretation and pedagogical flexibility (Case & Selvester, 2000; Reynolds & Trehan, 2003). It should always be borne in mind that metaphors can operate as much as *vehicles of obscuration* of our understanding as they can shed lucidity and insight, particularly if we fall into the trap of univocal ways of representing them. We should at all times be on reflexive guard against the ethnocentric expectation that everyone is inclined to "metaphorize" and "imaginize" in the same way that we are. Alertness to different ways of metaphorizing, moreover, not only carries anthropological but also ontological ramifications. We should allow ourselves the opportunity given by international communication to develop a profound respect for the **emic** imagination of the other and, as far as possible, be prepared to journey into differing social and cultural epistemologies that the other brings to the communication. The **ontological challenge**, moreover, simultaneously invokes an ethical challenge, being sufficiently ready to decenter oneself and one's perspective, so that a genuine encounter with the other (Levinas, 1969, 1998) becomes possible. In Levinas's terms, this entails rejecting an **unreflexive ontological position** that would either impose or project analytical or judgmental categories on the other. Such unreflexivity risks negating the other's essence of alterity in a quasi-colonial or imperious way. Rather, an ethics of the other should spring out of the relationship with the other and be realized through meeting the responsibilities that surge from the demands of an encounter with otherness.

International communication, in terms of, for example, international collaboration, would thus ideally involve an ongoing encounter with the collaborator as other, being mindful of the ethical responsibilities that come with the terrain. The moral challenge for anyone is to respond to the call of, and be prepared to *learn with*, the other. This can only happen if one is not seduced by the erstwhile securities of ready-made Anglo-centric categorizations, generalizations, classifications, rules, and obligations such as those that, in the wrong hands, might be seen to be offered and inscribed in Morgan's *Images*. This lies at the heart of the cautionary tale that stems from our teaching anecdotes. The implications of this for international collaboration and international management are not insignificant. To "learn with the other" would imply to liberate the other to imagine in unpredictable, nondomesticated ways, not only or simply to *translate* Anglo-centric metaphors but also to imagine with new metaphors rooted in other linguistic traditions. A few international management examples might serve to make our point in this regard. The word *kaizen* was originally used to mean the introduction of amendments and rectifications intended to bring about an improvement of some kind, but it became a seminal image to inspire the invention of modern concepts such as total quality management and quality circles. As another example, when conducting fieldwork in Italian corporations, one of the authors observed that the use of the word "family" (*famiglia*) by managers triggered representations of multiple images of organizing that were used to discuss international strategy in Italian corporations and business schools. Similarly, Dai (2015) shows how a modern Japanese term referring to corporate sustainability evokes much older Chinese characters (*gong qi*, 公器, "communal vessel"). This evinces qualities of containment and emptiness, meanings of sustainability that are not afforded by the English.

It is clear that Morgan-mediated image creation depends on multiple facets of international context, many of which are extremely difficult (and perhaps ultimately impossible) to fathom. This alerts us to the continuous negotiated malleability of the metaphors and the political economy of which organizational theory, embedded in particular relations of power knowledge, is a constituent. The following conclusions thus follow from our analysis and illustrative examples:

1) Those who use Morgan's metaphors are cultural ambassadors who, by mobilizing Morgan's metaphors in their practices, also reflexively represent and impart a cultural stance to people from other cultures.
2) Morgan's metaphors are not really "Morgan's" per se, but instead are appropriated by readers whose differing ethnicities mediate and modulate their meaning and application.

These conclusions lead us to consider that one should approach *Images* with humility, intellectual respect, and an appreciation of its sophistication. After years of engaging with the book, we are left with the impression that naïve and sometimes simplistic interpretations have attenuated the intellectual contribution of Morgan's work.

In retrospect, Morgan's work might ultimately go down as the last gasp of modernist organization studies, committed as it is to grand social theory (see, as evidence, the encyclopedic bibliographic notes in both editions of *Images*) as opposed to working through the micronarratives of a poststructural and postmodern sensibility (Lyotard, 1984). His book still serves as an extremely rich resource, but its application in international contexts reveals that the theoretical tapestry needs to be unraveled and its "teachers" must be prepared to work with surprising and unexpected interpretations of its images. We have sought, through the analysis and experiences related in this chapter, to promote a critical reappraisal of Morgan's metaphors, pointing to their totemic function and warning of the dangers inherent in their unreflexive and uncritical application in international settings.

Finally, we hope that this chapter constitutes an appreciation of Morgan's work and we wish to again express our respect, admiration, and gratitude for such a stimulating contribution to our field.

Key Terms

Actor-network theorists	Imagination
Animate or inanimate	Imagining
Approbative	Imaginization
Connotational field	Interpretative approaches
Cultural artefact	Magical metaphors
Dead metaphors	Mimetic objects
Dysphemism	Mimetic qualities
Emic	Modern period
Epigrammatically	Movement
Ethical relativism	Multifaceted replication
Ethnocentric	Ocular view
Homologous logic	Ontological challenge

Ontological relativism	Taboos
Ontology	Totemic characteristics
Postmodern	Totemic identification
Reflexive social anthropological stance	Totemic metaphors
	Totemic selection
Social constructionism and socially constructed	Totems
	Tour *de force*
Super-metaphor	Tropes
Synecdoche	Unreflexive ontological
Synecdochically	position

Note

1. We are grateful to Professor Kiran Trehan and an anonymous reviewer for comments on an earlier draft of this chapter. Thanks are also extended to Professor Anders Örtenblad for his editorial assistance and Professor Tuomo Peltonen (Turku School of Economics) for sharing his insights into teaching organizational theory using Morgan's *Images* in a Finnish context.

References

Alvesson, M., & Deetz. S. (2000). *Doing critical management research*. London, England: Sage.

Alvesson, M., & Spicer, A. (2011). *Metaphors we lead by: Understanding leadership in the real world*. Abingdon, England: Routledge.

Burgi, P., & Roos, J. (2001). *Naturally identifiable: Totemism and organizational identity* (Working Paper 6). Lausanne, Switzerland: ImaginationLab.

Burrell, G., & Morgan, G. (1979). *Sociological paradigms and organizational analysis*. London, England: Heinemann.

Callon, M. (1986). Some elements of a sociology of translation: Domestication of the scallops and the fishermen of St Brieuc Bay. In J. Law (Ed.), *Power, action and belief: A new sociology of knowledge?* (pp. 196–233). London, England: Routledge & Kegan Paul.

Case, P., & Gaggiotti, H. (2014). Italo Calvino and the organizational imagination: Reading social organization through urban metaphor. *Culture and Organization, 20*(3), 185–195.

Case, P., & Selvester, K. (2000). Close encounters: Ideological invasion and complicity on an international management master's programme. *Management Learning, 31*(1), 11–23.

Czarniawska, B. (2011). Narrating organization studies. *Narrative Inquiry, 21*(2), 337–344.

Czarniawska, B., & Hernes, T. (2005). Constructing macro actors according to ANT. In B. Czarniawska & T. Hernes (Eds.), *Actor-network theory and organizing* (pp. 7–13). Copenhagen, Denmark: Liber & Copenhagen Business School Press.

Dai, W. (2015). *The great vessel rarely completes: Translating corporate sustainability* (Doctoral thesis). Retrieved from https://ore.exeter.ac.uk/repository/handle/10871/15027

Durkheim, E. (1976). *Elementary forms of religious life*. London, England: George Allen & Unwin.

Evans-Pritchard, E. (1951). Kinship and local community among the Nuer. In A. R. Radcliffe-Brown & D. Forde (Eds.), *African systems of kinship and marriage* (pp. 360–391). Oxford, England: Oxford University Press.

Freud, S. (1913/1918). *Totem and taboo*. New York, NY: Moffat Yard.

Kamoche, K. (1995). Rhetoric, ritualism, and totemism in human resource management. *Human Relations, 48*(4), 367–385.

Kuhn, T. S. (1962). *The structure of scientific revolutions*. Chicago, IL: University of Chicago Press.

Kuhn, T. S. (1970). *The structure of scientific revolutions* (2nd ed.). Chicago, IL: University of Chicago Press.

Lakoff, G., & Johnson, M. (1980). *Metaphors we live by*. Chicago, IL: University of Chicago Press.

Letiche, H. (2004). "Talk" and Hermès. *Culture and Organization, 10*(2), 143–161.

Lévi-Strauss, C. (1962/1963). *Totemism*. Boston, MA: Beacon Press.

Levinas, E. (1969). *Totality and infinity: An essay on exteriority*. Pittsburgh, PA: Duquesne University.

Levinas, E. (1998). *Entre nous: Thinking-of-the-other*. New York, NY: Columbia University Press.

Lyotard, J.-F. (1984). *The postmodern condition*. Manchester, England: University of Manchester Press.

Martin, J. (1992). *Cultures in organizations: Three perspectives*. Oxford, England: Oxford University Press.

Morgan, G. (1980). Paradigms, metaphors and puzzle solving in organization theory. *Administrative Science Quarterly, 25*(4), 605–622.

Morgan, G. (1986). *Images of organization*. Beverly Hills, CA: Sage.

Morgan, G. (1997). *Images of organization* (2nd ed.). Thousand Oaks, CA: Sage.

Morgan, G. (2006). *Images of organization* (3rd ed.). London, England: Sage.

Morgan, G. (2011). Reflections on *Images of Organization* and its implications for organization and environment. *Organization & Environment, 24*(4), 459–478.

Morgan, G., & Smircich, L. (1980). The case for qualitative research. *Academy of Management Review, 5*(4), 491–500.

Morrill, C. (2008). Culture and organization theory. *Annals of the American Academy of Political and Social Science, 619*(1), 15–40.

Reynolds, M., & Trehan, K. (2003). Learning from difference: A critical perspective. *Management Learning, 31*(2), 163–180.

Šabanović, S. (2014). Inventing Japan's "robotics culture": The repeated assembly of science, technology, and culture in social robotics. *Social Studies of Science, 44*(3), 342–367.

Smircich, L. (1983). Studying organizations as cultures. In G. Morgan (Ed.), *Beyond method: Strategies for social research* (pp. 160–172). Beverly Hills, CA: Sage.

Taussig, M. (1993). *Mimesis and alterity: A particular history of the senses*. London, England: Routledge.

Tietze, S., Cohen, L., & Musson, G. (2003). *Understanding organizations through language*. London, England: Sage.

Trice, H. M., & Beyer, J. M. (1993). *The cultures of work organizations*. Englewood Cliffs, NJ: Prentice Hall.

Tylor, E. B. (1898). *Remarks on totemism, with especial reference to some modern theories respecting it*. London, England: Harrison & Sons.

Westwood, R., & Linstead, S. (Eds.). (2002). *The language of organization*. London, England: Sage.

Willmott, H. (1993). Strength is ignorance; slavery is freedom: Managing culture in modern organizations. *Journal of Management Studies, 30*(4), 515–552.

• Glossary[1] •

Actively viewing contemporary organizations: A combination of reading the text, seeing the visual elements, and looking for omissions.

Actor-network theorists: Scholars who employ a theory in which language comprises networks of interaction between human and nonhuman actors; thus, nonhumans have the capacity to act or participate in networks.

Affect: A socialized impulse, driving how people interact and connect with one another in social situations, often in seemingly spontaneous and unpredictable ways; a new metaphor that generates alternative understandings of new forms of organizations.

Analyst: A person who studies an organization or a set of organizations either to develop it or to do research on it.

Animate or inanimate: Having or lacking the features of living beings.

Applied metaphor approach: A research approach in which metaphor is applied to organizational analysis.

Applied research: Systematic inquiry that involves the application of scientific theories and methods for a specific purpose.

Approbative: Words or grammatical forms that express appreciation or approval of the speaker.

Big Data: Data sets so vast or complex that they defy conventional methods of analysis.

Bureaucratic leadership: Inspired by the machine metaphor, refers to centrality of rules, hierarchical power, and active supervision.

Cognitive perspective: An approach that focuses on knowing and perceiving; relying on cognitions or mental states.

Compactness: The quality of being concise or economical in generating ideas.

Comparison model: Comparing two concepts to identify discrete properties that apply to both of them; an alternative explanation for how metaphor works.

Complex metaphors: Using conceptual blending and elaboration to fit small pieces of a metaphor into a large whole.

Complexity science: The continual producing and reproducing of an organization out of a complex and causal interplay of forces.

Connectionist images: Images related to treating mental or behavioral processes as products of interconnected networks.

Connotational field: A setting in which a certain word is given a particular meaning.

Convergence: Integrating ideas through linking them across cultures, knowledge, industry, and economic boundaries.

Critical theory: A theory that addresses power, domination, and oppression and aims for human emancipation.

Cultural artefact: An object that conveys information and meaning about the community of humans that developed it.

Dead metaphors: Metaphors that are taken literally and no longer function as symbols.

Descriptive metaphor: A metaphor in which the target and domain concepts are very similar; a metaphor aimed at describing rather than generating images.

Digital turn: An increased academic interest in and focus on the digital and social media of organizing and organizations.

---

1. The definitions of these concepts correspond to their uses in particular chapters of this book. These terms may be defined differently in other books and articles.

Discriminant analysis: A statistical method used to find a combination of features/variables that separate one object from other objects for classification and interpretation.

Discursive approaches: Research approaches grounded in language and discourse processes.

Dis-integrated organizations: Transnational corporations that are assemblages held together by contracts, subcontracts, and sub-subcontracts.

Domain: A particular field of action or thought.

Domains-interaction model: A framework of extending meaning through a comprehensive connection between source and target domain for a specific organizational application.

Dysphemism: An expression that contains an offensive meaning about either the subject matter or the audience.

Eigenvalue: The amount of overall variance that a dimension in a factor analysis explains; a criterion used to determine a dimension and to eliminate nonrelevant factors.

Embodiment hypothesis: The preference for metaphors linked to the human body or human motor action.

Emic: Focusing on a local point of view in exploring and recovering knowledge; understanding practice from an indigenous perspective.

Emotional labor: Requiring individuals in an organization to engage in specific emotional displays in performing their roles and organizational tasks.

Empowerment: Distributing power and responsibility from leaders to followers.

Enact: To bring a phenomenon into being through performing or representing it.

Epigrammatically: To act in a pithy, satirical, or witty way.

Ethical relativism: A belief that what is morally right or wrong varies from person to person or from society to society.

Ethnocentric: Judging another culture through employing the values and standards of one's own culture.

Ethnography: The systematic study of an organization or community from the viewpoint of the people within that culture; data collection that employs participant observation, interviews, and archival data.

Fancy: Inventing the novel and unreal through reorganizing elements found in reality.

Fast capitalism: A rapidly changing, knowledge-based and global economy, driven by technological change and high levels of connectivity.

Figurative vehicle problem: Using the wrong metaphor; problems in making linkages between the source and target domains.

Framing: Creating a frame of reference; positioning elements in the figure as opposed to the ground of a mental frame.

Generative metaphor: Developing metaphor to create new insights and develop new meanings; metaphor in which the target and source domains are very distinct.

Generative value: The application of something, in this case metaphor, in ways that generate or cultivate new meanings and understandings.

Generic structure: The encoding of a metaphor (source domain) and the related target domain; the results or output of the first step of the domains-interaction model.

Ground: The features of one concept that become shared with another one in a metaphor.

Happiness: A feeling of joy, accompanied by higher levels of connectedness, love, compassion, fairness, pleasure, and satisfaction.

Hermeneutics: The process of interpreting texts; treating organizational life as a text that is to be read and interpreted.

Homologous logic: A logic that emphasizes similarities between divergent structures, positions, or states (e.g., between society and nature).

Human relations leadership: Inspired by the organism metaphor, a style of leadership that focuses on developing and nurturing social relationships.

Hyperspace: A multidimensional space.

Ideal types: Hypothetical constructions as prototypes that are based on ideal characteristics.

Image: A visible representation, form, or likeness, existing physically or conceptually; in persuasion, a rhetorical strategy that appeals to competing views.

Imagination: Creating images or concepts not immediately apparent to the senses; using images to sustain, elicit, or impose ways of organizing.

Imagining: Using imagination.

Imaginization: Intertwining the concepts of organization and imagination; to organize is to imaginize; using different approaches to organization to identify different images of organization.

Inferential structure: Using metaphor to make interpretations that flesh out rich organizational concepts.

Instituting imaginary: Situating new meanings in values, beliefs, and actions that alter established ways of organizing.

Integrated product-service systems (IPSS): A complex system that integrates and tailors products and services to meet individualized customer demands.

Integrated value proposition (IVP): A solution-oriented system of combining products and services that involves the customer in a value creation process to address specific business problems.

Integrating way of organizing (IWO): Transforming traditional organizations through shifting toward integrated value propositions; developing new routines of customer integration in patterns of organizing.

Interact: The process of one entity acting on or influencing another.

Interpretative approaches: Research that places the meaning-making practices of human actors as the focal point for scientific investigations.

Irony: The incongruity between what is expected and what actually occurs in a situation.

Knowledge economy: An economy in which the accumulation of wealth and value is based on the exchange of knowledge.

Knowledge interest: The reason or primary need that underlies the desire to know or understand something.

Knowledge work: Work that is grounded in knowledge-related tasks or information management; knowledge as the output or mode of work.

Laissez-faire leadership: The absence of active leadership through ignorance, neglect, or laziness; reactive rather than proactive leadership.

Language game: Enacting language patterns deemed incomprehensible to those unfamiliar with a given system.

Latent dimension: A set of variables that form a category inferred from analysis of data rather than being directly observed or measured.

Linguistically: Relating to language and the use of language.

Literal target problem: Using the wrong conceptualization of organizing and organization to develop metaphors; metaphors that fail to capture rapid changes and new forms of organizing.

Magical metaphors: Using metaphors grounded in mystery, the mystical, or the enchanted to exert influence.

Master tropes: Four primary classifications of figures of speech composed of metaphor, metonymy, synecdoche, and irony.

Meta-metaphor: An overarching metaphor that encompasses or serves as a category for other metaphors.

Metaphor: A process of using one element of experience to engage and understand another. Linguistic and other epistemological constructs characterized by the transfer of information from a relatively familiar domain (known as a source, base, or vehicle) to a new and relatively unfamiliar domain (referred to as a target).

Metaphorical: Applying a metaphor to phenomena, activities, behaviors, expressions, imagination, or theory development.

Metaphorical analysis: The deciphering or developing of metaphors in organizational contexts.

Metaphorical behaviors: Actions that illustrate the practices embodied in a particular metaphor.

Metaphorical expression: Phrases and words presented in metaphorical form.

Metaphorical imagination: Working across alternative images to create and engage with metaphors.

Metaphorical theory: Theorizing about organizations through using alternative images or metaphors.

Metaphors of the field: Metaphors offered intentionally or unintentionally by actors in the field that the analyst studies; metaphors derived from doing fieldwork.

Metonymical: Adjective form of **metonymy**.

Metonymy: Using words that represent parts or elements of a phenomenon to stand for the whole (e.g., using the term *crown* to refer to the *kingdom*); one of the four master tropes.

Mimetic objects: Imitations.

Mimetic qualities: The imitative characteristics of metaphor.

Mobilize the imagination: Productive use of imagination to engage people to organize in a desired way.

Modern period: An era or period of scholarship grounded in the inevitability of progress; the belief that science, philosophy, and religion form the foundation for the pursuit of truth.

Modifier: The source term in a metaphor that sets up a particular meaning for the target or subject. In the metaphor "the river of time," "river" is the modifier and "time" is the target, indicating that time is "like" a river.

Movement: The concept of motion, carriage, or transference integral to a metaphor; "a carrying over" or transference of meaning.

Multifaceted replication: Reproduction or imitation based on multiple features.

Network leadership: Inspired by the brain metaphor, a style of leadership that focuses on connections and interdependencies with other people.

Ocular view: Using the eye or seeing as a perspective.

Ontological challenge: Questioning the fundamental sense of being.

Ontological relativism: Adopting a relative stance to address questions related to existence and the nature of reality; a stance that varies by framework or situation.

Ontology: The study of being, existence, or the nature of reality.

Organizational actors: Individuals who work, interface with, and belong to organizations.

Organizational analysis: The study of an organization or set of organizations either to develop it or to do research on it.

Parallel structures: The semantic connection between a source and a target domain; developing a generic structure in the first step of the domains-interaction model.

Perception: Using the senses and cognitions to recognize and interpret stimuli or information.

Philosophical accounts of metaphor: Using metaphorical images to reveal truths or principles.

Phronesis: Acting morally, perceptively, and intelligently in a particular situation.

Political leadership: Inspired by the political systems metaphor, a leadership style grounded in power, competition for positions, ideologies, negotiations, and victories.

Positive psychology: A branch of psychology that focuses on the strengths and virtues of people that enable individuals, communities, and organizations to thrive.

Postmodern: An era or period of history that denies or critiques the foundational assumptions and universalizing tendencies of the modernist period.

Power relations: Ways in which different individuals and groups influence or control each other.

Primary metaphors: A basic and automatic way of forming links between target and source domains; the beginnings of developing metaphor.

Productive imagination: Treating imagination as a force that creates, distorts, or forges images beyond what was experienced.

Rational economic man: Treating humans in a mechanistic manner that maximizes self-interest through rational thinking; an approach that focuses on cost-benefit analysis.

Reading as metaphor: Being open to new understandings, reflecting on assumptions, and adopting an attitude of learning about organizations.

Reflective judgment: Using criteria or general principles to evaluate a particular case.

Reflective thinking: Maintaining a state of doubt, examining facts and prior knowledge, and critically examining one's own practices.

Reflexive social anthropological stance: Reflecting on and being aware of how cultural conditioning influences interactions with people in other cultures.

Reifies: The process of projecting human attributes or characteristics onto something that is nonhuman.

Root metaphor: A type of metaphor that underlies or lies at the foundation of other images.

Seeing as: Using metaphor as a frame of reference for interpreting an organization.

Semi-metaphorical expressions: Literal expressions tied to the features or elements of certain metaphors (e.g., "increased efficiency").

Social constructionism and socially constructed: A view of reality that treats it as constructed from interactions and meanings among people and groups.

Social imaginary significations: Assumptions that do not correspond with "real" referents shared by a society or an organization.

Social physics: A method for understanding behaviors based on analyzing Big Data.

Social systems: Groups of patterned relationships within an organization or entity.

Solution-oriented value proposition: Focusing on individualization or tailoring to customers, but with little mutual integration of product and service elements.

Source domain: The familiar or well-known concept in a metaphor that contains information to aid in understanding the target; see also **modifier** and **vehicle**.

Standardized value proposition (SVP): Focuses on equal product or services to a large number of different customers, but with little integration of products and services and a low degree of customer integration.

Standardizing way of organizing (SWO): Refers to how a business strategy grounded in a value proposition shapes routines, processes, or structures; aims to increase efficiency and optimization.

Super-metaphor: Using metaphor to function as organizational theories or paradigms.

Synecdoche: The substitution of the whole for the part (e.g., using the term "to Google" as a substitute for an Internet search); one of the four master tropes.

Synecdochically: Being characterized by **synecdoche.**

Systemic economic man: Treating human beings as physical, emotional, cognitive, social, cultural, and spiritual selves embedded in systemic interactions; creating personal as well as economic capital.

Taboos: Prohibited practices; actions too sacred or too dangerous for lay people to perform.

Target domain: The unfamiliar or less well-known concept in a metaphor; the concept that becomes understood through aligning it with a source.

Taxonomy: A classification system of related concepts based on general principles; scientific classification of key concepts; see also **typology.**

Temporal continuity: Characteristics of organizations that exhibit sameness over time.

Totemic characteristics: Features and qualities of totems.

Totemic identification: The act of identifying with a totem.

Totemic metaphors: Metaphors that have acquired the status of a totem.

Totemic selection: The act of choosing a totem.

Totems: Mythic structures that mirror the natural and the social; presupposed meanings that translate language, objects, and forms across cultures.

Tour de force: An exceptional performance or achievement.

Transformational leadership: A style of leadership characterized by inspiration and intellectual stimulation that challenges the status quo and encourages followers to explore new ways of doing things.

Trans-personal: Activities in which organizational members interact and connect with one another.

Trompe l'oeil: Tricking of the eye through using point of view or angle of vision to assume that an object is real.

Tropes: Figurative words, phrases, or images; a group of linguistic expressions such as metaphor, irony, metonymy, synecdoche, exaggeration, and understatement.

Typology: A categorization based on dimensions of a concept used in social sciences; typically includes ideal types; see also **taxonomy.**

Unreflexive ontological position: A stance on "what is reality" that is taken for granted or presumed as self-evident.

Value creation: Actions that increase the worth of goods, services, customer relations, or an entire business.

Value proposition: A promise of a specific value that a customer delivers and acknowledges that is connected to an organization's business strategy.

Variable: Treating metaphor as a given, focusing on obvious and similar features between source and target domain; also see **seeing as.**

Vehicle: A medium through which something is carried, conveyed, or expressed, such as meaning from a source to a target domain; see also **modifier** and **source domain.**

Visual turn: Focusing on the visual aspects of organizations, such as branding, images, and representations.

Vividness: Producing distinct, colorful, and intense images; acting clearly and vigorously.

Web 3.0: Smarter and individually tailored web-based products that deliver relevant content to users in automatic ways.

• Index •